WANDERING GOD

WANDERING GOD

A Study in
Nomadic Spirituality

Morris Berman

State University of New York Press

Grateful acknowledgment is extended to the following for permission to reprint copyrighted material:

Excerpt from "Little Sleep's Head Sprouting Hair in the Moonlight," from THE BOOK OF NIGHTMARES by Galway Kinnell. Copyright © 1971 by Galway Kinnell. Reprinted by permission of Houghton Mifflin Co. All rights reserved.

Excerpts from "The Last Hiding Places of Snow," from THREE BOOKS. Copyright © 1993 by Galway Kinnell. Previously published in *Mortal Acts, Mortal Words* (1980). Reprinted by permission of Houghton Mifflin Co. All rights reserved.

"The Opening," from ONLY TWO CAN PLAY THIS GAME by G. Spencer Brown. Copyright © 1977 by the Julian Press, Inc. Reprinted by permission of Julian Press, Inc., a division of Crown Publishers, Inc.

Published by
State University of New York Press, Albany

© 2000 State University of New York

For information, address State University of New York Press,
State University Plaza, Albany, NY, 12246

Production by Marilyn P. Semerad
Marketing by Dana Yanulavich

Library of Congress Cataloging-in-Publication Data

Berman, Morris, 1944–
    Wandering God : a study in nomadic spirituality / Morris Berman.
      p.   cm.
    Includes bibliographical references and index.
    ISBN 0-7914-4441-4 (hardcover : alk. paper). — ISBN 0-7914-4442-2
(pbk. : alk. paper)
    1. Spiritual life. 2. Consciousness—Religious aspects.
3. Paradox—Religious aspects.   4. Nomads.   5. Hunting and gathering
societies. 6. Social evolution. I. Title.
BL624.B4634 2000
128—dc21   99-26802
                                              CIP

10 9 8 7 6 5 4 3 2 1

The problem of modern man isn't to escape from one ideology to another, nor to escape from one formulation to find another; our problem is to live in the presence and in the attributes of reality.

—Frederick Sommer, *The Poetic Logic of Art and Aesthetics*

Men, incapable of liberty—who cannot stand the terror of the sacred that manifests itself before their open eyes—must turn to mystery.

—Carlo Levi, *Of Fear and Freedom*

CONTENTS

Contents

LIST OF ILLUSTRATIONS

ACKNOWLEDGMENTS

This work covers a rather vast canvas, and would not have been possible without the help and expertise of a good many colleagues and friends who were able to give me crucial feedback or relevant suggestions when these were needed. Two anthropologists in particular, Megan Biesele and David Spain, read the manuscript in its entirety and managed to save me from a number of egregious errors. Discussions with another anthropologist, the late Paul Shepard, helped the central theme of the book to crystallize in my mind over the years, and I owe him a great debt. I was also very fortunate to have the detailed and erudite commentary of sociologist Heribert Adam, who took the time and trouble to give the manuscript a very close reading.

In terms of specialized anthropological assistance, Erik Trinkaus was kind enough to go through an early draft of chapter 1, Richard Lee to discuss some of the ideas presented in chapter 2, and Robert Munroe to help me with some of the details on cross-cultural child rearing provided in chapter 3. Sociologist C. R. Badcock and biologist Gordon Orians also provided significant insights at timely moments, as did an old and dear friend, John Trotter, when I was living in New Mexico a few years ago. Early versions of the text benefited greatly from on-going discussions with my apparently tireless research assistant, John Whitney, who endeavored to keep me on my toes regarding matters of evidence, plausibility, and proof. Finally, my limited knowledge of the ancient world was greatly enhanced by the very generous efforts of Carol Thomas (ancient Greece), Ronald Sack (Mesopotamia), W. J. Murnane (ancient Egypt), and Richard Salomon (Indo-European origins). In all cases, as usual, responsibility for errors of fact or interpretation is strictly my own.

I received significant support in other ways as well. In 1992 I was the recipient of the first annual grant made by the Rollo May Center for Humanistic Studies, a division of the Saybrook Institute in San Francisco. Two visiting endowed professorships also gave me the time and financial support to pursue this research: the Amy Freeman Lee Chair in the Humanities at Incarnate Word College in San Antonio, Texas, fall semester 1993, and the Garrey Carruthers Chair in Honors at the University of New Mexico, which I held during the 1994-95 academic year. Finally, I am grateful to John Oliphant for help in preparing the illustrations included in this volume.

NOTE TO THE READER

To avoid repetition of certain phrases that occur in the text with some degree of frequency, I have occasionally employed the following abbreviations:

HG = hunter-gatherer
DR = delayed-return (economy)
IR = immediate-return (economy)
SAC = sacred authority complex
p.d. = planning depth
M.P. = Middle Paleolithic
U.P. = Upper Paleolithic
T.O. = Transitional Object
RV = *Rigveda*
ASC = altered state of consciousness

The reader also should note that I employ the name *!Kung* for the Bushmen of the Kalahari desert. In recent years, there has been a tendency in the anthropological literature to refer to the !Kung (or the San, as they are also sometimes called) by the name used in their own language, namely, *Ju/'hoansi*. Given the relative obscurity of the latter name outside of anthropological circles, however, I decided to retain the traditional terminology in this book.

Finally, there is a distinction between the use of the word "nomadic" in common parlance and in a technical anthropological sense. In this latter usage, nomads are those peoples who, like hunter-gatherers, move as a way of life but who have emerged historically within the context of agricultural civilization (this is discussed in chapter 5). However, HGs predate the phenomenon of pastoralism and animal domestication. Therefore, it can be confusing to refer to a "nomadic way of life" when speaking of HGs since "ambulatory" or "wandering" would technically be more accurate. On occasion, however, I do employ "nomadic," trusting that the context will make it clear when I am referring to HGs and when to nomadic peoples.

INTRODUCTION: THE EXPERIENCE OF PARADOX

This is not a journey for those who expect love and bliss . . . Having made this journey I now see clearly, that a dimension unmistakably exists beyond anything that could be described as the self's union with God—be it called spiritual marriage, transforming union, or whatever the terminology one may care to use. For the contemplative to regard such a union as the final or ultimate consummation of his spiritual life is a grave mistake.

—Bernadette Roberts, *The Experience of No-Self*

History is typically written in a linear and chronological form in textbooks and official accounts; in personal memory, however, it is largely anecdotal. "Where were you when Kennedy was shot?" we will often ask someone, knowing that the images of that moment, and later of the Zapruder film and of Jackie standing by the coffin not only define an era, but situate each of us in it as well, in an emotional sense. All of us who lived through that decade have, in addition, memories that may be less intense but that undoubtedly shaped our understanding of the nature of political power. Let me tell you two of my own.

The first event, coincidentally enough, also involved JFK: a rally in Upstate New York in 1960, when he was swinging by as part of his presidential campaign. Kennedy was an hour late, and the crowd waited patiently, in an atmosphere of charged anticipation. Behind me I heard a man say to his companion, "He's one of the few men in the United States worth waiting for"—an interesting comment, since beyond hearing some story about a PT boat in the Pacific, very few people at that time really had any idea of who the young senator was. Kennedy finally showed up and gave a short, impassioned talk. I have no recollection of the details of what he said, but I do remember the atmosphere, which was charged and electric as he spoke of a New Frontier in a rousing Boston accent. Looking back

1

at the event years later, I realized that it was essentially a revival meeting. The crowd loved it.

The scene now shifts to somewhere just outside of Washington, D.C.; it is 1968. I am again at a political rally, this time for Eugene McCarthy on the occasion of his bid for the Democratic presidential nomination. Senator McCarthy was on time, and his delivery was very low key. He talked about the problem of the arrogance of power (referring to Lyndon Johnson and the war against North Vietnam) and the need, as he put it, to err on the side of trust rather than on the side of paranoia and aggression. It was a reflective talk, notably lacking in charisma or fiery formulation. As the crowd dispersed, I again heard a man behind me, speaking to his companion. "Well, I'd never vote for *him*," he said to her. "Why not?" she asked. "No zip; no energy," the man replied; "he lacks the strength for the job."

As the years passed, I realized that these two vignettes epitomized the misunderstanding of strength that is so characteristic of American culture and, I argue in this book, of civilization in general. Not that JFK had no strength, but that it was largely submerged in what might be called "heroic" energy—which accounts, at least in part, for the American romance with the Kennedy dynasty and the glory of "Camelot." However, Eugene McCarthy was coming from a very different place, a nonheroic one. Since he understood that heroics had gotten us *into* Vietnam, he realized that heroics would probably not be able to get us out of there. He knew that true courage lay in questioning, in being tolerant of ambiguity, and was willing to live out of that space in a public way. But to an electorate long used to conflating strength and charisma, such a position could only appear weak and ineffectual. If you're not a hero, in this way of thinking, you must be insecure.

Our experience of politics has been conditioned by aberrant circumstances. The state—an autonomous political unit having a hierarchical, centralized government capable of levying taxes, making war, and enforcing laws—has been with us for only about six thousand years. The majority of human political experience has been relatively (though not entirely) egalitarian: small, nomadic bands of hunter-gatherers that had no chiefs and, in Pierre Clastres' formulation (*Society Against the State*) no relationship of command/obedience.[1] One of the issues I shall be exploring in this book is the origin of social inequality, that is, how the human race went from what might be called "horizontal" egalitarian relations to "vertical" hierarchical ones and what the stages were that existed between HG society and agricultural civilization. Before we can do this, however, we need to have a sense of an overview of politics and consciousness as they have existed during the last 100,000 years or so.[2]

Biological Baseline

There are certain experiences common to the human race—certainly to *Homo sapiens sapiens* (i.e., "modern" humans or Cro-Magnons—which includes ourselves—who go back ninety thousand to one hundred thousand years) and possibly to *Homo sapiens neanderthalensis* (Neanderthal man, who flourished from –130,000 to –35,000 years)—that constitute a kind of biological baseline. One of these is existential awareness, the perception of having a self separate from the environment, and from others, that commonly surfaces in the third year of life. According to what is known as the Object Relations school of psychology, which deals with very early infant experience, this moment of identity is also the moment of alienation, of distinctness from the rest of the world.[3] By thirty-five thousand years ago, for example, we find a sharp increase in artifacts such as personal ornaments and grave goods, suggesting the emergence of self-conscious awareness. In any case, the effects of this alienation are, and probably were to some extent, painful; and, historically, the human race has tried to grapple with it in three basic ways. The first is the mode of consciousness associated with HG civilization, which I shall refer to as "paradox," or the experience of "space." This is a diffuse or peripheral awareness, which can be characterized as being "horizontal" in nature, in the same way that HG politics is. It is not characterized by a search for "meaning," an insistence or hope that the world be this way or that. It simply accepts the world as it presents itself, and in that sense, it would seem to require a very high level of trust. One does not "deal with" alienation (the split between Self and World) as much as live with it, accept the discomfort as just part of what is. I shall say more about paradox below.

The second mode is very much about meaning and the process of being absorbed in it. I call this constellation the "sacred authority complex" (SAC); and despite what seem to be antecedents of it in Paleolithic times, I believe that its real flowering, certainly its institutionalization, coincides with agricultural, sedentary civilization. Trust in the world is now much less, and fear of death has assumed a prominent place. The human being has not so much a world as a world *view*; and the perception tends to be vertical in nature. In other words, whereas with paradox the "sacred," such as it is, simply *is* the world, in the case of the SAC sacrality has been projected upward, into the realm of the gods. Hence we get the great theocracies of the Near East, whose religious (and political) structures were embodied in pyramids and ziggurats reaching up to the sky. Atop these monuments, symbolically speaking, was a semidivine figure such as the pharaoh, who—like the pope, millennia later—was regarded as God's (or the gods') representative on earth. Validation of the national way of life was provided both cosmologically and politically, for both spheres partook of a sacred order that stood as the guarantor of reality itself. Explanations for all events in this vertical system were thus total, absolute, and it is no accident, for example, that the three thousand-year cycle of Egyptian history was subject to very little in the way of political rebellion. The SAC forms a kind of psychological cocoon, in which security is relatively assured and potential alienation kept under control.

Sometime around 2000 B.C. or after, the verticality of the SAC became even sharper. This was the emergence of what I have referred to elsewhere as the "ascent experience," although traces of it may have existed in the Paleolithic.[4] By "ascent experience" I mean the phenomenon of unitive trance or ecstasy, which is the most dramatic way of generating (temporary) psychological security. As I shall indicate later on, this mode of consciousness corresponds to a certain hero mythology that is endemic to recent civilization, though it does have certain antecedents (the Gilgamesh epic of Mesopotamia, for example, which dates from the third millennium B.C.). It is this mode of consciousness that the American psychologist Julian Jaynes popularized with his notion of the "bicameral mind." Although he incorrectly assigned it to all of agricultural civilization, it is more likely a heightened form of the SAC.[5]

In contrast to paradox, or the diffuse alertness of HG consciousness, ascent experience is vertical and intense; it provides "certainty" both in terms of its overwhelming numinous quality and in terms of the spiritual/political hierarchy it inevitably generates. In religious forms such as the Greek mystery cults, ritual practices were used to obliterate consciousness, to submerge the ego into the One, the Absolute. It was from these cults that Gnosticism, and eventually Christianity, flourished, and they had a heavy impact on Plato's *Dialogues* as well, which often entered Western civilization as a kind of countercultural, underground stream (the Neoplatonism of the Renaissance, for example).[6] All of this served to offset the pain of ego-consciousness by means of a mystical experience that merged the psyche with the rest of the creation, what Freud called the "oceanic experience." In his view, the experience was regressive, the attempt to return to a fetal state, or to the primitive, archaic mother. Jung, as is well known, regarded it as *progressive*, the contacting of a certain kind of primitive wisdom. Both were probably correct; and since the two views are irreconcilable, there is a conundrum within Western culture especially that sits with us, very uneasily, to this day.

The third way of dealing with ego-consciousness is the mode of industrial societies, what might rightly be called "dullardism"—*lowering* consciousness, in other words, "spacing out." Trance practice still exists in these societies, but only as a type of "heresy" among marginal or fringe groups. This is why drugs such as valium and Prozac are legal in the United States and Europe and why peyote (mescaline) and magic mushrooms (psilocybin) are not. With dullardism, the goal is simply to go unconscious, by means of tranquilizers, alcohol, TV, spectator sports, organized religion, compulsive busyness and workaholism, and so on (even though many of these do provide a short-term "high"). I won't be saying very much about this mode, inasmuch as it is not very interesting, and all too familiar, in any case. It is perhaps noteworthy, however, that civilization, whether agricultural or industrial, is a seamless whole. In both, political arrangements are vertical, and the sacred is elsewhere, "in heaven," with the leadership partaking of sanctity (a divine order) or imbued with aura, charisma. This is not to say that democracies don't often elect dull and unimaginative leaders, but the *ideal*, at any rate, is a heroic one, which accounts for the survival of monarchies in many democratic countries as well as the attraction to popular charismatic figures, such as the Kennedys. Hence the famous observation by the German sociologist, Max Weber, that we swing between bureaucracy and charisma. Indeed, the two seem to need each other.

As institutionalized entities, at any rate, vertical politics and consciousness have not been with us for very long. On an anthropological time scale, for example, the state is clearly aberrant. Whether one reads Oswald Spengler (*The Decline of the West*) or Joseph Tainter (*The Collapse of Complex Societies*), one comes away with a similar impression, that civilizations are *inherently* unstable; they *inevitably* collapse. Pursuing a vertical ideal, their center of gravity is too high. Unlike HG societies, which seem indefinitely sustainable, virtually all civilizations go the ironic route depicted by Percy Shelley in his famous poem, "Ozymandias," modeled on the figure of Ramses II of Egypt:

And on the pedestal these words appear:
"My name is Ozymandias, king of kings:
Look on my works, ye Mighty, and despair!"
Nothing beside remains. Round the decay
Of that colossal wreck, boundless and bare
The lone and level sands stretch far away.[7]

I shall have more to say about the SAC, heroism, vertical energy, and the like later on in this book. For now, let me focus on the first solution to ego-consciousness, that of paradox.

The Nature of Paradox

We thus have two modes of consciousness to deal with, two types of energetic configuration. The vertical, ecstatic mode has received virtually all of the scholarly attention. The historian of religion, Mircea Eliade, argued that it went back to the Paleolithic, and many have followed his lead in seeing animal paintings on the walls of Lascaux, Altamira, and so on, as shamanically inspired. There is also a fair amount of trance practice among present-day HG groups. Yet I can't help but wonder whether we may not be reading more recent forms of religiosity into those cave paintings and whether contemporary HGs have not absorbed the shamanic practices of their sedentary neighbors. I am not necessarily discounting the possibility of "mysticism" in the Paleolithic, as it were, but wonder whether we have overemphasized it because of its dramatic role in our own religious traditions. The dominant mode of consciousness among HGs today, as well as in the past, may not be unitive trance, but a diffuse, peripheral type of awareness that I am calling paradox. I suspect paradox is a very old genetic memory, in that it seems to be continuous with the kind of alertness that animals often display. In humans, as the word "paradox" suggests, it includes holding contradictory propositions, or emotions, simultaneously; sustaining the tension of this conflict so that a deeper reality can emerge than one would have if one simply opted, for example, for Self or Other. In the SAC, no paradox is present; one has "certainty" instead. And in unitive trance (ascent experience), Self dissolves into Other, and that is that. This latter process also can be fed into war, for example, in which the Other is obliterated in favor of the Self, even while the Self is dissolved into the nation or the cause. It would seem that these are psychologically infantile (or adolescent) solutions to the problem of bipolar (Self/Other) contradiction. What many HGs seem to display, by contrast, is a kind of mature ambiguity.

Figure 1. Rembrandt van Rijn, *The Syndics of Cloth Hall.* Courtesy Rijksmuseum Amsterdam.

In fact, there is nothing mysterious about paradox, but it is nevertheless difficult to define in any precise way. The following example from my own personal experience may possibly clarify what I am talking about.

In the summer and fall of 1991, I was living in Berlin. The Altes Museum in the former Eastern sector of the city mounted an exhibition of the work of Rembrandt—paintings, sketches, etchings. The artwork was collected from museums in Berlin, Amsterdam, London, and New York, and may have been the largest exhibition of Rembrandt up to that time. In a way, I was unprepared for what was about to hit me; I found it very difficult to leave the museum even after several hours. Many of the pieces had captured a single moment on paper or canvas—whether of a snail, or of Faust in his study, or of Rembrandt himself at age twenty-three—that was a moment in time and yet also, paradoxically, an eternity. For me this phenomenon was most striking in a painting that I had seen, reproduced countless times, on the Dutch Masters cigar box: *De staalmeesters*, or as it is sometimes rendered in English, *The Syndics of Cloth Hall*. The painting, which is quite large, shows six wealthy burghers, heads of the cloth guild in Amsterdam, sitting around their account book and staring out at the spectator of the painting (Figure 1). Nothing surprising there: in commissioned works of the seventeenth century, this was a typical bourgeois pose. But what is so astonishing is what Rembrandt managed to capture in their gaze. They seem to be saying: "Who *are* you?" and also, "Who are *we*, and what are we doing in these outlandish outfits?" There is in this look an eternal moment that is, at the same time, a very specific moment, quite unique.

This quality of the universal in the particular, and vice versa, is what the American author John Briggs refers to (*Fire in the Crucible*) as "omnivalence," in which the mind is moved to unfold itself in the space between contradictions. It is a moment of suspended animation, a particular type of paradox; a moment of pure "Is-ness" that cannot be framed in terms of any formula or ideology—not even the one of "Mystery"—and thus becomes the most radical or revolutionary statement of all. Such a moment peeks out between fixed forms, and reminds us of a very different mode of consciousness than the one we are used to. One might call this state "nonegoic," but that can be misleading, since it is a state of heightened self-awareness, one that is not about boundary loss, bliss, or the SAC in any way.[8]

I ran across one description of this state in a lovely book by Joanna Field (pseudonym of the British therapist Marion Milner), *A Life of One's Own*, in which she refers to it as wide, as opposed to narrow attention, and compares it to the hovering of a kestrel.[9] This mindset is actually well known in the anthropological literature. Here is the description given by Hugh Brody, who spent time living with native groups in British Columbia:

> Above all they are still and receptive, prepared for whatever insight or realization may come to them, and ready for whatever stimulus to action might arise. This state of attentive waiting is perhaps as close as people can come to the falcon's suspended flight, when the bird, seemingly motionless, is ready to plummet in decisive action.[10]

Similarly, in *Meditations on Hunting*, Ortega y Gasset wrote:

> It is a "universal" attention, which does not inscribe itself on any point and tries to be on all points. There is a magnificent term for this, [namely] . . . alertness. . . . Only the hunter, imitating the perpetual alertness of the wild animal . . . sees everything.

And Walter Ong, writing in the *American Anthropologist* in 1969, called it a "world presence" rather than a world view. The latter phrase, wrote Ong, suggests something fixed, a "major unifying perception." World presence, on the other hand, is about sensuality, immediacy, and "a certain kind of relevance."[11]

I call this consciousness "paradoxical" because it is simultaneously focused and nonfocused. It is hovering, or peripheral, rather than intense or ecstatic; and paradox also exists in the fact that a moment such as this feels completely individual and unique and, at the same time, universal. As a result, that which is most personal is also felt to be the most general, the most connected to other human beings. In addition, that which is fleeting is experienced as that which is most enduring.

Again, there is nothing mysterious about this. *New Yorker* staff writer Tony Hiss, in his discussion of urban planning (*The Experience of Place*), is well aware of this mode of consciousness and describes it in a number of ways:

> Our habitual style of thinking ... is a stream of consciousness pouring and pushing its way through the present; but this [other] feeling, which I call simultaneous perception, seems calmer, more like a clear, deep, reflective lake. Both the pinpoint focus of ordinary perception, which lets us shut ourselves off from our surroundings, and the broad-band focus of simultaneous perception, which keeps us linked to our surroundings, are inherited skills built into each of us. People sometimes get so good at blotting out the sights and sounds and smells around them that simultaneous perception, when it resurfaces, can catch them by surprise. But because this ability is always in operation, it's constantly available. And whenever we summon it, it's richly informative.[12]

In another passage, Hiss quotes art historian Anton Ehrenzweig, who refers to the experience as that of "utter watchfulness," paying equal attention to everything at once. Hiss says it involves "gaining a relaxed sense of our own outside edge ... [such that] we divide our attention equally between ourselves and things outside ourselves." This form of perception, he goes on to say, "putting at our disposal an evenhanded, instantaneous, and outward-looking flow of attention, acts like a sixth sense." When we diffuse our attention and relax its intensity, he concludes, we initiate a "change that lets us start to see all the things around us at once and yet also look calmly and steadily at each one of them."[13]

It is this kind of looking that opens the door to a very different experience of the sacred than that emphasized by agricultural civilization or by some tribal, shamanic cultures. It has some affinity with the Zen *satori*, the radical perception of the "suchness" of things; but because of its horizontality, its seeming ordinariness, it goes largely unnoticed. Once in a while, one runs across a reference to it in poetry. Although in the following excerpt from a poem by Galway Kinnell, the author is not making any specific references to hunter-gatherers or sedentary cultures, he does capture the essential difference between them in their views of what endures, what really counts:

> If one day it happens
> you find yourself with someone you love
> in a café at one end
> of the Pont Mirabeau, at the zinc bar
> where white wine stands in upward opening glasses,
>
> and if you commit then, as we did, the error
> of thinking,
> *one day all this will only be memory,*
>
> learn,
> as you stand
> at this end of the bridge which arcs
> from love, you think, into enduring love,
> learn to reach deeper
> into the sorrows
> to come—to touch
> the almost imaginary bones
> under the face, to hear under the laughter
> the wind crying across the black stones. Kiss
> the mouth
> which tells you, *here,*
> *here is the world.* This mouth. This laughter. These temple bones.
>
> The still undanced cadence of vanishing.[14]

In "Le Pont Mirabeau," a much older poem by Guillaume Apollinaire, the author contrasts the fleetingness of numerous lovers on the bridge, and their love, with the bridge itself—the solid, material object that endures. As I read it, the famous refrain of the poem is spoken by the bridge itself:

Vienne la nuit sonne l'heure
Les jours s'en vont je demeure.[15]

(The night comes, the hour sounds,
The days go by, I remain.)

Kinnell's advice is precisely the inverse of this: the bridge, a symbol of (material) civilization, is mere background, merely a stage. What is truly real is the newness of the moment, the "fleeting" kiss of the lovers. Do you get it? he is saying; *here*, here is the world, in this permanently ephemeral moment. *This* mouth, *this* laughter, these bones in my head, what I am feeling right now, not temple bones as relics in a temple—the religious trademark of agricultural societies, wherein they are worshipped as past artifacts or as prognosticators of the future. Bridges come and go, Kinnell is saying; the kiss or moment that is fully experienced lasts forever.

Shall we call this experience "sacred"? The problem with this is that it is a modern (i.e., civilized) way of relating to it. For HG societies, there was not a separate category of existence called "the sacred." When Native Americans refer to the Great Spirit, they often are (it depends on the tribe) talking about the wind. This spirit is "merely" the creation itself: water coming off a leaf, the smell of the forest after rain, the warm blood of a deer. This was a culture that lived, as Virginia Woolf put it, "between the acts"; alertness is the sine qua non of a hunting society. The great anthropologist Paul Radin, who did extensive fieldwork among the Winnebago Indians, argued that for such peoples, reality was heightened to such a pitch that the details of the environment seemed to "blaze."[16] This terminology can be misleading, in that it might suggest a kind of trance experience; but there is no loss of consciousness or "fusion with the Absolute" here. This is immanence, not transcendence; it involves heightened awareness, not "burning bush" experiences and boundary loss. In this world, the secular *is* the sacred, which is all around us. This is why I call it a horizontal perception.

The Coming of the SAC

The SAC, and later, unitive trance, are quite different from this. What (agricultural) civilization managed to do was to disenchant the world in a peripheral sense and then reenchant it in a focused or centralized sense. Vertical energy finally overwhelmed and replaced horizontal energy, and this is mirrored, as already noted, in the architecture of the great theocracies, such as Egyptian pyramids or Aztec temples. This energy is also the basis of religions and priesthoods. With unitive trance in particular, erotic energy, if you will, is expunged from the environment at large and then channeled into certain specific experiences, now regarded as cultural norms: romantic love, for example (which does not typically exist among HGs); heroism (Arthurian legends, the search for the grail); and the need to go to war. More than one writer since Freud has commented on the close relationship of these to death. For example, war is chronically irresistible to civilization because it provides situations of numinous intensity, so that one feels bonded to the universe, "alive." Sartre describes such a "religious" war experience in his novel *Nausea*; and Bertrand Russell, in his autobiography, recalls wandering around Trafalgar Square in 1914, just after war was declared, and being struck by how palpable was the excitement, the sense of physical relief that permeated the air. "I discovered to my amazement," he writes, "that average men and women were delighted at the prospect of war." He goes on, "What filled me with . . . horror, was the fact that the anticipation of carnage was delightful to something like ninety per cent of the population. I had to revise my views on human nature."[17]

In any case, we see that the structure of religion in civilization, particularly Western civilization (whether we are talking about heresy or orthodoxy), is a vertical one, with the mundane world regarded as being down here, below, and heaven up above. Starting at some point around 2000 B.C., and accelerating in the so-called Axial Age, after 1000 B.C. (see chapter 4), this verticality acquired its own dichotomy, a sharp division between the sacred and the secular, with salvation being a promise held out by the sacred sphere.[18] By contrast, I would argue, HG "religion" was for the most part nothing more complicated than the "magic" of everyday life. Why assume, for example, that Paleolithic cave paintings are reflections of mystical trance or oceanic experience? Nothing so exotic may be involved. It is at least as likely that our ancestors were "simply" celebrating energy, aliveness, such as can be seen in the vibrant colors and implied movement of the animals they painted. Although trance may have occurred occasionally, one does not have to undergo boundary loss to know the sacredness of life.

There is another issue here as well. Vertical experience, whether of the SAC or the ecstatic variety, has an unavoidable political counterpart. Jaynes regarded bicamerality as a quest for certainty, in particular, for authority or authorization. The psychic "certainty" of this experience was paralleled by the desire of agricultural civilization to possess certainty on other levels as well. A huge distortion ensued. With the rise of sedentary civilization, the human race went from paradox, a kind of kaleidoscopic consciousness, to fixed systems of religious "truth." This development, I believe, has had enormous consequences in terms of our political adherence to ideologies of various kinds. The net effect has not been salutary. During the last four millennia in particular, civilization has been preoccupied with transcendence, and this has led to a kind of absolutism in the way we live and think. "Cultural hypnosis" means not only that we take whatever paradigm we live in as real, but that we can only conceive of escaping that paradigm by installing another paradigm in its place. "Worship," even of a secular variety, continues to be the norm.

Trance and Agriculture

The possible association between ecstasy and agriculture, or urban/sedentary life, shows up in the great Mesopotamian epic, the Gilgamesh, which dates back to the third millennium B.C. and is among the very earliest literary works of Western civilization. It is also, I believe, the first hero tale. In this story, Enkidu, the highlander (or mountain man), is drawn into the ways of sedentary peoples. Here is the crucial passage, describing Enkidu's "first meeting with civilization," as Thorkild Jacobsen calls it:

> But Enkidu, who made his home in the mountains
> Ate grass with the gazelles
> And always sucked the milk of animals.
>
> The city dwellers set food before him, and he became uneasy;
> He gaped and looked.
> Enkidu did not know anything about eating bread,
> And he knew nothing about drinking *Rauschtrank*.
>
> The women began to speak to him.
> "Eat this bread, Enkidu, this is part of life!
> Drink the *Rauschtrank*, as is done in this country."
>
> Enkidu ate bread until he was sated
> And drank seven steins of *Rauschtrank*.
> His inner being became free and cheerful
> His heart became happy, and his face radiant.

He washed his hairy body with water
He salved himself with oil, and became a human being.
He clothed himself; now he is like a man.[19]

Of course, "human being" here is defined from the viewpoint of agricultural civilization, and it is interesting to note that bread—the economic symbol of that civilization—and *Rauschtrank* go together. But what is this *Rauschtrank*? The literal translation, from the German, is "ecstasy drink," which could include alcohol, mescal, or any type of hallucinogenic plant derivative. Whatever it might be, the crucial point is that it provides a *Rausch* ("rush"), a vertical/ecstatic experience, something Enkidu did not need when he was integrated with animal life and when all the world still shimmered for him. In sedentary civilization, that experience tends to get lost, and is compensated for by means of a megadose: seven steins of *Rauschtrank*, after which Enkidu is suddenly cheerful and radiant. All of this is regarded as natural, "human," in this society, in which paradox has disappeared, and in which some form of ecstasy serves as a heightened substitute. Even so, it remains the enduring power of the story that Gilgamesh "grows up," realizes that redemption cannot occur in some afterlife, and that this life is all we have. The epic concludes on a note of mature irony and self-acceptance. Gilgamesh is, perhaps, a different kind of hero than that common to later civilizations, such as Greece, or perhaps our own.

The theme of this book, in any case, is how the dominant perception of human beings shifted from a horizontal to a vertical one; how this shift is (for the most part) associated with the transition from nomadic to sedentary ways of life; how a kind of openness toward experience faded, only to be replaced by a search for "certainty"; and how we are now struggling with the consequences of these age-old developments. What might be done about all this is something I shall comment on toward the end of the book.

Apologia Pro Vita Sua

However, I do wish to insert some caveats here, and also give the reader some idea of why I would write what may seem to be a rather unusual book. One caveat is that the argument is quite tentative; I am floating a trial balloon, of sorts, an idea that I believe runs counter to most anthropological thinking about religion. This is because the phenomenon of paradox is virtually invisible in our culture, for the common understanding of breaking with the dominant (analytical) paradigm of Western thought is to shift to Gnostic insight, some form of mysticism or mythological thinking. This "transpersonal" viewpoint has no lack of enthusiasts, and I am not saying it is without a certain truth. I argued as much many years ago, in *The Reenchantment of the World*, though—thankfully—I put in a strong qualification regarding the politics of ecstasy at the end of the book.

As the years went by, however, I began to have doubts about "oceanic" solutions or about the excitement over a "paradigm shift" that might usher in a New Age. I wound up speaking on the subject at conferences that were little more than revival meetings, and wondered what I was doing there. It seemed to me that most of the supporters of the new holistic paradigm had no facility with the rational/scientific paradigm they fervently sought to discard; and I began to realize that the unthinking zeal that characterized this movement was the story of new paradigms down through the ages. No progress, in short, was being made in terms of seeing through the religious nature of paradigm itself. It was as though we were still in ancient Egypt, with the pharaoh now being replaced by a set of buzzwords.

Other things began to make an impression on me. Years of body work and meditation led me to believe that paradigm zeal is rooted in a denial of our somatic experience. Emotions, often painful, live in the body; paradigm-shift addiction (like substance addiction) enables us to escape these emotions and live in our heads. Carl Jung and the transpersonalists, despite some valuable insights, were (are) cut off from bodily experience; they created a larger mind than the dominant intellectual paradigm, but when all was said and done, it was still a mind. Their call for a renewed spirituality only went so far, in my view; clearly, we needed a renewed *corporeality* if we were not going to repress the body and fall into the trap of a new mythology, make a fetish out of our supposedly new spirituality. All of this became the subject of a subsequent book, *Coming to Our Senses*, the writing of which was an important journey for me.

However, the journey was hardly over; something was still missing, but I couldn't grasp what it was. The first hint came when I read *The Songlines*, Bruce Chatwin's book about his experience in the Australian outback. Chatwin was not an anthropologist, and there are all sorts of ethnographic errors in the book; but the book is really a kind of diary, an exploration of one particular theme, namely, the role of movement in the evolution of human life and consciousness. Chatwin believed that sedentary life spawned a host of illusions, religion among them, that were harmful to the human race and that were largely absent from HG and nomadic societies. The implication was that by going sedentary, we had shifted from a direct experience of life to the pursuit of substitutes, and that a certain kind of mental flexibility had gotten lost as well. To my mind, at any rate, it rang true.[20]

How I wandered from Chatwin's book to the text you are now reading is a bit blurry in my mind; the path certainly wasn't a linear one. But I recall reading Ray Monk's biography of the Austrian philosopher Ludwig Wittgenstein and recognizing that he had, during the second half of his career, stumbled onto paradox and spent the last two decades of his life elliptically describing an insight that no one around him could understand. At some point, I also read Bernadette Roberts' *The Experience of No-Self*, in which she describes the falling away of "God" and the loss of interest in Gnostic fusion with the Absolute, in favor of a particular kind of alertness that goes deeper than the *satori* of Zen Buddhism.[21] I began to see, even more dramatically than before, that freedom lay not in paradigms, which were just different versions of the SAC, but in a particular experience that was not endowed with any salvationist properties. I didn't know how this might apply to culture at large, but I saw that a very different understanding of reality was at least possible, and it seemed to me that HGs had had it and perhaps still did.

Much of this, then, revolves around the issue of sedentism. As I shall argue later on, being nomadic is something that culturally and physiologically reinforces kaleidoscopic or paradoxical perception, for the landscape is constantly shifting before one. Fixed abodes lend themselves to fixed perceptions, as well as a need for certainty, both religious and political. Given that the bulk of human experience on this earth is ambulatory, it seems likely that beneath our desperate need for certainty lies something much deeper, and that is our need for indeterminism, for the world to be *un*predictable, surprising, alive.

This brings me to a second caveat: this book is not a pitch for a return to HG society, which would, in the first instance, require a severe depopulation of the planet. Even beyond that, the formula of hunter-gatherers good, civilization bad is both simplistic and wrong. The reality is much more complicated than that, and the attempt to institute total egalitarian relations, or paradoxical perception (which probably cannot be "instituted" anyway), would be a very destructive undertaking. For better or worse, it is our fate to live in civilization, and our job is to do civilization well, not abandon it. In my view, part of that effort must involve exploring the dialectical tensions that exist between civilization and our HG past; simply "going horizontal" would only amount to more pathology. It would be a collapse of real thinking, a grasping of one horn of a dilemma and pretending that the other one didn't exist or that it would conveniently go away. This is not to say that certain key elements from our HG past are not valuable or worth trying to recover, and I shall be talking about this later on. But we need to have a sense of the complex relations that exist, or perhaps *should* exist, between the vertical and the horizontal if our culture is to move ahead with any degree of sanity, or even common sense.

A third caveat relates to the necessarily speculative nature of a project such as this one. In the main, it is about the nature and evolution of mental states and of a certain type of consciousness. Quite obviously, I have no way of interviewing Paleolithic peoples or of conducting evolutionary brain experiments; no one does, including those who, like Eliade, argued for the existence of Paleolithic shamanism. If this school of thought on Paleolithic religion projected modern depth psychology onto ancestors who are not here to speak for themselves, it is nevertheless the case that much of my own evidence is circumstantial. It is not that I have merely dreamt up some arbitrary scenario; as Walter Ong points out, there are clearly many cultures for whom the world is not an object or a paradigm, but "something dynamic and unpredictable."[22] But there is no way I can prove, for example, the existence of a solid evolutionary link between animal and human paradox, even though it seems likely enough. The upshot is that, empirical evidence notwithstanding, this book is as much a work of philosophy as it is of psychology or anthropology and ultimately makes sense (or does not) only when taken as a whole. Certainly, if my thesis regarding paradox is a delusion, the argument falls apart completely.

Finally, I am not arguing that paradox is our destiny. Certainly, we are at a crucial juncture as a civilization, and everybody seems to be saying this in one form or another these days. For me, there are at least two problems with this. First, I am not convinced that the human race actually *has* a "destiny," some sort of fate that is written down somewhere, which God, Hegel, and a few mystics have been privileged to know. There may *be* no unconscious purpose working itself out; life may just be life, going through various turns, occasionally hitting a dead end, sometimes making progress, and sometimes not. Second, I am no longer convinced that the institution of some new paradigm can really save us. Such a thing may come to pass, but like all of the previous paradigms, it too will have its problems; they too will be severe, and we shall have to deal with them as best we can. Perhaps destiny ought to be replaced by the notion that there is better, and there is worse, and that's just the way things are.

The role I see for paradox is thus not one of destiny. We are not going to get rid of the SAC very easily, and are undoubtedly heading for the next incarnation of it, which will (sad to say) probably involve an even *larger* transcendent outlook.[23] Paradox could even fuel this tendency, if attempts to institutionalize it on a large scale are nominally successful. A better role for it is not that of a new paradigm but that of a gadfly. For the form of consciousness that got rendered invisible by agricultural civilization will, I suspect, keep nagging at us until we are ready to look at our need for certainty with a more critical eye. If we can do that, and not make "uncertainty" into a new certainty, we might conceivably find ourselves in a less desperate place than we are now. "Certainties" of all sorts may reassure us psychologically, but they do that only by sharply restricting the range of our experience. Treated with nonideological integrity, as a lived (somatic) experience rather than a formula, paradox may teach us that broader possibilities exist. Theoretically, at least, there is hope for us yet.

1

THE WRITING ON THE WALL

> We have termed the ecstatic experience a "primary phenomenon" because we see no reason whatever for regarding it as the result of a particular historical moment, that is, as produced by a certain form of civilization.
>
> —Mircea Eliade, *Shamanism: Archaic Techniques of Ecstasy*

> Secularisation . . . is an age-old cosmological type . . . which need have nothing to do with urban life or modern science. . . . The idea that primitive man is by nature deeply religious is nonsense. . . . The illusion that all primitives are pious, credulous and subject to the teaching of priests or magicians has probably done even more to impede our understanding of our own civilisation than it has confused the interpretations of archaeologists dealing with the dead past.
>
> —Mary Douglas, *Natural Symbols*

I recall being asked, some years ago, by someone at a conference I was attending, what I was currently working on. Like many writers, this is a question I try to evade, since I have a fear that if I talk about my work I shall become less motivated to do it. So in response I murmured something about Paleolithic consciousness, thinking this would be sufficiently obscure as to discourage any further exploration of the topic. However, my questioner was not to be put off, and her rejoinder went to the heart of the matter. "What are you using for research?" she quipped; "psychedelics?"

It is a common notion, going back to the nineteenth century but kept alive by writers such as Carl Jung and Joseph Campbell, that primitive humanity was up to its eyeballs in trance, myth, and shamanism and that this was the "true" consciousness of the human race, its "natural mind." The assumption here is that the "natural" mind is a religious one; that transcendent experience of an Absolute, a "wholly Other," is the touchstone of sacred experience, absolutely necessary for human beings to exist in the world and have meaning in their lives. Openly or implicitly assuming the existence of a mythic substrate, or universal psyche, scholars such as Sir James Frazer (*The Golden Bough*) elaborated a comparative mythology, in which some so-called archetype—heroism, let us say, or sympathetic magic—is purportedly shown to be present in every primitive culture around the globe, past or present. Thus, Mircea Eliade, in his very influential book on shamanism, wrote that there was a dialectic of the sacred that tends to repeat archetypes, such that one hierophany was equivalent to any other, even if the two were separated by a thousand years. The process of sacralizing reality, Eliade asserted, whether of a tree, a rock, or a god, was always the same. The shaman's ability to leave his body and ascend to the heavens, he argued, was a primordial phenomenon; "it belongs to man as such, not to man as a historical being." Eliade held that at the dawn of time, there was a free and easy communication between humans and gods but that this got lost, and after the "fall from grace" only certain privileged persons had the power of transcendent or ecstatic experience. The shaman, he concluded, was thus part of a mystical elite that guarded the soul of the community.[1]

What might be the evidence for this? The fact is that the belief in the great antiquity of the "ascent" tradition, in which the soul goes up to heaven and merges with the "Absolute," is not merely the belief of a few easily persuaded New Age devotees or contemporary mystics; it has been held by a variety of scholars interested in Paleolithic art. Indeed, some form of religious explanation of cave art and related material seems to have been the rule for most of the twentieth century.[2] Thus, we find, in the cave of Les Trois Frères in the Pyrenees, a painting of a figure—often referred to as the "sorcerer"—wearing a mask and the antlers of a deer, which the eminent French scholar, the abbé Henri Breuil, took to be a Paleolithic god and which has often been regarded as a dancing shaman (Figures 2 and 3). On the walls of Lascaux, we see a stiff, prostrate figure lying on the ground and a symbolic bird on a stick depicted alongside it—clearly, to Eliade and others, a shaman in trance (Figure 4). At the Grotta Guattari in Italy, a Neanderthal cranium was discovered in 1939, of which the *foramen magnum* was enlarged, suggesting that the brains had been removed and eaten. The cranium also, supposedly, was found sitting within a ring of stones. And at Pech-Merle in the Dordogne, as well as at Le Tuc d'Audoubert in the Pyrenees, children's footprints appear in the caves, said by some archaeologists to bear witness

Figure 2. The "Sorcerer" of Trois Frères. From Paolo Graziosi, *Paleolithic Art.*

Figure 3. The "Sorcerer" of Trois Frères, Version by Henri Breuil. From Paolo Graziosi, *Paleolithic Art.*

Figure 4. Bison, Prostrate Figure, and Bird at Lascaux. From Mario Ruspoli, *The Cave of Lascaux.*

to the use of these places for ancient initiation rites. There would seem to be enough evidence, then, that my conference questioner was on the right track: Paleolithic consciousness was predominantly magical, heavily involved in the cultivation of altered states.[3]

Now to the extent that we can legitimately extrapolate backward from contemporary hunter-gatherers and other tribal societies, there seems to be good ethnographic evidence for such a conclusion. The shaman is obviously a major figure in many such tribes (the Arctic region is notorious for this), and in a survey done some years ago by the American anthropologist Erika Bourguignon, 90 percent of the 488 small societies she examined from around the globe proved to have some form of institutionalized religious practice involving an altered state of consciousness (ASC). In at least one case of contemporary trance practice—the *!kia* dance of the !Kung Kalahari Bushmen—we have rock art going back five hundred years that clearly depicts this shamanic behavior, down to details such as blood coming out of the nose. So the ethnographic parallels would seem to be fairly good.[4]

In consequence, I am not going to argue that Paleolithic humans did not have a spiritual life nor that things such as ecstatic trance, spirit possession, and sympathetic magic were necessarily absent from it. The traditional "religious" interpretation of the Paleolithic may indeed be true. The real problem is that regardless of what is painted on the walls of French caves, we cannot know what was going on beyond our own interpretations of those paintings because no one was running around the Paleolithic with a video camera, conducting interviews. More than religious interpretations are possible, and indeed, a number of scholars have made them.[5] As for ethnographic parallels, they are very suggestive, but we have no proof that what is going on today among HGs was also going on twenty thousand or forty thousand years ago. Contemporary trance behavior could reflect modern developments, for all we know. What I am going to propose, then, following the suggestion already made in the introduction, is that sacred experience did exist in the Paleolithic, but that for the most part, it was not the sort envisioned by writers such as Eliade. Instead, what was dominant was a more horizontal spirituality, a persistent "secular" tradition that is a lot less exotic, but that, because of its obviousness (and our own fascination with the exotic), has escaped our attention. This may, in turn, give us some insight into what our "spiritual birthright" really is, and what that means in political and religious terms. Before I can do that, however, we need to take a closer look at the evidence already presented and come to terms with the weaknesses of the vertical, and/or magical, religious approach.

Religion in the Paleolithic?

Part of the problem is the comparative method itself, which, as Eliade, Jung, and others admit, is not concerned with context. As Jane Harrison put it in her classic work, *Prolegomena to the Study of Greek Religion*, "mythologists are slow to face solid historical fact." It might be more accurate to say that they are oblivious to it. Thus the anthropologist Felicitas Goodman characterizes the approach as simplistic, one in which "snippets are cut from all sorts of religions which are then assembled into a collage of doubtful value." It is not that comparative methodology is faulty by definition; there are many good comparative analyses around. But the disconnection of psychological or religious practices from their historical embeddedness typically results in feelgood generalizations that have no basis in reality. To pick out any given item or pattern from a number of different cultures and insist that they are equivalent, or to force a single pattern onto a large body of material without historical qualification, is unacceptable from a social science point of view and usually violates common sense as well. Writers such as Joseph Campbell and Eliade, however, ultimately had no real interest in data; they were on vision-quests, not scholarly quests, and had their answer in advance. Their examples presuppose a universal mythic substrate and then, in circular fashion, are used to "prove" the existence of that substrate. If this gets a lot of people excited, it is almost invariably at the expense of intellectual integrity.[6]

Given this caveat, the evidence provided above for trance practice in the Paleolithic begins to look a little less convincing. Although certain cave paintings are very suggestive, they do have a Rorschach-like quality, in that we are projecting twentieth-century religious yearnings onto a screen, as it were. The prostrate figure at Lascaux, for example, was first interpreted (1952) as a shaman in trance by the German writer Horst Kirchner, based on comparisons with contemporary bird symbolism in some tribal cultures. But unless one *assumes* the existence of certain psychological universals as a fact, there is no way of proving that contemporary and Paleolithic bird symbolism have the same meaning. As Eliade himself admitted, at least one other scholar saw the bird on a stick as a memorial image, while Nancy Sandars (*Prehistoric Art in Europe*) regards it as a spear thrower. Kirchner also argued that certain unidentified objects found at prehistoric sites were shamans' drumsticks (*Kommandostäbe*), based (again) on contemporary ethnographic similarities. But this too is a case of modern projection; we simply have no way of knowing what such sticks were used for. Magical practice is only one possibility.[7]

A similar objection can be made regarding the "sorcerer" of Trois Frères, an image that has been taken to be hard-core evidence for ASCs in the Paleolithic. Indeed, looking at the abbé Breuil's reconstruction of it (Figure 3), it seems hard to avoid a sense of magical significance here, and the painting is commonly regarded as depicting a man wearing an animal mask and performing a ritual dance. For six decades, Breuil was the key figure in the documentation of Paleolithic art, and his views had an enormous influence. It is his tracings and copies that are reproduced in most works on cave art, illustrations that have become more familiar to us than the originals. Yet his ideas regarding that art were neither original nor profound, and they were devoid of any specific comment. Under the influence of writers such as James Frazer, Breuil adopted a religious or totemic view very early in his career and never wavered from it.

All human representations were seen as sorcerers or spirits; all Paleolithic caves had to be, ipso facto, sanctuaries for sacred activities. The result, write Paul Bahn and Jean Vertut in *Images of the Ice Age*, is that we are always getting the "Breuil version," "Paleolithic figures that have passed through a standard 'Breuil process': they are subjective copies, not faithful facsimiles." Breuil typically waited years—twenty, in the case of the Trois Frères "sorcerer"—to redraw his tracings for publication, and this led to numerous errors. Thus, he sometimes filled in missing elements or omitted lines that did not fit his magico-religious interpretation. Composite figures such as those at Trois Frères "were automatically and unjustifiably called 'sorcerers,' and were assumed to be a [sic] shaman or medicine man in a mask or animal costume." The truth is that we don't *know* what these figures represent; they may not be shamans at all. We also need to ask why, if shamanism were allegedly so important to Paleolithic peoples, such figures occur so rarely in Paleolithic art and are only schematically represented when they do appear.[8]

What Breuil did becomes evident when his popular reconstruction (Figure 3) is compared to a photograph of the actual cave wall (Figure 2). The figure is not necessarily dancing, as is commonly assumed (in Breuil's version it is often shown nearly upright); it could simply be crawling along the ground. As for the head, this barely appears in the original painting. The "Breuil version" is indeed an imaginative rendition, the product of the assumption of an "unreal, magical atmosphere in which the Paleolithic mind roamed," as art historian Paolo Graziosi once put it. Indeed, Breuil's reconstruction relies heavily on an ethnographic parallel, that of the Siberian shaman of the eighteenth century, which it closely resembles.

In consequence, I would like to suggest a more likely explanation, based on the notion that Paleolithic man was *not* wandering around in an "unreal, magical atmosphere," an explanation rooted in a very different ethnographic parallel: this is a representation of somebody hunting, one of the most obvious features of Paleolithic life. Thus, in southern Africa, in the nineteenth century, observers such as George Stow (*The Native Races of South Africa*) noted that hunters would often creep up on various herds or flocks, disguising themselves with the heads or hides of those animals and mimicking their movements. He found a number of paintings that depicted this, such as can be seen in Figure 5. This particular illustration is taken from a cave in the Herschel District, Cape Colony, and shows a Bushman hunter (far right) wearing an ostrich skin and feathers and stalking a flock. Such drawings, writes Stow, "would appear to any one not acquainted with the habits and customs of

Figure 5. Bushman Stalking a Flock of Ostriches. From George Stow, *The Native Races of South Africa.*

this old hunter race to be intended for symbolic, or supernatural deities, around which some ancient myth was embodied." But this, he goes on, would be a misconception. Disguises of this sort were used constantly for practical purposes, and it was probably later elaboration that gave this type of activity a mythical interpretation—in particular, in civilization, such as we find among the Egyptians or Assyrians, says Stow. At the very least, all this suggests that a shamanic interpretation of the figure at Trois Frères is very likely a modern projection, and as such, unwarranted.[9]

Consider also the Neanderthal cranium discovered at the Grotta Guattari, which is often cited as an example of primitive cannibalism and ritual behavior. As it turns out, a recent re-analysis of the cranium, the floor deposit on the cave, and the accompanying faunal remains, revealed that there was no evidence to support such an interpretation. Cut marks on the skull, for example, turned out to be made by animals (most likely, hyenas) rather than by human beings. In addition, the story of the ring of stones cannot be verified. The cranium was removed by workmen soon after the discovery; no archaeologist ever examined the untouched site. Based on a rumor, then, the ring of stones exists only in a hypothetical reconstruction of the site on display in the Museo Pigorini in Rome.[10]

The evidence of children's footprints in caves as proof of ancient initiation rites is probably one of the best examples of projection and stretched imagination around. At Le Tuc d'Audoubert, for example, we find heel prints of teenagers, modelled clay bison, and some sausage-shaped clay objects on the floor. Conclusion? The teens were instructed to magically wound the bison, put the ("obviously") phallic clay sheaths on their penises, and then march out of the chamber, throwing away the "sausages" when the ceremony (which some believe involved ritual dancing) was over. How fanciful such an interpretation must be, write Peter Ucko and Andrée Rosenfeld (*Paleolithic Cave Art*),

> is clear when it is remembered that no connection with the bison has been established, that the "phalli" may well have been intended for the modelling of animals . . . [and] that the correlation of age and heelprint size is a very doubtful matter especially when the relationship of body size and foot size of Paleolithic man is quite unknown.

In fact, they go on to say, heelprints "could well be the result simply of attempts to lessen the contact of the foot with wet mud when walking with a stoop in a low chamber." Archaeologist Randall White adds that what was probably going on was exploration, the excitement that children normally have in new situations. "Apparently," he writes, "children have not changed much since the Paleolithic; their prints are found in all sorts of nooks and crannies, while those of adults are restricted to paths that follow the middle of the galleries."[11]

Ucko and Rosenfeld come close to calling the shamanic interpretation of children's footprints "insane." At the very least, it is a good example of violating the principle of parsimony in science: don't create elaborate explanations for a phenomenon when a simpler one will do. It turns out that with one possible exception, no European Paleolithic caves contain any evidence of ritual performance, such as the presence of altars, implements, or signs of frequent human visitation. "There is no representation by these ancient gravers and painters of any sort of practice of curing another human being, nor is there any evidence of ecstasy or possession," writes the anthropologist Lawrence Krader. "The most careful conclusion we can draw," says another expert, "is that shamanism may have been missing in the earliest hunting cultures."[12] The point is that those scholars who have to have trance or initiation ceremonies going on in the caves are not, as they think, *finding* Paleolithic religion. Rather, they are *demanding* that Paleolithic human beings be religious!

The same thing can be said of Paleolithic burials, which conceivably could point to some kind of religious life. Grave goods have been found buried with some ancient skeletons, suggesting a belief in an afterlife. Or the skeletons were sometimes buried in a flexed position, supposedly in an attempt to confine the spirit to the grave. But how do we know this, inasmuch as we do not have access to the mental context of these events? The flexing could have been done to have the smallest possible trenches, for example. In general, parsimonious explanations for Neanderthal burials are not spiritual or ritualistic ones, and unequivocal associations of grave goods with Neanderthals are extremely rare. Too often, "simple and likely explanations have been ignored in favor of complex scenarios invoking enigmatic purposeful behavior."[13]

The issue of modern ethnographic parallels also poses a host of problems. Certain things, it seems to me, *can* be continuously traced back to the Paleolithic, but these are sociobiological in nature. On the one hand, all humans smile (the late twentieth and early twenty-first centuries excepted, I suppose); all are born from a female body, go through prolonged dependency, and are programmed to suck, to nurse at the breast; all have to eat to survive, and so on. If we cannot assume things of this sort, then we might as well pack up shop right now. On the other hand, tracing religious behavior back in time has a lot less validity because finally, continuity becomes just an assumption, and it could easily be incorrect. That Bushman rock art of five hundred years ago depicts trance dancing is fine, but 1500 A.D. is hardly the Paleolithic. In addition, present-day Bushmen of the Kalahari are not the descendants of the rock painters, who lived farther south (the /Xam Bushmen, who became extinct about one hundred years ago), and do not have a tradition of rock art themselves. There is also the problem that the percentage of rock art devoted to trance depictions is very small; in the Ndedema Gorge in the Natal Drakensberg, Harald Pager identified a total of thirteen dance scenes out of 3,909 individual paintings. Even then, this art could have been the result of neighboring Bantu (agricultural) influence, which has been present in southern Africa for nearly eighteen hundred years. Thus one observer, Dorothea Bleek, pointed out in the 1920s that the Bushmen of Angola were adopting prayers, dances, and fetish sticks from their Bantu neighbors. As impressive as the African rock art is, it cannot really tell us much about alleged religious ceremonies at Lascaux.[14]

However, what is an open question is whether the disposition to ASCs is psychobiological in nature. As Erika Bourguignon notes, a 90 percent figure for contemporary tribes certainly would point in that direction; but this may not be the crucial issue. The fact that many tribes *don't* practice it is no less significant, for it suggests that such beliefs and practices, even if wired into the brain in terms of capacity, get triggered only in certain cultural contexts. These contexts may be pathological, for all we know, and possibly confined to the Neolithic era. The "10 percent crowd" could be the *healthy* group, the ones we should be looking at. Thus, Peter Wilson argues (*The Domestication of the Human Species*) that ASCs emerge in contexts of group stress where no fission-and-fusion pattern (the freedom to leave the community and regroup) is present. Possession trance, writes Wilson, "or its frequency, relates to the extent of community life and hence may be involved with the increasing intensity of problems that emerge with daily group life." In turn, this would be a function of population pressure and population density—things that were not problems prior to the Neolithic Revolution.[15]

There is also the problem of the definition of the ASC, and Bourguignon has been taken to task by the British anthropologist I. M. Lewis for making theoretical distinctions in her analysis among possession, trance, and possession trance, which, he argues, cannot be sorted out in actual practice.[16] But once we admit that they might be all jumbled up, then it is quite possible that we are not necessarily talking about altered states. For example, "trafficking in spirits" might be equivalent to animism; but what is animism? Is the (secular) celebration of animal vitality that we see on the walls of Lascaux "animism"? Then the word would lose the totemic meaning that is being assumed for it. Such a framework, of course, has a good pedigree: Emile Durkheim, the eminent French sociologist, took Australian totemism to be the prototype of all religion. But as Ucko and Rosenfeld point out, modern tribes have undergone enormous changes; "it does not follow just because the Australian aborigines are totemic so, therefore, were Paleolithic men." "Almost invariably," they write, "the [ethnographic] parallel which is chosen by the archaeologist as the most meaningful one has some esoteric or ritual association," but there is no justification for this unless the context and content of the art itself warrants a religious, as opposed to a secular, interpretation.[17] When a local French official (Jean-Marie Chauvet) discovered a Paleolithic cave near Avignon in 1994, complete with paintings of animals that rival those of Lascaux, the report in *Time* magazine was—perhaps surprisingly—very astute. "We can assume," wrote the *Time* reporters, that these paintings "had a symbolic value, maybe even a religious value, to those who drew them, that they supplied a framework of images in which needs, values and fears . . . could be expressed. But we have no idea what this framework was, and merely to call it 'animistic' does not say much." In fact, the overwhelming impression conveyed by the roughly three hundred animal figures at Chauvet is not one of religious feeling, but of a vivid and direct naturalism.[18]

Recall Paul Radin's comment that primitive subjective experience of the natural world was so intense that things often seemed to "blaze." Should we call this "animism" or "spirit possession"? It may be that "heightened awareness" is a more accurate description of what is going on than "altered state." We begin to see, in Bourguignon's case at least, the problem of relying on ethnographic parallels.[19]

Finally, there is another way in which religious ethnographic parallels are problematic, and that is that we are caught up in our *own* religious framework. In a very trenchant critique of Western biblical ethnocentrism, S. N. Balagangadhara argues that the notion of a society without religion is something we find disturbing because we ethnocentrically equate religion with experience of the sacred. Yet, he says, some societies are capable of sacred experience without having to generate any sort of religious world view at all. On what basis, he continues, can we argue that early humans were religious? Funeral practices won't work for the reason already cited: they may not be *religious* practices. And if we want to argue that religion *had* to exist among our Paleolithic ancestors because it is a universal hedge against death, we overlook the possibility that our ancestors might have simply regarded death as death, not as something terrifying or mysterious (this is in fact true of some HG societies today). There is no evidence that they would invent a god or a transcendent world, just because *we* do. As Nicholas Thomas and Caroline Humphrey demonstrate very convincingly in their volume *Shamanism, History, and the State*, shamanism "is more of an exotic essence, a romanticized inversion of Western rationalism, than a scholarly category that can stand up to any sustained interrogation."[20]

The consciousness of Paleolithic peoples, then, including their experience of the sacred, is not likely to be the same as ours projected backward in time. Trance and spirit possession certainly could have existed, but I would like to try to make the case for paradox, as defined in the introduction, as a more likely candidate for the mindset at Lascaux. There is no absolute "proof" here, as already stated, and I am going to have to extrapolate backward as well, but I believe that the argument below is more parsimonious and convincing than the "religious" alternatives.[21]

What You See Is What You Get

Let us return once again to the issue of cave art. In *Prehistoric Art in Europe*, Nancy Sandars points out that with very few exceptions, books on the subject are more concerned with possible religious interpretations of the art than with the subject of what is actually portrayed.[22] But consider, she says, the relief engraved on the rock face at Roc-aux-Sorciers, located not far from Poitiers. (Figure 6) It dates from about 12,000 B.C. and depicts three nude female figures from the waist down. The effect is quite erotic, and Sandars comments on how *naturalistic* it is: "The most extraordinary thing about the figures is the mastery of perspective and the three-quarter view as they half-turn, like dancers in line, ready one by one to peel off and join the movement."

This same naturalism can be seen in the engraving of a horse from Schweizersbild in Switzerland (Figure 7), in which line and shading technique is used to suggest the contour of the animal under matted hair, and to give the appearance of weight and volume. The horse's head at Lascaux (Figure 8) also has similar qualities. The "aim of this art," says Sandars, "was truth to nature and the illusion of a thing seen." It is "frivolous," she goes on, to call the sketches of the three women "Venus figures," or to read symbolic interpretations into any of this material. The women are women; grazing deer are grazing deer. The "facts revealed by the art itself," write Ucko and Rosenfeld, "suggest that many Paleolithic representations were intended to have a visual effect," even those placed in remote regions of caves. Even the superpositioning of one painting on another, which occurs from time to time, "could well have had the specific aim of creating an impression of 'animalness' or 'vitality' which need not have been due to repeated and unconnected acts of magical representation."

As in the case of the footprints at Le Tuc d'Audoubert, parsimonious explanations lead us *away* from symbolism, not toward it. What we are seeing on these walls is not only an appreciation of vitality but also the product of classic HG alertness. If this is "animism," it would seem to be a very secular variety of it. It consists mostly in a sense of the awareness of Presence, of the "magic" that exists in Self being differentiated from Other; of the awareness of Self *as* one is aware of the Other. I put it to you that this *was* HG spirituality, experience of the sacred—a horizontal experience, not a tale of souls ascending to heaven.[23]

Agriculture and sedentism changed all of this. Studies done of HGs versus farmers show strong tendencies for the former to be "field independent" and the latter to be "field dependent." This

Figure 6. Three Women at Roc-aux-Sorciers. From N. K. Sandars, *Prehistoric Art in Europe.*

Figure 7. Horse at Schweizersbild, Switzerland. From N. K. Sandars, *Prehistoric Art in Europe.*

Figure 8. Horse's Head at Lascaux. From N. K. Sandars, *Prehistoric Art in Europe.*

occurs for adaptive reasons and reflects the fact that HGs are alert to details, have the ability to focus on specific items in the landscape ("field") even as they scan it as a whole, whereas sedentary farmers tend to blur on details, see parts of a field of vision as merged with the whole. Peter Wilson says that domestication was a major modification here, altering the ability of humans to pay attention. HG societies, he says, "are marked by an emphasis on 'focus' in contrast to domesticated societies, which are distinguished by an emphasis on the boundary." Survival is the underlying issue here: among HGs and nomadic peoples, survival depends on being able to distinguish a bird from the surrounding, dense foliage of a tree, or to spot a snake several hundred yards away. In a word, they are much more alert.[24]

Paying attention, living in paradox, being alert to the movement of animals—all of this had great survival value and is rooted in a sociobiology that I believe is traceable back to the Paleolithic. *Homo sapiens* had assimilated animal alertness into the structure of its brain long before it developed the capacity for self-awareness, and hardly lost that once self-awareness arose. Put self-awareness together with alert observation of the Other, the environment, and something like paradox is what results, a perception that carries its own type of aura.

It is at this point, however, that things get a bit complicated, because it would appear that based on what we know of the experience of infancy, the potential for vertical religious experience and for paradox has its roots in the first few years of life. "Aura" of whatever variety, in other words, would seem to be at least partially derivative from a situation that is psychobiological in nature. Much of our need for that aura can be traced to the phenomenon of prolonged dependency and the process of coming-into-consciousness that all human beings go through. This is part of our sociobiology; and while it probably cannot be traced back to, let us say, *Homo erectus* (1.5 million years ago), it nevertheless has a fairly long ancestry. This means that although Object Relations theory—that part of psychoanalysis that deals with very early Self/Other relations—is, as already noted, a twentieth-century "invention," some of its basic premises can be applied to Paleolithic life in the same way, say, that Darwin's theory of natural selection can (even though formulated in the nineteenth century); or (presumably) Freud's theory of the Oedipal relations of the family; or, for that matter, Newton's law of gravitational attraction (to close approximation), and so on. These things are obviously not in the same category as Eliade's "mythic substrate," although early Object Relations can shape the potential for mythic elements to emerge.

The dialectic of aura experienced as paradox, as secular/immediate presence, versus that which is experienced as vertical sacrality, "in heaven" and outside of us, is in many ways the theme of this book. The two modes give rise to two very different kinds of religious and political configurations. Inasmuch as the vertical forms of these—the state, the sacred authority complex, mystery cults and monotheisms—have not been with us for very long and are circumscribed by the Neolithic era (i.e., date back only a few thousand years), the argument for paradox as being our "baseline spirituality" would seem to be valid. But it is not the whole story, and working out the network of relationships is no easy task. Factors in the story include the nature of human ontogeny (coming into consciousness); child-rearing patterns among Paleolithic vs. Neolithic peoples; the evolution of mind, and the historical emergence of self-awareness in the human race as a whole; the role of physical movement versus sedentism as a way of life; and the impact of population pressure. We shall have to look at all of these things in the pages that follow. For now, let me say a few words about human ontogeny and the evolution of mind.

The Birth of the Ego

As far as Object Relations theory goes, what we are talking about is the emergence of cognition, specifically, the crystallization of an ego, or self-conscious awareness, out of an unconscious matrix.[25] A new-born human—and we can assume this is the case for an infant born in the Paleolithic caves of southern France as well as for one born in a hospital in Paris—does not make much of a distinction between Self and Other. Although much has been written by now on the infant's ability to recognize parents very early on (the ability to imitate gestures and so on), it is doubtful that this and related abilities represent true self-awareness or interiority, that is, the consciousness of one's own consciousness. What has been called the "psychological birth of the human infant" typically occurs during the third year of life, when the child realizes that he or she is a separate entity, a Self in a world of Others. This is the core of Object Relations. Standing in front of a mirror now, the child knows that the "playmate" in the glass is really "me," a specular image. But this realization does not happen all at once. Self-awareness is a nonlinear process, something that grows in fits and starts, and the presence of an existential identity with a reflective internal life (something that does not happen for the rest of the animal kingdom) takes a bit of time to stabilize. If the truth be told, it is a process that is never really complete.

In any case, the process/event of understanding that you are "in here" and that the other person (or in general, your environment) is "out there" is the birth of individual identity, but also of alienation from the world. The birth of real self-awareness tears the psyche in two, creates what one psychologist (Jacques Lacan) called "the gap," or what another (Michael Balint) referred to as the "basic fault." A lot of how this is negotiated depends on the immediate surroundings, and if they are benevolent, so much the better for our feelings of being at home in the world. But there is always a tear, a pulling away from a primal unity; and it is in the search to mend that, to fill in the gap, that much of our sacred yearning is rooted. A "lived distance" now divides us from the world, and to varying degrees, we find it painful.

There are various ways of dealing with that pain; the one that is universal is the breast. In HG society, breast-feeding often goes on up to age four, and this undoubtedly accounts for the healthy psychological outlook that the individuals in undisturbed forager societies seem to have. But weaning of any sort means that something has to take up the slack, and this is where the possibility for paradox *or* for addictive attachment—the root of the SAC—both open up. The Freudian term for this is *cathexis,* and in our own culture the most familiar form of it in weaned infants is the teddy bear, generically speaking; what the British psychoanalyst Donald Winnicott called the "Transitional Object." The T.O. becomes a breast substitute, the intermediary between Self and World. It is for this reason that such objects are, for children, quasimagical, endowed with aura (just try to pry a T.O. loose from an infant, and you'll see what I mean). Winnicott argued that we didn't lose our tendencies for cathexis later on in life; we merely found more sophisticated substitutes—for example, religions and ideologies.

All of this opens up a host of questions. What about the role of child-rearing in the formation of attachment? Do all cultures have T.O.s, or do HGs cathect something else, beyond the breast? Given the diffuse quality of paradox, how did it manage to emerge at all? Is Object Relations true for all time? And if not true for *Homo erectus,* just how far back can we reasonably extrapolate it? A lot obviously depends on the answers to these questions. I shall say a bit more about the matter of attachment and its relationship to the SAC below; for now, we need to deal with the question of the universality of Object Relations theory. Specifically, was there a time when the human race awoke to its own interiority, stepped from what we might call "proto-paradox" into something else? When did interiority—"mind"—come into existence?

This last question is absolutely crucial, because the greatest discontinuity in terms of the emergence of culture has to be the phenomenon of self-objectification. There is archaeological evidence for this going back quite a ways, as I shall discuss below; but things such as art, personal adornment, or burial with certain types of grave goods, which emerge for the first time with any regularity in the Upper Paleolithic (say forty thousand years ago), would seem to be good indicators that a serious mental discontinuity has occurred. Julian Jaynes speaks to this issue quite eloquently when he writes, "It is as if all life evolved to a certain point, and then in ourselves turned at a right angle and simply exploded in a different direction." Animals live in the eternal present, a kind of proto-paradox. To realize that one is operating in a time stream is to possess a radically different consciousness. The American anthropologist Irving Hallowell saw art, for example, as clear evidence of self-awareness, because it involves abstraction and representation, the conveying to others what is in your individual mind (self). He regarded this as proof of a generic type of personality organization that had not existed hitherto. "By the time we reach the Upper Paleolithic," he wrote, "the infrahominids have been left far behind."[26]

What, then, is this distinct psychology, this new "generic type of personality organization" that emerged during the Late Paleolithic? Although I believe Jaynes' dating of these events is very much off (he places it at 1300-900 B.C.), his description of this new consciousness is one of the best I have come across. Briefly, Jaynes' principal characterization of the new mental configuration is that of a metaphorical mind space, including a sense of past and future, which allows us to see ourselves in the "story" of our lives. In other words, when we are conscious in this self-reflective sense, we possess what he calls an "analog 'I'," a metaphor we have of ourselves that can move about in our imagination. We "see" this imago, this self, doing things in the world, that is in space and time; and on this basis, we make decisions regarding the imagined outcomes that would be impossible if we *couldn't* imagine this self. We can observe this self, in our mind's eye, from the outside (as we sometimes do in a dream), or from the inside, looking out on the environment. In either case, a narrative is present in our minds, of past or future events, involving what we did or intend to do.[27]

Animal alertness is, of course, the ground of our consciousness; it represents our evolutionary origins, our genetic or ancestral "being," as it were. In such a state, there is no reflection or anticipation, but only an immediate awareness of the environment and a reaction to it—as I said, a proto-form of paradox. The entry of a time scale, of a metaphorical "I" having goals in the world, changes all of this. Not that alertness is automatically lost, but that reflection is now also present, and this conflicts with a purely alert state (human paradox means living inside and outside of a time frame simultaneously). It puts the human race on a path that takes it out of the animal state, and that eventually gets manifested in the creation of history and culture.

Before we turn to the issue of attachment/dependency and its role in generating a need for the sacred, we need to understand very clearly how dramatic a shift the events of the Upper Paleolithic represent in terms of human mental functioning. If it is the case that sharp Self/Other differentiation cannot be pushed back a million years, it is almost certain that it can be applied to the men and women of forty thousand years ago, if not a bit earlier. To see how remarkable was the change of mind that occurred across what is known as the "Middle/Upper Paleolithic transition," we need to undertake a brief excursion into paleoanthropology.

The Birth of Culture

Consider the data presented in Table 1 below, which I have entitled "Outline of Hominid Biocultural Evolution."

What I have assembled here is the consensus of expert opinion on this subject that can be gleaned from works published over the last twenty years or so, substantiated by empirical studies in archaeology, anthropology, and paleontology. It is, I believe, the most plausible evolutionary picture of hominids that can be synthesized at the present time.[28]

What is perhaps most striking about this compilation, at least to my mind, is how *logarithmic* the cultural development is; the bulk of the "action" occurs when the modern (Cro-Magnon) human being, or *Homo sapiens sapiens*, appears on the scene. In fact, the relative suddenness, and recentness, of human culture has been commented on for decades now, from the anthropologist A. L. Kroeber in the twenties to archaeologists Lewis Binford, Paul Mellars, and Randall White in the eighties and nineties. Beginning with Kroeber, scholars have not been able to separate the dramatic developments of the Upper Paleolithic from the nature, and possibly evolution, of mind, no matter how elusive the latter may be. For what we see in the artifacts is the physical expression of human consciousness, even if interpretation is nearly always controversial or difficult.

The crucial issue in this development is the relentless, and finally explosive, cumulation of intent, or goal orientation; what archaeologists refer to as "planning depth" (p.d.). This in turn implicates the kind of consciousness described by Jaynes, the ego awareness necessary to see oneself in a story, in future time. Conscious tool making implies the ability to impose a mental template (arbitrary form) on unworked (i.e., formless) material. Thus Lewis Binford defines p.d. as the amount of time between anticipatory actions and their results, and the investments humans make in these actions.[29] However, we need to be cautious here because tool use certainly exists among apes and monkeys (as well as some other animals); they can abstract the objective consequences of an action and store them in a form accessible to mental control. Apes, for example, will stack boxes to reach food on a roof or put short sticks together to make a long one. Some conceptual and behavioral continuity thus exists between humans and apes. Nevertheless, it is the *dis*continuities between humans and apes that are the most striking. Apes can work only with "real world" perceptions; it is at the future/imaginary level that their constructional capacity is lacking. Hence, they can stack boxes, but they do not look at a stone flake and imagine an arrowhead. This is why ape "art" displays no symbolic pattern, whereas for example, children will quickly arrange generic face cutouts (nose, mouth, etc.) into a face pattern. Thus there clearly exists, as Peter Reynolds points out (*On the Evolution of Human Behavior*), "a phylogenetic discontinuity in the human ability to direct motor acts in terms of an image of a final product that is being produced by the action."[30]

Table 1. Outline of Hominid Biocultural Evolution

Years Ago	Hominid Form	Culture/Technology
4+ million to 1.2 million	*Australopithecus* ("man-ape;" bipedal walker)	Lower Paleolithic. This hominid form in existence long before appearance of Stone Age tools. Scavenging. No language or fire.
2.2 million to 1.6 million	*Homo habilis* ("handy man")	Oldowan; pebble tools.
1.6 million to 0.5 million	*Homo erectus*	Acheulean (1.5 million years ago in Africa, 1 million years ago in Europe); pebble tools; biface hand axes.
400,000 to 250,000	*Homo sapiens*	Seasonal huts and hearths; control of fire.
130,000 to 35,000	*Homo sapiens neanderthalensis*	Middle Paleolithic (Mousterian). Blade and flake tools; rare ceremonial burial. Big-game hunting from ca. 100,000 years ago (systematic only from Aurignacian period).

Table 1. Outline of Hominid Biocultural Evolution *(continued)*

Years Ago	Hominid Form	Culture/Technology
100,000 to present	*Homo sapiens sapiens* (Cro-Magnons)	
35,000		Upper Paleolithic/Aurignacian
28,000		Gravettian/Solutrean/ Magdalenian (see discussion in text)
10,000		Neolithic; domestication of animals, planting of grain

When we consider the "Culture/Technology" column in Table 1, we need not get too excited about the existence of pebble tools or hand axes of 1 to 2 million years ago. The use and even manufacture of tools can be so basic as to function only in immediate, practical situations. P.d. is quite frankly minuscule in the Oldowan and Acheulean "industries" (as they are called) and faint even in Mousterian technology (usually associated with Neanderthals). There is not a single tool from forty thousand years ago that was not already present sixty thousand years before that, and in addition, Mousterian sites reveal no artistic activity. Neanderthals did very little planning; for example, they did not exploit cyclical events such as the migration of fish or reindeer. All that would come later. As Lewis Binford puts it, we also need to distinguish between curated and expedient technologies. "Curation" is maintenance behavior, that is, activities such as repair, designed to give tools long life, whereas expedient technologies refer to on-site, reactive use. Thus, curation is an advanced level of p.d. (one can have p.d. without curation but no curation without p.d.). As p.d. increases in human evolutionary history, so do the number of tools and the number of manufacturing steps necessary to produce them. Finally, we get tools designed to repair other tools, which means that the degree of p.d., of futurizing, has become quite sophisticated.[31]

Turning to the cultural record, Oldowan technology is completely expedient. Tools are found where they were used, not where people resided and to which they returned with their tools. Early hominid technology, says Binford, reveals stasis, great similarity over vast areas, pure biology rather than culture. This is mostly true even of the Mousterian period. With very few exceptions, says Paul Mellars, "Middle Paleolithic tools do not appear to have been produced with clearly defined preconceived 'mental templates' about the final, overall form of the finished tools." Or, as Binford puts it, prior to symboling, the ability to anticipate events and conditions not yet experienced was not a strength of our ancestors. It is for this reason that materials such as bone and ivory, which are tougher than stone and take time and effort to modify, are rarely used in the Mousterian. Activities such as carving and polishing date only from Aurignacian times, and the eyed sewing needle first appeared around –20,000 years. In general, compared with the Middle/Upper Paleolithic transition, previous patterns are tedious and unchanging.[32]

Big-game hunting, of course, is closely related to tool development, and as a group activity it is something, as we have said, that requires advanced planning, futurizing, and mental imaging. It is a complex event, requiring a great amount of social orchestration, as well as conscious awareness: one probably needs to have a mental picture of oneself throwing a spear into an elephant and bringing it down in order to then go out and do it. Until about 1980, it was believed that hunting was associated with the stone tools found alongside animal bones and therefore that it went back a very long time. Subsequent research showed that this was actually scavenging, that the tools were expedient, made on site so as to enable people to carve up the animal carcass they had run across. Very little p.d. was involved in this, and in fact big-game hunting arose just prior to the earliest emergence of *Homo sapiens sapiens*, say about one hundred thousand years ago. Even then, it may have been rare. We see numerous spear points in the Upper Paleolithic and very few in the Mousterian. Indeed, the most conspicuous gap in the Mousterian "tool kit" is the absence of items such as projectiles for procuring large game. By contrast, obvious projectile elements are found in every European Upper Paleolithic context, and the spear thrower (which extended the hunter's throwing arc dramatically) was invented around –20,000 years. In a detailed study of the Mousterian in west-central Italy, evidence that medium and large game animals were successfully hunted shows up only after –55,000 years, and evidence for major discontinuities in foraging patterns occurs only when we leave the Mousterian altogether. Major kill sites in Europe date from the Gravettian period, that is, after –28,000 years.

All in all, recent scholarship on hunting reveals that prior to the Upper Paleolithic, humans did not have much ability to anticipate events. The dominant pattern, after all, had always been one of *gathering*, with hunting probably being a kind of extension of that. Gathering, like scavenging, requires much less p.d., and the faunal remains of the Middle Paleolithic show only small-game hunting, scavenging, and the avoidance of dangerous prey. It is only in the U.P. that culture, fueled by intent, swiftly starts replacing biology as the chief agent of human survival.[33]

Tools and planning depth are not the only indicators of changing mental constructs. The dramatic increase in personal ornamentation around −35,000, when almost none existed before, suggests a different type of mental functioning, as does the emergence of art and abstract design. The elaboration of burial (mortuary treatment) is another indicator. In a study of thirty-five Middle Paleolithic and twenty-four Upper Paleolithic burials, Sally Binford found that items of adornment—beads, pendants, and necklaces—occurred in great numbers in the latter and were completely absent in the former. (No "art" has ever been found associated with buried Neanderthals.) On the reasonable assumption that distinctions made in death are symbolic of those made in life, the presence of such items in the U.P. suggests an increasing tendency toward status differentiation, something that must surely reflect a distinction now being made between Self and Other. In general, the issue of personal adornment weighs in heavily with respect to self-definition, psychological identity, social display and so on. Furthermore, beads and pendants show up rather suddenly in the archaeological record. The emergence of the technology for making such items is also abrupt, and the technology is complex and full-blown. It is very hard to avoid the conclusion that once into the U.P., we are dealing with a different kind of human existence, a different world.[34]

Part of that new world is the framework of historical time. This represents a whole new dimension, a break with the "eternal present." However, the point is that in the shift from *Homo sapiens neanderthalensis* to *Homo sapiens sapiens*—that is, the demographic replacement of the former by the latter that was largely complete by the onset of the Upper Paleolithic—we are already moving toward a historical state and mindset. Indeed, it may be the case that Magdalenian culture (−18,000 years to −11,000 years) is actually the world's first civilization, and we should note that 80 percent of all known Upper Paleolithic art dates from this period.

"Civilization," in any case, means more than just art; it also means the existence of a social organization capable of passing knowledge on from one generation to the next, which was clearly going on if—as was indeed the case—the people of Upper Paleolithic Europe had a body of technological knowledge as sophisticated as that of any modern HGs. In general, the pattern from −35,000 years is one of almost continual change.[35]

What we see in all of these events—technology, burials, adornment, hunting, and artistic/symbolic representation—is basically a shift from the exterior world to the mind. It is essentially with the rise of modern *Homo sapiens* that ideas about *non*material phenomena, such as death or personal identity, begin to get externalized. Before this, the limit of cognitive ability, of p.d., was the externalization of ideas pertaining to physical material alone. Neurally modern humans, according to Randall White (it's a controversial point), emerged by −100,000 years, after which we start to see the slow imposition of mental form on the external world—"image-driven constructional action," as Peter Reynolds calls it. Glimmerings of this, such as Mousterian burials, start to occur after this, and then, between −35,000 and −30,000 years, something new crystallizes: hominids step from biology into culture. And culture, in essence, involves self-conscious awareness and intent. By the time we arrive at the Neolithic, with the planting of grain, the experimentation with animal domestication, and the almost constant preoccupation with survival—activities that involve enormous degrees of planning depth—paradox is virtually lost. Feeling at home in the world is now going to require stronger spiritual medicine; religion, in fact.[36]

This review of cultural prehistory hopefully serves to show that with *Homo sapiens sapiens*, the Self/Other split, or self-objectification, that had been slowly germinating prior to −100,000, now came rapidly into its own. Lived distance is now part of the human process, on both the individual and the cultural level. This split between Self and World creates a need for "mending," and it is this that gives rise to the phenomenon of attachment. Attachment, in turn, takes various forms; paradox was probably the most common, and also the least "attached." With the nursing of infants running to four years in length, HG children did not develop attachments to T.O.s, but cathected the whole environment instead, giving it a kind of subjective radiance, which is what (I believe) we are for the most part seeing on the walls of Lascaux. The Mbuti Pygmies of Zaire, made famous by Colin Turnbull in *The Forest People*, don't worship anything; they "merely" regard the forest, their universe, as alive, friendly.[37] The SAC, which is a Neolithic phenomenon, represents a very different sort of energy. It arose under different circumstances, ones that accentuated the Self/Other split.

The Phenomenon of Attachment

Let us talk, then, about the sources of sacred energy.[38] If we wish to talk about psychobiological constants, there seems to be a dyadic pattern of "attachment behavior" between mother and infant that is virtually universal, given the fact of prolonged dependency among human beings, and which exists among other primates as well. In the 1950s, for example, the American psychologist Harry Harlow became famous for conducting a series of experiments with Rhesus monkeys which showed how these animals had to have a "soft" parent surrogate—even a cloth-covered dummy would do—to cling to in order to survive. Bare wire surrogates would not work. Having a soft figure to cling to was more significant for the monkeys than was feeding. Behavior such as sucking, grasping, clinging, and crying are biologically hard-wired; and among humans all of this—to which we would have to add smiling, vocalizing, and the "shadowing" of the mother—apparently must take place within the context of an intense one-to-one relationship that exists between the infant and a (m)other. This crucible, it would seem, is the source of all human health—and human neurosis.

The zero-to-five-year stage of life has, as we have seen, been the focus of Object Relations theory, and it is also the major concern of what is called "attachment theory." Both of these have their roots in Freud. The infant's first love object, wrote Freud in 1905, is the breast, and this early sucking relationship is the prototype of all later love relationships the infant will have. "Anaclitic love"—dependency, leaning on another person—from Freud's viewpoint, at least, has orality, or feeding, at its core. In 1938 Freud reiterated this, saying that the relationship with the mother was "unique, without parallel," and (again) prototypical of all later love. His daughter, Anna Freud, similarly argued that feeding was central to symbiotic security, while the psychologist Margaret Mahler conceived of object and ego differentiation emerging only slowly from a state of dyadic unity, a completely fused state of self and other.

But is feeding *really* the "dyadic glue," as it were? Harlow's work, for example, points to warmth and holding, rather than feeding, as the crucial issue, and two experts in child development, John Bowlby and Donald Winnicott, argue that the same is true for human beings. Nevertheless, the one thing everyone seems to agree upon is the centrality of the mother/infant dyad for healthy primate life, an attachment that Bowlby calls "monotropic." Monotropy, as Bowlby defines it, is a "strong bias for attachment behavior to become directed mainly towards one particular person and for a child to become strongly possessive of that person." Attachment, he claims, is biological; it exists in an evolutionary context. For the human race to have survived despite the period of infant dependency, says Bowlby, attachment and reciprocal care behavior must exist as a stable configuration. Culture can vary, but underneath it all is a species-based biological drive for infant attachment and maternal reciprocation, that is, for a dyad. In short, this is ethological, a matter of "imprinting," and probably occurs during the "window" of one to eighteen months after birth. Without this match between infant programming and maternal response, the capacity for attachment, for what the eminent psychologist Erik Erikson calls "basic trust," is permanently lost.

Of course, this is where neurosis (or worse) comes in. If a child is separated from its mother before it is capable of sustaining the attachment, adverse effects result. The phases that result in response to this, according to Mary Ainsworth, are protest, despair, and finally, detachment. Detachment ensues if the separation is long enough, something often observed in institutional settings. The child will be described as being "back to normal," that is, superficially social and cheerful, but when the mother visits, the child no longer seeks interaction with her. All the empirical data, Ainsworth concludes, show that interaction with a mother figure, and resulting attachment, are absolutely essential for psychological health.

From where does the sense of basic trust arise? In an article on "The Development of Ritualization," Erikson makes explicit the link between the SAC—in particular, unitive trance—and the bond between mother and infant.[39] Arguing that there are "connections between seemingly distant phenomena, such as human infancy and man's institutions," Erikson suggests that ritual behavior "seems to be grounded in the preverbal experience of infants," in particular, in the mutuality of recognition that is reenacted over and over again between mother and infant. Erikson suggests "that this first and dimmest affirmation, this sense of a *hallowed presence*, contributes to man's ritual making a pervasive element which we will call the 'Numinous.'" It is this first dyadic, numinous experience, he says, that the individual will try, later in life, to capture repeatedly, through experiences of fusion such as romantic love, immersion in a leader's charisma, or religious observance. "The result is a sense of *separateness transcended*." The structure is that of a particular ontogenetic beginning and its subsequent (adult) elaboration, which form "parts of a functional whole, namely, of a cultural version of human existence."

It is interesting that Erikson describes this process as *a*—that is, one possible—cultural version of human existence, because it means that although the dyadic factor is always present, there are going to be child-rearing situations that are not so clear cut as this one. In the pattern of the exclusive dyad, the "sacred" is going to come off as a sharp, vertical experience; nothing else will do. It is in infancy that our spiritual destiny is set, and our relationship to "God" largely determined. Yet as we shall see in chapter 3, other cultural versions are possible, and in them romantic love, religion, war, vertical spiritual experience, and charisma seem to be absent, aberrant, or muted because infants in those societies are not the object of such exclusive (narcissistic) intensity.

Given the fact that some *Angst der Kreatur*—"creature anxiety," as the German psychoanalyst, Karen Horney, called it—is always present, and that the mother's role is always crucial, it is nevertheless the case that there is a great deal of lability possible with respect to child-rearing practices and the infant psyches that they shape. But under what would become the stress and insecurity of Neolithic life, what is a *natural* spiritual life—love of the world as it presents itself—moves aside to make way for the shaman, for ecstasy, myth, ritual, charisma, and in general, vertical religious experience. The fear of death that is generated by that life, and the altered child-rearing practices that often accompany it, make transcendent solutions (and explanations) increasingly attractive. As the British psychoanalyst Ernest Jones once put it, "The religious life is a dramatisation projected onto the cosmos of the fears and desires arising from the child-parent relation."[40] Causally speaking, it is larger than this, of course, but you get the point.

If the dyadic pattern and the "hallowed presence" phenomenon were the world historical (and contemporary) norm, no alternatives to the vertical religious pattern would be possible. Infants raised in such a context would (and do) grow up imprinted for charismatic experience, learning to view sacred authority as the highest "truth," which would then serve to reaffirm the vertical social order. This is, of course, what is known as "civilization." Thus, Nicholas Thomas and Caroline Humphrey note that Mircea Eliade's classic model of north Asian shamanism looks very different when seen in political context, in which the claim to be able to ascend to the sky and obtain esoteric knowledge was "a politically highly charged matter." What *seem* intrinsic features of shamanism, they say, are actually historically contingent. For political power, even in state systems, operates through ideas such as the knowledge of destiny.[41]

But it doesn't have to be this way, and for much of our (pre)history, it wasn't. If the mother/infant bond and Object Relations are core phenomena, they are nevertheless plastic as well. What

Philip Slater once called "steep-gradient" psyches—those nurtured by the "hallowed presence" into oral dependency and transcendent yearning—have not been dominant for HGs; and as we shall see, the phenomenon of movement has a lot to do with this. Felicitas Goodman notes that whereas agriculturalists seek transformation (the stuff of myth and ritual), HG's are interested in *balance*. It is only when we examine patterns of comparative child-rearing that we are able to obtain a sense of what the other possibilities are and what the sources of this balance might be.

However, it will be necessary to postpone such a discussion to a later point. Before we can meaningfully talk about religious verticality and its relationship to child-rearing practices, which exist on a microlevel, we have to have a sense of what goes on around this—that which exists on a macrolevel. Religious verticality exists in the context of *political* verticality. It is to this subject that we must now turn.

2

POLITICS AND POWER

The human condition is about poverty, injustice, exploitation, war, suffering. To seek the human condition one must go . . . to the barrios, shanty towns, and palatial mansions of Rio, Lima, and Mexico City, where massive inequalities of wealth and power have produced fabulous abundance for some and misery for most. When anthropologists look at hunter-gatherers they are seeking something else: a vision of human life and human possibilities without the pomp and glory, but also without the misery and inequity of state and class society.

> —Richard Lee, "Art, Science, or Politics?
> The Crisis in Hunter-Gatherer Studies"

Let me hear no more of our kind's natural necessity to form hierarchical groups. An observer viewing human life shortly after cultural takeoff would easily have concluded that our species was destined to be irredeemably egalitarian except for distinctions of sex and age. That someday the world would be divided into aristocrats and commoners, masters and slaves, billionaires and homeless beggars would have seemed wholly contrary to human nature as evidenced in the affairs of every human society then on earth.

> —Marvin Harris, Our Kind: Who We Are,
> Where We Come From, Where We Are Going

I recall, some years ago, reading a discussion by the American psychologist Abraham Maslow of a course he had taken in graduate school in abnormal psychology. Maslow had forgotten the name of the course textbook, but the images on the dust cover remained engraved in his memory. At the top, said Maslow, was a photograph of newborn infants in a nursery, the glow of birth still hovering over them, looking out at the spectator with wide-eyed curiosity. At the bottom was a photograph of commuters on the New York subway system returning

49

home from work, hanging onto the straps, their bodies bent over, a depressed look on their faces. In between the two pictures was a banner headline consisting of two simple but dramatic words: WHAT HAPPENED?

Maslow never says what was actually *in* the textbook, but my own reaction is that the drama depicted on the dust jacket is one of *normal* psychology, not abnormal; it shows the fate of humans in civilization, that is, in societies organized around class and power. "Normal," of course, is not the same as "healthy," yet this eventual wearing down of the spirit is fairly common within cultures such as our own. However, what happened is a theme that needs to be applied not merely to individuals, but to large-scale historical shifts. As the quotes from Lee and Harris above would suggest, anthropologists have not been unwilling to do this. The question of the shift from HG life to civilization, and of the origins of social inequality, has been a hot topic for some time now.

One of the earliest attempts at a solution (in this century, anyway) was that of the Australian archaeologist V. Gordon Childe. In *The Dawn of European Civilization* (1925), Childe, following Marx, put forth a "global" division based on the introduction of agriculture. HG societies, he said, are egalitarian; agricultural civilization, complex (i.e., hierarchical). If you want to find the origins of social inequality, on this view, you need look no farther than the nearest seed.[1]

The Childean concept of a "Neolithic Revolution," and the broad dichotomy he posited between foragers and domesticators, set the framework for much of the anthropological thinking of the next four or five decades. (Claude Lévi-Strauss' binary classification of the raw and the cooked, for example, is an obvious echo.) For Childe's concept addressed a very real anthropological puzzle: How is it that after 1 to 2 million years of a very different way of life, characterized by movement and foraging, agriculture and sedentism were almost universally chosen over this in just a few short millennia? What Childe did was to integrate the famous argument of the eighteenth-century minister Thomas Malthus, that population was determined by food supply, with the thesis of the nineteenth-century anthropologist, Lewis Henry Morgan, that cultural evolution occurred in stages that were determined by technological change. Hence, said Childe, the development of Western civilization was the result of a series of technological revolutions leading to population growth and social change, amounting to the adoption of agriculture as a way of life. Agriculture was thus a *conceptual* revolution, for Childe; the introduction of new knowledge, perhaps at an opportune moment in history, which then revolutionized human existence itself.[2] Childe further argued that it was this change from food procurement to food production that paved the way for civilization, that is, for class society and the state, because only agriculture was capable of guaranteeing a surplus large enough to maintain a "nonproductive" class. It was thus in the crucial split between those who domesticated plants and animals, and HGs, who did not, that the roots of civilization could be found.[3]

It is important not to underestimate the conceptual power of Childe's argument, even to this day, for he was the first (following Marx) to pose the notion of a global and radical opposition between two types of socioeconomic organization and to locate the origins of civilization in that opposition. We need only contrast the civilization of Sumer in 3500 B.C. to the band societies of, say, 20,000 B.C. (i.e., what we know of them archaeologically) to realize that we are looking at two utterly different worlds. Virtually all scholars agree that food production, that is, "the use of domesticated plants and animals as the primary basis of subsistence . . . is the economic foundation upon which the state and modern civilization are built and maintained."[4]

Yet research during the last two decades or so has mounted a serious challenge to the Childe thesis on a number of levels, to the point that some scholars now doubt that a Neolithic Revolution ever took place. At the very least, it is by now abundantly clear that social inequality antedated the deliberate cultivation of the first sheaf of wheat. Let us look, then, at some of this material.

Agriculture as a Gradual Development

The revision of the Childe thesis revolves around two crucial questions: (1) Exactly how revolutionary *was* the Neolithic Revolution?, and (2) Were Paleolithic HGs truly egalitarian? As we shall see, there is a profound connection between these two issues.

To take the first question first, it is by now generally accepted that techniques of plant and animal domestication were fully known before 9000 B.C.; that hunters understood the mechanics (or "organics") of planting well in advance of the rise of agriculture as a new type of economy. The use of plants existed on a continuum. Hence, the invention or knowledge of agriculture and pastoralism (the management and exploitation of herd animals) is not the issue; what *is* significant is its acceptance. Motivation, not knowledge of techniques, is the central point here. Archaeological evidence from the Near East and Mesoamerica shows agropastoralism appearing not as an economic revolution but as a long and gradual transition, as part of a "mixed economy."[5]

One of the reasons for this is that agriculture is not a monolithic phenomenon, but something that exists in degrees. Thus, Childe had argued that agriculture generated a surplus and that it was the phenomenon of surplus that got the machinery of social inequality going. But, as noted, many foraging societies had the technical knowhow to generate a surplus and chose not to do so, which is why they have sometimes been called the "original affluent society."[6] The same is true of a number of agricultural peoples, such as Amazonian Indians prior to the arrival of European settlers. The technological means to generate a surplus were present, but the social mechanisms to do so were not.[7] In addition, archaeological evidence from Peru, as well as from Puebla and Oaxaca in Mexico, shows the existence of what might be called "simple farming," a pattern in which the beginnings of agriculture did not alter the amount of food being produced in any significant way. Instead, agriculture was inconspicuously integrated into the foraging economy and initially proved to be of minor importance, without any corresponding changes in mobility patterns, sedentism, population growth, or social inequality. Thus, the anthropologist Barbara Göbel argues that agriculture must be *established* for it to make a difference, not just added on to an economy, and this means the large-scale cultivation of plants rich in calories (e.g., maize). Hence, the existence of agriculture is not synonymous with the existence of an agricultural economy as such. The shift to agriculture must be seen not as a rupture or a concrete event, but as a long, drawn-out, and occasionally nonlinear, process. Studies of settlement patterns, demographic changes, and shifting subsistence patterns make it clear that "Neolithic Revolution" is a phrase that masks millennia of cultural development.[8]

Delayed versus Immediate Return

Refinement and closer examination of Childe's thesis, and the increasing awareness that neither agriculture nor foraging were monolithic ways of life, in neat opposition to one another, was long in coming; but it was not until the work of the British anthropologist James Woodburn that the weaknesses of that thesis became clear. Woodburn's writings, based on fieldwork he did among the Hadza HGs of Tanzania in the late fifties, brings us to our second question, that of HG egalitarianism. The fundamental split, said Woodburn, was not between foraging and agriculture, or between primitive and civilized, but between peoples caught up in what he called a "delayed-return" economy as opposed to an "immediate-return" one. Some HGs, said Woodburn, actually fell into the former category. We thus have to look for complexity (hierarchy, social inequality) not in the development of agriculture, but within HG society itself.[9]

What Woodburn discovered in Tanzania was that the Hadza do not experience any severe food shortages and that they are unconcerned about the future. The population density is low, and groups move camp often, perhaps every two or three weeks. Although all Hadza consider themselves to be kin, they have few obligations to each other and are not bound by commitments. This is, Woodburn wrote, a major source of their strength. Everyone has direct access to valued assets, and this provides security for all. In Hadza society, you can separate yourself from those with whom you are in conflict without incurring any loss. Dependency, let alone hierarchy, is not part of the Hadza way of life. I shall say more about this below, but it is important to ponder that what is perhaps the popular image of HG societies—close, warm communities that are simultaneously very supportive and very conformist/restrictive—may be off the mark. Instead, what we often find is a great deal of autonomy and independence—freedom, in short—although not that of the bourgeois version of individualism of, say, nineteenth-century England. Woodburn also believed that the Hadza were not unique, that "this relative lack of sustained reciprocal load-bearing relationships is widely characteristic of the social organization of nomadic hunter-gatherers." Indeed, it usually goes by the name of "fission and fusion" and is a common pattern.[10]

What accounts for this freedom? The difference, according to Woodburn, lies in the mode of production. Immediate-return (IR) systems reject the notion of a surplus. Tribes such as the Hadza, the !Kung, and the Mbuti Pygmies of Zaire do not accumulate property. In such societies, even if you don't participate in a particular hunt, you have the right to eat, and individual hunters have no future claims on those they feed. One is not constrained by group decisions, and these societies either have no leaders or have leaders who wield no coercive power.[11] Delayed-return (DR) societies, which are based on the accumulation of surplus, inevitably lose their egalitarianism; there is a preferred status for those who arrange and manage the surplus for the rest of the tribe. Such systems also create dependency on specific persons so that one is caught up in a network of binding ties and corporate groups that can determine one's survival. This is typical of agricultural civilization, but, says Woodburn, it is also the rule for DR foragers as well. Thus, sedentary or semisedentary HGs, such as the Haida or Kwakiutl of the Pacific Northwest; the Plains Indians, who invest time in keeping horses; Australian aborigines, among whom the men retain long-term rights over women (through marriage brokering, etc.) are all DR and characterized by social inequality. Aboriginal society is laced with obligations, conflicts, an elaborate religious life, secret societies of (male) elders, and so on. All of this is more similar to the hierarchy (and the misery) of agricultural civilization than it is to the life of IR hunter-gatherers.[12]

In evolutionary terms, there was undoubtedly some switching back and forth between DR and IR; we know, for example, that there were substantial sedentary communities in existence prior to the Neolithic. But DR systems could not have made a sudden appearance on the Paleolithic scene; they had to have evolved from IR societies. Hence, says Woodburn, "There must presumably have been a time when all societies had systems based on immediate return." Only HG life, he asserts, permits so great an emphasis on equality, although a number of foraging societies have inequalities which are even greater than those of some agricultural or pastoral societies.[13]

Central to the IR economy—or at least, a necessary condition for it—is the phenomenon of movement. Movement works heavily against any tendencies toward surplus building and accumulation, which suggests that sedentism is a key factor in the origins of social inequality. In addition, the nomadic life is one that acts as a natural leveler of social conflict, which becomes a major issue once human beings start to create permanent settlements. In an article on "Egalitarian Societies," Woodburn examined six foraging societies with IR economies: the Mbuti, the !Kung, the Pandaram and Paliyan of southern India, the Batek Negrito of Malaysia, and the Hadza. In all six, he says, movement is fundamental. There are no fixed dwellings or base camps; people live in small camp units of twelve to twenty-four individuals and move frequently. The groups are flexible, with composition changing constantly, and individuals have a choice of whom they associate with (this is the "fission-and-fusion" pattern referred to above). Conflict, when it does arise, is resolved by simply moving away, and no one's livelihood is jeopardized as a result. Movement thus enables social ties to be manipulated without strain, and the Hadza move at the drop of a hat. No one is in charge, and this is modeled within the family as well. The values taught are ones of personal autonomy and sharing, not dependency and authority. All of this works against the formation of hierarchy and social inequality, as well as against the possibility of farming. The sharing ethos means that fields get "raided" before the grain is harvested, and once harvested, there exist great pressures to share, rather than accumulate. Motivation to invest in farming is thus very low, and hence in order to understand how agriculture did develop, we need to look more closely at delayed-return HGs, "who have the values and the organisation to facilitate the transition." Woodburn thus pushed the locus of social inequality back from agricultural civilization to HGs, but the question still remains as to what led IR egalitarian systems to change, to become DR systems with hierarchical arrangements.[14]

The Role of Storage

A closer look at the phenomenon of surplus has been the principal contribution of the French anthropologist Alain Testart, who locates the rise of social inequality in the phenomenon of storage among certain groups of HGs. Unfortunately, Testart's work does not account for the *origins* of storage, any more than Woodburn's accounts for the origins of DR economies, but it does push deeper into this new, post-Childean territory (the whole investigation has the flavor of the hunting of the snark). Testart identifies four types of social organization among hunter-gatherers:

1. Mounted HGs (those of central Asia, Argentina, or the Plains Indians of the United States) who are nomadic and relatively nonegalitarian;
2. storing HGs (e.g., the Indians of the Northwest Coast in the United States, Southwest Coast in Canada), who are sedentary, dense in population, and nonegalitarian;
3. nonstoring, sedentary HGs, who are virtually nonexistent, but who may have, in the past, formed a bridge for the transition to agriculture;
4. nomadic HGs, who are egalitarian, but who are subordinate to surrounding agricultural peoples and dependent on them economically (e.g., most Asian HGs and African pygmies).[15]

For Testart, storing HGs challenge the notion of a Neolithic Revolution, by sharing three essential characteristics with agricultural society: sedentism, high population density, and social inequality.

To begin with, Testart distinguishes between intensive (large-scale) storage and more limited storage. The latter does not necessarily entail a sedentary way of life since, within limits, food can be carried. At some point, however, quantity precipitates a shift in quality, and one finds storage, sedentism, and hierarchy all rolled into one. In addition, says Testart, many historians regard storage as a preadaptive feature leading to the invention of agriculture in the Near East. Sedentism per se makes possible the accumulation of light goods, while village life allows for structures and items that tie people down, such as mortars, grinding stones, containers, and durable dwellings. The shift to storage, he believes, involves an important mental shift: a distrust of nature, which is echoed (and, I would say, accompanied by) a distrust of human beings. For the nomadic way of life involves a fundamental trust in the ability of the natural world to provide, and along with this, an ethos of sharing with others in the band or group. All this is violated once storage gets going in a large-scale way. All in all, Testart's work, which includes a fairly convincing ethnographic examination of forty storing HG societies, demonstrates that "the relevant factor for the development of inequalities is not the presence or absence of agriculture, but the presence or absence of a storing economy, whether it be hunting-gathering or agricultural." Or, in Alan Barnard's words, storage "is probably the most significant factor in the origin and development of social inequalities."[16]

Testart's work strikes me as a real benchmark in our understanding of human cultural evolution, and although one can fault it in a number of ways, it is clear that he is onto something in his emphasis on storage, rather than agriculture, as being the crucial factor in the emergence of hierarchical structures. With this concept, says Testart, we have introduced, contra Childe, an important continuity back into human prehistory. Yet, as already noted, a major problem remains, for we have only managed to push Childe's rupture further back in time. It is not that there was no rupture, nor is it the case that this rupture is explained. For whence cometh storage? As one anthropologist has noted, Testart fails to show how an egalitarian, nonstoring HG society is transformed into a nonegalitarian storing one, and that remains the crucial issue. The snark still slips through the net.[17]

Politics and Autonomy among Contemporary HGs

Although, as in the case of religious history (above, chapter 1), there is a potential problem with extrapolating backward into the Paleolithic, it will be helpful to have a look at the political situation with respect to contemporary HGs before we continue our search for what happened just prior to the establishment of agriculture. The anthropological consensus on the subject seems to be something like this: there are a (very small) number of HGs alive on the planet today who do, or did until recently, display a number of characteristics that, from the vantage point of modern civilization, appear quite enviable. These include egalitarian sharing patterns; anti-authoritarian tendencies; respect for individuality combined with an emphasis on cooperation; flexible living arrangements; permissive child-rearing practices; and a system of "generalized" (as opposed to "balanced") reciprocity. These societies have achieved a greater degree of equality of wealth, power, and prestige than any other societies we know of. They are based on immediate-return economies and the discouragement of accumulation. They do not create dependencies on specific persons, and their emphasis on sharing works against the development of agriculture because it undermines the possibility of savings and investment, which agriculture requires. Finally, in such societies individuals do not have power over one another.[18]

This material is not a matter of political theorizing or wishful romantic thinking, but is based on the ethnographic experience of many researchers, as well as on correlations of ethnographic data. In a very important study published in 1991, the American anthropologist Peter Gardner used George Murdock's *Atlas of World Cultures* to examine the emphasis that HGs put on individual autonomy. Defining HGs as peoples with 0 to 5 percent dependence on agropastoralism, Gardner found a number of characteristics that they had in common: mobility, IR economies, an absence of leaders, egalitarian age and gender roles, emphasis on individual decision making, and an emphasis on the nuclear (as opposed to extended) family structures. Furthermore, these traits overlap in a mutually reinforcing way. Nomadism and factors pertinent to egalitarianism show a strong correlation, in the same way that Testart's data show a significant relationship between storage and social stratification. As it turns out, only 22 percent of the HG societies that Gardner examined have what he identifies as an "individual autonomy syndrome" (characterized by self-reliance within a community setting); but in today's world, this is perhaps nothing short of a miracle. Nor, as Gardner points out, is it useful to argue that these societies fall short of "true" egalitarianism. Tribes such as the Paliyan or Mbuti may not achieve perfect egalitarianism, but what they do achieve is absolutely remarkable.[19]

Although much more is involved in this than the classic Marxist issue of the mode of production, it is clear that the latter clearly plays a part. As Richard Lee notes, central to the foraging mode of production is an ideology of sharing and egalitarianism. Under the influence of their Bantu-speaking agropastoralist neighbors, the !Kung Bushmen have been experimenting with farming and herding. But it hasn't worked out very well, because there is a basic contradiction between the two modes of production. Central to !Kung life is sharing and generalized reciprocity. Central to Bantu life is saving, the husbanding of resources. And while there are small-scale agricultural or pastoral societies that are more or less egalitarian, they have a hard time staying that way because built into these DR economies is a dynamic that pushes them toward complexity. Increase population, and hierarchy starts to become an issue. Thus, writes Lee, many foraging societies have existed for hundreds of thousands of years without moving toward hierarchy, but no simple farming formation has lasted more than a few thousand years without developing social inequalities.[20]

What many contemporary HGs, as well as semisedentary cultures, display, in any case, is a radically different understanding of power: they know it can be organized in noncoercive ways. Our best source for this is probably the work of the French anthropologist Pierre Clastres, who lived among a number of such societies in Paraguay and Venezuela in the sixties and summarized his findings in a seminal work entitled *Society Against the State*. Perhaps more than any other single text, Clastres' study elucidates what the phenomenon of paradox looks like when translated into the political arena.[21]

From a modern point of view, HG societies would seem to be apolitical. What Clastres argues is that such a viewpoint is the bias of a culture that equates politics with the state.[22] From the viewpoint of Western ethnography, in other words, power is identical to coercion, or violence; it is "the ability to channel the behavior of others by threat or use of sanctions."[23] A society that doesn't operate on such a basis is, in our terms, regarded as a society without power. Yet throughout Mexico, as well as Central and South America, Clastres argues, there have been and still are Indian or native societies headed by caciques who do not possess power in the classical Western sense. As Clastres puts it, "No relationship of command-obedience is in force." The notion that coercion, subordination, and hierarchy constitute the essence of political power, in all times and all places, is merely the bias of vertically organized cultures. It is for this reason that the first European explorers felt psychologically at home in the Mexico of the Aztecs or the Peru of the Incas; these empires wielded power in the way that people from monarchic nations understood it. But when the same explorers encountered, for example, the Tupinamba Indians of Paraguay, they were completely disoriented, describing them as "people without god, law, and king."

From the very beginning, says Clastres, our ethnography has been skewed; we have taken our own definition of power as the yardstick of meaning and then gone out into the field to see how stateless societies measure up. What we find is a "lack," when what we are really doing is displaying our own conceptual poverty. What this approach misses is the political achievement of those cultures that practice the power of nonpower because, from the outside, it looks like nothing. And, in a sense, it *is* nothing; but as Clastres shows, this is a very rich nothing, a nothing which, like the "empty hand" of karate, actually contains enormous power.

So the way we in the industrial West organize relationships of power is seen (by us) as the apex of a certain political or historical progression, and groups such as the Tupinamba are classified to the degree to which they approximate this ideal. We also believe in a continuity between these various forms. Hence, the political organization of HGs is referred to as an "embryonic" form of power, implying that we constitute the adult stage. Or we claim that the Sioux Indians failed to achieve what was attained by the Aztecs. As Clastres points out, this is ideology, not scientific investigation.

What would genuine scientific investigation consist of, in this field of research? It would mean, among other things, being open to the possibility that negation does not necessarily signify nothingness, that power might exist totally separate from coercion or hierarchy, and that our own task as scientific investigators is to solve the paradox of a "powerless" power. For Clastres, political power is universal and inherent in *all* social reality, and the statist/coercive model is only one particular configuration of it. Our job as social scientists is to examine the noncoercive case and figure out how the absence at the center functions in a political way.

Clastres identifies three essential traits of the Indian leader that recur throughout North and South America:

(a) the chief is the peacemaker, the tribe's moderating agency; (b) he is completely generous with his possessions and cannot reject material demands made on him; and (c) he is a good orator.[24] Now there are two comments that need to be made at this point, in addition to the observation that the ethnographic evidence tends to document the presence of these three features.

First of all, it is the case that the noncoercive model switches to a coercive one during wartime. During war, the chief (or the war chief, if it is a different person) commands substantial power. Hence the coercive model is adopted only in exceptional circumstances, namely those of an external threat. This is interesting: it suggests that since civilization uses the coercive model as the norm, it is, in a strange sense, always in a state of war (or mobilized for it). In HG society, the normal role of the "chief" is maintaining the peace.

Second, the prestige of the chief is closely bound up with his generosity. But this is, in effect, a kind of bondage. Rather than having power in our sense, the chief is in a constant state of obligation. Across all of South America, says Clastres, "greed and power are incompatible."

But why have a chief who has no (coercive) power? That would mean he is—apparently—merely a figurehead (for *what*?). Of course, this is the way "ranked" or prestige societies work, and one can perhaps see ranking as a step on the road to real social stratification. Often, the chief is the only male allowed to have more than one wife, which is further compensation for his role; but it remains the case that he can't compel anyone to do anything. According to Clastres, this paradoxical situation is quite deliberate: by having a chief who has no coercive power, the tribe displaces power from the center to the periphery. It exists, but no one can find it. These tribes, says Clastres, have an intuitive understanding that allowing power to be vested in a person "conceals a mortal risk for the group . . . [and] is a challenge to culture itself." So what they did was create a paradoxical way of neutralizing the potential threat of the coercive model. "They chose themselves to be the founders of that authority," writes Clastres, "but in such a manner as to let power appear only as a negativity that is immediately subdued." In other words, by having a chief whose power is effectively nothing, the group displays its radical rejection of authority. By refusing coercion as an option, this "choice" on the part of the tribe becomes intentional.

Why have a chief at all, then? Clastres comments that in fact, a number of tribes do not, and that in the language of at least one tribe, the Jivaro, the word "chief" doesn't even exist (this was also true of the /Xam Bushmen of southern Africa, who survived into the early twentieth century).[25] But the powerless chief is more typical because his existence as a person serves to embody the paradox of native political arrangements. In a sense, he is the group's prisoner. After all, says Clastres, these tribes are hardly unaware of the possibilities of coercive power and are in fact fascinated by it: "The affluence of the chief is the group's daydream." To thwart that, power is paradoxically venerated in its impotence, and the chief is set up as the physical embodiment of that paradox.

We see, then, the mistake of referring to "primitive" society as politically "lacking" something, as though the state were the inevitable destiny of every society. It is more likely that we have lost touch with our own remarkable possibilities and that the shift to coercive structures that occurred on the civil or political level was an immense loss. Primitive politics is in fact about mastery, but not in the coercive sense of the term. What we are witnessing is political genius, even if it has proven to be very fragile.

Leveling Mechanisms

But how do we know Clastres is seeing the situation correctly? Unfortunately—at least in this work—he has not interviewed any of his subjects, has not asked them what they think they are doing. It remains rather speculative, until we realize that what are called "leveling mechanisms"—social techniques designed to keep pride and self-aggrandizement in check—are known to be a common feature of HG social and political life. One of the most compelling stories in this regard is Richard Lee's famous tale of "Eating Christmas in the Kalahari." Lee decided to buy the !Kung Bushmen, among whom he was living, an ox for Christmas. He was grateful to the Bushmen for their cooperation in his researches, and managed to procure the largest, meatiest ox that was around for the upcoming feast. The reaction was not what he had expected. His first visitor, a sixty-five-year-old mother of five, called the animal a "bag of bones," claiming it was old and thin. Next, a delegation of young men came to his evening fire, complaining that the ox was "an old wreck," "thin to the point of death." The third round was a cattle owner who showed up the next morning, shaking his head and telling Lee, "I'm surprised at you; you've lived here for three years and still haven't learned anything about cattle."

And on and on. One of the best hunters, Tomazo, came by to tell Lee that he should buy a different cow, one with fat on it; a !Kung elder worried that if Lee served such a scrawny animal, fights would break out among groups that had feuded in the past. Lee was ready to pack it in and leave, but curiosity got the better of him, and he decided to stay for the slaughtering and see what, indeed, was under the skin. As the animal was cut, and thick layers of desirable fat burst forth, the tribesmen rolled on the ground, nearly paralyzed with laughter. Then the men packed large chunks of beef into the cooking pots, muttering all the while about the worthlessness of the animal. They danced and ate for two days and nights.

Realizing that he had been had, Lee decided to seek out /gaugo, one of the young men who had derided the ox at Lee's evening campfire the previous week. "Why did you tell me the ox was worthless," he asked the young man, "when you knew it was loaded with fat?" "It's our way," replied /gaugo. "A Bushman who has been hunting, for example, must not come back and announce a big kill. He must sit in silence until someone asks him about it. Then we all go out to look at the animal, and tell him it's just a bag of bones, but that we'll slaughter it anyway, even though it's hardly worth it."

Similarly, Tomazo explained to Lee: "It's about arrogance. When a member of the tribe kills much meat, he can come to think of himself as a chief, and the rest of us as his servants. Someday, his pride will lead him to kill someone."

All of this gave Lee a lot to think about, about the "Clastrean" choice that the !Kung had deliberately made, to reject vertical power relations. "Was it this independence of spirit," he wondered, "that had kept the Bushmen culturally viable in the face of generations of contact with more powerful societies?"[26]

The same orientation is described by James Woodburn as the pattern for the HG societies he investigated. A Hadza hunter, for example, returns to camp and sits down, allowing only "the blood on his arrow shaft to speak for him." Sanctions also exist in these societies against any form of accumulation. The point is, they *know* what vertical power is, and they don't want it; they know it will rip their culture apart. Clastres argues, for example, that the role of torture in initiation ceremonies was to send (and embody) the message: "You are no more and no less than anyone else." He also points to the prevalence of stories and folktales in which the shaman is made to look ridiculous. All of this, it would seem, is about the power of nonpower.[27]

Of course, most of these cultures did get ripped apart, reorganized along vertical lines. That there are a handful of even partially egalitarian societies left, that 22 percent of remaining HG societies efficiently combine self-reliance with community (Peter Gardner's work, above), is nearly unbelievable. But again, assuming this was the pattern back into the Paleolithic, how are we to account for the change? Why would any society abandon "equality and justice for all" for vertical relations in which a small number of elites run the show? Who, except for that small number, would benefit by such a change?

The answer, of course, is that the change was not a voluntary one. Rather, it was toward the end of the Paleolithic, if not before, that certain developments occurred that rendered this shift inevitable. Having examined some facets of contemporary HG egalitarianism, we are now in a position to pick up the thread of our original inquiry.

The Role of Population Pressure

The most convincing explanation to date is the body of work generated by two American anthropologists, Mark Cohen and Robert
Carneiro. Their explanation for this momentous shift and for the rise
of the state neatly interlock. In a nutshell, they argue that population
growth, leading to population pressure in a "circumscribed" area—
one socially or environmentally bounded in such a way that an ex-
panding population has nowhere to go—leads to conflict, war, and
the search for more calories per unit space. Out of these circumstances,
social inequality emerges as a matter of course. The stage is then set
for agriculture and the state.

To take Cohen first, then: the argument here is that world human population was building over the course of the Pleistocene and,
on the eve of the Neolithic, the world was effectively saturated. Agriculture, sedentism, and political centralization, he says, then followed ineluctably. For while the foraging strategy is that of adjusting
people to resources (via mobility), the agricultural option is that of
adjusting resources to people, which requires governments. Population pressure, says Cohen, eliminated the first option; the HG way
of life is not one that can support large or dense populations. The
search was then on for more food, that is, more calories per unit
space, which is why storage first occurred in pre-agricultural,
semisedentary contexts. Eventually, various forms of centralized authority arose, to manage the new system (e.g., the redistribution of
food) and to provide security against risk.[28]

Do the archaeological data support the notion of steady population increase throughout the Pleistocene? Cohen claims that such
is the case, although there is the familiar problem of "soft" data disappearing, which can create misleading impressions. Thus, he notes
that standard demographic techniques for dealing with the Pleistocene, especially when this involves nonsedentary populations, are
faulty. The archaeologist typically takes as a parameter the number
of sites or acres occupied, or (say) the number of shellfish remains,
as representative of the population at some point in time, and then
does the same for another point in time. Supposedly, the two figures
represent relative population sizes. However, the method assumes a
fixed relationship between the number ascertained and population
size, but this is questionable; nor is it likely that this parameter has
been recovered in its entirety. In addition, with nonsedentary populations, temporary campsites are often not preserved, as in the case
of sedentary groups. Hence archaeological studies tend to emphasize
agricultural populations rather than HGs. The result is that the data

can easily create the impression of a population explosion accompanying agriculture, when all that has exploded is the availability of
reliable data.[29]

This tendency to underestimate the potential for population
growth among nonsedentary societies, says Cohen, leads to a Malthusian bias, such as we see in the work of Gordon Childe: that is,
populations seem stable prior to the emergence of agriculture; then
they suddenly take off. But it may be the case, in contrast to
Malthus, that population regulates food supply rather than the reverse. We can assume the existence of population pressure, says
Cohen, when the archaeological evidence shows a shift from eating
large mammals to smaller ones, or to birds, or to plant foods; or
when there is a greater focus on regional resources; or when
sedentism and storage arise; or when the evidence shows an increasing amount of disease, which can be traced to stress and to a reduction of variety in the diet. Although the appearance of a single
one of these factors does not prove the existence of population pressure, a convergence of several of them makes it extremely likely.
Agriculture, in particular, is preceded by a cessation of territorial expansion, increased sedentism, and a high concentration on fish and
plant foods. What the archaeological record shows is that such trends
go back a very long way, and that the Mesolithic period, that is, the
time between the Paleolithic and the Neolithic, saw the culmination
of these trends. It is for this reason that agriculture and the state
arose at independent locations throughout the ancient world within
such a relatively short period of time. Population pressure is the only
factor that is nonlocal, which would therefore explain such a trend.[30]

In Cohen's view, egalitarian or band society could not handle
two problems: reduced mobility and high population density. Loss
of mobility meant the loss of time-tested "homeostatic buffers," in
particular, the fission-and-fusion method of conflict resolution. The
new buffers included hierarchy, prestige (ranked society), religion
and ceremony, and food storage, and we find that a number of complex HG societies, such as the Tlingits of southeastern Alaska, the
Peruvians of 3000 B.C., or California and Pacific Northwest Indians,
existed in antiquity. The new buffers, says Cohen, enabled the
marginalization of large groups of people; the ability, on the part of
newly appearing elites, to stereotype these people, screen them out—
something that is hard to do if face-to-face contact is the norm.[31]

But (again) is Cohen's assessment of world demography in fact
correct? Certainly, the notion of the ubiquity of population pressure,
climaxing at the end of the Paleolithic, is a controversial one, and
has been much debated in the anthropological/archaeological litera-

ture.[32] When combined with Robert Carneiro's work on the origins of the state, however, the argument for population growth as a key factor in the creation of social inequality (even if it doesn't exactly follow Cohen's "bottle" theory of the earth gradually "filling up") seems fairly persuasive. Carneiro followed the suggestion made by the German sociologist Georg Simmel, in 1902, who argued that when a group exceeded a certain size, it had to develop certain organizational features for its maintenance or else split into smaller groups. Carneiro examined the data for forty-six single-community societies, consisting of autonomous bands and villages, and found that the number of such organizational traits did increase as the communities grew. Complexity became inevitable, suggesting that population density was a crucial factor in the process. Thus, Carneiro pointed out that the Plains Indians had a pattern of minimal political organization during most of the year except during the summer, when the bands, which (Clastrean-style) had only powerless "chiefs," came together for the buffalo hunt. This added up to several thousand people. As a result, the chiefs would quickly form a council and elect a chief with real authority, that is, coercive power. But once the hunt was over, the whole structure was immediately dissolved.[33]

Carneiro also argued that war played a decisive role in the formation of hierarchies, especially the state, as can be seen in the early stages of Mesopotamia, Egypt, India, and elsewhere; but that it was not a sufficient condition for state formation. The key to the process, he said, was "circumscription": a situation in which areas are set off by mountains, deserts, coasts, and so on, such that one could not escape by moving away. This environmental form of circumscription, however, was not the only way an area could be closed off; there also could be a social circumscription, in which the presence of nearby populations made nomadic behavior—the fission-and-fusion pattern of HG societies—impossible. Since a tribe in this situation could not expand horizontally, vertical arrangements were the only alternative.[34] In her book *Farmers as Hunters*, Susan Kent summarizes what is by now the general consensus regarding the origins of complexity: that population packing and restricted mobility lead to sedentism, and when this happens in an environment that has the potential for storage and surplus, a need for power differentiation arises. Someone is needed who can settle disputes that can no longer be solved by fission and fusion. Hence, differences of social status arise, for the position of arbitrator is a privileged one. As for *formal* leadership, this *can* arise in nomadic HG contexts, but sedentary societies simply cannot exist without some form of centralized leadership. The only way to avoid this is to start moving again, and that may no longer be possible.[35]

According to Cohen and Carneiro, then, conflict plays a crucial role in the emergence of vertical structures. Of course, there is no way to know for certain how Paleolithic HGs dealt with conflict, except that all the evidence points to the use of the easiest conflict resolution mechanism of all, namely, movement. While it is true that contemporary groups such as the !Kung practice elaborate means of negotiation, in addition to the use of various "leveling mechanisms" described above, we have no way of knowing whether these are fairly recent developments, the result of mobility becoming increasingly unavailable as a solution.[36] The norm seems to be that when conflicts flare up, the parties involved separate, go elsewhere; and in IR economies, in which there is no dependence on specific persons, no sacrifice of vital interests are involved—which is why people *choose* avoidance as a mechanism; they are free to do so. Thus, James Woodburn notes that intragroup conflicts among the Hadza are solved quite easily by self-segregation and attract little attention because band units are highly unstable anyway, always involved in a rhythm of dissolution and regrouping. The point is that in HG societies such as these, people are not coerced (i.e., do not coerce themselves) into "community"; the system is much more laissez-faire. When a conflict arises, people simply pull up stakes and move on. This is the path of least resistance, which is why we can imagine it stretching back into the Paleolithic, when immense spaces were available.

Woodburn also points out that such arrangements work against the development of authority. We have to divest ourselves of the belief that given the opportunity, people will form into the sort of tightly knit groups that are found among farming peoples. Human beings may not be all that social, and may find the cooperative long-term commitments inherent in farming or DR economies oppressive. Such is true, apparently, of the Hadza; and anthropologists Allen Johnson and Timothy Earle see it as common for family-level (band) society in general. Thus, they point out that when band society expands, what happens is a shift from control *over* aggression to control *by means of* aggression. Ceremonies and leaders also increase; sporadic violence becomes endemic. The "domestication" of people into interdependent groups, they say, is closely tied to warfare and competition. Family-level households, they conclude, are "amazingly independent . . . They are capable of mustering all the necessities and most of the desirables in life through their own efforts. And they like it that way: other people just get in the way."[37]

Studies of the !Kung Bushmen show quite clearly the relationship between conflict and population density and why band societies prefer the small, independent way of life. Significant differences
in political centralization and violence have been mapped for sedentary, newly sedentary, and nomadic Bushmen, in terms of what
we would expect: the nomadic ones are egalitarian and nonhierarchical, with only occasional violence; newly sedentary groups (i.e., those
formed during the last twenty-five years) show patterns of centralized leadership. In 1972, Richard Lee reported that the large seasonal gatherings of Bushmen, which occur around water holes in
dry seasons, were plagued by disputes and that this was a function of population density. Thus, serious disputes only occurred
three to four times a year at water holes with populations of forty
to sixty people, but rose to twice a month once the population exceeded one hundred.[38]

All of this suggests that Pierre Clastres' attack on "Eurocentric"
ethnography may be correct in theory but possibly irrelevant to the
actual historical situation. For if population growth, population density, and the resource stress that typically accompanies these in circumscribed situations played so great a role in the emergence of
social inequality, and if their appearance were historically inevitable, then so were vertical political arrangements. Thus, "radical
democracy," to the extent that it existed, would seem to be a very
fragile flower, quite easily disrupted; and there is both demographic
and biological evidence to suggest that this is the case.

A Biological Basis to Egalitarianism?

The most dramatic evidence for the (negative) influence of resource
stress and population density in biological terms emerges from the events
surrounding chimpanzee feeding practices at Gombe National Park in
Tanzania, made famous by the fieldwork of Jane Goodall. According to
the Canadian anthropologist Margaret Power, some wild chimp groups
are foragers, in the same way that human HGs are; they are "groups
without one permanent leader that follow a nomadic pattern of fission
and fusion, and live off wild food."[39] The chimps are functionally egalitarian, she says, and conflict is often resolved by a pattern of fission and
fusion that also serves to prevent any fixed leadership from arising.
This egalitarian system, writes Power, "is characteristic of both (undisturbed) chimpanzees and (undisturbed) humans who live by the 'immediate-return' foraging system." Prior to 1965, when a change in the
feeding pattern was instituted at Gombe, Goodall's reports showed that

the chimps there were nonaggressive, nonhierarchical, and nonterritorial, without any one leader or alpha male; and this has been corroborated by all researchers who have used naturalistic feeding methods. All observers, says Margaret Power, have found that the fission-and-fusion pattern is characteristic of chimpanzees; and in 1965, Goodall stated that wild chimps did not form separate communities but united freely from time to time.

In 1965, a change was instituted that made the existence of fluid independent communities impossible, and what resulted was total bedlam. The new system was that of human-controlled banana feeding, which fostered direct competition among the Gombe chimps for limited food. It involved making the chimps wait in groups for the food to be released, introducing elements of temporal uncertainty, irregularity, and population clustering. The result was a sharp increase in the number of aggressive interactions. In fact, the whole foraging social order broke down, and the chimps began to kill each other. What rapidly evolved was a ranked society, with great emphasis on territoriality. By 1972, groups of apes began patrolling the peripheries of their home range, brutally attacking the outsiders they encountered. The year before, one group of chimps had left the Gombe area and moved south. This was known as the Kahama group; the ones that remained were the Kasekala group. Between 1971 and 1976, the Kasekala males sought out and killed all of the members of the Kahama group.

These are dramatic events, and it is a pity, as Margaret Power notes, that reports on and from Gombe argue for innate territoriality, hierarchy, and aggression, when chimp behavior prior to 1965 clearly contradicts this. Change things such as food supplies, population densities, and the possibilities for spontaneous group formation and dissolution, and all hell breaks loose—no less for apes than for humans. If people or chimps want community, they want it on their own terms, not under conditions of obligation and dependency.

However, this does not amount to an every-man-for-himself society. Band societies are based on sharing, on the allocation of goods and services without calculating the returns. Sharing may be closely related to our biological nature, rooted in the mothering of children by adults. Because it is based on intimate linkages and biosocial attributes, it doesn't work for large populations. When it hits the "public sector"—that is, goes much beyond band level society—it is transformed into a system of redistribution.[40]

All of this suggests that our natural propensity is at least partly egalitarian, but not especially communitarian. Band societies are nomadic; they value individual autonomy; and they do not form person-specific economic dependencies. For the most part (the !Kung example notwithstanding), conflict is not resolved by working things out, but by throwing in the towel. All of this suggests that community, at least as understood within the conceptual framework of the last ten thousand years, is unnatural. The basic model for human relations is the family, and this cannot be extended much beyond twenty-five or thirty people. As population growth creates population density in circumscribed areas, all manner of attempts are made to reduce conflict, but the biological basis for "getting along" is very weak. This is where hierarchy enters the picture.

One of the first researchers to recognize the importance of group size for social organization and to document this in terms of specific numbers and ethnographic situations was Joseph Birdsell, who did fieldwork in Australia. Birdsell saw five hundred as a kind of magic number for tribal cultures. Apparently, this number represents a statistically significant "equilibrium" value for several HG groups throughout the world. In terms of Australia, Birdsell showed that tribal populations across the entire continent had a number of distinct structural similarities. Thus, every "tribe" was composed of local groups, each of which numbered about twenty-five members; each "tribe" amounted to about five hundred members; each tribal zone spanned a predictable amount of land; and so on. The same data came up in work done on the Shoshone (USA), the Andaman Islanders, the Birhor of India, and the !Kung. According to Birdsell, the numbers can vary; this was not a rigid, mechanistic rule. Yet twenty-five and five hundred did tend to recur in the data, and Birdsell was able to show that this was not due to external or environmental factors. What, then, was the cause?[41]

According to Birdsell, the constraints had to be imposed socially, from within. The key, as we have already seen, is the opportunity for face-to-face communication. Birdsell defines a "tribe" as "an aggregation of local groups in spatial proximity [that have] a common dialect." In arguing this, Birdsell is hardly alone. As Richard Lee puts it, "When the size of the local group grows beyond the scale where everyone knows everyone else well, new modes of behavior and new forms of social organization must crystallize in order to regularize the added complexity." Classifications arise which usually spell the end of egalitarian relationships, but which are necessary if social coherence is to be maintained when the population goes much beyond 350 or 400 individuals.[42] A survey of George Murdock's *Ethnographic Atlas* shows that for any cultures having communities consisting of more than four hundred people, there are no egalitarian-like qualities; whereas for communities of less than four hundred, only seven

of the 862 Murdock catalogued had some kind of hierarchy (and
these seven were without significant class distinctions). Thus, it
would seem that group size is a significant regulator of the amount
of social inequality that can be present at any one time.[43]

Emergence of the State

To conclude this survey of the causes of the rise of social inequality,
it would appear that agriculture is far less of a "culprit" than was
hitherto imagined. Distinctions of prestige (ranking) as well as wealth
(stratification) took root in certain HG societies well before agriculture
ever arrived on the scene. The "breakdown," then, occurred within
HG society itself, and over time it became the norm. Once formed,
complex institutions have their own agendas. "Our kind" started with
band society, in which the typical size was about twenty-five to thirty
people, leadership was context-specific, war (as opposed to aggression
or impulsive homicide) was nonexistent; and ritual was largely ad
hoc. The archaeological evidence suggests that most of the world's
population was organized in this way prior to 10,000 B.C.[44]

The second level of development was that of the local group,
when storage and some degree of sedentism appeared. Typically, this
arrangement has a headman, who often serves to redistribute the
surplus, and when headmen begin to vie for this role, you get the
Big Man, the charismatic figure. At this level, the village population
has risen to anywhere from three hundred to eight hundred persons,
it has a clan structure, food sources are domestic, and ceremony has
become significant. Out of this, given enough of a population increase, chiefdoms gradually evolve, and this is a new order of mag-
nitude. The size is anywhere from one thousand to one hundred
thousand, and ceremonial centers, hierarchy, and stratification—un-
equal access to the means of production—are clearly in evidence,
along with hereditary leadership. The evolving pattern, say Johnson
and Earle, is fueled by population growth and agricultural expansion (which represents opportunity for economic control). The state
now emerges as a function of increasing size.[45]

The state is thus like a chiefdom, only more so: bureaucracy,
state religion, and police are added on, along with kingship, codified
law, taxation, and a military draft. At some point, the tribesman paying tribute to a chief becomes a peasant paying rent to a lord. Thus,
the "progression" is one from a social organization grounded in the
nurturance and trust of the family, to one based on prestige and hi-

erarchy, and finally, to one run by bureaucracy. The rest, as they say, is (literally) history.

All this is not to say that agriculture was incidental to this process. In rough outline, Childe's thesis actually remains intact. What agriculture and sedentism did was solidify these trends, render them irreversible. Thus, ranked society usually involves domesticated food sources, while no full-fledged states arose before agriculture became the major source of subsistence (with the possible exception of the Peruvian coast). Once HGs become storing and sedentary, they can adopt agriculture without any major changes in their way of life. But it is agricultural intensification that enables an incipient class stratification, linked with storage, to evolve into a class society, a civilization. This is why we see states, writing, and steel-making in agricultural society, but not before. In the same way, the shift from swiddens (impermanent fields) to terracing and irrigation is a move toward permanent cultivation and settlement. All of this involves stratification, and stratification and rule by elites are endemic to states. Both communism (such as it existed until recently) and democracy decorate this truth with an egalitarian ideology, but the reality since we left band society is elite control and differential access to resources. Civilization has many benefits, and it is also the case that some civilizations are better than others. But what they all have in common, that is, what defines them structurally, is a system of triage.[46]

There are, then, reasons to believe that contemporary HG egalitarianism represents a survival of tendencies that can be traced back to the Paleolithic. Foraging remains a distinct mode of life, what the British anthropologist Tim Ingold calls a "radically alternative mode of relatedness."[47]

Problems with the Egalitarian Argument

However, it is not *quite* so rosy as this, and before we can resume our hunt for the snark, some qualifications of the above argument must be made. Rousseau's contention, that humans were free in a state of nature and that inequality showed up only with civilization and the emergence of the state, does have a lot of validity, but it is only true up to a point. Certain data compel us to modify this.

For example, it is all well and good to point to the egalitarianism of chimpanzees, and note that they are our closest primate relatives; but the hominid evolutionary line obviously contains other primates as well, such as vervet monkeys and baboons, and these live by very definite group patterns of hierarchy and dominance. In fact, what we see in their behavior is a state of continuous tension; they constantly focus on who is on top of the pecking order and how to avoid threats. Michael Chance, in *Social Fabrics of the Mind*, calls this the "agonic" mode (*agon* means "contest," in Greek) and says it is marked by a preoccupation with hierarchy and security, whereas the "hedonic" mode of chimpanzees is focused on creativity, exploration, and free choice in relationships. As the evolutionary outcome of at least two very different types of primates, humans have both tendencies embedded deep within them.[48]

Second, it becomes difficult to take one's Rousseau completely straight, as it were, in the face of Francis Harrold's comprehensive study of Paleolithic burials, which he carried out in the seventies. We have already referred (chapter 1) to Sally Binford's work along the same lines, which showed that status differentiation starts to appear with items of personal adornment in Upper Paleolithic burials. In the case of Harrold's work, we have even stronger evidence for status differentiation increasing across the Middle/Upper Paleolithic transition, but with an important twist: the evidence from grave goods indicates status differentiation by gender going back into the Middle Paleolithic (i.e., –75,000 years)! This levels out somewhat as we enter the U.P. (despite the *overall* context of increasing status differentiation), but as far as the M.P. goes, we have some evidence that egalitarianism did not include women.[49]

Gender aside, however, both studies make it clear that some degree of status differentiation goes back to 33,000 B.C., and this among societies that were presumably IR, nonstoring, and nomadic. And this is crucial for our investigation, because it suggests that ultimate answers regarding power relations are rooted in psychological issues that arise from the cognitive/emotional split between Self and Other referred to in chapter 1, and no amount of Rousseau can make this go away. (I shall return to this below.)

Finally, can the cultural evolutionary pattern discussed above, that of band/tribe/chiefdom/state, be verified conclusively? Is it true that the human race went from relatively egalitarian band society to hierarchical statehood in a more or less linear progression? When we look at egalitarian patterns among many present-day HG societies, are we *truly* witnessing behavior that has continuity stretching back to the Paleolithic? This has been the subject of a rather heated debate in anthropological circles over the past few years, and while my own answer to these questions is a qualified yes, the reader needs to be aware that the whole thing is not an open and shut case, and that these issues will continue to dog the egalitarian argument. Somewhere between the two extremes of utopians and cynics lies the truth, and although I am personally more persuaded by the "utopian" camp, it remains a murky utopianism at best. Again, we cannot have our Rousseau-ianism straight.[50]

To continue with our snark hunt, in any case, we have now accumulated a veritable catalogue of exogenous causes for the origins of social inequality. We know about circumscription, population pressure, storage, delayed return and the like. And this is all well and good, but, ultimately, it doesn't go far enough, because one crucial factor has been omitted: deliberate human intention. The Carneiro/Cohen model rules out subjectivity or voluntarism; mechanically, as it were, human beings are squeezed by forces beyond their control until hierarchy finally "pops out." But people are not only acted upon, they also *act*, based on perception, evaluation, and opportunity; they are culture creators as well as culture bearers. If hierarchy is forced on human beings, it is also created by them. Thus, Morton Fried writes that the potential for stratification is present within egalitarian societies, just waiting for the right context to spring it. This potential lies in the existence of what I would term an "aggressive subgroup" that comes forward to claim power. So we need to have a look at what this kind of human intentionality entails, and ultimately, at the *unconscious* motives that may be driving the whole show.[51]

Taking Charge: The Aggressive Subgroup

We are now getting closer to the causes of social inequality than purely exogenous factors are able to take us. Yet it must be said that the suggestion of some sort of inherent "will to power" is found scattered, in muted form, in the writings of a number of anthropologists who argue for exogenous factors. It is as though, on some level, everyone knows that something voluntaristic and/or psychological is going on, but that most are reluctant to give it more than a passing reference. "One has to ask," writes Alain Testart, "why intensive storage is adopted in the first place . . . Although I have stressed the importance of technique, it is the pursuit of wealth and the will to increase inequality and exploitation that determines the intensification of food production above basic needs." Similarly, the Canadian archaeologist Brian Hayden comments that storage and other exogenous factors "only constitute the permissive conditions for the expression of the human pursuit of wealth and power." Storage, he says, is symptomatic of deeper changes in society.[52]

In one form or another, Mark Cohen, James Woodburn, Morton Fried, Allen Johnson, Timothy Earle, and a number of other scholars have effectively stated that band-level society contains the potential for social inequality; which, of course, has got to be the case, evolutionarily speaking (where else *could* it have come from?).[53] Dominique Legros, who did fieldwork among the Tutchone Athapaskans of the Subarctic—a poor nomadic HG group—makes this as explicit as possible.[54] Legros had expected to find an egalitarian society, but this was not how it turned out; and since it can be demonstrated that storage and other manifestations of social inequality among the Tutchone were not the result of proximity to Northwest Coast society,

> one has to conclude that a nomadic hunting and gathering economy, and a poor one at that, provides just as many opportunities for the development of inequalities and of a "storage economy" as a sedentary hunting economy in a rich environment . . . In consequence, I . . . take the position that all societies of hunters and gatherers have provided possibilities for the development of social inequalities in the full sense of the term . . . [55]

It is generally recognized, he continues, that societies of HGs did not *have* to institute inequalities, but that in the past, some did, with or without a rich environment and with or without the adoption of agriculture. Hence, "there is no point in trying to link the adoption of nonegalitarian structures to particular kinds of ecology and/or productive techniques." The crucial factor, in his view, is "the simple initiative of some subgroup in a society," such as he saw occurring among the Tutchone, where a particular subgroup appropriated valuable stores as their own private property. While exogenous factors are obviously crucial, this point of the role of an aggressive subgroup takes us to the threshold of human intention and psychology, which is where, I believe, we may at last bag the snark.

One of the most comprehensive studies undertaken of this subject is that of Brian Hayden and Robert Gargett, who did original fieldwork among communities in the Maya area of Mesoamerica.[56] These communities, which had been extremely isolated in the early twentieth century, experienced a series of crises during that time. Interviews conducted with older individuals who had lived through these events produced independent testimony that was unequivocal: incipient elites, or what the authors call "accumulators," provided no aid to their communities other than actions designed to consolidate their own power and wealth. Across the board, the "accumulators" made usurious loans, sold food at very high prices, and bought children to work as servants or slaves. In other words, emergence of elites was strictly a response to the opportunistic possibilities for self-aggrandizement; and the authors argue that this is the norm, that all human populations contain individuals with competitive, acquisitive personalities who try to rise to the top. "Accumulators everywhere," they write, "appear to be primarily skilled manipulators of social relationships, production, and debts."[57]

All of this is very revealing, but even if we do solve the problem of what motivates some individuals to seek power, we are left with a problem that is equally significant for our inquiry, namely: What enables them to get away with it? Why does the rest of the community submit? Assuming egalitarianism were the norm, say Hayden and Gargett,

> How, then, does the process leading to socioeconomic inequality even get started? How is it possible for a few individuals to persuade the vast majority of the community to moderate or even abandon rigid egalitarian ethics, to give up communal access to any important resources, and to let a few individuals exert disproportionate influence on the decisions and behavior of the majority of the community?

Hayden and Gargett attempt to answer this with an appeal to cultural ecology and natural selection, but for me, at least, this won't work, because it is only a restatement of the argument that opportunistic behavior gets triggered when the material conditions are right, which although true still begs the question. More relevant is Marvin Harris' remark, that the desire of the Big Man for prestige is actually the search for a love substitute.[58] I shall pursue this possibility in chapter 3. For now, I wish to return to the issue left hanging at the end of chapter 1, namely the relationship between political and religious verticality.

Cultural Stress and the Need for Sacred Authority

I have mentioned, in passing, that the protective mechanisms that an HG society employs to maintain social cohesion start to disintegrate under conditions of resource stress and population pressure. Circumscription and sedentism play particularly important roles in this as well, for along with the other factors, these additional ones mean that the best mode of conflict resolution known to man—taking off—is foreclosed as an option. When group size exceeds five hundred, in particular, hierarchical mechanisms come into play, generating prestige (if not power) for certain individuals; and all of this is significantly, and synergistically, reinforced by ritual and ceremony. Religion, trance, and/or the sacred authority complex step in to promote social cohesion. With this, the political mystification of human experience follows as a matter of course.

Two things inevitably happen under conditions of sedentism and agriculture: a change in a society's relationship to movement and a change in its relationship to time. But the shift in time frame—which is really the shift from paradox to the constellation of futurizing and intent—is not so much dependent on agriculture per se as it is on the existence of a DR economy. All of the anthropological data we have supports the notion that cultures with IR economies tend to entertain charismatic behavior largely under conditions of stress. Otherwise, the focus is on *this* life; "the sacred" is merely what is present in front of them. Such cultures do not generate prophets or guru figures; "worship" is simply participation in the here and now. This is difficult to do in the context of a DR economy. This difference with respect to time orientation is especially noticeable in the area of attitudes toward death and an afterlife. In a revealing study of this subject, James Woodburn reports on his survey of such beliefs among the Hadza, the !Kung, the Mbuti Pygmies of Zaire, and the Baka Pygmies of the Cameroon. All four of these HG groups live near farmers and are aware that their neighbors have very negative feelings toward the HG practices associated with death. Indeed, it must be very threatening to be around people who think death is no big deal. The Hadza don't mark their grave sites; many of them say that when one dies, one rots, and that is that. Similarly, the Baka don't believe in an afterlife, ghosts, or spirits. They say: "When you're dead, you're dead, and that's the end of you." Until recently, they left their dead in the forest to be eaten by animals. As for the Mbuti, when missionaries or agricultural neighbors come to talk to them about the afterlife, they say: "How do you know? Have you died and been there?" None of these groups have chiefs or shamans who administer death rituals.

Some of this is changing, especially under the influence of agricultural neighbors, with whom these HG groups are often forced into economic relationships. Under Bantu and missionary influence, the Baka now speak of the "soul" and say that upon death, it goes to reside in the "Big Village." Under economic pressure, it doesn't take much to turn HGs into Christians and Gnostics; and with the sharp increase of death and disease in sedentary situations, there is a corresponding tendency to resort to sorcery. However, Woodburn points out that the nomadic life in itself cannot guarantee freedom from all of this spiritualism because groups such as the Australian aborigines and Andaman Islanders have elaborate death rituals. The key, once again, is whether the economy is one of immediate or delayed return. IR economies have very simple beliefs surrounding death, and, significantly, questions of succession and inheritance are almost nonexistent. In IR systems, no one benefits from a death, and no one believes death will hurt them.[59]

Colin Turnbull's work with the Mbuti Pygmies provides an equally dramatic case study here.[60] Reading through his account of Mbuti life (IR economy), one cannot help but be struck by the "Isness" of it all. Unlike the neighboring Bantu villagers (DR economy), the Pygmies have a "sacred" reality that is no more sacred or esoteric than the forest in which they dwell. There is a notable absence of any preoccupation with political power, magical rites, and "hidden realities," which is the stuff of Bantu village life. The Mbuti regard all of this as superstition. Their central "religious" ritual, the *molimo*, is a cycle of songs sung in times of crisis and accompanied by the playing of a long wooden trumpet. But the trumpet is not regarded as a "sacred object"; in fact, the Mbuti sometimes use a metal drainpipe for the same purpose(!), and the song cycle is devoid of any magical components. It is just something that is done. When something goes wrong in the village, the inhabitants believe that sorcery is the cause. When something goes wrong in the forest, the Pygmies believe that the forest fell asleep; so they sing to it to wake it up. The forest, writes Turnbull, is "presence," or "God," and communion with it is all that is necessary. This is not a vertical god; Turnbull's narrative makes no mention of ecstatic states or anything resembling a sacred authority complex. As for the practice of magic, the Mbuti regard it as manipulative, egoistic, and antisocial. While the villagers are soaking in magic and ritual in an effort to get the spirits to do their bidding, the Pygmies "believe in a benevolent deity or supernatural power which identify with the forest." They do have a concept of *pepo*, a life force, which they see as animating all moving things; but this is no great mystery. In fact, the word has connotations of "breath" and "wind." Turnbull writes:

> The perennial certainty of economic sufficiency, the general lack of crisis in their lives, all lead the Mbuti to the conviction that the forest, regarded as the source of *pepo* and of their

whole existence, is benevolent, and that the natural course of
life is good. The absence of magic . . . is simply an indication of
the normal absence of crisis.[61]

Concomitant with this is the absence of any vertical authority.
"The overall picture," writes Turnbull,

> is one of a society where the lack of formal structure is so
> evident that one wonders why there is not complete disinte-
> gration. There are not only no chiefs or councils of elders, but
> no ritual specialists, and no lineage system that in any way
> contributes directly to order and cohesion. There is no legal
> system, and no body of belief in supernatural sanctions.[62]

All of this changes under the pressure of sedentism and community. Trance practice does, as already noted, exist among the
!Kung Bushmen, although it has a very democratic structure: one-
half of the adult males, and one-third of the adult females, learn to
do the trance dance, and *!kia* dancers have no special status in daily
life. Teachers will be uncles or brothers, for example. But this cannot be maintained under sedentary conditions. Thus Susan Kent
reports that among the Ghanzi Basarwa (i.e., Bushmen) who became
sedentary, trance dancers became candidates for emerging leadership
roles, and the whole thing acquired a political dimension. (Again,
the influence of Bantu agriculturalists is a key factor here.) Some
dancers became paid professionals and were soon regarded as potential leaders. A similar pattern exists among the Mbuti, who were
forced into sedentary farming by the government of Zaire between
1951 and 1972. Hierarchy, competition, and belief in spirits and
witchcraft all arose together. Paradox and egalitarianism are extremely fragile flowers; it doesn't take much for religious and political hierarchy to overwhelm them. Hence the comment of Charles
Lindholm (*Charisma*) that a "Weberian charismatic authority figure . . .
lies very near the surface of even the determinedly egalitarian Bushman collectivity." As in the case of the rise of an aggressive subgroup, if conditions are right, verticality gets "sprung."[63]
     Sedentism, of course, increases the amount of community life
that is forced on the individuals involved. We have already seen that
conflict and hierarchy arise in situations of newly imposed sedentism
and greater population density, and the same is true with respect
to religious behavior. Thus Peter Wilson notes that shamanism and
trance seem to occur frequently among groups such as the !Kung
that have an intense community life, one that presumably figures

large in the establishment of individual identity. Among the Hadza, says Wilson, or the Naiken of the Nilgiris (southern India), there is very little reliance on any form of community life. A Hadza, for example, may go on walkabout for a long time. The suggestion is that "possession trance, or its frequency, relates to the extent of community life and hence may be involved with the increasing intensity of problems that emerge with daily group life." Leave people alone, in short, and they don't need sacred authorities.[64]

A drift toward religious verticality, and its relationship to political hierarchy, is well known and well documented by scholars the world over. The consensus is that "sanctified charismatic leadership is . . . a universal feature of the early state"; that ceremonialism and shamanism grow in proportion to the need to control large groups; that ritual, the codification of myth and legend, the elaboration of symbolism, and the manufacture of prestige goods, are the roots of civilization; and so on. In his article, "Sacred Power and Centralization," anthropologist Robert Netting points out that when population pressure hits fixed resources, leaders arise and rapidly acquire a special status, whereupon the centralization of such leadership under a religious aegis suddenly becomes adaptive. Extensive studies demonstrate conclusively that the following aspects of religious belief and practice are correlated with a high degree of cultural complexity: belief in a high god, possession trance, priests and religious hierarchies, calendrical rites, frequent group ceremonies, and more elaborate funerals. As Carlo Levi once put it, "The farther the state is removed from each individual, the mightier it grows in boundless leviathanic capacity, the more it breeds an all-pervasive sense of sacredness."[65]

We have already observed that community bonding beyond the level of the family—say, twenty-five or thirty people—is unnatural, and that under population pressure and resource stress, complexity emerges as the easiest way to control the inevitable conflicts. Given what we have said about vertical sacrality, it becomes clear why it too would be adaptive in these circumstances. Trance, in particular, is binding energy, and for the most part it and the SAC are not particularly adaptive when HGs are not sedentary or circumscribed and can freely make use of the fission-and-fusion option. When "f & f" is no longer possible, vertical "sacred" relationships come forward and serve as a homeostatic buffer, in much the same way that social inequality does. This is why the two patterns, the sacred and the secular, mesh so well. Unitive trance keeps communities together that ordinarily wouldn't stay together, *and* it serves to validate the hierarchy at the same time. In addition, magical systems arise to provide certainty, while ritual serves to reinforce group participation in hierarchies. In this context, charisma makes "sense"; it is attributed to those who establish ascendancy over others, either by force or by an "inner state"; which, either way, amounts to vertical power relations. As Caroline Humphrey has written, "[Mircea] Eliade's concept of an Ur-shamanism, based on the idea of the shaman's ascent to celestial abodes, looks rather different when it is realized that this very ability was contested by political leaders."[66]

Failure to understand the nature and long history of paradox can lead to some very warped assessments regarding the nature of vertical religous experience, in ways remarkably similar to what Pierre Clastres points out regarding the nature of political hierarchy. Thus, Grant Jones and Robert Kautz (*The Transition to Statehood in the New World*) assert that all human society requires ultimate sacred propositions and that this sanctity is a principle of hierarchy. Charisma and hierarchy both become "natural," on this way of thinking, in much the same way that the state is seen as natural. Similarly, anthropologist Roy Rappaport writes that "sanctity has permitted the progressive centralization of regulatory hierarchies," which he apparently regards as both good and natural.

> When we consider further that religious beliefs and practices have frequently been central to human concerns and when we reflect upon the amount of time, energy, emotion, and treasure that men have expended in building religious monuments, supporting priestly hierarchies, fighting holy wars, and in sacrifices to assure their well-being in the next world, we find it hard to imagine that religion, as bizarre and irrational as it may seem or even be, has not contributed positively to human evolution and adaptation.[67]

Of course, Rappaport is making the point that in an evolutionary sense, religion has been adaptive, has had a payoff. But this is to assume no change in its essential nature between the Paleolithic and the Neolithic and thus to ignore the fact that the word "positively" comes off in a rather peculiar light—as when "healthy" and "normal" are used interchangeably. That religion is adaptive in a warped context doesn't make it a positive thing. All of this is, in my view, a good demonstration of how far we have strayed from what really *is* natural. Clastres called for a "Copernican Revolution" with regard to our political perceptions; it seems clear enough that our religious sensibilities could use a similar overhaul.

Movement as a Biological Baseline

I need to say just a bit more here about the phenomenon of movement, the real core of HG life. Movement is not only crucial in terms of fission and fusion, conflict resolution, and low population density; it is also important from a physiological point of view. Thus, in *The Songlines*, Bruce Chatwin argues that movement is not only a leveling mechanism, something that prevents the emergence of social inequality, but also something that is central to nomadic consciousness, to human fulfillment, and that serves to make life so rich here on earth that there was no need for many or most HGs to create religion or concepts of an afterlife. Wandering, says Chatwin, reestablishes an original harmony (read: paradox) that existed between human beings and the universe. He argues that it is an instinctive migratory urge, something we carry with us in a genetic or inherent sense.[68]

It is precisely the nomadic (i.e., ambulatory) aspect of HG life that sustains the perception of paradox and the fluidity of mind that was lost when the human race sat down. The HG way of life, with its evolutionary basis in movement and animal alertness, adds up to a kind of process psychology: the going is the goal. The wandering life is not about finding permanence, securing a beachhead against change or insecurity. Rather, *movement is the physiological substrate of the paradoxical experience*, of embracing life as it presents itself, rather than exclusively through the filters of myth and ritual, which are mistakenly taken to be, in sedentary societies, the fundamental sources of aliveness. In this sense, HGs were the first phenomenologists, or "non-ists," if you will, and this outlook corresponds to more than 99 percent of the human experience on this planet. Indeed, if walking is the leveling mechanism that keeps verticality at bay, we have to remember that hominids have been doing it for something like 4 million years. Probably nothing else in our evolutionary history has such continuity.

The truth is that we have never cut the "cord" connecting ourselves to animal alertness because that cord is part of us and probably part of the circuitry of the brain. Not all intent or futurizing is bad, of course; we would hardly be human without it. The problem arose when—as in Andrew Bard Schmookler's *Parable of the Tribes* or in the situation known as "Prisoner's Dilemma"—the "quick kill," the narrow focus, was consistently chosen over the expanded, peripheral one. The effect is destructively synergistic because everyone else is forced into similar behavior in order to survive. Thus, DR systems (probably), the SAC, culture/civilization, and power politics (social inequality) all arise at roughly the same time and accelerate rapidly. In a cultural sense, they get naturally selected for. So the "ascent of man," in Jacob Bronowski's perhaps unfortunate phrase, is the story of increasing intent, futurizing, and the suppression of alternative forms of awareness and behavior.[69]

It is for this reason that when civilization finally does destroy or sedentize the handful of remaining HGs, the victors will, ironically enough, prove to be losers as well. To live like this is to live on shaky ground, for the historical record is absolutely clear on this: civilizations are inherently unstable; they do not last (although some have obviously had some very long runs).[70] Culture and planning depth, while certainly constituting aspects of that which is essentially human, also represent (to the extent that they attempt to sunder or repress the link with paradox) something of a distortion, something that has to be defended all the time. Within the context of civilization, easing away from that pattern may be no less scary than attempting unilateral disarmament. Not that doing this would be identical to a return to pure animal alertness, but rather to an alertness that is highly plastic, simultaneously focused and contextual. But this is a vulnerable position to be in, and the historical fate of both contemporary and Paleolithic HGs provides a clear example of how high the stakes really are. Thus, the dilemma is clear enough, for one way of interpreting the record of repeated civilizational collapse is to say that on a logarithmic curve, planning depth (or what has also been called "hypercoherence") finally does itself in. This is why contemporary calls for religious renewal that argue for the resurrection of myth, transcendence, or ecstatic experience are ultimately pseudosolutions, for they can only trap us in more verticality, perpetuating a game of heresy versus orthodoxy that we have been playing for millennia.[71] In controlled contexts, such as exist among some HGs and small tribal cultures, this might make some sense; within an industrialized context, the typical result is the generation of authoritarian regimes.

What are we left with, then? It seems to be something like this: we have pushed exogenous factors back as far as we can. We have finally arrived at the inner psychic threshold. The potential for verticality of both a political and a religious sort may possibly be inherent in human makeup, but apparently it gets (or got) triggered in HG societies for the most part only under certain stressful conditions. When that happens, a certain aggressive subgroup comes forward to take power, and this pushes the rest of the group into a prisoner's dilemma situation: get on the bandwagon or get left behind. Morton Fried, for one, did not believe that a drive for power was an innate quality of human life, but believed that the power relations of stratified society were foreshadowed in the organization of the family.[72]

I believe that with issues of child rearing and family organization, we get down to the nitty gritty of power relations that exogenous factors cannot finally explain. Granted, the data might be nebulous, but we have to feel our way around in this area if the puzzle of social inequality is ever to be solved. What we need, according to the German anthropologist Antje Linkenbach, "is an approach which allows us to get detailed information on the main relationships of man—to nature . . . to the Other, and to the Self."[73] It all points to the "Big Man," damaged in childhood, seeking prestige as a love substitute, using (or becoming) a shamanic healer, and getting the rest of the group to buy into a bipolar game of dominance/submission. In *Charisma*, Charles Lindholm quotes Eugene O'Neill—"Man is born broken. He lives by mending."—and a Mazatec Indian shaman: "I am he who puts together."[74] Are we all broken from a very early age? Is child rearing a universally traumatic process? If alternatives to hierarchy are at all possible, this much seems certain: we are going to have to know a lot more about the nature of human infancy, and the possibilities that are inherent in *that*.

3

AS THE SOUL IS BENT:
THE PSYCHO-RELIGIOUS ROOTS
OF SOCIAL INEQUALITY

> It is not something specific in the world for which the human being feels *Angst*, but simply the uncanniness of existence, which breaks out as anxiety.
>
> —Otto Friedrich Bollnow, *Das Wesen der Stimmung*

> From the child of five to myself is but a step. But from the new-born to the child of five is an appalling distance.
>
> —Leo Tolstoy

Let me begin by reviewing what was said in chapter 1 about Object Relations, alienation, prolonged dependency, and the need for maternal care. This will then set the stage for a comparison of child rearing in HG versus agricultural societies.

All human organisms go through two early processes, or events, that rupture the primordial experience of unity with the mother and with the world. The first is physical birth; the second, which is much more tenuous and prolonged, is psychological birth. The second rupture is what concerns us here, for it marks the beginning of the journey toward individual identity, self-conscious awareness, and the experience of fear and alienation. This begins the dialectic of Self and Other, and even under the most benevolent child-rearing conditions, fear and alienation are going to be present. It is this primary rupture to which Eugene O'Neill and the Mazatec shaman are referring (at the conclusion of the previous chapter). There are conditions of birthing and of early child rearing that are much less traumatic than those of the Western industrial nations, but the nugget of "uncanniness" that the German philosopher Otto Bollnow refers to—Karen

Horney's "creature anxiety," which is the strangeness of being alive *at all*—lies at the core of the human condition. Camus' *Stranger* and Sartre's *Nausea* are perhaps the most extreme portrayals we have of this, but the sociobiological evidence (discussed in chapter 1) takes some kernel of it back to the Middle Paleolithic.

As the infant grows and comes into self-conscious awareness, it has people and things in its environment that mitigate this uncanniness, act as a memory of that primordial unity in some way. Foremost among these is the mother's breast and, to be sure, the mother herself. In a HG situation, there are also forests, rivers, trees, and animals, and from the Late Paleolithic, domesticated animals. There are also, of course, members of the family. Such cultures may not create dependency on Transitional Objects, and even infants in our own culture who are breast-fed on demand and weaned late (by our standards) apparently do not need these. Thus, the degree of separation and cathexis spans a broad spectrum of intensity from culture to culture, and even within the same culture; but the constellation of alienation and attachment itself, as a raw fact of life, is a constant for human life going back a very long time.

The mother/infant dyad also shows up as a constant as well, even among (nonhuman) mammals. This is directly related to feeding and survival, of course, but warmth and holding are just as important. Given the human phenomenon of prolonged dependency, the infant deprived of these will die. This is John Bowlby's "monotropy," attachment to a specific caregiver in a one-to-one, dyadic relationship, that provides the organism with reassurance, basic trust in the world. Thus while multiple caregiving—a larger-than-dyadic context—is quite common throughout the world, and very likely to have been the historical norm as regards child-rearing practices, all kinds of comparative studies come back to the truism that "there ain't no one like mom." While we cannot know anything definite about patterns of Paleolithic child rearing, these studies do provide us with strong sociobiological clues. Thus, in one study that Herbert Barry and Leonora Paxson did of child-rearing patterns in 201 societies from around the world (which included HGs), it turned out that almost all of them ranked the mother as being of great importance, regardless of how multiple the caregiving pattern actually was. Research with nonhuman primates also indicates that separation is much more traumatic for peer-raised individuals than for mother-raised ones. As Mary Ainsworth puts it, attachment behavior and maternal reciprocity may be labile, but they remain instinctive nonetheless.[1]

That being said, the lability of the human psyche, its plasticity under the impact of different child-rearing practices, is as impressive as the instinctual aspect. For our own purposes, the crucial comparison will be the career of the psyche in HG versus agricultural child-rearing contexts (or more specifically, if we can find the data, under IR versus DR regimes). It will be valuable more generally, however, to look at the broader category of Western versus non-Western societies. Multiple caregiving and community child rearing are strongly characteristic of the latter and so might conceivably provide an interesting contrast to the "hallowed presence" phenomenon that Erik Erikson regarded as being universal.

Child Rearing in Western versus Non-Western Cultures

The greatest difference between First and Third World patterns of mother/infant interaction lies in the emphasis on somatic attention, in the latter case, as opposed to visual and vocal attention, in the former. That is to say, both Western and non-Western societies provide their infants with what Donald Winnicott calls a "holding environment," but in one case the holding is largely tactile, while in the other it is primarily emotive/interactive (verbal and visual). This pattern has been confirmed by numerous studies, including ones that have used video equipment to document the details of mother/infant interaction. It can be seen in HG societies, in agricultural societies such as those of rural India, or in an industrial society such as Japan. We have to wonder what difference this shift in emphasis makes.

Let us take the Japanese case first. In Japan, the primary emphasis on child rearing centers on the first three years of life. Indeed, the Japanese have a special word for this period, referring to it (I am anglicizing it here) as "ajasic," thereby avoiding the loaded teleological term "pre-Oedipal." A Japanese saying has it that "the soul of the three-year-old lasts till one hundred." Hence, the crucial importance of this formative period.[2]

Unlike the situation in the West, where the goal of child rearing is to cultivate autonomy and separation, the Japanese emphasis is on *amae*, or dependency; although weaning typically takes place after one hundred days and is thus far from the HG pattern of two to four years. Mother sleeps next to baby, who must have as little anxiety as possible. In fact, the aim of Japanese child rearing is to avoid any direct confrontation leading to bad feelings and to establish a primary foundation of basic trust. The infant is never left to

cry, and the Western practice of having the baby sleep in a separate room and cry itself to sleep is shocking to Japanese mothers.
To the latter, physical contact is regarded as being indispensable.[3]

One thing we see is that despite the centrality of the biological
mother/infant tie, cultural expectations begin to shape the infant by
the third month of life. One study of thirty Japanese and thirty
American infants found that preferred patterns of social interaction
were unconsciously imposed by the mothers from the moment that
their children were born. True to form, Japanese mothers spent a
great deal of time with their infants, emphasized physical over verbal interaction, and had a passive/contented baby as their goal. In
general, a Japanese child will sleep with its parents until ten years
of age; in the United States, the infant typically sleeps alone shortly
after birth. Whereas the American model is that of seeing the infant
as a dependent organism that needs to become independent in order to mature, the Japanese regard the infant as a separate organism who needs, from birth, to be drawn into interdependent
relations. Thus, mother/child symbiosis is "pathology" in New York,
"health" in Tokyo. While the American mother typically looks at her
baby and "chats" with it, the Japanese mother carries, rocks, and
soothes it.[4]

What is the result? The Japanese goal is to create a being that
is compliant, oriented toward harmony, hierarchy, and the group,
with a deep sense of emotional ties and family responsibilities. Even
if we were to regard all of these traits as desirable, it turns out that
this pattern has a dark side to it as well. For contrasted with the
warmth of belonging is the terror of ostracism, and the Japanese individual knows that the alternative to symbiosis and interdependence
is exclusion, being regarded as a nonperson. Fear of ridicule is enormous in this culture, and it works to keep people in line. The Japanese are not notorious risk takers, and the split between inner
feelings and social mask is quite extreme in comparison to most
other cultures. At the same time, the Japanese are brilliantly subtle
in their mode of communication, which is heavily nonverbal and
which relies frequently on emotion and intuition. By contrast, American babies are raised to be more active and exploratory, and this
shows up in cultural style as well.[5]

Being an American, I have, no doubt unfairly, made an unfa-
vorable judgment in comparing Japanese and American styles; I'm
not much of an admirer of a symbiotic, passive/hierarchical culture
and personality. However, I am aware that many Japanese do not
think much of American culture and personality either. Perhaps a
less culturally loaded evaluation is that of the Israeli social worker

Mordechai Rotenberg, who chose to view the Japanese style as one of "reciprocal individualism," which he characterized as harmonious, fulfilling human needs for affiliation and nurturance. By contrast, he regarded the "alienating individualism" of Western Puritan societies as competitive and egoistic, a pattern of being driven by the need for achievement, which finally issues out in loneliness.[6] Now both of these pictures (mine and Rotenberg's) are "true," as far as I can see; both have an up side and a dark shadow. Which is "better" may depend on where you were born. But my point here is that given the dyadic core of mother/infant interaction common to both, very different societies and personalities can be erected on the same biological foundation; this is what is meant by "lability." So great is the variation here, the plasticity of what can be done with the instinctual (dyadic) base, that Americans and Japanese often regard each other as coming from different planets. A great deal of cross-cultural interaction, not just that of Americans and Japanese, is like that.

The case of India, and of Hindu child rearing, provides another sharp contrast in terms of mother/infant interaction. One study, conducted by Hélène Stork in 1980, was based on observations of four middle-class Hindu families in the south of India, using film to analyze gesture and behavior in detail.[7] Stork also spent time filming mother/child interactions in France, and in general she substantiates the essential East-West difference: holding is physical in Pondicherry, visual in Paris. Indian child rearing involves the permanent presence of a mother or caregiver; nursing on demand; security of gesture in holding; and great sensitivity to the infant's needs. The difference in kinesthetic stimulation that she found between India and the West was particularly striking, and Stork observed that the Indian infants she studied seemed very open and secure with themselves. The Hindu conception of mother/infant dyadic unity, she says, assures the continuity of the mother's body with that of the infant, and words and voice are used in place of body contact when the infant is put in a cradle. But the major sources of security and support are communicated physically. For example, bathing of the infant is done by hand, with the baby held on the mother's body.

Films of French mother/infant interaction show a very different pattern. Communication is not primarily kinesthetic but visual, involving smiling, talking, and looking with great intensity. The infant is bathed with a sponge, and put on a table during the activity, which again means less touch and more looking. "La parcimonie des échanges cutanés est . . . frappante," remarks Stork. (Free translation: The low amount of skin contact is striking.) Interestingly enough, Transitional Objects are not a big part of the

Hindu infant's world, a development that can be attributed to breast-feeding on demand and prolonged body contact between mother and infant. T.O.s tend to assume great importance, says Stork, when child rearing lacks these features and when the infant is left to itself. The Indian baby's relations are not with toys, but with persons, family members. She believes that early separations of mother and infant in Western societies occur before the infant can handle these psychologically, thereby interfering with the attachment process.

Of course, it might well be argued that Stork's data base—four families—is too narrow to be regarded as definitive in any sense. Yet the comparative analysis of child rearing in France versus that in India in terms of film is a premier contribution to seeing the contrasting cultural patterns in action and in detail; and as already noted, the anthropological generalization of "somatic in the East, visual in the West" is fairly well established. Stanley Kurtz, for example, in *All the Mothers Are One,* drives this point home again and again, because he believes it is essential to understanding the group psychology of Hindu culture. Winnicottian "mirroring," says Kurtz, is simply not the Indian pattern; "the Hindu mother is careful not to load her physical care with the kind of attention or 'mirroring' it would carry in the West." This combination of physical attention and emotional restraint, he claims, is quite deliberate, serving to push the child toward the group. The absence of any emotional mothering also leads to religions that idealize the notion of a detached, spiritual self, something for which India is famous. The mother, says Kurtz, is present for feeding and rocking the infant, but is otherwise emotionally distant. She puts no great emphasis on the child as a unique individual. All of this serves to reassure the child of the world's benevolence *and* to move it away from a too-direct link with the mother.[8]

What about mother/infant interaction in HG societies? Annette Hamilton, who lived among the Anbarra aborigines of Arnhem Land (Australia), reported that the period of six to eighteen months is one of intense attachment to the mother. Although many adults will handle an infant (especially a newborn one), the real mother is the breast-feeder and the most important person. Hamilton found that children of less than two months of age are fed about every thirty-five minutes; those from two to six months, about every ninety minutes. Infants between the ages of birth and six months, she found, are rarely out of physical contact with an adult, and nursing, in particular, is accepted in this society as the infant's right, whether for milk or for pleasure. In general, comparative statistical studies of world cultures demonstrate that in early infancy, at least, degree of bodily contact is higher among HGs than among agricultural peoples.[9]

Similarly, the American anthropologist Melvin Konner found that the mother/infant bond among the !Kung Bushmen is close and of long duration. During the first year of life, says Konner, the infant is in physical contact with the mother 70 to 80 percent of the time and in contact with someone else almost all of the remainder. Comparative studies of two to five year-olds here and in London reveal that English children are more likely to be put face-to-face with the mother than !Kung children. Emotional contact—in particular, vocalization and smiling—between the !Kung mother and her infant is fairly high for a tribal people, but Konner acknowledges that this is exceptional.[10]

What emerges from all of this, as a kind of biocultural constant, is (a) the primacy of females as caregivers (there are a few contemporary rare exceptions to this) and, again, (b) the primacy of physical contact in non-Western cultures (especially HG cultures), and probably in the West until the High Middle Ages, when the cradle was introduced in Europe, inaugurating the regular separation of infants from adults.[11] The world norm is for the infant to be on or near the mother (or a female caregiver) day and night, and this was very likely the Paleolithic pattern as well. Dr. Spock and other child care experts have typically been concerned that all of this early physical holding promotes dependency, but just the opposite has proven to be the case: interference with early somatic needs, and the imposition of "autonomy" before a child can handle it, creates a sense of absence where there should be a primary experience of relationship. In effect, if one gets punished or reproved for being human, what will result is a pervasive sense of anxiety, confusion, false independence and (often hidden) overdependence. Miss this early phase of holding, and you remain caught in dependency needs forever. In such a world, domination and hierarchy become very attractive, "natural," the "human condition."[12]

As for the pattern of the dyadic core, how modifiable is it? The particular arena in which cultural variation is perhaps the strongest is that of the pattern of multiple mothering, which throws the notion of the absolute centrality of the mother/infant dyad—Bowlby's "monotropy"—into some doubt. More precisely, you can shape a child via the monotropic model, but it is only one possible self (and cultural style) among many, and it is not necessarily the best. Granting both the crucial importance of somatic security and of a primary female caregiver, we need to examine how child rearing can be modified in nondyadic directions.

Nondyadic Child Rearing

In terms of cultural modifications, it turns out that strictly dyadic mothering is once again the exception rather than the rule. Monotropy would seem to be a European pattern, one that weakens in multiple caregiver situations. Data from Uganda, for example, reveal that the mother/infant bond is weaker in proportion to the number of people in the household. This is the common pattern, in worldwide terms; and in addition, in such contexts, infants and toddlers tend not to have attachments to Transitional Objects. The availability of other people mediates the nature of maternal care and—we would have to conclude—the dyadic energy pattern as well.[13]

It may also be the case that attachment figures, at a certain point in a child's development, may be fairly interchangeable, indicating some degree of pliability in this area. Thus Mary Ainsworth notes that some research has demonstrated that a baby may become attached to several caregivers before, at the same time as, or shortly after it becomes attached to its mother. She also notes that too many attachment figures work against the formation of attachment to any one figure (the pattern of the Israeli kibbutz), but she argues that in general, spreading the attachment over several figures may be healthy and adaptive.[14]

Narcissism, of course—which Philip Slater says is characteristic of the "steep-gradient" personality (see below)—begins at home, and, conversely, so does the more diffuse, community-oriented personality. Two factors (which tend to go together) make the latter possible: multiple caregiving and having the infant on the periphery rather than at the center of adult activities. This pattern is especially true of HG societies. Thus, while the mother/infant bond among the !Kung Bushmen is close and of long duration, it also exists within a dense social context, and by age three or four the infant "graduates" from this strong bond with the mother to a multi-age child group.[15] Melissa Heckler, who spent some time living among the !Kung, reports how, by six months of age, the !Kung infant could "be found on the hips of anyone . . . who happened to wander by . . . It was less clear to a visitor who the mother was . . . Nurturing is provided by all and sundry, male and female." In this society, the infant is passed from one adult to another, to be held and played with; hence the oft-quoted African proverb, "It takes an entire village to raise a child."[16]

A similar pattern was observed by Annette Hamilton among the Anbarra aborigines, to which I have already referred. Hamilton notes that the Anbarra father often can be found holding his child within a few hours of its birth, and that a baby less than a day old is passed around the extended family group. Any passerby, she says, interacts with the infant, who starts to smile very early in life. As in virtually all HG societies, and some agricultural ones as well, infants are not the central focus; they only exist "as appendages to their caretakers' activities." In fact, the Anbarra attach no significance to infant development; they do not sit around eagerly awaiting the baby's first steps. In Anbarra culture, says Hamilton, "the infant's experience of sociability from the first is not confined to its biological mother alone."

> The Aboriginal child is placed immediately into a group relationship characterised by excitement and diffuse emotionality among many . . . Since the child does not attach exclusively to its mother, nor equally to each member of the group, a kind of balance emerges between the child as a separate individual in relation to its mother and as a member of a group of women and children.[17]

This notion of a "diffuse emotionality" ought to catch our attention; it spreads out the energy contained in what Erik Erikson referred to as the "hallowed presence" of the mother/infant dyad and is, again, a kind of world norm.

Further discussion of the diffuse pattern among HGs is provided by Gilda Morelli and Edward Tronick in their study of the Efé Pygmies of Zaire (seminomadic foragers). Among the Efé, multiple caretaking begins at birth. In fact, the majority of daytime caretaking during the first six months of an Efé infant's life is nonmaternal. The authors hypothesize that this pattern fosters the capacity to relate to many individuals and the development of multiple bases of security and attachment. Efé society, they say, probably needs people who can form trusting relations with a number of people, and their child-rearing pattern makes this possible. Thus, Tronick and his colleagues argue that the theory of monotropy is a rigid overgeneralization, and that while dyadic child rearing creates a sharply focused pattern, multiple mothering promotes one that is more diffuse. Since each person the Efé infant interacts with has a different style, the infant must learn to adjust to each. As a result, its social repertoire is flexible and broadly based, not locked into one stylistic set of stimuli. And as in the case of the !Kung and the Anbarra, Efé mothers and other caregivers have other involvements, such as work. They are not, as in many agricultural and industrial societies, "professional mothers."

Interestingly enough, Tronick et al. believe that the Efé child-rearing pattern produces good personality boundaries as well as good orientation to present events. The pattern of having to relate to a number of different caregiver styles teaches a more rapid and complete pattern of Self/Other distinction; and, in addition, it renders the child more oriented to present time. With only one caregiver, say the authors, the tendency is to base current events on past history—what is called "transference" in psychoanalysis. Multiple caregiving teaches that not everybody, or every situation, is the same.[18]

Examples of this kind are easily multiplied. The American anthropologist JoAnn Campbell, who did work with Nigerian children, found that multiple caregiving diffuses sibling rivalry by providing each child with someone special. This results, she says, in less intense experiences of object loss and loss of love and generates less anger and frustration than does the dyadic pattern. Barbara Rogoff's study of Mayan peasants in Guatemala revealed that "toddlers were in the company of many people who were engaged in the business of life" and that they routinely observed activities of sewing or weaving or accompanied their mothers out to the fields. In urban communities of Turkey and the United States, by contrast, toddlers are at home with mothers whose economic activity is homemaking, or are in settings in which the mothers' activity is to tend *them*! In such situations, children cannot learn by being embedded in the activity of adult members of the community.[19]

What Western or urban children get is a child-rearing pattern that is atypical on a world scale and that amounts to a double whammy. This is not to say that the multiple caregiving pattern is problem-free or that it creates perfect societies. Far from it. But if we are focusing on the issue of basic trust and psychic stability, it is clear whence the drivenness and pervasive malaise of narcissistic cultures originate. With a lack of very much somatic holding and a caregiver pattern that is dyadic and exclusive, we get an adult who is typically brittle and high-strung; the "center of gravity" is too high. Such a zero-sum personality (all-or-nothing psychology) is largely erected around fear, around a hole, one might say, and this is why Object Relations is particularly accurate in its description of the contemporary Western personality. And although *some* degree of fear and alienation is always present in the human psyche, this nonsomatic/dyadic pattern creates a tremendous need for hierarchy to generate (pseudo)stability. It doesn't work very well, of course; domination produces a chain reaction without end, and this has a parallel in the outside world.

Before clarifying the differences between HG and agricultural child rearing, which will serve to bring the importance of nomadic existence sharply into focus, a few words about the problems of multiple caregiving are perhaps in order, at least as they show up in sedentary contexts. Of course, the extreme of this would be orphanages and other institutional situations, which really do not count here since they are outstanding for a *lack* of mothering, but which are instructive examples since at this end of the spectrum what shows up in the children is lack of affect or emotional withdrawal. But the outstanding experiment with multiple caregiving in modern times is that of the Israeli kibbutz, which was specifically designed to break the grip of the intense, one-to-one dyad and create personalities that were emotionally more diffuse, more "horizontal." In this, the originators of the experiment were very successful, yet they wound up being a bit ambivalent about their success.

Children of the Dream

The originators of the kibbutz experiment were largely East European Jews who had known very little beyond the life of the ghetto. Walled in in this way, they had learned to become intimate with themselves and a few others, self-absorbed, inward, and often depressed. As settlers in Israel or Palestine, their goal was to create a new person in a new land; to rid the individual of this inward-oriented, self-conscious personality so characteristic of Eastern Europe. Thus, when the famous child psychologist, Bruno Bettelheim, went to live on a kibbutz in the sixties, he found adults who had a strong group identification, with multiple attachments, who were not haunted by fear of love or object loss. He regarded the experiment as largely successful, yet he felt that it was a weird kind of success. If kibbutzniks had a strong group consciousness, it was also the case that their individual attachments were not very intimate; and Bettelheim attributed this to the fact that the kibbutz infant did not have a continuous relationship with one caregiver. If the kibbutznik had very little fear of object loss, he or she also had very little ability to be close to anyone at all. The older generation got what it wanted—diffuse personalities—but discovered that the new breed didn't have a whole lot of depth. You pays yer money, and you tykes yer choice.[20]

In terms of the exact mechanics of this process, Bettelheim observed that "imprinting" by caregivers and other babies begins in the first days of life. It is only during actual nursing at the breast that the infant's mother emerges as a separate and special person for the infant; and, in any case, most kibbutz infants are weaned within the first six months. Dyadic attachment is very dilute. Generally, if an infant experiences separation anxiety, it is around the absence of a peer, not the mother. Caregivers constantly shift, so the child learns that single individuals are unreliable but that the community itself never is. In such a context, says Bettelheim, things never get as bad as they *can* get between the lone mother and infant, but they also never get as good: the infant, from a Euro-American perspective, has something missing from its personality. Multiple mothering, Bettelheim continues, interferes with the depth of mutuality that is found in our own situation, that of great intimacy at the earliest stage of personal development. A further difference, he points out, is that while for kibbutz children, "life" is always within easy reach, it lacks introspection or intellectual sparkle. Although the Euro-American model is, in Bettelheim's view, imbalanced in the other (narcissistic) direction, it is nevertheless the case that the kibbutz ego is much less rich, complex, or personalized. On the kibbutz, he says, individuals seek intimacy but don't really attain it since they don't know how to be intimate with themselves. One is finally alone with one's pain. Adult kibbutzniks, according to the American anthropologist Melford Spiro, "seem to be enveloped within a shell, from which their psyches rarely protrude."

So the kibbutz experiment "succeeded": the children lost their parents' defects, but they also lost some of their parents' positive qualities. They became less neurotic but also less curious about life. The kibbutz-reared personality, says Bettelheim, is "flat."

Kibbutzniks *do*, however, have a great deal of basic trust, and we see quite clearly here that such security can be achieved outside of the dyadic format. Kibbutzniks escape the existential despair common in the West, and from cradle to grave, they never feel useless or isolated. But they pay a price, having little ability for emotional intimacy and little interest in individual achievement. They feel no need to explore, says Bettelheim, to push ahead,

> but neither do they have the impulse to push anyone down. While such people do not create science and art, are neither great leaders nor great philosophers nor innovators, maybe it is they who are the salt of the earth without whom no society can endure.

This business of not needing to push others down is crucial to our inquiry. For following Object Relations theory, I have been assuming something about the root cause of social inequality, namely that the need to dominate others is a way of handling one's own insecurities, one's creature anxiety and alienation. Hierarchy is one way to stabilize that insecurity—both for the rulers and for the ruled. But leaderless group loyalty is another way, and although it is hardly a problem-free solution, theoretically, at least, it does not generate games of power and resentment. Due to the ontological uncanniness of life, human beings may indeed possess a will to power; hence the evidence of status differentiation that Francis Harrold and Sally Binford found, going back to the Paleolithic. If ranking and domination are false solutions to the problem of human insecurity (i.e., they reflect the fear rather than work through it), it is clear enough that they go back a long way. Even then, it is instructive to see that the will to power, no less than the constellation of separation and attachment, is labile: in both cases, nonvertical solutions are possible. Societies can mitigate these things in various ways, and they will be very different types of societies.

All of this is perhaps no great breakthrough; the reader is probably wondering if I'm now going to reveal that the pope is Catholic. Yet we have to remember that there has been a real reluctance on the part of traditional anthropology (some of it justified) to go out on a limb with these sorts of generalizations—in particular, generalizations based on the attempt to marry macrophenomena with inner states that cannot be tracked in any precise or objective way. But I remain convinced by Erik Erikson's assertion (quoted in chapter 1) that there are "connections between seemingly distant phenomena, such as human infancy and man's institutions" and that it makes sense to suggest that monotropy, the "hallowed presence" of the dyad, produces a psyche that is driven to generate vertical structures that then have to be defended from collapse. This is not to insist on single-factor explanations or on having a perfect, one-to-one correspondence between the microlevel and the macro; things are never that easy. But in some way, what happens in the nursery really *is* mirrored in the pattern of the larger culture. The dyadic pressure of intense, "sacred" energy leads to an energetic configuration on the individual level that finds its parallel in Ozymandian-type societies, societies that in turn raise individuals with a vertical, narcissistic energy pattern, who then reproduce those types of societies, and so on. The alternative is to cultivate an energy that is a lot closer to the ground, as it were, which is what both kibbutzim and HG societies do, with varying results. Bettelheim thus begins his book *The Children of the Dream* with the question: "How intimate is the link between the nature of a society and how its children are raised?" Even if we accept the fact that simple, monocausal answers are not possible, the question still comes off as rhetorical.

Of course, one wonders whether the uncreative, group-loyal kibbutznik and the aggressive Tel Aviv businessman are the only choices available. But even beyond this, there are legitimate reasons why anthropology traditionally has been wary of "interior" explanations: cause and effect are often murky. Working with the Navaho in the forties, Clyde Kluckhohn, one of America's greatest anthropologists, finally threw up his hands in despair, noting that despite the fact that the infants were breast-fed on demand and raised permissively by very affectionate parents, the anxiety level in Navaho society was extremely high.[21] Anne Hamilton found that the Anbarra are trained not to be curious (their language doesn't even have a word for "Why?") and to accept things as they are, which makes them present-oriented and leaderless, but also timid and conformist. In the case of small agricultural societies, multiple mothering is no insurance against the development of dominance and hierarchy, as a number of case studies have shown. Individuals in those societies commonly turn out to be dependent and conformist in their behavior, and the societies are often characterized by priesthoods, centralized governments, and social stratification. Multiple mothering, then, is no guarantee of anything, and one-dimensional explanations will not work.[22]

That being said, there exists enough evidence to suggest that the child-rearing practices that correlate with sedentism versus mobility, and with DR versus IR economies, do produce very different results. The factor of movement proves to be of enormous importance, having a huge impact on population, birth spacing, and weaning. But even beyond this, it does seem that sedentary/DR societies generate different personality types than nomadic/IR societies do, especially as this relates to the issue of fear and the consequent need for dominance and hierarchy.

Hunter-Gatherer Child Rearing

The single most important study along these lines was conducted by Barry, Child, and Bacon.[23] Their general hypothesis was pretty straightforward: any given society will employ child-rearing practices that tend to produce the particular type of personality that is functional for adult life in that society. Their goal was to examine the relationship of such practices to the subsistence economy, using categories such as collecting, hunting, fishing, cultivation, and stock raising.

The authors had a more specific hypothesis in mind, however, one that (shades of Alain Testart) regarded the degree of accumulation of resources as the key variable. Both agriculture and animal husbandry, they argued, involved investment in future food supply; and all of this required adherence to certain routines. Stock breeders had to follow procedures that served to maintain the health of the herd; farmers had to follow rules for harvesting and storing. In such cases, reasoned the authors, individual initiative would be maladaptive because changes could lead to disaster (in particular, famine). Ergo, such cultures might be expected to put a premium on obedience to tradition, and the faithful performance of routine.

Turning to hunting and fishing, just the opposite might be expected to obtain. With no practice of storage, individual initiative would be likely to be the adaptive factor, because variations would lead to immediate results, which would reveal whether this was a good or bad path to take. If you live on a day-by-day basis, you might go hungry occasionally, but you won't be wiped out. In such a context, innovation would be a plus.

Hence, the more precise form of the hypothesis reads as follows: in societies with low accumulation, adults will be individualistic, assertive, and adventuresome. In societies with high accumulation, they will be conservative and compliant. What is most important, the child-rearing practices in each case will move in the direction of promoting behavior useful to that economy. The authors used George Murdock's world ethnographic sample, rating 104 societies from all over the world, separately for boys and girls ages four through twelve, for six aspects of child rearing: obedience, responsibility, nurturance, achievement, self-reliance, and general independence. The results were all they could have wished for: child-rearing practices were clearly correlated with the degree of food accumulation. Overwhelmingly, societies with high accumulation showed a strong pressure toward responsibility and obedience and low tendencies toward achievement, self-reliance, and independence—regardless of gender. High accumulation went with compliance; low accumulation with assertion. The factor of accumulation proved to have a higher correlation with these patterns than any other cultural variable.

This is a dramatic piece of research, as it establishes quite clearly that the self of the forager is (for the most part) a different creature from that of the agropastoralist, and certainly from the individual living in civilization. HG society works because its members are risk takers. Imagination counts for much more than past experience. However, civilization works because its members do what they are told; and they accumulate not only food, but "wisdom," which they pass on through stories, proverbs, and tradition. From here it is a short step to myth and ritual, literacy and numeracy, and, usually, ideology and dogma (and ultimately, it must be added, to science, which—at least theoretically—abhors dogma!).

Clearly, then, sedentism makes an enormous difference. This shows up quite markedly in a study conducted by John Berry, which compared the Temne rice farmers of Sierra Leone with the Eskimo of Baffin Island. The former are high food accumulators and discipline their children very strictly, not allowing them to assert their individuality. The latter are hunter-fishers, low food accumulators, who value self-reliance and are lenient in their child-rearing practices. Berry conducted a psychological experiment among members of each group, designed to test susceptibility to peer pressure and group norms. As anyone might have guessed, Temne subjects fell in step with these without a murmur, regardless of what they personally may have believed, whereas the Eskimo subjects had almost a total disregard for the choices made by other members of their tribe. In each case, mode of subsistence, child-rearing practices, and personality structures neatly interlocked.[24]

Exactly how new child-rearing patterns, storage and sedentism, and the emergence of civilization go together is unclear; certainly, we have no way of knowing how such changes occurred toward the end of the Paleolithic. Herbert Barry regards it as a chicken-and-egg problem, a set of mutually interacting (or reinforcing) patterns. Child rearing may adapt a person to the economy, he says, but it also could be that when environmental pressures move a society toward food production, the society most adaptable to such a move might be the one that already has a stronger compliance training in place. The British sociologist Christopher Badcock sees such a mutual pattern as unavoidable. DR societies, he says, necessarily involve discipline and the postponement of gratification, and this would make new modes of child rearing virtually inevitable. Earlier weaning and the creation of greater dependency (by violating organic patterns) would contribute to this, and we might expect this as much among herders as cultivators, since both are involved in delayed-return economies.[25]

One of the most direct comparisons of forager versus village life, which is somewhat complicated by the factor of male parenting, is Barry Hewlett's study of the Aka Pygmies of the Central African Republic and their neighbors, the Ngandu farmers. The Aka have very few status positions; are fiercely independent, practicing no coercion of others (including children); employ leveling mechanisms against prestige behavior; and share their food. Aka infants are nursed on demand and held constantly, in a pattern of multiple caregiving, but adults do not interrupt their own activities to deal with the children. The children are autonomous and independent from an early age and are not socialized to respect their elders. So great is the prohibition against striking children that if one parent does this, the other might ask for a divorce. The Ngandu pattern is very different: they typically boast, draw attention to themselves, and accumulate wealth. They practice no multiple caregiving as such; children are physically punished for lack of obedience, and deference to elders is extremely important. In each case, we can see a clustering of certain child-rearing patterns with a particular kind of social structure.[26]

So although the results are somewhat mixed, and multiple caregiving cannot be separated out as a single, causal variable, there do seem to be some broad strokes that can be painted here. Yes, the passivity of the kibbutz does occur, and this suggests how problematic it is to abstract one variable from HG society and attempt to import it into a sedentary, DR system. Utopian schemes typically backfire, and we cannot socially engineer civilization into becoming uncivilization; this will not work. But in terms of analysis, the overall pattern does seem to be autonomy and initiative in HG societies, conformity and conservatism in agricultural ones, with political arrangements appropriate to each.

Birth Spacing and Population Growth

The issues of child-rearing practices, accumulation and storage, dominance and insecurity, and so on are all closely intertwined with the factor of birth spacing and population growth. This is also something that shows up as a contrast between sedentary versus nomadic life and points to the biological and demographic constraints that limit human choices with respect to social values and corresponding adult-infant patterns of interacting. Once again, the constellation of factors is important. Population growth leads to complexity, and as Barry, Child, and Bacon discovered, this evokes a different set of values and corresponding child-rearing practices than those found in simpler situations. Nomadic situations make frequent birthing maladaptive. Every time a !Kung woman moves, she has to carry all of her children who are less than four years old. Over a four-year period, she will carry a child nearly five thousand miles. If she has a child two years after the previous one, it will be a great burden to her. To maintain birth spacing, !Kung parents refrain from sexual relations during the first year of their infant's life. But once sedentism occurs, a woman can shorten the interval between births and still give each child adequate care because she is now required to carry her children much less often. Thus, sedentism can act as a trigger for population growth.

Also operative in the HG case is the factor of prolonged lactation, which suppresses ovulation. This means that sexual activity doesn't lead to conception. Such lactation often continues for as long as four years, because HGs do not have soft foods available for infants, such as agropastoralists do (notably grain and milk). The availability of such foods typically leads to earlier weaning, with concomitant return of ovulation and subsequent conception.[27]

The impact of all of this on child rearing is not difficult to imagine, for the pain of earlier weaning and sibling rivalry is quite traumatic. Wide birth spacing means that for the nomadic !Kung, each child gets its mother's (and family's) attention for forty-four months, thirty-six of which includes breast feeding. For the child weaned at twelve months instead of at thirty-six, the trauma of separation is fairly severe. Richard Lee reports that the effects of the mother's pregnancy on a young child are striking, that a two-year-old with a sibling on the way is miserable and sullen, and that the family situation goes out of kilter. This scenario, he says, "is in marked contrast to the relatively placid scenes of infant care in the nomadic camps documented by [other anthropologists]." This pattern of much earlier weaning among agricultural peoples is a crucial distinction between them and HGs. The wide birth spacing typical of HGs enables "the raising of what might be called fewer children of higher quality." Prolonged lactation and holding and the absence of sibling rivalry mean better care and greater psychological stability; and one sees this stability among !Kung adults. "With short birth spacing," he says, "the circle is broken and the emotional economy is put under stress."[28] Apparently, a stressed emotional economy runs parallel to a stressed financial economy. Insecurity and the need for domination eventually become the order of the day.

The subject of breast-feeding, and its role in lactational amenorrhea (absence of menstruation during lactation), has been the focus of much recent study. Apparently, it is the sucking stimulus itself, and not the production of milk, that is the crucial issue. In human terms, it has a contraceptive effect. In the case of the !Kung, for example, the infant suckles even while the mother sleeps, and the !Kung show a mean birth interval of 4.1 years (the same interval as exists among chimpanzees, which are the primates closest to human beings).[29] But we now have studies that are even more precise. In one case, bottle-feeding women began to menstruate eight weeks after delivery, whereas breast-feeding women menstruated after thirty-three weeks. No woman in this sample ovulated if she were breast-feeding more than five times a day or for a total of more than sixty minutes a day—which is quite typical among HGs. In general, the HG pattern is one of weaning at four years or more, whereas the agricultural pattern is less than two years.[30]

The impact of the birth of a sibling and consequent early weaning on the life of the family is quite devastating. Indeed, Christopher Badcock claims it is the single greatest threat to the life of an existing child within the Third World and HG cultures.[31] Thus Annette Hamilton, commenting on her experience with the Anbarra, says that a birth spacing of, say, eighteen months means that the older child must give up its attachment to its mother before it is equipped to do so. An older baby is never breast-fed once a younger one arrives on the scene. Among the Anbarra today, she reports, weaning occurs at around two years of age and is accompanied by clinging and temper tantrums. It is a period of fear and misery for the child. The shift is often abrupt, and the peer group then steps in to function as emotional compensation for loss of the breast.[32]

The power of all of this in biological and demographic terms is important to keep in mind because it strongly suggests that the Neolithic configuration of sedentism, population pressure, food accumulation, frequent birthing, and early weaning—factors that I personally believe enhance human insecurity and are behind the drive for dominance and hierarchy—is very recent in human history and quite unnatural. However, before we can elaborate on this theme in any detail, is necessary to insert an important coda into the discussion. For all one can say of a positive nature about the quality of HG child rearing and HG society in general, this quality was achieved by having fewer children to care for; and that often meant killing off the ones you *couldn't* take care of.

Coda: The Role of Infanticide

This is a very touchy subject, to say the least. Joseph Birdsell and Lewis Binford regarded infanticide as the key to HG population control, estimating that it may have been as high as 50 percent in the Pleistocene. Certainly, it is found among the majority of HG peoples, from the !Kung in the Kalahari desert to the Copper Eskimo of northern Canada. A conference, Infanticide in Animals and Men, held at Cornell University in 1982, came to the conclusion that in many populations, infanticide is quite normal and adaptive and in fact is widespread in the animal kingdom. In certain species of birds, for example, the first-hatched chick proceeds to kill its younger siblings. All of this, observe the editors of the conference proceedings, is ultimately related to the competition for resources. In the case of human society, it is done to improve the mother's chances for survival or that of the older offspring; and short of infanticide, especially under conditions of stress, nurturance may be reduced and offspring neglected. The editors write, "Virtually every category of infanticide which has been described for other animals can be documented anecdotally for the human species." Thus, when John Whiting and his colleagues examined infanticide in eighty-four societies, they found that it existed in about one-third of these, as a way of eliminating defective offspring or dealing with too-frequent birth spacing. Among seventy-two of these societies, more than one-third (36 percent) reported the practice of killing an infant born too soon after its older sibling. This was more likely among HGs, less likely among agropastoral societies. The general anthropological consensus, originally suggested by Birdsell, is that "infanticide by parents has deep roots in human history, and has probably been part of an adaptive repertoire since Pleistocene times."[33]

Marjorie Shostak, in her biography of a !Kung woman named Nisa, has the latter describe how the issue of infanticide came up when she was between three and six years of age (1924–1927). Nisa was weaned when her mother was pregnant with Kumsa, her younger brother. She was too young to be weaned, and the process made her miserable. One day, she and her mother left camp to gather food. Her mother sat down under a tree and gave birth to Kumsa. Then she told Nisa to go back to camp and get her (i.e., mother's) digging stick, so she could bury Kumsa. Nisa cried and said she wanted her brother to live. They argued; finally, it was agreed that they would keep the baby and that *he* would nurse, not Nisa. Shostak believes that infanticide occurred rarely among the !Kung, even in traditional times. Today, Bantu law (the Tswana government) prohibits it—as all civilizations do. But the point here is that among !Kung women it was a viable option. Nursing two children was literally impossible. The decision was not taken lightly, but when there was no choice, the women would give birth alone and bury the child almost immediately. The traditional !Kung did not consider a child a true person until it was brought back to the village (camp), so infanticide was not regarded as homicide in that culture.[34]

We may find this shocking, or worse, but it is important not to impose our own framework on that of the HGs. Overpopulation wreaks havoc, violates the biopsychic basis of human life; the abandonment of an infant is not necessarily the same thing as callous-ness. Studies among Eskimo, for example, revealed that the children who were allowed to live were dearly loved. The problem of defining infanticide is similar to defining the beginning of life in the abortion debate. In most societies, it takes place before the infant has the status of a real person. Among contemporary cultures, at least, ethnographic research makes it clear that infanticide, as in the case of the !Kung, is never taken lightly, and done only when it makes adaptive sense. As in the abortion debate, we have to ask whether the proliferation of unwanted and abused children is the better choice.[35]

The point remains that the human biological inheritance is de-signed for a higher quality of life than that provided by agricultural civilization, with its early weaning and traumatic treatment of infants. It is this insight that may have motivated Garrett Hardin's notori-ous "lifeboat" thesis, predicting that overpopulation could lead to a system of triage—something that civilization, with its mechanisms of dominance and hierarchy, has already instituted in any case. Simi-larly, Margaret Mead pointed out that civilized values had painted us into a corner. In the extreme case, that of institutional care, Mead noted that because we demand that every individual be saved, we generate large numbers of adults who are damaged and antisocial, making civilized life even more unstable. In the HG case, allowing children to die when you simply cannot care for them means that those who do make it are cared for in a loving and personal way; that is the ethnographic record. When we talk of the glories of ma-ternal-infant care in primitive societies, said Mead, we are really talk-ing about those babies who survive, which could be as few as 50 percent. Again, civilized values of compassion do not permit such solutions (who, for starters, would be making the decisions?), and neither Hardin nor Mead was arguing any such thing. But their work, as well as what we know of HG life, does point to a dilemma endemic to sedentary society and to a major source of violence and dominance as it exists among the world's cultures today. All of these factors discussed above push urban society in the inevitable direc-tion of creating a life of psychological misery as a kind of norm. In other words, HGs practice quick death, while civilization, being more sophisticated, does it a lot more slowly.[36]

While not identical, then, triage and status differentiation ex-ist on a continuum. They are not issues the human race ("civi-lized" or not) has escaped or ever will, and if we are going to look back at the "good old days" of hunting and gathering, we have to realize that while such days were real, they were based on a brutal process of selection. But it seems to be the case that once the selection was made, it was probably a better life, one largely free from the ideology of hierarchy and manipulation.

The Psychology of the Aggressive Subgroup

With fewer people, then, we could have a life of much higher quality. More love and resources and space per person means that primordial fear and alienation can be managed within band society, by means of paradox or generalized cathexis of the environment. The personality is simultaneously diffuse and autonomous, something we have a hard time even imagining. Once the Neolithic constellation of population pressure, circumscription, sedentism, storage, frequent birthing (sans infanticide), and early weaning occurs, not to mention the shift from constant holding and multiple mothering to reduced somatic attention and intense dyadic child rearing, we are practically talking about a different species of human being. Vertical religion and politics follow (or are concomitant) as a matter of course; what else, indeed, *could* possibly handle such changes? A DR economy, more calories of poorer quality per hectare (plus chronic anxiety over potential crop failure), a constantly stressed-out psyche—all of this cannot float indefinitely without the culture falling apart. It requires top-down management, and thus the stage is set for the emergence of an elite, an aggressive subgroup that claims power and leadership roles. In such a context, egalitarian intersubjectivity is too fragile to endure; arranging things in a religious and political pecking order stabilizes what is otherwise unmanageable.

We shall never know the inner drama of the Paleolithic, of course, but there are a number of contemporary psychological studies and ethnographic parallels that might possibly shed some light on it. Marvin Harris tells a story that provides a useful clue. A study was done some years ago of the "Big Men" among the Siuai, a village people who inhabit the Solomon Islands of the South Pacific. Every boy in the tribe wanted to become a big man, or *mumi*, whose status was displayed by the hosting of feasts. This was all about prestige, says Harris; the *mumi* had no coercive powers, but he always had an entourage of disciples around him. On one occasion, Soni, who was one of the great *mumi*s, gave away so much food that his closest followers had to go hungry. However, Harris reports, they didn't seem to mind. "We shall eat Soni's reknown," they said.[37]

We have here, in a nutshell, the first glimmerings of the SAC: I myself am nothing, but I become something by basking in the reflected glory of our (semidivine) leader (or later, the social/religious order). This is what I mean by not having to work through the primordial fear. The "gap," the "basic fault," gets covered up for the followers, who can fill themselves with "Soni's reknown." Soni, for his part, can compensate for the love *he* didn't get in infancy by having a crowd of adoring disciples (he eats their adoration). It's all hype, of course; prestige in either direction, up or down the vertical ladder, will not heal the narcissistic wound suffered in childhood, and that is why there is no end to chasing it (or wealth, or power, etc.). It's a little like trying to feel full by shoveling food into the mouth of an idol. Since that's not where the actual hunger is, the amount required is literally infinite.

The implication of what I have been saying, and of Harris' anecdote, is something that the famous Austrian psychiatrist Alfred Adler talked about many years ago: social relations in the context of civilization are essentially sadomasochistic. That is to say, those in the aggressive subgroup mask their fear and inadequacy by becoming the rulers; those that acquiesce in this political process mask *their* fear and inadequacy by becoming the ruled. The core of the whole arrangement is the damaged self, and this is where economy and spirituality perversely converge: storage and abundance provide material "validation" of a differential spiritual status (Calvinism in the Stone Age, as it were). I can't prove any of this, any more than, say, scientists who argue for a chemical basis to dominance behavior (serotonin levels and so forth) can prove *their* case; but it seems quite reasonable just the same.[38]

In more recent times, the sadomasochistic dynamic used by Adler conceptually to explain why the ruled tolerate domination by a small (self-declared) elite has been carefully explored by the American psychotherapist Jessica Benjamin in *The Bonds of Love*. This study, based on an extension of Object Relations theory, is too complex to explicate in any detail at this point, but Benjamin's essential argument is that the balance of Self and Other that exists between mother and child in early infancy is typically difficult to maintain. There is a tension inherent in equality (a tension HGs endeavor to maintain), and it becomes easier to resolve it by means of a hierarchical pattern. This then has repercussions on the macrolevel, for the payoff inherent in inequality exists no less for the ruled than it does for the rulers. Plainly put, submission gives the ruled an "identity"; in losing one's Self, one gains vicarious access to a more powerful Other ("eats Soni's reknown"). Citing Dostoevsky, Benjamin says that the Grand Inquisitor (in *The Brothers Karamazov*) pointed out to Christ that people didn't want freedom and truth; rather, they wanted miracle, mystery, and authority. But the training for transcendent (i.e., vertical, power-based) solutions, as opposed to paradoxical tension (which is a dynamic "nonsolution"), begins in early infancy. Child rearing can teach you that Self and Other can remain in balance; or it can teach you that there is room for only one ego in any relationship. In the latter case, one dissolves the Self, ecstatically, into the power of the Other; on the macrolevel, vertical politics is a foregone conclusion.[39]

The Urge toward Transcendence

We are now in a position to pull together the strands of our argument relating to the shift from paradox to the sacred authority complex, or from horizontal to vertical energy, with which this book began. Recall our tripartite schema of how, historically, human beings have dealt with the split between the self and the world: paradox, the SAC (including unitive trance), and dullardism. Among HGs, for whom— occasional infanticide notwithstanding—the quality of nurturance is probably the best, unitive trance and "religion" may exist occasionally, but for the most part, they are superfluous. Secure in the world already, these immediate-return cultures tend to entertain charismatic behavior mostly under conditions of stress. Their child-rearing pattern of multiple caregiving means that individuals are raised with a diffuse energy pattern; their vertical needs are much less, and they grow up with a focus on life itself, not on "God" or an afterlife. HGs typically do not generate prophets or guru figures; the "sacred" is simply that which is present in front of them. To be alive, to participate in life in the here and now, *is* worship for these cultures.

In the case of the SAC, and in particular, of unitive trance, we should recall Erikson's comments on the "numinous" experience that an infant, in a dyadic situation, will have of its mother. By trying to recapture this experience later in life, through things such as religion or immersion in a leader's charisma, the individual obtains a sense of transcending his or her separateness. The two levels of self and society merge here, because social integration is sustained beyond the family level by means of this "sacred" extension of the self, which has now (supposedly) recovered its original wholeness. This plasticity of the self, with its origins in the early boundary conditions of infancy, is what gives sacred politics its enormous power. Add to this the Neolithic condition of the DR economy and the consequent rise of the "professional mother," whose major concern is not her own social and economic activity but the activity of her offspring—all of which intensifies the "hallowed presence" effect enormously—and the setup for verticality is virtually assured.

All of this indicates how historical, or contextual, our urge toward transcendence really is. Recall the discussion by S. N. Balagangadhara (chapter 1, above) that our insistence that primitive humans were religious is essentially a reflection of our own bibliocentric bias. By following writers such as Jung and Eliade, we can easily be deluded into thinking that this kind of religious need is prototypical and that if we ever did have a society without religion, "new forms of worship would erupt to fill the vacuum." Strange, I guess, that the Hadza and the Mbuti, among others, are not rushing to fill this terrible hiatus in their spiritual lives with some kind of transcendent deity so that they can defend themselves from the Abyss. The possibility that death is *not* scary, that it is *not* a mystery, never seems to enter our heads, because within the context of DR economies and substitute love activity, we have never really lived; hence the show has to go on forever because we can never fill the gap. It's all a mirage, and this makes death terrifying, since the fulfillment we may have experienced in life was only occasional, transitory.[40]

In an interesting discussion of the psychological basis of religion, Brant Wenegrat (*The Divine Archetype*) argues that religious beliefs are Transitional Objects, that the "mother archetype" (goddess, Great Mother) is latent in the infant's attachment behavior, and that the attachment dynamics that are emphasized in child rearing determine how adults view their gods. Although (see below, chapter 4) I do not believe that there was any kind of unified Great Mother religion or culture in Europe or Asia, dating back to the Late Paleolithic, it is the case that with the shift to agriculture a corresponding emphasis on the feminine did seem to take place. Nor should this surprise us. If relative gender equality was more common in the Paleolithic, then a sedentary situation with frequent birthing and a new emphasis on the woman as a mother first and foremost is going to drive a balanced gender situation toward one that starts to see the mother as an archetype. This is the "Great Mother in the nursery," as it were; and as the "hallowed presence" becomes more intense, the Great Mother begins to emerge as an object of veneration. Instead of remembering paradoxical consciousness, the emphasis now shifts to lost primal unity, the intensity of which is now echoed in the SAC and later, in unitive trance. That war shows up in the Late Paleolithic is also no surprise.[41] Under these historical pressures, if the female is transformed into an archetype, then so is the male. Once a scavenger-hunter, perhaps, he is now a hunter-warrior, specifically, a hero. This dynamic becomes particularly sharp in

the relationship between mothers and sons. For with the woman ultimately denied much of an economic role in sedentary/agricultural society (having previously brought in most of the calories in HG
society),[42] she is forced to live vicariously, through her son. It is for
this reason that issues of gender are central to the whole problematic
of vertical religion and social inequality. For the most part, it has been
only men who have been allowed, in a public or visible sense, to make
history, to shape civilization; the "aggressive subgroup" discussed earlier is typically male. It is time to ask why this is the case.

Mother and Son: The Great Mother in the Nursery

Once again, I am going to call on Galway Kinnell to help us sort
things out. Here is an excerpt from his poem "The Last Hiding Places
of Snow," which is a tribute to his mother:

I have always felt
anointed by her love, its light
like sunlight
falling through broken panes
onto the floor
of a deserted house: we may go, it remains,
telling of goodness of being, of permanence.

So lighted I have believed
I could wander anywhere,
among any foulnesses, any contagions,
I could climb through the entire empty world
and find my way back and learn again to be happy . . .

My mother did not want me to be born;
afterwards, all her life, she needed me to return.
When this more-than-love flowed toward me, it brought darkness
she wanted me as buried earth wants—to heap itself gently upon
              but also to annihilate—
and I knew, whenever I felt longings to go back,
that is what wanting to die is. That is why

dread lives in me,
dread which comes when what gives life beckons toward death,
dread which throws through me
waves
of utter strangeness, which wash the entire world empty . . .

no matter what fire we invent to destroy us,
ours will have been the brightest world ever existing . . .

Even now when I wake at night
in some room far from everyone,
the darkness sometimes
lightens a little, and then,
because of nothing,
in spite of nothing,
in an imaginary daybreak, I see her,
and for that moment I am still her son
and I am in the holy land
and twice in the holy land, remembered
within her, and remembered in the memory
her old body slowly executes into the earth.[43]

This poem so accurately captures the ambivalent legacy of the mother/son bond, and the intensity of the confused boundary relations that lie at the root of civilization, that it is tempting to do a line-by-line exegesis of it. How powerfully Kinnell expresses the sacred quality of the dyadic relationship, the coupling of the numinous (Erikson's "hallowed presence") with death and dread, and the implication that it is precisely this constellation that is responsible for the glory of our civilization ("the brightest world ever existing")! The larger context of this is that of skewed gender relations, a point Freud made many years ago in his essay "The Psychology of Women." "The mother," wrote Freud, "can transfer to her son all the ambition she has had to suppress in herself" and then live vicariously through his heroic life.[44] The fact is that the brilliance of civilization, from Egypt and Mesopotamia to India and China to Classical Greece and the Renaissance to twentieth-century America, is dependent on this gender inequality and on the "holiness" of the mother/son dyad; it depends on sharp, vertical energy for its cultural fuel. Nor will we be able to give up this vertical set of arrangements without an immense sense of loss. Let us look, then, a bit more closely at the mother/son bond.

One of the most insightful, and devastating, investigations of civilization and its pattern of cultural achievement was provided by Philip Slater in his book *The Glory of Hera*. Ostensibly a study of familial relations in classical Greece, it is also a speculation on whether heroic/narcissistic culture has its roots in the energy of the mother/son dyad. In this work, as well as in *Footholds*, Slater argued that the exclusion of women from any civic life or arena of

importance in ancient Greece meant that dominating their children
was the only outlet for their urge for autonomy. In particular, there
was a tendency on the part of the mother to project longings for
her own life or destiny onto her son, who would be her hero, live
the life she was never free to live. In short, says Slater, the boundaries were all blurry. The Greek mother did not respond to her son
as a separate person, but as a cure for her narcissistic wounds (eating Soni's reknown). This created ambivalent feelings in both parties. The boy wished to "save" his mother (give her the life she
never had), but he was also terrified by the intensity she focused
on him. The mother gloried in his achievements, but also, on some
unconscious level, she sought to destroy him, for those very
achievements represented the denial of her own power. Given such
an arrangement, the resulting male self was quite precarious; honor
in Greece was linked to a deep pessimism. Furthermore, says Slater,
the nature of this neurotic, dyadic intensity created personality
types that might be called "steep": people who put all their eggs
in one basket, as opposed to "level" people (what I have referred
to as the "diffuse" personality) who are capable of treating many
things as a source of gratification. Dyads produce steepness, says
Slater; multiple caregiving is more conducive to levelness.[45]

The resulting Greek culture was based on the precariousness of
this steep-gradient (zero-sum) personality. A man grew up feeling
that unless he were some type of hero, he was nothing at all. Pride
and prestige defined the ethos of classical Greece. Nor is this limited to Greece. Slater obviously sees contemporary America as a narcissistic, achievement-oriented culture, but he also refers to Ruth
Benedict's study of the Kwakiutl Indians—HGs involved in storage
and sedentism—as illustrative of the same thing. Benedict's work revealed a culture whose men were devoted to self-glorification, economic display, and the humiliation of rivals. What is significant
about any culture is its energetic configuration: Kwakiutl narcissism,
says Slater, looks a lot more like fifth-century Athens than the typical contemporary "primitive" society. At the heart of this energetic
pattern is a deprivation of pleasure, of physical joy in the world,
that leads the men in these cultures to renounce love—which they
feel they cannot really get—and then disguise their despair in self-
aggrandizement and ambition. The cycle continues when such a
person looks down on his wife, becomes a poor husband, and effectively forces his wife "into the arms" of her son; who then fears
women, needs to succeed, and so on.[46]

Was the glory of Greece worth it, asks Slater, if it required this
narcissistic personality structure to make it possible? For the most

part, his answer is no. In ancient Greece, or twentieth-century America, we have great art and technology and a large body of knowledge, but the suffering on a deep emotional level was/is correspondingly great. This degree of narcissism, says Slater, means that life is never savored, that "the joys of the many are sacrificed to the achievements of the few." The majority of people in these cultures are left bitter because they operate out of the same value system, yet can't achieve heroic status. And even heroes don't get to enjoy very much because what they have done is channel sensual pleasure and experiential immediacy into "transcendent" realms, such as mastery and glory. According to Slater, it is not that we should try to eliminate narcissism altogether, but the point to which cultures such as Greece or America took it or have taken it is at the far end of the spectrum.[47]

The connection between intense mothering and the culture of achievement does seem to be intuitively correct, and it has some psychoanalytic data to support it. Freud wrote that a son who is his mother's special pride (as he himself was) will retain "the feeling of a conqueror" throughout his life.[48] In her own research on this relationship, Carole Klein found that "when we study the lives of famous men, over and over again we find the son who has been singled out by a fiercely determined mother." Similarly, the work of Victor and Mildred Goertzel, *Cradles of Eminence*, which is a study of the childhoods of eminent men, shows that the mothers involved often had heroic dreams for their sons. Many politicians had adoring mothers, and one study of male politicians revealed that they were driven by an agenda of "conquering" the world. The Goertzels found that military sons had great difficulty in separating from their mothers and that the overpossessive mother of a peer-rejected child, especially when relations with the husband are poor, "is most likely to rear . . . a military hero who enjoys the carnage of battle." This should not be all that surprising. War offers numerous opportunities for ecstatic experience, the peak intensity that, of course, reproduces the "hallowed presence" of dyadic infancy. It is another way, as Galway Kinnell would say, of entering the "holy land." The problem with vertical energy is that you can never get enough of it. There is no end to achievement and no end to war ("what gives life beckons toward death"), as civilization has found out. All of this, it seems to me, should give us some idea of who the aggressive subgroup is. Heroes are made, not born, and they are certainly not timeless archetypes.

I am assuming, then, what the psychologist Clara Thompson argued several decades ago and what feminist scholarship now regards as an obvious fact: ambition, the drive for power, is found in women as well as men; and if culture is arranged in such a way that this drive has no direct outlets, it will get channeled into indirect ones. Even more, if women are stuck in a situation of economic dependency, then they have no security beyond that of a love relationship. Love becomes their "career"; being loved becomes their "profession."[49]

What we need to examine more closely, then, is how this asymmetrical structure gets perpetuated and maintained on the microlevel of child rearing, what Nancy Chodorow calls the "reproduction of mothering." One of the best analyses of this is that of Dorothy Dinnerstein (*The Mermaid and the Minotaur*), which points out that regardless of the gender of the infant, the primary caregiver is invariably female, and this has consequences for how women are perceived in any culture and for the relationships between the sexes. Of course, Dinnerstein is talking about dyadic arrangements and doesn't have much to say about multiple caregiving or HG societies. Nevertheless, if we can agree that *some* degree of "monotropy" is always present and is keener in sedentary cultures (which is a debatable issue; see note 22), then Dinnerstein's analysis of the source of vertical energy in civilization would seem to work.

In essence, boys and girls have a very different problematic to deal with in terms of the "hallowed presence," of the powerful figure of the mother in the nursery. Being of the same gender as Mom, girls find their identity by identifying with the mother, whereas boys find it by *separating* from her. So boys grow up learning to fear this energy, learning to become "rational" and to distance themselves from their bodies and their emotions, which are seen as female. (Falling in love, falling for charismatic leaders, going to war, or becoming alcoholics are often the only exceptions men will make to this distancing behavior.) But girls are nervous about this energy as well and grow up fearing that they can never fulfill the "goddess" role that their mothers modeled for them on the unconscious level. So, as women, they choose to collude in patriarchal arrangements, since the unstated premise is, Let go of the gates of reason and logic, and all hell will break loose (which in our culture is absolutely true). "Paternal authority," writes Dinnerstein,

> is a sanctuary passionately cherished by the essential part of a person's self that wants to come up . . . out of the drowning sweetness of early childhood into the bright dry light of open day, the light of the adult realm in which human reason and human will—not the boundless and mysterious intentionality,

the terrible uncanny omniscience, of the nursery goddess—can be expected, at least ideally, to prevail.[50]

The result is that women are deprived of power in our society. They are assigned the function of representing the "soft underbelly," the zones of touch, emotion, intuition, and so on, while men represent the "outside world," the life of mastery and adventure. Once again, this gives women too much power in the nursery; and Dad, by contrast, gets to represent the healthy "rational breeze" that blows through the family unit. The next generation picks up this bipolar lesson quickly and in turn passes it on. Clearly, then, we cannot really understand the psychogenesis of dominance and hierarchy without referring to gender relations. Under conditions of such dyadic intensity, men are driven not merely to dominate women (and nature), but to prove their masculinity by dominating other men. A satirical title of a few years ago—*Real Men Don't Bond*—captures the tragic truth of all this. For both sexes, the fear of a large, dark, irrational chaotic (and, in my view, primarily Neolithic) energy just seething below the surface, waiting to erupt at any moment, and only dimly perceived, is enough to make social inequality and hierarchical arrangements—the guarantors of order and stability—extremely attractive. Dinnerstein concludes that only by drawing men into the child-rearing process can the female domination of the nursery be broken and women's terrifying, mythological status be reduced.

Was this situation part of the Paleolithic scenario as well? Dinnerstein writes that "prehistoric children, like more recent and contemporary ones, lived their early lives under predominantly female auspices." As we have seen, however, big-game hunting showed up in a dramatic way (at least in Western Europe) only during the Upper Paleolithic, primarily during the Gravettian (i.e., from about 30,000 B.C.). For the larger record, the correct label is GH—gatherer-hunter—rather than HG. And Dinnerstein is fully aware of this. The digging stick, she says, may have been more central than the spear, and if so, "the female contribution to the beginnings of human culture is apt to have been more substantial." Big-game hunting works against gender equality; the process whereby the female is turned into a second-class citizen, and thus, of necessity, a "professional mother," is thereby triggered. Sedentary arrangements, of course, with accompanying narrow birth spacing, accelerated this trend exponentially. Under conditions of gender equality, the infant is peripheral to a busy, meaningful adult (female) life. Introduce a major socioeconomic role for the man and a correspondingly lesser role for the woman—both of which agriculture eventually does—and the infant moves from periphery to center, becoming the focus of the mother's life and giving rise to the narcissism already described.[51]

It is for all these reasons that "fusion" and "Oneness" lie at the heart of the SAC and the religious configuration of agricultural civilization and why paradox became so difficult to sustain. We need, then, to take a closer look at that configuration and at the complex relationship that developed between women and agriculture. Having done this, we shall be in a better position to understand the subsequent reemergence of nomadic consciousness that occurred a few millennia later, but now in a very different form.

4

AGRICULTURE, RELIGION, AND THE GREAT MOTHER

...The farmer I will marry,
The farmer who grows many plants,
The farmer who grows much grain.

—From "Dumuzi and Enkimdu: The Wooing of Inanna";
Sumerian poem, second millennium B.C.

I have been arguing for the existence, historically, of two basic constellations: HG society (or more precisely, immediate-return economies)— whose conception of the sacred is diffuse, paradoxical, and horizontal—and agricultural civilization (or more generally, delayed-return economies)—whose notion of the numinous is vertical, ranging from a generalized sacred authority to the intense experience of unitive trance. I have also argued that the pattern of horizontal versus vertical religious experience is, not coincidentally, roughly duplicated in the pattern of (relative) egalitarianism versus social inequality and that all of this, in turn, is tied into child-rearing patterns. Multiple caregiving tends to create a less "steep-gradient" child, and, in addition, the mother in HG societies focuses on the infant much less because she is directly involved in the social and economic activities of her society. In DR economies, the woman's economic role is much reduced; she becomes a "professional mother," especially with the narrow birth spacing that is concomitant with a sedentary lifestyle. This entails a too-strong focus on the infant, giving rise to the "hallowed presence" phenomenon discussed by Erik Erikson. To complete the cycle, infants raised in such a context get imprinted for charismatic experience; that is, they learn to see sacred authority as expressive of the highest "truth," which then serves to reaffirm the vertical social order. Men caught up in this configuration feel the need to be heroic; and when we combine this with the fear and insecurity that is endemic to DR economies, and with sibling rivalry and the need for

117

intense parental investment, we get a configuration of aggressive subgroups, command/obedience relations, and prisoner's dilemma situations that characterize the power structures of the Neolithic age and
beyond. This is, of course, a kind of rough-hewn outline, but on the
whole it would seem to be a fairly accurate summary of the negative
aspects of life in civilization.

What I wish to do in the present chapter is flesh out this outline, and the modifications of it that might be necessary, in greater
detail. For the point I am leading up to here is that we are living
within a (Neolithic) mindset that has some validity in terms of cognition and perception, but that also represents a serious distortion.
It's not merely that we have lost spontaneity in favor of institutionalized life, but that since the Late Paleolithic, our very thinking process has been skewed in a "religious" direction, something that is
generally hard for us to recognize. The insistence on certainty (sacred authority) that characterized the Neolithic now shows up in the
daily newspapers of the Western industrial nations and in the
speeches of their politicians, who can seem to think only in formu-
las. Indeed, Ronald Reagan saw nothing wrong, as president, in re-
plying to questions at press conferences by reading slogans off of
flash cards that he had assembled in front of him. More to the point,
the American public found his replies acceptable, even "wise." And
when we turn to those who seek to change the dominant culture—
"new paradigm" advocates or promotors of postmodernism,
multiculturalism, and the like—we don't seem to do much better. It's
oppositional logic and a new set of slogans all the way. (A different reality, but with "our crowd" now in charge.) Whether modern
or postmodern, our world is caught up in a consciousness that has
its origins in the SAC as the source of truth. We are all, in Eric
Hoffer's memorable phrase, true believers.

In order to escape from this "entrancement," as it were, we need
to look at a number of things. One is the possibility that pre-agricultural societies had a different mode of consciousness; and I have
discussed the notion of paradox at length. Another is the question
of how this got lost, both on a macro- and a microlevel; and this
was the subject of the last two chapters. We also shall have to talk
about attempts to resuscitate nomadic consciousness, which I shall
discuss later on. What I wish to do right now is provide a closer
look at the details, the mechanisms, of agricultural civilization.
Specifically, how did the SAC function, and where does the worship
of the Great Mother come into this, if at all? What are the relations
among the Great Mother, agriculture, fertility, sexuality, rebirth
eschatology, unitive trance experience, ideology, and social inequal-

ity? Answering this is a tall order; obviously, I shall not be able to fill it. But let's have a go, in any case, and see what transpires. I'll begin our inquiry with the religion of the Great Mother.

Unfortunately, this is no easy topic to discuss. Thomas Friedman, in *From Beirut to Jerusalem*, remarks that it is difficult to assess the situation in the Middle East because the minute the topic is raised, people become temporarily insane. The situation is not very different in the case of "the Goddess." On the level of popular culture, great numbers of people have uncritically absorbed a Jungian/feminist mythology about a goddess religion whose basis in historical reality is, with a few exceptions, quite shaky, but that has therapeutically become so central to their identities that any critique of that mythology is too threatening for them to entertain. Therefore, some degree of stripping away of the accreted layers of this pseudohistory will be necessary if we are to establish the reality of the Great Mother in agricultural civilization and determine what her actual role has been in the development of Neolithic culture.

The Jung Cult

The core problem, as indicated in chapter 1, is that of a fallacious methodology, namely that of comparative mythology; the tendency, as the eminent Assyriologist Leo Oppenheim once put it, to compile "smoothly written systematizations decked out in a mass of all-too-ingenious comparisons and parallels obtained by zigzagging all over the globe and through the known history of man."[1] This approach goes back to James Frazer and J. J. Bachofen in the nineteenth century; in the twentieth, the leading figure has been Carl Jung, with Mircea Eliade and Joseph Campbell following close behind.[2] But as so many scholars have shown, the assumption of a mythic substrate or "collective unconscious" is just that—an assumption. Imported into history or anthropology, it amounts to no more than an attempt to force the record of the past into a framework previously decided upon; and this problem is endemic to all Jungian work. A much more realistic approach is the one captured by an old saw from gestalt psychology: "Our goal is not to *make* things happen; it is to see what actually *does happen*." The same cannot be said of the "comparative mythology" school, whose methodology is just the opposite.

With that in mind, let me turn briefly to the work of Carl Jung proper, before we look more specifically at the issue of the Great Mother, because so much of the methodology involved in the "goddess craze," as Mary Lefkowitz calls it, is ultimately rooted in Jung's peculiar brand of psychohistorical misinformation.[3]

The most recent and outstanding analysis of this particular problem is the work of the historian of science Richard Noll, in his recent book *The Jung Cult*.[4] Noll shows that Jung's argument for the existence of a common mythic substrate for all humanity was heavily derivative from *völkisch* and Teutonic concepts current in nineteenth-century Germany, the same wellspring that was to feed much of Nazi ideology. Two sources in particular formed the basis of Jung's historical outlook. The first of these was the study by the Belgian scholar Franz Cumont of a Hellenistic solar mystery cult known as Mithraism. The initiation into this cult, which was very dramatic, was also practiced in the cult of Cybele, the Magna Mater (see below). In the central rite of the *taurobolium*, the initiate stood in a pit below a grating, on which a bull was slaughtered, and then emerged drenched in blood. Cumont traced the cult, which flourished from 100 to 400 A.D., to Persian/Iranian roots dating to 600 B.C., but he hinted at an even greater antiquity for it, a tribal prehistory. Jung saw Mithraism as an *Urreligion*, a primal nature religion involving a fusion experience with the "true" god, that was the basis of all of the ancient mystery cults, and the basic mythic substrate that, he argued, we all possess. The cult was structured like a Masonic lodge, with ranked grades of initiation, and was very popular among the Roman army. This Indo-Iranian (Aryan) religion, said Jung, was our true biological heritage, which Christianity had overlaid for two thousand years.[5]

The problem with this is that recent scholarship has discredited Cumont's work. Mithraism, it turns out, cannot be traced to Persian roots, thus denying it the primal antiquity he and Jung claimed for it; and in addition, we do not have, and never have had, a single account of the central myth of this religion. Any reconstruction of it is pure fantasy. However, this did not constitute an obstacle for Jung, for whom acts of imaginative reconstruction were the key to historical understanding. The image of a solar, Aryan "truth" lying at the root of everything, access to which could only be had via occult initiation run by an "enlightened" elite, was irresistible to him; and this whole structure was in fact duplicated in Jungian analysis, with Jung serving as the high priest of his own "mysteries."[6]

Jung's second source was that of the Swiss writer J. J. Bachofen, *Das Mutterrecht* (mother right, or matriarchy), published in 1861. Bachofen argued, without any solid evidence, that the human race had gone from matriarchy to patriarchy, an argument that virtually no present-day anthropologist accepts as valid. In his own time, however, even though he was regarded as a kind of Erich von Däniken figure (citing him in scholarly work could have ruined one's career), Bachofen's ideas had great popular appeal. So although Jung barely referred to him, he nevertheless used Bachofen's work to combine biological vitalism with an Earth Mother cult. Parts of his *Psychology of the Unconscious* are pure Bachofen, and they set the stage for Jung's discussion of hero myths and their relation to the mother complex. Bachofen becomes the key to a psychoanalytic history of the human race, which is supposedly recapitulated in the ontogeny of the individual human being. The myth of the hero, wrote Jung, is the myth of our (by which he meant "male") suffering unconscious, which longs for the Mother, and, through her, for "communion with infinite life." All of this followed the schema of the mystery cults, such as that at Eleusis in ancient Greece, in which the initiate was reborn via a descent to the underworld of the mothers. The solar hero, said Jung, descends into the dark realm of the mothers, does battle, and emerges reborn. This realm, Jung argued, was the deepest stratum of the unconscious.

Two things strike me as being very important here. The first is that although Jungianism is a patriarchal world view, grounded as it is in the mysteries of an all-male cult, it fits very well with matriarchal mythology and the notion of a universal female deity. For although the Jungian odyssey is a male one (the heroic journey, the man's search for his "anima," the man's process of individuation), the would-be hero climbs the ladder of initiation only by virtue of a descent into the realm of the archetypal feminine. For Jung, the unconscious is female, and it is only through the temporary obliteration of consciousness, the dissolution of the ego into the Absolute (= womb of the Great Mother), that the initiate gets his solar/ heroic wings. He undergoes psychic death and rebirth and becomes, in some sense, immortal. This was apparently the process of the mystery cults, as far as we know, and thus in an *archetypal* sense, even if those mysteries are "male," it is the encounter with the Great Mother that is the crucial point. Influenced by Bachofen's work, Jung claimed that a female voice spoke to him in trance in 1913, and that it was that of an archaic goddess from the (supposed) early matriarchy. In a visionary experience he had later the same year, he claimed he had been initiated into the Hellenic mysteries and that his anima, "Salome," told him he was Christ.

Second, in both the mysteries and the Jungian world schema as well, hierarchy and elitism were/are central to the whole project. Jung, according to Noll, would be the charismatic prophet of the "Jung cult," the collection of disciples/initiates who would "individuate" so that they could become just like Jung(!). Jung's fantasy, writes Noll, was that of a hierarchical organization led by a priesthood that was privy to esoteric knowledge by rising through the ranks via initiation. But we should be clear by now that shamanic practice is, as Nicholas Thomas and Caroline Humphrey demonstrate, largely about personal and political power. Thus, the American anthropologist Walter Goldschmidt writes that the purpose of the Plains Indian vision quest was success in a social context. Among the Blackfeet, he says, personal achievement led to material wealth; the Crow Indians bragged about their personal exploits; and so on. As I trust the previous two chapters have made clear, religious verticality is about political verticality; the two go hand in hand. Nor was Jung unaware of this; in 1928 he wrote that the "vast majority [of humankind] needs authority, guidance, and law." Shades of Plato, as Karl Popper told us, and of course, the Grand Inquisitor as well.[7]

As in the case of Frazer and Bachofen, Jung hopscotched from culture to culture to "prove" his thesis regarding the existence of a collective unconscious. In his case, however, it was worse than mere anthropological naïveté: he lied. So obsessed was he with this theory that he falsified the dates of his key case study, the so-called "Solar Phallus Man"—this even in a televised interview on the BBC (in 1959)—and consistently maintained that the patients of his clinical studies had no knowledge of alchemy, Mithraism, or occult lore. Yet none of this was true: Jung's patients, including his British and American ones, were well-educated and versed in mythologies of various sorts. Not only had such material been popular for decades, but many if not most of those patients had been involved in occult traditions and had even read Jung's works. Material on the "collective unconscious" often was gathered from the study of a single individual. In the case of Jung's famous essay, "Individual Dream Symbolism in Relation to Alchemy," the subject was the physicist Wolfgang Pauli, a man of great erudition; and in the case of his "Study in the Process of Individuation," the subject was the American Jungian Kristine Mann, who had been a Swedenborgian and exposed to alchemical ideas long before she ever met Jung. All in all, says Noll, Jung's data base was both biased and minuscule.[8]

Commenting on Freud's fixation on repressed sexuality as the root of all human difficulties, Jung remarked how important it was for the researcher to have some ability for self-examination, to ask himself *why* he was obsessed with any given idea. Strangely enough, Jung exempted himself from this test; he never asked himself why the Great Mother, the collective unconscious, and the shotgun comparative method so overwhelmingly possessed his soul. But, of course, there is nothing strange about this: Jung was critical of *Freud's* obsession, not his own. As Noll puts it, Jung was into mystery, not history; and history, he adds, "is not the bread of the faithful." What we get, instead, is pseudohistory, built upon the shaky foundation of an alleged universal psyche. Nowhere is this configuration more evident than in the literature on an ancient matriarchy or goddess religion, to which I shall now turn.[9]

The Myth of the Goddess

The classic work on the Great Mother remains the book of the same name by Jung's most talented disciple, Erich Neumann.[10] In fact, the book is dedicated to Jung, and the epigraph to part 1 is taken from the work of Bachofen. However, Neumann at least made the attempt to modify Bachofen's notion of a matriarchal stage: it exists, he says, not as an actual *historical* entity, but only as a stratum of the psyche. What Neumann then reproduces is a large number of plates—of "Venus" figurines, statuettes, murals, vessels, and so on—spanning the period from the Late Paleolithic through the sixteenth century A.D., serving as examples of worship of a goddess and bearing the characteristics of this female archetype. He says, the sequence is designed to reveal "the unfolding of the Archetypal Feminine," which (he adds) displays an obvious unity. Again, Neumann's self-admitted goal is therapeutic rather than historical, his purpose being to achieve psychic wholeness for Western culture by balancing its overly male orientation with an exposure to the feminine world. Thus, he is not concerned with history as such, and he makes this explicit:

> If we offend against "history" by removing documents and representations from their cultural context, we hope to compensate by correlating our archetypal investigation with a "psychohistory," that is to say, with the stages in the development of the human psyche. Taking the development of consciousness as the decisive phenomena [*sic*] of human history, we arrive at an arrangement of the phenomena that does not, to be sure, coincide with the usual sequence of historical events, but makes possible the psychological orientation we require.

The problem with this is that the historical record does not exist for the purpose of any particular school of psychological thought and cannot be "raided" arbitrarily for the latter's benefit. This mode of argumentation is a closed circle, because the Q.E.D. has already been drawn up. It is also the case that disclaimers notwithstanding, if you are using historical materials, it is hard to avoid making assertions about real historical events. Thus, Neumann argues that the "Venus" figurines demonstrate that a goddess stood at the center of Late Paleolithic and early Neolithic group life—that is, did so *historically*; but how can we know this? Certainly not through archetypal analysis; and as we shall see below, more likely interpretations of the "Venus" figures exist than Jungian or religious ones. As for Neumann, he claims in one breath that he is not referring to social structures; then he proceeds to talk in terms of historical stages, ones that are, not surprisingly, generated by merging Bachofen with Jung, so that human history is identified with the history of consciousness and then seen to fall into a specific sequence. We start with a "primordial" period; move on to the Great Mother stage, as evidenced by the "Venus" figurines; and then finally conclude with patriarchy. Neumann's contribution, really, was to show that the idea of the feminine is central to the human psyche, and in that sense, his reproductions are impressive. Thus it is undoubtedly true that male civilization has ignored its female side, has suffered as a result, and that recovering that side would be a salutary thing. I agree; I think we need to do it. But it is more a statement about the present than the past. There simply is no concrete evidence for continuous goddess worship or Paleolithic fertility cults, and while Neumann's plates are suggestive, they ultimately don't amount to a new historical record.

A similar argument, but now unequivocally imposed on the historical record, was mounted by the anthropologist Marija Gimbutas in a series of monographs such as *The Goddesses and Gods of Old Europe*, *The Language of the Goddess*, and *The Civilization of the Goddess*. Like Neumann, Gimbutas reproduces pictures of "Venus" figurines and other female images, including statuettes of pregnant women with pendulous breasts. Across "Old Europe" (the area stretching from the Aegean and the Adriatic north and east to Czechoslovakia, Poland, and the Ukraine, 7000–3500 B.C.), says Gimbutas, the concept of the feminine was dominant, and the Goddess was worshipped as the Source. This became stronger in the Neolithic era, during which the culture was agricultural, sedentary, peaceful, and egalitarian because of the primacy of female values. We see (she claims) evidence of the goddess culture not only in the Venus figures, but also in a whole host of symbols, such as moon crescents and bulls' horns. With the Neolithic, "a separate deity emerged, the Goddess of Vegetation, a symbol of the sacred nature of the seed and the sewn field, whose ties with the Great Goddess are intimate." This was a society dominated by the Great Mother. Unfortunately, Gimbutas tells us, this happy state of affairs was not to last. Between 4500 and 2500 B.C., Old Europe was invaded in three waves by Indo-European, or "kurgan," culture, as she calls it (*kurgan* being the Russian word for pit-grave, or burial mound), which was patriarchal and warlike. The civilization of Old Europe was destroyed by the patriarchal element; the Goddess was replaced by male deities, and Old Europe never recovered.[11]

This basic schema, of a peace-loving goddess culture (matrilocal if not actually matriarchical) destroyed by patriarchal invaders is quite popular today and has been picked up by a number of writers. Thus, Riane Eisler, in *The Chalice and the Blade*, projects a world of neat black and white, binary opposition, of male versus female; but there is more. For example, we have *The Myth of the Goddess* by two Jungian analysts, Anne Baring and Jules Cashford, whose footnotes refer us to Campbell, Jung, Eisler, and Gimbutas; Anne Barstow's essay, "The Prehistoric Goddess," which tells us that there was a single goddess who stood for female power and the earth (which we "know" because her figurines are faceless and without feet); and the popular video released in 1989 by the National Film Board of Canada, *Goddess Remembered*, which celebrates the "ancient goddess-worshipping religions" that are now "energizing contemporary women's spirituality." All of this popular narrative expands on Gimbutas and takes the tack that the past tells us that a unified goddess culture existed, as evidenced by the archaeological remains, that it was peaceful and egalitarian, and that it was destroyed by patriarchal nomads. Before turning to the scholarly evidence of what the "goddess culture" actually was, we need to look at this argument a bit more closely, so as to have a clear understanding regarding its claims to historical validity.[12]

Gimbutas contends that we have thousands of extant sculptures that provide evidence of Great Mother worship. Consider a late sixth-millennium figure carved from bone, found in a grave near Bucharest (Figure 9). The two rounded protuberances are apparently folded arms. The abdomen and pubic area is emphasized. "This little sculpture," she tells us, "is probably a portrayal of a Great Goddess in a rigid position . . . a type encountered in graves throughout the Old European period and in the Cyclades of the third millennium B.C." Or consider fourth-millennium clay models of shrines from the Ukraine. In one case, the model shows an oven, to the right of which we find a female figurine with her hands on her breasts. By another wall, we find a figure of a woman grinding grain. This type of

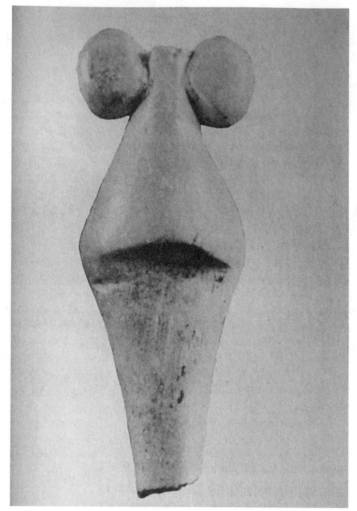

Figure 9. Bone Figurine from Romania. From Marija Gimbutas, *The Goddesses and Gods of Old Europe.*

juxtaposition, she says, suggests the performance of religious ritual. We also find the cross on Neolithic and Chalcolithic (Copper Age, ca. 5000–3500 B.C.) pottery, elaborated into fourfold designs, symbolizing the four corners of the cosmos. Gimbutas comments:

> The cross and its various derivative symbols are frequently encountered in the incised or painted ceramic decorations of each Neolithic and Chalcolithic group. Their consistent appearance on dishes, bowls, vases, stamp seals and the crowns of

Figure 10. Decoration on a Vessel from Macedonia. From Marija Gimbutas, *The Goddesses and Gods of Old Europe.*

figurines strongly suggests that they are ideograms necessary to promote the recurrent birth and growth of plant, animal, and human life . . . The fourfold compositions, archetypal of perpetual renewal or wholeness and the moon in the symbolism of Old Europe, are associated with the Great Goddess of Life and Death, and the Goddess of Vegetation, moon goddesses *par excellence.*

In addition to cross imagery, she writes,

Parallel lines, V's, chevrons, belts of zigzags, and groups of parallel lines are frequently found on figurines, stamp seals, cult vases and vase lids. Their consistent appearance on figurine masks and bodies, anthropomorphic vases, miniature cult vessels and zoomorphic containers suggests the existence of a coherent system of symbolic expression: the relationship between the depiction of rain torrents, the mythical bear and the Bird Goddess is obvious.

As an example of the bird goddess, we have a decoration on a vessel from Macedonia, dating from circa 5500 B.C. (Figure 10), as well as a sculpted head from Bulgaria, five hundred years later (Figure 11).

Figure 11. Sculpted Head from Bulgaria. From Marija Gimbutas, *The Goddesses and Gods of Old Europe.* Courtesy Stara Zagora Regional Historical Museum, Bulgaria.

Finally, the symbolism of the bull's horns, seen at a number of cult sites in the Neolithic, has (she says) a strong similarity to human female reproductive organs (Figure 12), which Gimbutas regards as a "plausible if esoteric explanation for the importance of this motif in the symbolism of Old Europe, Anatolia, and the Near East."[13]

Before the reader shakes her head in utter disbelief, it should be stated that this compilation of icons and running commentary *is* Gimbutas' evidence. *Language of the Goddess* and *Civilization of the Goddess* are essentially picture books, collections of images in the Neumann style, with a goddess interpretation tacked onto each image. The examples I have chosen are quite representative

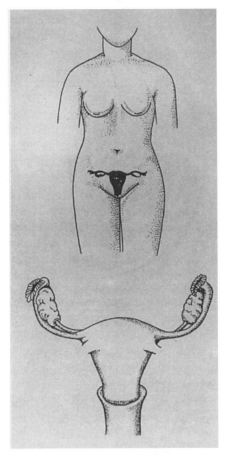

Figure 12. Bull's Horns Compared with Female Reproductive Organs. Figure 7-35 from *The Civilization of the Goddess: The World of Old Europe* by Marija Gimbutas. Copyright © 1991 by Marija Gimbutas. Reprinted by permission of HarperCollins Publishers, Inc.

of this mode of argumentation; they are hardly exceptional. But do we really see a goddess in Figure 9? On what basis? This object would certainly seem to be female, but beyond that—? In the case of the shrine-oven-model mentioned above: What conclusions might we draw? Undoubtedly, that women in this culture are associated with grain, or at least with the baking of bread. The hands-on-breasts probably suggests more, namely, mothering, feeding. Does this make this a ritual performance? Does it make the female figures goddesses? On what basis? Does cross imagery reasonably translate into "moon goddesses *par excellence*"?

Similarly, chevrons and zigzags on vessels may indeed suggest "the existence of a coherent system of symbolic expression," but how does this get translated into rain, bears, and a bird goddess? Does the reader really see such a goddess in Figures 10 and 11? And isn't the equating of bull's horns with female organs little more than a Rorschach test?

This is the crux of the problem: what we learn about from these books is not, for the most part, the nature of an early Neolithic goddess civilization, but the nature of Marija Gimbutas' psyche. For the "goddess" in these images is surely in the eye of the beholder; it is not in the images per se. Just as Joseph Campbell was obsessed with issues of (his own) heroism, so was Gimbutas preoccupied—for whatever reason—with issues of femaleness. And such obsessions are fine, if the researcher stops short of passing off personal (or even "archetypal") projections as historical fact. But the intuitive-comparative methodology is a siren song; it says, in effect, if your intuition tells you such is the case, then it is probably true.[14]

A similar point has been made by the archaeologist Brian Hayden, who notes that Gimbutas treats everything, including symbols that are clearly phallic, as symbols of the Goddess:

> [O]blique parallel lines, horizontal parallel lines, vertical parallel lines, chevrons, lozenges, zigzags, wavy lines, meanders, circles, ovals, spirals, dots, crescents, U's, crosses, swirls, caterpillars, double axes, chrysalises, horns, butterflies, birds, eggs, fish, rain, cows, dogs, does, stags, toads, turtles, hedgehogs, bees, bulls, bears, goats, pigs, pillars, and sexless linear or masked figures are all viewed as symbols of this goddess. One wonders what is left.

The famous fish/human sculptures from Lepenski Vir, in Yugoslavia, he points out, are taken by Gimbutas as a central example, while (it turns out) the archaeologist who excavated these indicated that they represented a male deity. Gimbutas similarly takes bulls, rams, and he-goats to be symbols of the Goddess; when she is forced to admit that some of the objects are masculine, she claims they did not exist prior to agriculture—a claim that is unfounded. Or she will insist that purely abstract symbols are those of the Goddess. All of this, says Hayden, is "verifiable only with the eye of faith. Nowhere is there even a mention of methodology, testing, statistics, chance variation, assumptions, or rigor."[15]

An equally incisive critique is provided by Margaret Ehrenberg in *Women in Prehistory*, which methodically discredits the goddess thesis step by step. Referring to "dubious feminist literature, which is based on ignorant and undiscriminating use of archaeological evidence," Ehrenberg begins by pointing out that there "is no obvious connection between the existence of goddesses and the roles and status of real women." Images of the Virgin Mary, for example, hardly reflect the status of women in our own society—something that Gordon Childe pointed out nearly fifty years ago. Female figurines by themselves are only suggestive, at best. What the "goddess crowd" fails to tell us, she says, is that these objects are part of a much larger group of Paleolithic statuettes, *most of which appear to be sexless*. Even in the case of the obviously female figurines, according to an analysis done in 1996, it is more likely that the "exaggeration" of sexual characteristics is not about religious messages, but rather is the image one gets of a pregnant female looked at from her own (i.e., top-down, or foreshortened) perspective, as part of an effort Paleolithic women made to obtain knowledge of their own bodies and the reproductive process. The authors of this study write:

> The idea that women sought to gain and preserve knowledge about their own bodies provides a direct and parsimonious explanation for general as well as idiosyncratic features found among female representations from the middle European Upper Paleolithic . . . It is possible that the emergence and subsequent propagation of these images across Europe occurred precisely because they played a didactic function with actual adaptive consequences for women.[16]

Turning to the Neolithic group of figurines, says Ehrenberg, many are female, but some are animal, some male, and a great many are asexual. When we examine, for example, the eighty-one figurines found at Knossos in Crete, dating from 5500 B.C. to 3000 B.C., we find that thirty-three are female, six are male, and no less than forty-two are without gender. Among the seated figures, the males have proportionately heavier hips than the females. Nearly all of these figurines were found in rubbish pits; none came from shrines or burial sites. For all we know, these objects could have been used for sorcery or magic, or simply have been dolls for children. In general, concludes Ehrenberg, "the likelihood of a significant continent-wide cult of a Mother Goddess has been greatly exaggerated."[17]

The problems with the goddess argument do not stop there, however. Even if we were to grant the existence of such a cult, where is the evidence that these Old European cultures were peaceful and egalitarian? This used to be the view of Minoan civilization

on Crete, for example (discussed below), and a case can still be made
for it being a more peaceful type of society than that of the Greek-
speaking Mycenaeans, on the mainland; but excavations in the 1970s
have forced a reconsideration of this picture. Fortifications were not
so unusual for Minoan Crete as previously thought. A number of
cities had protective walls; weapons have been discovered on Crete,
as well as evidence of human sacrifice and even cannibalism. Minoan
murals show armed warriors, and some people were buried with
hammers and maces in hand. Nor should we idealize Minoan relations with foreigners, captives, or slaves. All in all, it seems to be
the case that there have been "overstated descriptions of pacifism"
for this culture. As for egalitarianism, Minoan Crete certainly had a
privileged class. At its climax, says Brian Hayden, Old Europe was
rich, hierarchical, and competitive.[18]

What about the theory of the destruction of these societies by
"kurgan" invaders? Frankly, the subject of Indo-European origins has
to be one of the murkiest and most controversial topics ever tack-
led by prehistorians, not one that any scholar has been able to unravel successfully. I shall say more about it in chapter 5, when we
consider the possible Aryan invasion of India. However, what *is* clear
by now is that all invasion theories of societal collapse have proven
to be simplistic; there is always more than meets the eye. Was
Minoan civilization simply overrun by warlike Mycenaeans (main-
landers) in the mid-second millennium? Possibly, but it's a bit too
easy. Crete (and nearby Thera) were rocked by devastating earth-
quakes; there may have been a Minoan naval domination ("thalas-
socracy") of the Aegean, possibly including taxation of the
Mycenaeans and exclusion of them from foreign markets, against
which they revolted; we have no solid evidence of Mycenaean political control of Knossos; and even our knowledge of the Dorian invasion of Greece proper (twelfth century B.C.) is largely based on
legends. All in all, the question of outsider versus Cretan relationships has never been resolved. When looked at more closely, invasions often prove to have symbiotic elements, such as intermarriage,
trade, and slow intermingling.[19]

In the case of much of the goddess literature on "kurgan" waves
of barbarians, the whole thing has a kind of paranoid flavor to it, a
myth of female purity overrun by phallic evil. As anthropologist
David Anthony points out, the argument ignores the possibility that
the "goddess civilization" may have already been crumbling from
within. Societal collapse is a recurrent process; it cannot be explained
by a random variable that operates, says Joseph Tainter, like a pol-
tergeist, a *deus ex machina*. I would also add that if, as Gimbutas and

others wish to argue, human cultural evolution somehow follows a female-to-male pattern, we are at a loss to explain the historical origins of these male, warlike societies. These people were not cardboard figures, so where did *they* come from, culturally speaking? On the invasion theory, says Tainter, collapse is seen to be "caused by mysterious troublemakers, whose behavior is inexplicable." Such theories, he concludes, "provide a clean, single resolution to a distressingly convoluted problem."[20]

It is finally time to ask: Will the real Great Mother please stand up? Having cleared away some of the confusion that has bedevilled goddess scholarship, we need to clarify what actually *were* the relationships among agriculture, religion, and the Great Mother.

The point at which the association between goddess worship and agriculture becomes unequivocal is the second millennium B.C. This is the beginning of what is sometimes called "Axial" civilization, as I shall discuss below. With these changes came the mystery cults with their initiation rites and the search for salvation; and here, a Jungian approach *is* valid. We get the process of dissolution of the ego into the Great Mother (as psychological archetype) and the subsequent resurrection or return. The SAC has narrowed itself down to ecstatic trance practice, with a goddess figure in the various mystery religions now tied to personal salvation. We see hints of this in the civilization of the Aegean, briefly mentioned above. Before we turn to the mystery religions per se, it might be useful to say just a bit more about the Minoan world.

The Great Mother in the Aegean

It is in the region of the Aegean during the Bronze Age and after that the argument for a pervasive, generic female deity (or deities) seems to have some validity. For the island of Crete, as already noted, this culture is known as Minoan and runs from about 2900 to 1200 B.C. For the Greek mainland, the parallel culture is Mycenaean, running from ca. 1550 to 1100 B.C. Although it is a bit dated and in need of some qualification, Martin Nilsson's *Minoan-Mycenaean Religion* remains the classic study of the spiritual life of these cultures. Nilsson reproduces plates of a variety of objects, such as vessels and jewelry, that constitute fairly solid evidence for ritual practice associated with female deities in a specific region of the world.[21]

Although most of the Minoan artifacts are from the second millennium, we do find possible goddess objects (e.g., vessels with "breasts") on Crete in the third millennium, in tombs, connected to

Figure 13. Seal Impression from Knossos, Crete. From Nanno Marinatos, *Minoan Religion*. Courtesy University of South Carolina Press.

a cult of the dead. The concept of a nurturing goddess who protects the dead and insures the regeneration of life may have been established during this time; notions of natural cycles and renewal were central to Minoan religion. As William Taylour tells us, it is generally held that this chthonic religion, which regarded Mother Earth as the primal source—"a form of worship natural to a settled, agricultural community"—was the religion of the Aegean before the Greeks.[22]

The evidence gets better in the second millennium, which is the "palatial" period, when large religious structures were built at Knossos and elsewhere. Numerous seals and gold rings from this time show a Minoan goddess, with her breasts bare, in the context of flowers, trees, or animals (see Figure 13). She may not be a single deity, says the Greek archaeologist, Nanno Marinatos; that we have no way of knowing. But there does seem to be a single *concept* running through these images, that of a nurturing goddess of nature. Shifting to settlements on the mainland, we find little clay figurines of a standing woman, by the thousand, all over Mycenaean Greece. While it is unclear exactly how to interpret these, it is hard to avoid the notion of a generic female presence, even though the Mycenaean period is not characterized by a uniform goddess.[23]

Figure 14. Epiphany Scene on a Ring from Crete. From Nanno Marinatos, *Minoan Religion*. Courtesy University of South Carolina Press.

The really striking thing about some of the goddess imagery depicted on the seals and rings from the second millennium, however, and what Marinatos regards as the unique feature of the Minoan cult, is ecstatic visionary epiphany. The iconography here is remarkable, often showing one or more worshippers having an encounter with a deity (Figures 14 and 15). There is a kind of "burning bush" quality to these images, which sometimes include orgiastic dancing. This strikes me as being unequivocal evidence of goddess worship; the images are so clear here that there is little question of projecting an interpretation onto them, as far as I can see. In addition, all of this would seem to prefigure the mystery cult at Eleusis, which apparently involved the cultivation of ascent experience and oceanic dissolution of the ego. It also suggests that Eliade's "shamanism" (discussed in chapter 1) is actually a recent phenomenon, mostly dating from the second millennium. I shall say more about this below.

As for the agricultural connection, a civilization does not have to have a maternal goddess religion in order to believe in the cycles of vegetation; Egypt is a case in point. But I suspect that in the ancient world, this constellation occurred more often than not. It is apparently a strong feature of Minoan Crete; we see it unequivocally in the Eleusinian mysteries, with Demeter, the central figure, as corn goddess; and the literature and religious rites of Mesopotamia

Figure 15. Goddess Worship/Epiphany Scene on a Ring from Isopata, Crete. From M. P. Nilsson, *The Minoan-Mycenaen Religion*. Courtesy Almqvist & Wiksell International.

strongly point to connections among the breast, the vagina, the field, grain, female deities, and death and rebirth. A few words about Mesopotamia are in order, then, since the connection is so explicit here, in what traditionally has been referred to as the "cradle of Western civilization."

Mesopotamia: The Goddess-Agriculture Connection

The first high civilization, then, and one of the six "pristine" states to arise, was that of Sumer, what the Greeks and the Hebrews knew as Babylonia. It had the first urban centers, political centralization, ziggurats, commerce, and writing. The land itself, which corresponds to the southern half of modern Iraq, was first settled circa 5000 B.C. by an agricultural people known as the Ubaidians. The Sumerians themselves date from the fourth millennium B.C. Gilgamesh was an early ruler and became the first hero figure of the ancient world. Besides the invention of writing (circa 3500 B.C.), Sumer's key achievements were in agriculture: techniques of farming, and the creation of an intricate system of canals for irrigation.[24]

According to Samuel Noah Kramer, Sumer was wealthy, and this wealth was based on agriculture and stock breeding. "Sumerian culture," he writes, "fostered an obsessive drive for wealth and possessions—that in an agricultural and pastoral economy could be maintained only by fertility of the land, and fecundity of the womb." Hence, an "obsessive veneration" pervades Sumerian literature. In the text known as "The Curse of Agade," for example, we find references to full granaries and silos. Over and over again, the documents "underline the obsessive concern of the Sumerians with grain-laden fields, vegetable-rich gardens, bulging stalls and sheepfolds, milk, cream, and cheese in profusion."[25]

Sumer had both male and female deities. As Tikva Frymer-Kensky tells us, goddess worship was not a separate religion there, not part of a "women's cult."[26] In other words, we are dealing with a patriarchal culture, whose goddesses were subordinate to a male pantheon; yet one is left with the sense of there being a very strong "female aspect" to this civilization. The goddesses were in charge of three economic activities that Mesopotamia considered to be absolutely fundamental: the weaving of cloth, the eating of grain, and the drinking of beer (cf. the Enkidu vignette from the Gilgamesh epic, discussed in the introduction). They were also in charge of the storing of surplus. Thus Nisaba, the goddess of vegetation, was associated with grain and identified with the great storage room. Since storage on this scale requires a bookkeeping system, the goddesses were involved in administration, in running the temple complex. The Sumerian word *agrig*—"manager," "housekeeper"—was applied to a number of Mesopotamian goddesses. This is why agricultural civilization, at least in this case, seems to be "female"; significant economic activities were minutely regulated by female deities.

But the female role—at least on the divine level—is even more significant than this. To keep cosmos and culture operating harmoniously, without conflict and confusion, the gods devised the *me* ("Tao" might be one possible translation), a set of universal laws (or "cosmic offices"), which had to be obeyed by everybody and everything; and the "Queen of all the *me*," as she is described in a Sumerian poem, was the goddess Inanna (Ishtar, in Semitic languages), a complex figure whose various roles included the preservation of order itself. Nevertheless, her key function was to guarantee the fertility of the land, and this was accomplished by means of an annual new year's ceremony, the Sacred Marriage Rite, in which the king repeated the story of an ancient fertility cult by marrying, as Dumuzi (the biblical Tammuz), a priestess playing the part of Inanna.

This rite, which was celebrated all over the ancient Near East for at least two thousand years, dates to the fourth millennium B.C. The story includes Inanna's descent to the underworld, as well as the death and resurrection of her consort; and the core of the rite, accompanied by ecstatic love songs, was the sexual union of the king and the goddess-representative, to promote agricultural fertility. In essence, the sacred marriage ritual was a prayer for abundance.[27]

The most famous part of this story is given in a poem entitled "Dumuzi and Inanna: Prosperity in the Palace," in which the goddess presents herself as an agricultural metaphor, a well-watered field. Inanna's first choice for husband was a farmer, Enkimdu (not to be confused with Enkidu of the Gilgamesh epic); but Dumuzi, the shepherd, persuades her to change her mind by telling her he can give her more food. Again, we see how preoccupied civilization is with abundance and also with status (two earmarks of a vertical society). Inanna hesitates because she has misgivings about Dumuzi's pedigree, and he has to convince her of his background and rank. She then recites her famous invitation to him:

As for me, my vulva,
For me the piled-high hillock,
Me—the maid, who will plow it for me?
My vulva, the watered ground—for me,
Me, the Queen, who will station the ox there?

[The answer:]

Oh Lordly Lady, the king will plow it for you,
Dumuzi, the king, will plow it for you.

[She responds:]

Plow my vulva, man of my heart!

[They cohabit, and vegetation flourishes around them:]

Plants rose high by his side,
Grains rose high by his side . . . [28]

Once married, Inanna promises to take care of Dumuzi's storehouse. The marriage, writes Frymer-Kensky, "enables the true surplus abundance upon which urban civilization depends."[29]

Who exactly *is* Inanna? Frymer-Kensky claims that she is not the Great Mother, but rather the nondomesticated woman, "the very embodiment of sexual attraction and lust." Yet many scholars of the ancient Near East do see her as a mother/goddess figure, and in fact, in Mesopotamian mythology, she is the actual mother of Dumuzi as well as his wife.[30] This is a recurrent motif: in Greece, Gaia mates with Uranus, who is also her son, while in Egypt Isis sleeps with her brother Osiris. My guess is that this incest, especially the overlap of mother/lover, is part of the ambiguity generated by agricultural civilization, with its overlapping focus on food and sexuality; and it is also part of the "Dinnerstein syndrome" of women losing power in one sphere and then compensating for this in another one. For if so many of the goddesses of Mesopotamian civilization had real economic power, it is still the case that for the most part, actual women did not.[31] As noted in chapter 3, what we have instead is the rise of the professional mother.

So we see the agriculture/sex connection in Inanna's exhortation to "Plow my vulva," but the identification of her with nurturance in general seems to be present as well. Here is an excerpt of a hymn to her, originally written in the Akkadian language, second millennium B.C. (I am translating from a German translation):

> A goddess sings, especially awe-commanding among
>   goddesses!
> She, attired with swelling power and attractiveness
> Has the fullness of fruitfulness, seductive charm,
>   and ampleness
> Honey sweet are her lips, her mouth is life.
> Her colors are beautiful, and her eyes colorfully
>   shimmering.
> One finds wise counsel from this goddess
> She holds all skills in her hand.
> Where she looks, arises happiness,
> Life force, splendor, and strong fertility of
>   man and woman.[32]

One thing I find striking here is the calculated ambiguity of the text, which bespeaks a world vastly removed from that of HGs. For there is a possible blurring of nurturing and sexuality here. Inanna (Ishtar) is both seductive and fruitful, and the word "ampleness"— *Üppigkeit* in German—refers to both the sumptuousness of a meal *and* the voluptuousness, "curvaceousness," of feminine sensuality. One might say that Inanna is a red-hot momma, and power in agricultural civilization is rooted in oral dependency and who can satisfy it (whether male or female). Not without relevance, it seems to me, is the fact that at some point around 2500 B.C., Inanna's "duties" were enlarged: in addition to being the goddess of love, she also became the goddess of war. Civilization really *is* all of a piece![33]

Religious Experience in Pre-Axial Civilizations

There is still the question of the nature of consciousness that prevailed as part of the religious configuration, or SAC, that was represented by festivals such as the Sacred Marriage Rite or in similar rituals that occurred in, say, Egypt. What was the state of mind of the respective populations? Were the onlookers "glazed out," in a state of unitive trance? For the whole structure of these states was based on vertical, sacred/charismatic authority; that is how they functioned. But exactly what did that mean in terms of individual consciousness? Before we move on in time to the "Axial Age" and the mystery religions, we need to consider this question.

What seems to be the case for the Egyptians, writes the German scholar Erik Hornung, is that they "evidently never experience a longing for union with the deity. They keep their distance from the gods."[34] Unlike the Greeks, the Egyptians did not see their gods as inhabiting an immortal, transcendent world; for them, "departure into the eternal would be a departure into nonexistence." While it is true that they believed in an afterlife, had an elaborate pantheon of gods and a system of magical practice that permeated nearly every facet of daily life,[35] it is nevertheless the case that the

> Egyptians remain detached and balanced, and avoid . . . abrogating the self by surrendering to an unlimited state of nonexistence in which everything is possible . . . Several writers have stressed quite correctly that no trace of mysticism can be found in ancient Egypt. The Egyptians never succumbed to the temptation to find in the transcendence of the existent release from all imperfection, dissolution of the self, or immersion in and union with the universe. They remained active and often, to us, startlingly matter-of-fact; any sort of ecstasy appears quite alien to their attitudes.

He goes on to say that scarcely any other civilization has been able to integrate the "Nonexistent" into its way of life so perfectly, without falling prey to it. In Egypt, concludes Hornung, "one cannot speak of a true transcendence that would raise a deity above space, time, and fate and extend his being into the realms of the absolute and limitless."[36]

As for Mesopotamia, it was (like Egypt) soaking in exorcism, sympathetic magic, and the like, but this does not tell us much about the real nature of religious life. Mesopotamian religion, says Oppenheim, is not of the revealed variety. A private person could not approach a deity through dreams or visions—an "Axial" development that began to occur (in the form of oracular utterances) late in Mesopotamian history, and then only in peripheral areas (outside Babylonia proper), possibly under Western influence. "Manifestations of religious feelings," writes Oppenheim, "as far as the common man is concerned, were ceremonial and formalized rather than intense and personal." Tension between individual consciousness and society in Mesopotamia was resolved by submerging the former into the latter; the human being was assimilated into the external and objective universe. Thus, concludes Oppenheim, *ecstasis*—direct communion with God—did not have the sort of position that it did in Syria and Palestine. On the fringes, you do get oracular pronouncements ("channeling") from Assyrian prophetesses of the goddess Ishtar (Inanna), a form of religious practice that was deeply alien to the mainstream Mesopotamian attitude. The absence of shamanistic concepts in Mesopotamia, says Oppenheim, is noteworthy.[37]

The issue of the ceremonial and formal is, I think, the key to this, and it meshes well with Jaynes' notion of bicamerality: people on automatic pilot, as it were. Not that there was no self-conscious awareness in Egypt or Mesopotamia: whoever composed the text that has Inanna calling out to Dumuzi, "Plow my vulva!" can hardly have been living in an unconscious fog. But the general atmosphere of these civilizations is one in which the individual is submerged in a larger whole. We do not have the "individual autonomy syndrome" of HGs discussed in chapter 2 (Peter Gardner), or the training for innovative thinking mentioned in chapter 3 (Barry, Child, and Bacon). This is not unitive trance practice but rather a kind of "group mind" that serves as the psychic glue of these civilizations. This is what made the later change in Greek and Hebrew cultures so dramatic, because they broke with this "totality" of the SAC, which they found suffocating. At least in the Jewish case, we have a putatively pastoral or nomadic people effectively saying, "We're outta here." The Exodus was not merely a departure from the Nile valley; it was also a rejection of the ceremonial-formalized-sedentary way of life. "We were slaves to Pharaoh in the land of Egypt," Jews still say every year at the Passover seder; slaves to the world of myth, in other words, of bicameral group mind. Thanks, but no thanks, the Hebrews declared; you can keep your pantheon. We'll bake some *matzoh* and hit the road!

It is for this reason that Rachel Levy, in her classic work, *The Gate of Horn*, comments that the defiance of the Greeks and the Jews was not hurled, in satanic fashion, against the world order. *Their* order was one of destiny and individualism—strong self-conscious awareness. Thus, the Hellenic and Hebrew revolutions, she says, were profoundly creative.[38]

The Axial Age

The term "Axial Age" was coined by the Swiss-German philosopher Karl Jaspers years ago to denote the period and events of the first millennium B.C.[39] During this time, a number of civilizations arose or were transformed along the lines of a sharp vertical split between heaven and earth; what the Israeli sociologist S. N. Eisenstadt calls the "transcendental" and "mundane" orders. This included ancient Israel, Greece, Iran, China, and the cultures of Hinduism and Buddhism. If we extend this backward in time to include the emergence of the mystery cults and the breakdown of bicamerality, and forward in time to include Islam, the Axial Age is really something like 1800 B.C. to 700 A.D., about twenty-five-hundred years. Yet the most turbulent period, as Jaspers said, does remain the one thousand years preceding the birth of Christ.

The idea, then, is that of an ordinary or secular world "down here," and a perfect or divine world "up there." As this is vertical sacrality, the trademark of the Neolithic, it would seem that nothing new is really going on. This is the SAC of Egypt, Mesopotamia, and the other early states and chiefdoms, no? Well, say Jaspers, Eisenstadt, and other Axial scholars, not quite. In the pre-Axial civilizations, they maintain, the two orders of the mundane and the supernatural are homologous. That is to say, the higher world is structured symbolically along the same lines as the lower one. The two realms are parallel and even embedded in one another. Thus, the gods in these cultures quarrel, fight, experience jealousy, deceive each other, go hungry, and even die, as we do here on earth. The powers of the gods were limited. In Egypt, Osiris was slain, and Ra grew decrepit (he was even tormented by a snake bite).[40] In the Axial civilizations, something else has happened. If nothing else, the upper world has become transcendent; it is the realm of eternity, and the gods live forever.

Once this disjunction got institutionalized, the question arose of how to bridge the gap between the two worlds; and with this came the problem of salvation. Again, note the difference from the pre-Axial mentality. In the pre-Axial civilizations, there was no salvation as such—redemption of the soul, continuity of the spirit, and so on. The focus was on *physical* continuity into the next world, which is why, for example, Egyptians embalmed the dead and buried them with food (especially bread and beer), toilet articles, and weapons.[41] In the mystery cults of ancient Greece, or the oracular prophecy of late Mesopotamia, something else is going on. Continuity can (and should) occur, but it is now based on the reconstruction of the personality. We are at the edge of Gnosticism here: the mundane world is regarded as inferior, and human beings, via certain kinds of occult practices, can become like gods. And by the process of such reconstruction, the mundane world can perhaps be remade on the basis of the transcendent one. This shows up in Plato and in Jung and is the "ascent" tradition of later agricultural civilization. The Goddess is not merely a ritual or ceremonial figure any more; she is "Diotima" (in Plato's *Dialogues*), or the Great Mother archetype, into which consciousness is dissolved and with whom fusion of psyche and divine is made possible. Julian Jaynes comments on this era:

> The collective cognitive imperative becomes weaker (that is, the general population tends towards skepticism about the archaic authorization), [and] we find a rising emphasis on and complication of the [trance] induction procedures, as well as the trance state itself becoming more profound.[42]

What starts to occur now is ascent experience and oracular prophecy, which show up as early as 1800 B.C. at Mari, in Assyria (modern Tell Hariri, in the middle Euphrates area), and continue to gain momentum. Letters in the Mari archives (*Archives royales de Mari*) refer to oracular messages given through a *maḫḫûm*, or "frenzied person." They report that someone prophesied or was in an ecstatic state (*immaḫû*). In five or six cases, this occurred in a temple context, although noncultic individuals also could obtain divine messages while in ecstasy.[43] However, all of this is very early. It is only with the clear breakdown of bicamerality, well into the Axial Age, that we have unequivocal evidence of organized cult practice of an ecstatic nature. Thus, by the seventh century B.C. we have female prophets, or *raggintu*s (literally, "those who cry out"), "channeling" the voice of the goddess Ishtar—a development that had no place in traditional Mesopotamian life.

Linked to this search for salvation, moreover, was the drive for utopia; the two are part of the same impulse. As a result, the Axial civilizations developed the notion of an Event (e.g., the coming of the Messiah) that would come along and close the gap between the mundane and the transcendent once and for all. In effect, the mundane order will be destroyed; a notion not present in pre-Axial civilizations.

All of this millennnarianism had a lot of proselytizing zeal attached to it and, along with this, an intolerance for other modes of salvation. This intolerance was rooted in the uncertainties generated by the two-world split itself. So you get the emergence of orthodoxies, which in turn generate challenges to themselves, and the challengers are typically as intolerant as the establishment. Axial civilizations share a totalistic view of change; there is always the attempt to remake the world according to the prevailing transcendent vision. For Eisenstadt, then, the Axial Age marks the birth of ideology.[44]

With the exception of desultory references to mysticism and esoteric practice in the Western Axial civilizations, the literature on the Axial Age fails to make the crux of the change explicit: what was going on in the search for salvation and the reconstruction of personality was initiation involving unitive trance practice, the obliteration of personal history by means of the dissolution of consciousness. This apparently occurred in the second millennium in Minoan Crete and was in particular the province of the mystery cults, cults that were clearly tied to agriculture and a goddess figure. As the SAC of the pre-Axial civilizations begins to split into two separate realms, and self-conscious awareness (interiority) begins to dominate the mental arena, unitive trance (fusion with the godhead) steps in to sew the two realms together and to reembed the individual in the cosmic order. If sacred authority provided certainty before, trance practice created an ideological zeal that would tolerate no other versions of truth. The last piece of this puzzle, then, lies in the mystery cults that arose during the Axial Age.

The Mystery Cults

The earliest organized mystery cult was probably the one located at Eleusis, fourteen miles west of Athens. The earliest actual building we have associated with the Eleusinian mysteries dates from the second half of the second millennium; but, in fact, excavations at Eleusis have provided no evidence that the mysteries can actually be dated to the Mycenaean period. Although it might seem logical that Demeter's role as corn goddess would derive from the indigenous religion, most of the evidence suggests *dis*continuity, making the mysteries a much more recent phenomenon. There is, for example, no evidence of Minoan influence; a full one thousand years separate Minoan and Eleusinian artifacts. Mycenaean tablets mention the names of various deities, but Demeter and her daughter Persephone are not among them. And while the mysteries are, as in the older cult practices, directed toward agrarian prosperity, the emphasis eventually shifted to a new goal, namely, giving the initiate a better lot in the afterlife. The innovation of the mysteries was the enactment of a divine drama as the central feature, involving psychic death and rebirth.[45]

In *non*ecstatic terms, however, the ancestry of the mystery cults goes back much further, to the ritual relationship between agriculture and goddess worship, as existed in Minoan and Mycenaean religions, and in Mesopotamia as well. All this is part of the SAC. As Joan Engelsman puts it, "there is a strong agrarian element in the mysteries." At Eleusis, the goddess Demeter is an earth mother figure, celebrated as the giver of grain and the goddess of vegetation. Kore, her daughter, became Persephone, who had to live in the underworld for two-thirds of the year, but she was reunited with her mother for the other four months, during which time crops flourished. Hence, we have a clear association between agricultural rites and the theme of death and resurrection; although, as we shall see, the notion of salvation was added sometime after 650 B.C. In general, the historical pattern of the mysteries is one of original worship of a vegetation deity, onto which was subsequently grafted "the worship of a spirit of intoxication." In either context, however, Demeter was seen as the goddess who bestowed grain as the basis of civilized life. In fact, one disclosure of the Eleusinian mysteries by an initiate was that as part of the sacred rites, he was shown an ear of grain.[46]

Of course, there were a number of mysteries, and in general they were centered around earth goddesses and female deities:[47] Demeter and Kore at Eleusis, a series of goddesses (including Gaia) at Delphi (despite the centrality of Apollo there), Cybele in Phrygia (and later in Rome), and so on. As far as the Eleusinian mysteries go, they involved a procession from Athens to Eleusis and an offering of the first crops of the harvest. The initiate drank the *kykeon*, a soup consisting of meal, water, and mint, and handled certain sacred objects.[48] In

Alexandrian days, a winnowing fan, symbolic of agriculture, was also employed. The agriculture/female connection was almost always in evidence, both before and after the cultic shift to salvation and redemption. Dionysus' mother, for example, was Semele, an ancient Thracian earth goddess, and Plutarch commented that Dionysus and the cult of Demeter embodied the life of nature witnessed by agriculture.[49] Dionysus is described as being followed around by worshipping women, and the instruments of his cult were supposedly his mother's. "The Mother and the Son," writes Jane Harrison, "were together from the beginning."

According to Harrison, the "spirit of intoxication," the *enthousiasmos* that got grafted onto the old vegetation worship, was a missionary faith of Thracian origin. This cult of Dionysus held the belief that through physical intoxication, and later (historically), spiritual ecstasy, a person could be transformed from the human to the divine. Not much later, the Orphic religion added to this the possibility of complete fusion with the godhead, taking Eros and Dionysus as its two divinities.

Much the same thing happened to the Isis cult of Egypt. Isis was a very old goddess, but it was not until about 300 B.C., in the Roman empire, that her worship took the form of a mystery religion. What emerged was a closed society of adherents who celebrated sacred and secret rites, into which one could be initiated to obtain the wisdom made possible by the goddess and to attain redemption and salvation. Apuleius, in *The Golden Ass* (see below), wrote that she had the power to let a person be reborn and attain immortality.[50]

The timing of all this—generally from the seventh century B.C. on—is significant, for it corresponds to Jaynes' notion of the breakdown of bicamerality and to Bruno Snell's assertion (*The Discovery of Mind*) of the discovery of the individual around this time. Walter Burkert thus emphasizes the role of private initiative in the mystery religions, the voluntary decision to undergo a change of personality through the experience of the sacred. One of the few descriptions we have from an Eleusinian initiate is something along the lines of, "I felt like a stranger to myself." In the *Phaedrus*, Plato uses details from the Eleusinian mysteries to create a picture of the soul ascending to heaven and undergoing a purification that allows new powers to enter it. The theme of death and rebirth is a constant one.[51]

Let us take a closer look at the nature of the initiation process. Ecstasy and temporary "insanity" are the crucial features. Edith Weigert-Vorwinkel, in her essay on the Great Mother, points out that the word "fanatic" is derived from the mysteries, inasmuch as the Latin word *fanum* means "sanctuary," the place where the initiation was carried out. Hence, the followers of the Phrygian goddess Cybele (Magna Mater in Rome) were called *fanatici*. Those who wished to become priests in her cult, the Galli or Galloi (Corybantes in Greece), used dance and music to enter ecstatic states. As Lucretius described it (first century B.C.), this was accompanied by self-flagellation. At the peak of their frenzy, the initiated castrated themselves. Their genitals and clothing were then carried into the *fanum*, or inner shrine (also called the "bridal chamber of Cybele"). After that, the Galli wore women's clothing, wandering the countryside, performing ecstatic dances and breaking into prophecy. "To be filled with the Great Mother, to be possessed by her, was the only form of life they desired."[52]

All of this is corroborated by contemporary sources. Plutarch (first century A.D.) gives a description of the cult practice of Isis; Apuleius gives us the fullest description of initiation into her cult, in which ecstasy and fusion with the goddess are clearly implied. After a ten-day fasting period, Lucius, the initiate, says:

> I drew near to the confusion of death, treading the very threshold of Proserpina [i.e., Persephone, Demeter's daughter] . . . At the dead of night, I saw the sun shining brightly. I approached the gods above and the gods below, and worshipped them face to face . . .

A "Hymn to Isis" written during the time of Hadrian (117–138 A.D.) refers to an underground marriage, the "birth of plants," an "unspeakable fire," and "the birth of the little child."[53]

Once again, the timing of this with the "discovery of the individual" is noteworthy. E. O. James writes (*The Cult of the Mother Goddess*) that the Eleusinian mysteries acquired a personal dimension—bliss and immortality for the individual—only after the union of Athens and Eleusis that occurred between 650 and 600 B.C. The mysteries, he says, then "acquired an urban character and a more profound sacramental significance, giving to those who underwent the experience a new philosophy of life that transcended the things of time and space." The original agricultural rites had been transformed into a ritual of death and resurrection, centered in the pledge of immortality.[54]

According to Walter Burkert (*Ancient Mystery Cults*), the mysteries offered a chance to escape from a barren and predictable world, to create a sense of meaning in a banal life, by means of an experience of a great rhythm, in which the individual psyche could be integrated through a large, sympathetic event.[55] No doubt. But what if life were *not* barren and banal? What if the environment were *not* experienced as adverse? What if, in short, one were a hunter-gatherer? Would one then be impelled to die, be reborn, become a hero?

The Axial Age is a desperate one, and we are, effectively, still living within it. Ascent is a recent phenomenon; for the most part, it is rooted in alienation, in not finding this world as enough. In their article "Deprogramming," Thomas Robbins and Dick Anthony argue that spiritual ecstasy is "hostile to mankind's deepest aspirations."[56] This is an intriguing statement, sure to send many spiritual devotees into a fury of ecstatic rage. The interesting thing here is that it is *un*true, in the sense that if your life is barren, perhaps a good dose of "God-realization" is just what you need to glimpse the larger possibilities. To know the possibilities of boundary loss can be a good thing; fusion does contain a certain type of truth, in that the primordial connection to the mother is part of our biological heritage. But the statement is *true* in that (a) human life should not *be* barren, and if it is, something has seriously gone awry, and (b) if we get hooked on ecstasy and heroic "rebirth," there is the likelihood that we shall never get down to the deeper layer of paradox. As I said earlier, it becomes a way of getting trapped in a world view and thus ultimately prevents us from finding the world.

The Axial Way of Life

With the rise of the mystery cults, and the institutionalization of unitive trance, the SAC is taken to its apogee. Apparently, it took a higher degree of sedentism and urbanization to do this, though like Jaynes and Eisenstadt, I have no clear answer as to why such a profound shift occurred. But its preparation goes back, in any case, to the changes of the early Neolithic. Women's political and economic power declines. Birth spacing decreases. Mothering, once a part of female life, now becomes the focus of that life. Multiple mothering and diffuse energy patterns are weakened, and the child basks in the "hallowed presence" of the mother's aura and attention. If it is a male child, he will now get the message that his job is, in some way, to serve his mother and "save" her; to give her, through heroic acts, the life she can lead only vicariously. He will search for charismatic energy everywhere, saying, "This is real." He will (in Mesopotamia) worship Inanna, goddess of sexual love and war combined. War, romantic love, the SAC, and finally unitive trance will all go together, "make sense" on an energetic level. ("Love and War are the same thing," wrote Cervantes in *Don Quixote*.) He will be "steep-gradient," in Philip Slater's characterization, and vertical power structures will come naturally to him. ("It Doesn't Take a Hero," wrote General Norman Schwartzkopf, meaning just the opposite.) The mythic properties of the mother in the nursery that Dinnerstein talks about will, not coincidentally, show up in his goddesses and their mythologies of sexualized mother/son relationships. On a visceral level, goddess cults and initiation rites will ring true for him. At one extreme, literally then and symbolically now, he will castrate himself, wear women's clothing, dissolve into the Great Mother. At the other extreme, he will become a conqueror of men and his own feminine impulses. He will enjoy war and the energetic rush it provides. War, sacrifice, death, charisma, heroism, love, and Arthurian legends—all of this will (strangely) be what life is about. He will extol warriors and the "warrior archetype." He will love women, but he will resent them as well. He will, as Paul Shepard says, remain a permanent adolescent and feel, on some level, brittle, perhaps even a bit haunted.

So this is the link to our previous chapter. The force of the Great Mother image derives from unconscious memories in infancy; this is what makes mothering and issues of gender equality so significant for culture at large. A possessive goddess is quite congruent with an infantile society; and the link with agriculture is, as we noted in chapter 3, one of obedience as a lifestyle. Jaynes had to posit auditory hallucinations as the controlling agent here, but in fact, nothing so exotic is required. If you are trained from infancy into the SAC, you'll do what you're told.[57]

You will also get enchanted by ideologies of various sorts, tend to swallow things whole, and call your beliefs certainties. Existential and psychological certainty will be, on an unconscious level, your number one concern. This is strongly connected to the oral dependency of agricultural society and Great Mother culture. In his book, *Ego, Hunger and Aggression*, the gestalt therapist Fritz Perls introduced the notion of "introjection"—not quite the Freudian version of this, but more along the lines of an infant, who doesn't discriminate and swallows everything whole.[58] This is, in fact, how children get enculturated or learn language. But adulthood involves a healthy balance between suspicion and trust, and balance is not what agricultural civilization or Great Mother worship is about. Consider, then, the accumulated historical sources of "certainty" and ideology in sedentary and urban cultures:

- delayed-return economy and accompanying insecurity
- sacred authority complex; unitive trance
- One-on-one dyadic mothering ("hallowed presence")
- female agricultural deities
- oral dependency
- gender inequality
- search for salvation and rebirth; heroism
- increasing population density and narrow birth spacing
- fear of death
- (etc.)

The result of all this is what Roy Rappaport, referring to social structure, calls "hypercoherence"; but it seems clear enough that this applies to group behavior and individual personality as well.[59] Surely, ideology is a major part of hypercoherence, and paradox in such cultures is a long-lost possibility, a dim memory at best. Hypercoherent societies are rigid: everything is predictable; all the options are foreclosed. As Walter Truett Anderson points out, it takes virtually no time in our culture for an idea to become a religion, and he cites as evidence the latest manifestation of Great Mother worship, namely, James Lovelock's "Gaia" hypothesis, as an example. Anderson says that while the theory does have a real scientific core to it, the popular Gaia bandwagon could care less about such things. Instead, a collection of myths and metaphors of the earth as alive, as a goddess, as having a mind of its own—these "are the turn-ons, and they are what is being transformed into a new *faith*, a kitsch ecotheology, complete with its doctrines and its priests and priestesses."[60] This is Perls' "introjection" to the *n*th degree, the cognitive/emotional process of an infant. As Perls himself put it, "Hunger for mental and emotional food behaves like physical hunger . . . [This structure of impatience] is responsible more than anything else for the excessive stupidity we find in the world."[61] We only think we are thinking; the truth is that we spend most of our time organizing our lives around mental theme parks, going from one "paradigm" to the next and congratulating ourselves on our insight. There's gotta be a better way.

Put it all together, then, and you get a pattern of rigidity in civilization that operates on both a socioeconomic level as well as a psychological or philosophical one. It is all too cloying, and the desire to break out of that shows up in the modern world, for example, in things such as paramilitary organizations and rodeo/rancher culture—which are pathologies of another sort. Historically, the SAC and the totality of urban/sedentary/agricultural life, with the Great Mother thrown in later, provoked a response, an experiment designed, by means of physical movement, to do two very important things: to reject the suffocating totality and ideological "certainty" of agricultural civilization, and to restore paradox to the center of human consciousness. This was the phenomenon of nomadism.

5

THE ZONE OF FLUX

A tent dweller [buffeted(?)] by wind and rain . . .
Dwelling in the mountain . . .
The one who digs up mushrooms at the foot of the
    mountain, who does not know how to bend the knee;
Who eats uncooked meat;
Who in his lifetime does not have a house;
Who on the day of his death will not be buried.

—From "The Marriage of the God Martu,"
Sumerian poem describing the Amorite
nomads, late third millennium B.C.

People wish to be settled; only as far as they are unsettled is there any
hope for them.

—Ralph Waldo Emerson

So it turns out that not everyone is happy with the sedentary life, and
this should come as no great surprise: it's not our genetic heritage.
States, sedentism, and agriculture are all latecomers, apparently forced
upon us by a combination of external circumstances and a latent drive
for power and inequality. Although pastoralism has a relatively long
history and evolves out of the early domestication of animals, it eventually becomes a form of movement, not just a form of food production. As the great Russian authority on nomadic peoples, Anatoly
Khazanov, once put it, "Pastoralism is not only a way of *making a
living*; it is also a *way of living*."[1] And it is a way that takes us back to
our hunter-gatherer roots. In this latter development, which is the
reassertion of movement, we find both the deep rejection of sedentary
life—along with its values—and the attempt to recapture core elements of the lost HG life: egalitarian social relations, self-reliance and
autonomy, paradoxical consciousness, a "nonreligious" way of being,
and the world of immanent brilliance, perpetual surprise.

153

Still, there was no way it could have remained "pure"; nomads are not hunter-gatherers. Too much happened since the Neolithic Revolution, so nomads carry a difficult and complicated baggage of (sometimes) vertical religious belief and (often) war and aggression. All of this muddies the story. The result is that with nomads, we don't get paradox in an unsullied form; some nomadic experience even contradicts it. And yet the nugget of paradox remains and gets passed on as a spiritual legacy, a memory of the "uncertain" life. I call this the "Zone of Flux."

There are four topics I wish to discuss in this chapter, then: (1) the history and evolution of the nomadic phenomenon; (2) its dual character of war and paradox; (3) its values and how they are expressed in social structure and individual personality; and (4) its legacy for today. It is hoped that in this way, we shall get a sense of how nomadism acts as a bridge phenomenon, stretching back to our HG ancestry and forward to a certain type of rare, yet still surviving, spiritual flexibility. Typically, nomads have been regarded by historians as marginal, outside the mainstream of civilization, and in some sense this is true. But the deeper truth is that nomads embody a crucial historical and emotional tension, one that we are still living with today.

The problem, obviously, is how to sort this out. Not merely are nomads, by definition, elusive, but the research on them is elusive, as a number of scholars have pointed out.[2] We have tons of empirical case studies that finally don't tell us what nomadism *is*, generically speaking, and a few attempts at typologies of nomadic behavior (animal husbandry, transhumance, seminomadic pastoralism, etc.) in which the realities of nomadic life are constantly escaping from the established categories. In addition, nomadic studies tend to be dominated by nineteenth-century intellectual frameworks that generate clichéd pictures of nomadic life that we are not yet free of: that pastoral nomadism arose from HG society; that it is (as one German scholar put it) nothing more than *Raubwirtschaft* (theft economy, pillage), the absolute antithesis of sedentary life; that it is entirely, or even primarily, motivated by ecological and economic conditions; and that in cultural or historical terms, it "doesn't make sense" because change is supposedly progressive/developmental, and nomads don't seem to be "going" anywhere. I shall be addressing these issues in the discussion that follows, but before we deal with the history and evolution of the nomadic phenomenon, it will be useful to say a few words about it as a way of living, as Khazanov characterized it; as an expression of values that are deeply felt—by nomads and by sedentary peoples alike.

Nomadism, writes the British archaeologist Stuart Piggott, has a dual character. It is a way of life; it is also—at least since about 1000 B.C. or a bit earlier—a destroyer of other ways of life.[3] It is for this reason that the French philosophers Gilles Deleuze and Félix Guattari subtitled their book on the subject, *The War Machine.*[4] Nomadism is the attempt to pull the rug out from under the fake security of agricultural civilization, but—consciously or unconsciously—in the interest of what it sees as a deeper truth. "They were, those people, a kind of solution," wrote the Greek poet C. P. Cavafy, a sentiment voiced a few decades earlier by Ralph Waldo Emerson (see the epigraph, above).[5] In other words, there has been a haunting undercurrent within sedentary culture that nomads, even though despised as the classic Other, are an answer to the ills of civilization. They are free agents, in short, which is how nomads have tended to view themselves.[6]

The essence of nomadism was captured just a few years ago in a strangely perceptive action film entitled *Point Break*, starring Patrick Swayze and Keanu Reeves (dir. Kathryn Bigelow, 1991). An unlikely candidate for an Oscar, the film nevertheless generates a tremendous amount of tension by pitting two basic ways of life, nomadic and sedentary, against each other. Of course, in Hollywood, as in modern (Neolithic) life, sedentary civilization has to triumph, so the ending is quite predictable: the outlaws and disturbers of our settled way of life—the "bad guys"—lose. But in the course of the tale, the nomadic position, both in its reactive aspect (the war machine) and in its positive aspect (the search for the "point break" that occurs while surfing, what Deleuze and Guattari call "smooth space," and what I have called "paradox") is quite brilliantly elaborated.

The story takes place in Southern California. Every summer, a wave of bank robberies is pulled off by a small band of crooks calling themselves the "Ex-Presidents," named for the rubber masks they wear representing Reagan, Nixon, Carter, and Johnson. They are quite good at it, raiding their targets in ninety seconds flat, never being too greedy, and getting out before the cops can arrive on the scene. Twenty-six robberies, and the FBI doesn't have a clue as to who these men are.

One FBI agent, however, has a theory, based on a few scraps of evidence: these men are surfers. Their goal is not wealth, but a certain lifestyle, which they seek to maintain at the expense of average, law-abiding citizens. Hence, they descend on Los Angeles every summer, surf and rob, and, when Labor Day comes, hit the road. When young Johnny Utah (Keanu Reeves) comes aboard as a new FBI recruit, the plan is hatched for him to learn to surf and, hopefully, penetrate the gang.

It is an arduous process. Learning to surf is not easy, and it is not until the new agent gets it "spiritually" that he is able to ride the crest of a wave. It is only when that moment of paradox comes for him, and he is atop the wave, moving with it, and yet fully aware of himself and his surroundings, that his female surfing coach falls in love with him. The leader of the pack, played by Swayze, goes by the name of "Bodhi" (short for Bodhisattva); and when we first meet him, he is slowly turning on the crest of an immense wave, motionless in the midst of turbulence, completely at ease with the power of the ocean. Nor is Bodhi unaware of the meaning of it all, for he tells Johnny that surfing is not actually about surfing, as such, but about one's relationship to oneself, and to the natural world.

Later on in the film, when it is revealed that he is the leader of the Ex-Presidents, Bodhi delivers a speech to his followers, to the effect that bank robbing is not about money but rather constitutes a political statement, one being made to and about the commuters patiently crawling through traffic jams on the L.A. freeway to get to jobs they hate so that they can pay off the mortgage on a tract home in the suburbs. This is drudgery, says Bodhi, not life. If surfing is the positive pole of nomadism, the pole that would recapture the experience of space or paradox (the point break), then bank robbery is the reactive pole, the one that would stick it to sedentary, landowning society at the very same time that it symbiotically lives off the latter's wealth.

Two other points: unlike most HGs or nomadic peoples, Bodhi increasingly starts pushing the moment of paradox toward a vertical high, unitive trance. In a word, he becomes an "edge junkie," an excitement addict. He keeps talking of the ultimate rush, of riding the waves at Bell's Beach in Australia the following year, which will see a tidal wave such as occurs only once in a half-century. The group also pursues sky diving, which Bodhi describes as a "100 percent adrenalin rush." Finally, they undertake to do one last, superfluous bank robbery, instead of quitting for the season, and go for the big money in the vault. This takes more time than the usual ninety seconds and proves to be their undoing.

The second point is the symbiotic relationship between the nomads and the sedentists—something that *is* true to life. We see this not merely in the phenomenon of the nomads raiding the Establishment, living off the fat of the land, but also in the subtle inability of Swayze and Reeves to bump each other off when they have the chance. These two somehow need each other, in more than just an economic sense. When Johnny finally catches up with Bodhi on Bell's Beach, slapping handcuffs on him, the latter tells him he'd rather die than be caged, and Johnny consents to let him go to his death, riding the wave of the half-century.

The Philosophy of Nomadism

Nomadism is the attempt to restore paradox to the center of human consciousness, a perception that got lost in the shift to a sedentary way of life. It recognizes that sedentary civilization cripples us emotionally, in consequence of the damage it does in social, psychological, and even physiological terms, and nomadism seeks the wholeness and integrity that we had prior to the constellation of narcissism and dependency fostered by political hierarchy and the sacred authority complex. It is an attempt to "reterritorialize on deterritorialization," as Deleuze and Guattari put it, to attack the rigid organization of agricultural civilization and expose its alleged security as an Ozymandian facade. The goal is to smash "the system" in favor of a deeper, nonmanufactured security, which is rooted in movement and is part of our genetic memory. Since the system is already in place, however, the nomad cannot, like the HG, simply be oblivious to it; rather, he must reveal the phoniness of the civilized project at the same time that he draws his living from it. ("Raids are our agriculture," as one Bedouin proverb has it.) In contrast to dependency and the hierarchical law of the *polis*, nomadism displays auto-nomy, self-rule, the distributive law of the pasture—*nomos*, in Greek. From *nomos* we also get the word "nemesis," divine justice or retribution. Nomads are the nemesis of sedentary civilization.

For the state, on the other hand, nothing must be vagabond, nothing must be allowed just to follow the natural meandering of things.[7] It seeks to fix everything by means of categories, not to follow the intrinsic evolution of a phenomenon, its intuitive conditions. Nomadic thought, conversely, dwells in the midregions, the grasslands and the steppes. Its function is to *destroy* images (iconoclastic). The model is that of a tribe in the desert, of relays and intermezzos, rather than that of establishing a universal subject. In the nomadic mind, the tent is not tied to a territory but to an itinerary. Points are reached only to be left behind. The road to truth is always under construction; the going is the goal. We are back to the impermanence of the Pont Mirabeau and the eternality of the transient kiss. Life is dictated by content rather than form, and it is partly for this reason that metallurgy, especially the working of gold, was raised to a high art by nomadic peoples, in what Bruce Chatwin calls the snapping "animal

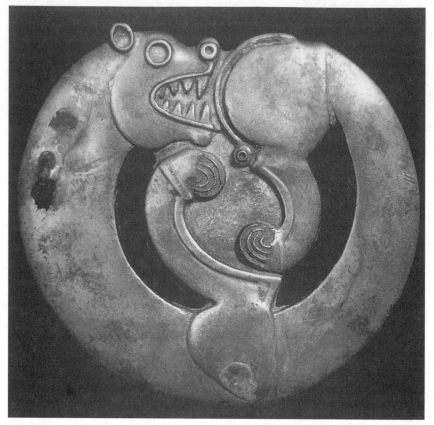

Figure 16. Scythian Ornament from Horse's Harness, Siberia. From V. N. Basilov (ed.), *Nomads of Eurasia.*

style" of the Scythians and Sarmatians,[8] with their jewelry that to this day crackles with compressed energy (Figure 16). Such pieces are illustrations of pure mobility; they flash in the light. As in Galway Kinnell's comment on the lovers' kiss, the message is "here, *here* is the world . . ."

I shall return to the philosophy of nomadism at the end of this chapter. What we need to consider now is how nomadic pastoralism came about in the first place.

The Evolution of Nomadic Pastoralism

As the anthropologist Philip Salzman defines it, pastoral nomadism is "a way of life at least partially based upon movement of people in response to the needs of their herds and flocks." Khazanov's definition is perhaps a bit more precise: "a distinct form of food-producing economy in which extensive mobile pastoralism is the predominant activity, and in which the majority of the population is drawn into periodic pastoral migrations." We can see from this how it might be logical to think that nomadism evolved out of hunting and gathering. Both nomads and HGs are, by definition, mobile; and HGs had already tamed the dog by something like 12,500 B.C. Taming, however, is not equivalent to domestication, which involves stock breeding, that is, regular reproduction; and this is something HGs did *not* do. For domestication requires sedentism and plant cultivation, in order to have vegetal products for fodder, which is stored. Put another way, nomads are food *producers* (delayed-return economy), HGs food *extractors* (immediate-return economy). The domestication process, in other words, was initiated by incipient cultivators engaged in sedentism and storage, which is a prerequisite for stock breeding.[9]

As far as we know, this is the general pattern. In the Near East, for example, farming preceded the domestication of goats and sheep (circa 6500 B.C.) by one thousand to fifteen hundred years.[10] The earliest appearance of cereal cultivation occurs in the ninth to eighth millennium B.C. in places such as Mureybet and Jericho; pastoral sites occur in northern Arabia and Africa about a thousand years later. In general, our best dating for the domestication of sheep and goats in Mesopotamia and nearby areas, based on the available archaeological evidence, is the seventh millennium, following cereal agriculture and settled village life. Pastoral nomadism, in short, has a Neolithic basis; it arises out of a mixed farming economy. The evidence we have suggests that the herding of animals existed in nearly every village in the Near East from the seventh millennium on, and that Semitic pastoralists appeared in the steppe and desert areas of Mesopotamia by 6000 B.C.[11] *Why* this occurred, we shall never know, beyond the likely possibility that it was a way of filling an available ecological niche; a mode of economic diversification, in short.

Was this really nomadism? Granted that the progression looks something like this,[12]

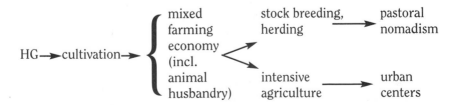

it is not entirely clear at what point we are talking about extensive movement, regular migratory patterns. This is where the attempt to establish a typology of nomadism becomes important, because there is movement and there is movement. Some forms of pastoralism remain, to this day, "agricultural supplements"; they are just part of settled village life and can hardly be characterized as an ideological rejection of it. Site data show that pastoral people were in the area of present-day Iran by 6200 B.C., for example, but that the degree of symbiosis between them and cultivators was so high as to form a single cultural and economic system.[13] Pastoralism becomes nomadic only when continuous settlement becomes impossible; in this sense, transhumance (discussed below) doesn't really qualify, although it is an essential intermediate step.

Part of the problem in trying to construct a history or typology of nomadism is the familiar error of projecting modern images onto the past. In the popular imagination, the typical nomad is a warrior, someone like Genghis Khan, for example. But the "Mongol hordes" of the Asian steppes date from the thirteenth century A.D., and this kind of nomadic empire is radically exceptional anyway. Almost by definition, nomads do not form states, and when they do, the states are highly unstable.[14] Khazanov himself is a bit of a purist, identifying "pure nomadism" as the mounted horse/warrior variety of the first millennium B.C. and after. It is only around this time, or just a bit before, that horse and camel riding start to occur with any degree of regularity. So we have to be careful about projecting the image of warrior states onto an age that was characterized by animal husbandry in villages and (later) very tentative experiments with seminomadic pastoralism. Even if we can agree that pastoral nomadism enters a radically different phase around 1000 B.C., there is still the issue of movement and seasonal migration as representing (millennia earlier) a new aspect of Neolithic life. It may not have been particularly dramatic, but it obviously had to start somewhere, and these are the terms on which we have to understand it.

Khazanov's typology, in any case, involves three "developmental" phases (which nevertheless continue to coexist even today) prior to the appearance of the more dramatic, horsemen-of-the-steppes variety: transhumance, or herdsman husbandry; semisedentary pastoralism; and seminomadic pastoralism.[15] His approach is to evaluate the degree of emphasis on agriculture in each case. With "pure" nomadism, for example, we have an absence of farming activity, and a major part of the motivation for raiding or trading is the acquisition of grain and other agricultural products. With seminomadic pastoralism, which is much more common, agriculture exists in a supplementary capacity. In one variant of this, the same groups in society are engaged in both farming and herding; in another, there are groups occupied with agriculture and others occupied primarily with stock breeding. And between pure pastoralism and the seminomadic variety, says Khazanov, there are many transitional forms.

In the case of semisedentary pastoralism, agriculture really is the economic base. Migrations are much shorter, and there may be small pastoral subgroups. With transhumance—the earliest date for which we have being circa 3500 B.C.—the majority of the population lives a sedentary life, and a subgroup of herdsmen maintains the livestock at a distance from the town or village. This is usually a "vertical" displacement: in *yaylag* pastoralism, as it is called in Russian, the livestock are kept in mountain pastures for part of the year and then moved down at another time. Finally, with straightforward sedentary animal husbandry, we are really talking about farming, with the keeping of a few animals thrown in as an economic supplement. No movement is involved.

In historical terms, the picture is thus one of plant domestication followed by animal domestication, with the subsequent slow addition of movement and herding: animal husbandry, transhumance, semisedentary pastoralism, and so on, until one gets a discontinuous jump to mounted horse riders on the Eurasian steppes. This is not to deny the very real antagonism between nomads and settlers, but only to note that nomadism didn't *begin* in an oppositional way (as far as we can determine), and it continued to have a symbiotic relationship with sedentary society into the twentieth century. We also have to keep in mind that, allowing for the use of donkeys as pack animals, the major part of nomadic history— even including raiding—occurred *on foot*. Since it is movement per se that I am dealing with in this book, to restrict nomadism to the Scythian or Mongol variety would be far too narrow. Thus Khazanov would exclude the Amorites who beseiged Sumer (see below) from the nomad category, which makes no sense to me. As Roger Cribb argues in *Nomads in Archaeology*, Khazanov's search for a "pure" nomadic society needs to be replaced by the recognition of nomadic tendencies being manifested in varying degrees in a wide range of societies. "Nomadic" and "sedentary" (or "pastoral" and "agricultural") are perhaps best conceived of as ideal types; the lived reality is that of a continuum. We may not, in short, be able to find the precise "origin" of nomadic pastoralism. By definition, it is outside the main line of cultural evolution. It is a highly fluctuating phenomenon, says Cribb, with probably many origins in many places at many times.[16]

This notion of fluctuation, marginality, and overlapping categories is crucial not only to an understanding of nomadism but also to the theme of this entire book. What I am talking about is a frame of mind that breaks with fixed forms without simultaneously establishing itself as another fixed form (i.e., becoming the fixed form that breaks with fixed forms). By the fourteenth century, the Arab historian Ibn Khaldun had already recognized that nomadism was an oscillatory, not a progressive, phenomenon. Nomads, he believed, possessed a group solidarity (*asabiyah*, in Arabic) that enabled them to expand and conquer, but that led to sedentism and "softness," or decadence, whereupon they might be taken over by another nomad group, or a breakaway movement might develop from within their ranks. Social life was thus an oscillation between *badawa*, nomadism/ruralism, and *hadara*, or urbanism. But as Philip Salzman points out, we have a difficult time seeing nomads for what they are because of a nineteenth-century intellectual framework that views change as progressive/irreversible as well as discrete. That is, the notion is that of the crossing of a clear boundary: some quality x (e.g., sedentism) disappears, and another quality y (e.g., nomadism) replaces it. But this neat set of evolutionary stages does not, for the most part, apply to the history of movement. The more typical pattern of that history is one of alternating phases. As Dan Aronson puts it, "Nomads have been settling and desettling themselves repeatedly throughout history."[17]

And the archaeological record bears this out. We find evidence of mixed economies, including some degree of mobile pastoralism, in the early Neolithic in Mesopotamia, that was all part of a mixed subsistence strategy of hunting and herding and horticulture. Mobile pastoral groups become common during the Late Chalcolithic, or Copper Age (after 3000 B.C.), which also sees a coexistence of sedentary village and mobile pastoral camp. The lines may harden as we move from prehistory to history, but the pattern of alternation and crossover remains. Thus, Brian Spooner, in what seems to be a moment of perplexed exasperation, writes: "Nomads and peasants hate and despise each other, and yet we know that nomads become peasants, and peasants become nomads."[18] Go figure.

That being said, let us look a bit more closely at the historical record.

Nomads first emerge into the historical record in Sumerian documents of circa 2600 B.C. as "Martu," or "Amurrum" in the Akkadian language. Hence the name *Amorites,* a Semitic people whose homeland was the northern Syrian desert, west of the mid-Euphrates area. They put constant pressure on the cities of Mesopotamia, and the literature of this time describes them as beseiging Uruk, and as having ravaged the Sumerian-Akkadian countryside. The portrait in these documents is one of contempt, as the Amorite is referred to as a man without a home or a god ("does not know how to bend the knee"), who eats raw meat, and who will not be buried when he dies. Texts refer to sheepherders, "the Martu, [a] people of raiders, with animal instincts, like wolves." "The description of the Amorites given in the literary sources," writes the Italian scholar Giorgio Buccellati, "shows both contempt and fear; the year[ly] [entries] give a hint of how unremitting was the threat of nomads at the frontiers." References to war or battles with the Amorites also occur in these texts, and circa 2250 B.C. they were (for a time) defeated by a punitive expedition conducted against them by the armies of Akkad, for having engaged in raiding. Around 2050 B.C., the king of Ur began building fortifications to protect Mesopotamian cities, and letters from this time refer to an "Amorite wall," which was completed circa 2035 B.C. We also have lists of booty taken from the Amorites by the kings of Ur. But at some point around 2023 B.C., the nomads overran the wall. This was the beginning of the end of the Third Dynasty of Ur; although, given the internal divisions of that kingdom, nomadic invasions can hardly be held solely responsible for it.[19]

So the very first mention of nomads in the historical documents would seem to verify the traditional picture of invading hordes, even though the previous archaeological evidence speaks for coexistence and symbiosis. Which version should we believe?

The answer is that war and raiding certainly occurred, but this is not the major part of the story. Rather, they were part of a much larger pattern of infiltration and assimilation that is especially typical of the Middle East and that speaks more accurately to the complexity of nomadic/sedentary relations. Following the lead of the great scholar of China and Mongolia, Owen Lattimore, Michael Rowton refers to a system of "enclosed nomadism" that involves a "dimorphic structure" of intratribal relations and also tribal/state relations. Lattimore saw nomadic/sedentary relations along the Chinese frontier as one of very sharp boundaries (a position he was forced to modify later on), whereas the situation in the region of western Asia was a lot more fluid. Pastoral land in this part of the world was often encircled by urban settlement, with grazing areas sometimes located in the sedentary zone. Seasonal migration necessitated close interaction between tribe and state. For example, in Mesopotamia the steppe area is arid during the summer, and sheep have to be brought into the sedentary zone, a situation latent with potential conflicts.[20]

All of this was present in the region around Mari (briefly referred to in chapter 4), the westernmost outpost of Sumerian civilization and for long time the center of Amorite culture. The term for the Martu in the Mari archives is not quite "nomad," and it is significant that the Sumerian and Akkadian languages do not in fact have such a word. The word used is *nawûm*, "migratory group," which can also mean "pasture" or "encampment." The ambiguity of the language here reflects the fact that in an enclosed, dimorphic situation, the same tribe typically will have a nomadic "wing" and a sedentary one. Also suggestive is the fact that the Akkadian word *alu*, "city," is closely related to the Hebrew *ohel*, "tent." All the evidence suggests that Mari nomadism was symbiotic: between nomadic and sedentary wings of the tribe, and between tribe and state. So although the conflict was real, so was mutual need. In fact, in the story "The Marriage of the God Martu," quoted in the epigraph to this chapter, Martu, the Amorite "barbarian" god, winds up marrying the daughter of a Mesopotamian townsman![21]

Contacts between sedentary Mesopotamians and the Martu thus run the spectrum from full-blown war to peaceful coexistence; and this, not merely hostility, is the overall pattern. But it goes even further than this, as the "Marriage of Martu" implies. Plainly put, the Martu "conquered" Mesopotamia more by love than by war. The process of infiltration went on for over six hundred years. They became townspeople, engaging in farming, leather work, and metallurgy, being reknowned as bronze workers. If they remained nomadic, it was probably in a transhumant sense, and they are described in some administrative texts as suppliers of sheep and goats. In Sumer, they increasingly appear as assimilated residents, especially after 2000 B.C. Eventually, the texts stop referring to them as Martu at all; we know their identity only by means of their characteristic Amorite names. They just became part of Babylonian society, often drifting to cities to find work. Even before this, the fear and hostility that Sumerians felt toward them did not impair the position of those Amorites who lived within the sedentary Babylonian world. They held administrative positions, pursued professional careers, and intermarried with the Sumerian population. A few even became royal envoys, and in one remarkable case an apparent Amorite became the king of Larsa, a Sumerian state.[22]

All of this is not to diminish the "war machine" aspect of pastoral nomadism. Dimorphism means complicated forms of social relations, of which assimilation is one pole, war the other. On the ideological level especially, we do not lack for evidence, in a generic sense, of deep rivalry and cultural contempt between nomadic and sedentary ways of life. Ibn Khaldun saw *badawa* and *hadara* as implacably opposed: "All the customary activities of the Bedouin," he wrote, "lead to wandering and movement. This is the antithesis and negation of stationariness, which produces civilization."[23]

"In the eyes of nomads," writes Khazanov, "an agriculturalist is a slave because he is tied to one place and is enslaved by his own arduous labour." Their deepest value is freedom, which is underwritten by movement; on this view, to stay in any one place would be little better than imprisonment. As for sedentists, they have been peculiarly obsessed with getting nomads to *stop* moving. In 2325 B.C., the Egyptian pharaoh Pepi I directed a local governor to round up the nomads of the Eastern Desert, and in the second century B.C. the Numidian king Masananes instituted a policy of compulsory sedentization in North Africa—a policy that was continued by the Romans. The attitudes of modern states are not very different.[24]

It is not, then, merely raiding that is the source of sedentary animosity toward nomads; on a deeper level, it is movement itself. Nomads are elusive, and it is precisely this quality of not being pin-down-able that, says I. M. Lewis, many nomads like to flaunt. Lewis notes that they "regularly make a defiant parade of all those attributes which they know are most calculated to annoy their sedentary neighbours and rulers." To those neighbors, the nomads appear completely irrational, even an expression of evil, the "hosts of Gog and Magog," in the words of the Bible ("locusts" is another favorite appellation). To the nomads—as in the movie *Point Break*—village or urban dwellers are docile drudges who have sold their souls for an illusory stability.[25]

It is necessary to underscore this so as to avoid what I regard as a common anthropological mistake (and one not made by Owen Lattimore), that the nomadic phenomenon is governed for the most part by economic considerations. Ideology is no less important, and nomads often wear it like a badge, as do sedentists. Thus, the Chinese classified the nomads on their borders as "raw" or "cooked" depending on how much they had been influenced by Chinese civilization. Han dynasty officials (second century B.C.) refer to nomads at one point as "beasts to be pastured, not as members of the human race." Among sedentists, there is the belief, says Thomas Barfield, that movement itself is pathological and that "civilized life is only possible with a fixed address and a respect for bureaucratic boundaries." ("They have no respect for the laws of the palace!" scream the writings of an Egyptian scribe, late second millennium B.C.) Even their tents, Barfield adds, are an irritant, for they are symbolic of the ability to move at will, to throw off unwanted constraints. As we have seen in the case of HGs vs. agriculturalists, mobility (or lack thereof) affects the very structure of human personality and cognition; nomads and sedentists live in differently perceived environments. "The tradition of the camp-fire," wrote the Jewish philosopher Martin Buber, "faces that of the pyramid." It is a compelling image.[26]

As in the case of HGs, the great differences between moving and stationary peoples shows up in a variety of contexts: religion, personality, and social structure. Following Buber, we might say that if there is such a thing as "pyramid" religion, personality, social structure, we can also identify a "campfire" religion, personality, and social structure. Before we can talk about the evolution of nomadic society into the war machine, it is necessary to say a few words about these three aspects of nomadic culture. I have argued that sedentism and the desire for certainty help to generate the SAC that is so central to civilization, whereas HGs have a more horizontal experience of the presence of the natural world. Is this true of nomadic peoples as well?

Nomadic Religion

As already indicated, in a Neolithic context, things get compromised. The war machine syndrome and heavy interaction with sedentary society have produced vertical religious structures in many nomadic cultures, so it is difficult to speak of them as unsullied bearers of paradox. Yet the latter still exists, along with other patterns "inherited" from HGs, so it is nevertheless still possible to speak of many nomads as having a spiritual experience of the world that is horizontal rather than vertical and ritualistic. The Norwegian anthropologist Fredrik Barth, in a classic study entitled *Nomads of South Persia*, claimed that for the Basseri nomads of Iran, pastoral migration *was* their religious rite. What I would like to suggest (following Bruce Chatwin) is a bit different: in the case of such nomads, as with HGs, it is movement that makes religious ritual superfluous. Movement across the landscape is such a vivid, immediate experience that the need for anything more complicated than paradox is largely obviated. To see this more clearly, it will be helpful to summarize Barth's conclusions and observations, along with the comments on his research by the eminent British anthropologist Mary Douglas. For in her reflections on Barth, Douglas goes to the heart of the paradoxical phenomenon and the ultimate security of needing no mirroring, no self-representation, in order to feel at home in the world.[27]

Figure 17. Encampment of Basseri Nomads, Iran. From Fredrik Barth, *Nomads of South Persia.*

Barth lived with the Basseri nomads of Iran from 1957 through 1958. These are tent-dwelling pastoralists (Figure 17) who are politically centralized under a chief. Officially, the Basseri are Shiite Moslems, but as Barth was to discover, this religious affiliation doesn't amount to very much. They are, Barth learned, "generally uninterested in religion." They have very few ritual activities, observe no communal prayer, and tend to ignore Islamic feast days. Even Ramadan attracts very few participants. But being a tribal people, reasoned Barth, they *must* be religious; so what is their ritual?

Barth concluded that migration was "the central rite of nomadic society." In the case of the Basseri, he said, they were heavily invested, emotionally speaking, in the annual spring migration. The search for pasture was of secondary importance to the symbolism of this event, which revolved around spatial mobility, the freedom to migrate. Barth noticed that in the course of the migration, tension and excitement built progressively; and when he and the tribe came over the last pass and saw the mountains toward which they had been heading, all of the women spontaneously broke out in song. We are confused, said Barth, if we think that an economic activity cannot also be a religious one. The response of the tribe here was not to the utilitarian aspects of the event, but to "the movement and its dramatic form."

Now Mary Douglas' discussion of this, in her book *Natural Symbols*, is much wider than that of ritual nomadic migration, and bears directly on our previous discussion of "religion" among Paleolithic cave painters and the like (see above, epigraph to chapter 1). It is, in particular, about as far from the arguments of writers such as Jung and Eliade as one can get. Douglas argues that a situation in which people are not constrained by group loyalties, but only by rules of reciprocal transaction, leads them to avoid framing reality in transcendent terms; to not separate mind from matter, revering one and despising the other. Their outlook is really secular; and we make a mistake, she says, if we associate the latter term with science and modernity alone. Anthropologists such as Barth—and he is clearly a good one—tend to get confused by the existence of secular tribal cultures, which violate the anthropological "canon." When an anthropologist meets an irreligious tribe, says Douglas, he or she typically tries to squeeze the data harder. So in order to argue that the Basseri really *were* religious, Barth convinced himself that the annual migration was endowed with symbolic meaning, that it conceptualized space and time. But suppose this were not the case at all? Suppose the "meaning" of the migration were just . . . the migration?

With this we come to the heart of the matter about paradox and the SAC, which I have been arguing with respect to HGs, whether in twentieth-century Zaire or at Lascaux, and which I think also can be said for a number of nomadic societies. *"Should not one suppose,"* writes Douglas, *"that a society which does not need to make explicit its representation of itself to itself is a special type of society?"* Indeed; and the same applies to individuals as well. The constant need of human beings in civilization to create ideologies, religious beliefs, political hierarchies, and the like, investing these with meaning ("My name is Ozymandias!") so as to feel mirrored, real, validated, part of some larger, transcendent reality—all of which we commonly regard as healthy—is largely the product of dependency and sedentism and does not (for the most part) appear in societies that value autonomy and mobility. In its most recent historical manifestation, the need for this kind of self-representation takes the form of millennarian beliefs, expressed in unitive trance. The idea is that matter will be replaced by spirit, by ultimate, undifferentiated goodness. Hence, says Douglas, "the millennialist goes in for frenzies; he welcomes the letting-go experience . . . He seeks bodily ecstasy which, by expressing for him the explosive advent of the new age, reaffirms the value of the doctrine."

Of course, this is the dynamics of Axial civilization; it speaks to the "strain" that exists between the transcendent and the mundane. We commonly think that primitive people were religious or "spiritual," and that civilized people tend to be secular; but with the possible exception of the last few hundred years, this may not be the case. The notion of a progressive decrease in magic, for example, accompanying the rise of civilization, says Douglas, may be an "optical illusion."

Barth's need to squeeze Basseri migrations into a religious framework, his difficulty in grasping the celebration of life *as life*, reminds me of a service I attended some years ago at a very small church, in the Pacific Northwest, to honor the completion of an altar engraving that had been done, on commission, by a Native American artist. The engraving showed two fish in a circular pattern, beautifully carved in wood. Everybody, the artist included, sat for forty-five minutes as the pastor went on and on about the symbolism of the fish, their Jungian and Christian associations, the balance of yin and yang, the integration of male and female principles, etc. etc. When he concluded his sermon, exhausted but flushed with pride from a job well done, he turned to the artist—I'll call him "No Bull"—and asked him to come up to the front and explain his engraving. No Bull did as requested, put his hand on one of the fish, and turned to the audience.

"This here," said No Bull, pointing to the eye of the fish, "is the eye." "And this, this here," he said, indicating the fin, "is the fin." "And this right here," he concluded, tapping the tail, "is the tail." Whereupon No Bull returned to his seat and sat down. The silence in the chapel, as you might imagine, was deafening.

Religion, wrote Bruce Chatwin, is a response to anxiety, and it is at least possible that movement, by eliminating anxiety in a whole number of ways, removes the need for religion as well. The great religions, says Chatwin, arose among settled people who previously had *been* nomads—such as Jews, Arabs, or Zoroastrians—and whose ceremonial is filled with pastoral metaphors, notions of pilgrimage, and so on.[28] But my point is not merely a Marxist (or Freudian) one of religion being an opiate; rather, it involves an issue that Marx would never have imagined: that under conditions of movement, autonomy, and egalitarianism, a perception of the world is present that is both natural and remarkable, a perception that was the norm for most of human existence. It still exists, vestigially, in nomadic people who retain those values; and had Fredrik Barth not been so caught up in a "sednocentric" framework, he would have seen what was right in front of his nose. The Basseri are not trying to make a symbolic statement to the world. What they *do* know how to do is to be paradoxically present in it.

I shall deal with nomadic religious belief in a moment, but first let me briefly review the evidence for the lack of such belief. In the case of the Basseri, we have a headman structure, politically speaking, without a corresponding structure of unitive trance practice or the SAC. Khazanov's own comprehensive survey led him to conclude that this is more the rule than the exception, that while sedentary chiefdoms tend to have a theocratic form of government, corresponding nomadic polities do not. Khazanov adds that many field workers have commented that the Bedouin only maintain the appearance of Islamic observance; it's not where their hearts are. In the late eighteenth century, a French traveler (C.-F. Volney) wrote of them that "they are so lacking in religious rigour, so slack in the devotions, that in general they are regarded as infidels, knowing neither the law nor the prophets." Joseph Hobbs, in his study of Egyptian Bedouin, maintains that the value system of the Ma'aza tribe with whom he lived is grounded in immanent, material practice. They take pride, he says, in the "lightness" of their life, as opposed to the life of settlers. In just a few minutes, a Ma'aza family can break camp and pack everything they own on a single camel. Their ideological commitment is to having few belongings and great mobility. Walter Goldschmidt similarly observes that pastoral ceremonial life is meager and that ritual, gods, and spirits are more typical of horticulturalists.[29]

However, there is a great deal of evidence for just the opposite, for deep religious belief among nomads, although there is no way to know how much of this has been influenced by their own agricultural practice and their involvement with sedentary societies. So the evidence comes off as a mixed bag. A study by Gerhard and Jean Lenski, for example (*Human Societies*), found that herding economies could be correlated with the belief in a single, moralistic sky god; but the data base was from agrarian societies that had varying percentages of their subsistence derived from pastoralism.[30] According to Khazanov, Genghis Khan introduced to the Mongols the notion of a supreme divine power, which he borrowed from sedentary societies; but Khazanov adds that the Scythians certainly had such a concept and that it is a characteristic notion of nomadic states of the Eurasian steppes. David Morgan (*The Mongols*) points to the practice of shamanism among these people, but he questions what it really amounted to. "Religious belief as such," he says, "seems to have set rather lightly on the Mongols" because they generally adopted the religions of their conquered subjects, and had so great a policy of religious tolerance that the eighteenth-century British historian Edward Gibbon compared their religious laws to the writings of John Locke(!). But this, says Morgan, is an exaggeration; the real situation was more one of religious indifference than one of religious tolerance. In an interesting comparison of Mohammed and Genghis Khan, Khazanov points out that although the Mongols had the belief that charismatic leaders were in contact with a supreme god, known as Tengri, they had (unlike the Moslems) no interest in a universal religion or claims on an ultimate "truth." He adds that the Mongols were purely nomadic, whereas the Bedouin were linked with sedentists, and that Mohammed himself preached against the nomadic way of life. In general, says Khazanov, nomadic society had a low level of tension between the transcendental and the mundane orders. Mongol shamanism, adds Morgan, was purely practical.[31]

The issue of practical versus ecstatic shamanism is an interesting one, and the case of the Scythians, who had a whole pantheon of gods, is instructive here. Herodotus wrote that "the Greek custom of indulging in Dionysiac orgies is, in Scythian eyes, a shameful thing; and no Scythian can see sense in imagining a god who drives people out of their wits." He went on to recount the story of Scylas, a son of the Scythian king Ariapithes, who got himself initiated into a Dionysian cult and was subsequently beheaded by his own people for this. Similarly, the Scythian philosopher Anacharsis went to Athens in 590 B.C. and was initiated into the Eleusinian mysteries. Upon returning home, he was killed by his brother when the latter caught him practicing the cult of Cybele. We can conclude from this that ecstatic fusion with the godhead did not have much popular support among these nomadic people (although the case of the Aryans, discussed below, would lead to a very different conclusion).[32]

Whether from sedentary influence or not, there is good evidence for vertical gods and the SAC being present among many nomads. The Nuer and the Dinka of the Sudan have no eschatology or magical practice, but their religion is one of pastoral monotheism. I. M. Lewis, who did fieldwork in Somaliland from 1955 through 1957, found that the northern pastoral Somali, who have no chiefs or central political authority, are devout Moslems and that Islam permeates their culture. In general, there are wide variations in the degrees of "orthodoxy" among Islamic nomads, and the same can probably be said of nomads in general.[33]

What is the source of this variation? As we shall see below, egalitarian social structure among nomads is greatly compromised by their contact with sedentary society, and it is very likely that religion is similarly influenced. But a big factor, apparently, is the degree of social stress. Richard Tapper, who lived with the Shahsevan nomads of northwestern Iran, found that unlike the Basseri, they are deeply involved in Shiite Moslem rituals. The celebration known as Moharram, which includes a near-ecstatic ritual known as *rowzäxani*, is extremely important to them. But when Tapper looked more closely, the reason for the differences with the Basseri became clear. For one thing, a lot of government pressure had been brought to bear on this tribe, whose structure subsequently disintegrated and whose pasture estates had fragmented into individual holdings. Conflicts over grazing rights and political authority had become so bad that the community was constantly in danger of splitting. Whereas the Basseri have great flexibility of organization and use fission and fusion to deal with structural conflicts, this option is apparently not available to their Shiite counterparts in the north. So while the Basseri ignore the Moharram celebration, the Shahsevan observe it with great enthusiasm. It brings them together, reaffirms group solidarity and the authority of the chief—for a while. It serves to keep oppositions within the tribe from developing into full-blown factions. By way of contrast, Tapper refers to a study that was made of the Al-Murrah Bedouin, which showed that the primary interest of the latter was in independence rather than social solidarity, so they had little interest in big celebrations to bring everybody together.[34]

This matter of valuation of independence versus social solidarity or conformity brings me to the issue of personality structure among nomadic peoples. We saw, in the case of HGs, the existence of an "individual autonomy syndrome" (Peter Gardner) and the correlation of child-rearing practices with independence among HGs, obedience among agriculturalists (Barry, Child, and Bacon). Studies of the nomadic personality produce, perhaps unsurprisingly, similar results, which also have implications for paradox and alertness, what we briefly referred to in chapter 1 as "field independence." Let me, then, say a few words about these findings.

The Nomadic Personality

One of the most comprehensive studies of the nomadic personality was the Culture and Ecology Project, directed by Walter Goldschmidt of UCLA and carried out by Robert Edgerton from 1961 through 1962. This involved interviews with four East African peoples: Sebei, Pokot,

Hehe, and Kamba. In all four cases, the groups had agricultural and nomadic pastoral "wings," making for a total of eight groups in all, more than five hundred people. Goldschmidt and his associates administered a variety of psychological tests, including the Rorschach. What showed up was a clear difference of personality structure not along ethnic lines, but rather along ones of subsistence. That is, the farmers of all four groups had similar values, which differed sharply from the pastoralists in all four groups (who were, in turn, similar to each other). But, clearly, the key difference between the two sets was the availability or nonavailability of movement. To summarize briefly, the pastoralists expressed anger and other emotions directly, whereas farmers stuffed it. The farmers hated others, including figures in authority; pastoralists did not harbor hostilities, and they respected authority, although this latter characteristic was perhaps more ideal than real, inasmuch as they relied heavily on the option of fission and fusion. Pastoralists' networks of interdependence were not person-specific; they saw no need to maintain relations with those they disliked. Fear of poverty, jealousy of wealth, and desire for friends were dominant in the agrarian psyche; the pastoralists prized independence and self-reliance above everything else (the correlation between this and pastoralism was 92 percent).[35]

All of this tallies very well with the farmer versus HG study of Barry, Child, and Bacon, which found that independence and innovation were characteristic of HGs, while conformity and obedience were characteristic of agriculturalists; it also corresponds to John Berry's study of Temne rice farmers versus Baffin Island Eskimo, which showed great differences with respect to peer pressure (see above, chapter 3). We need not stop there, however; the whole thing can be taken into the realm of perception and cognition—the mental structuring of the world itself—which also can be applied to HG populations and which has obvious implications for the question of paradox and alertness. As the anthropologist Joseph Berland explains it, "field independence" (or f/i) is the tendency to see parts of a perceptual field discretely, as separate from the whole, whereas field dependence (f/d) is a holistic perception, in which parts of a field are seen as merged with the whole. The former is especially valued in HG and nomadic societies, for survival often depends on being able to see things quickly and at a great distance. However, holistic perception is more adaptive in sedentary society, where group pressure and conformity serve to make these societies "work." And, in fact, Berland reports that cross-cultural studies clearly demonstrate that a high degree of f/i correlates well with the greater individual autonomy that is characteristic of more egalitarian societies, while f/d shows up more typically in societies that are hierarchical in nature. Again, the key variable here is mobility: high mobility goes with f/i, low mobility with f/d. Of course, in some activities, such as distributing food among an HG band, it is f/d skills that are adaptive, so we can see that context is always going to be a factor. Nevertheless, HG and nomadic groups are quite markedly at the f/i end of the spectrum.[36]

The nomadic groups studied by Berland (in Pakistan, in the 1970s) are not, as it turns out, pastoralists, but they do have highly mobile lives. These are the Qalandar, who are peripatetic entertainers and animal trainers, and the Kanjar, who are nomadic artisans, dancers, and prostitutes. Berland compared these with two sedentary groups: the Lahoria, urban merchant families, and the Jats, farmers. The result: the Qalandar and Kanjar are significantly more f/i than the Lahoria and the Jats. The usual pattern of socialization also obtains. That is, the Qalandar emphasize individual autonomy, include children in most spheres of adult activity, feed infants on demand, praise their offspring frequently, and so on. Among the Jats, men are more highly valued than women, child-rearing practices emphasize obedience, self-reliance is discouraged, and interdependence is rewarded. All that we would expect, but the difference in cognitive approaches to the world—differentiated vs. holistic—is the most striking outcome of this research. In brief, mobility correlates with alertness to the natural world; and given studies of HGs that demonstrate the same correlation, we can see that this mode of cognition constitutes a bond of continuity between band and nomadic society. The former do not have much of a war machine mentality, but beyond that the value systems and perceptual patterns of the two types of societies are quite similar.[37]

Nomadic Politics

The other point of similarity is that of egalitarian social structure. Again, nomads are compromised by their historical position in the Neolithic, so their egalitarianism is not as direct as that of HGs, but it is instead usually embedded in convoluted structures that are themselves determined by the war machine mentality. However, it does come off quite favorably in comparison with the hierarchies of sedentary agriculturalists. The key terms to understanding nomadic social and political organization are "fluid," "elusive," and "ephemeral," qualities that lie at the heart of nomadic egalitarianism. Nomadic leadership, for example, is temporary; alliances are shifting; and when social stratification or state formation does occur, it is unstable and leaves no lasting mark. There are economic reasons for all of this, such as issues of herding and herd composition, which are constantly changing; but once again, one senses something deeper, a commitment to flux itself.[38]

Thus, the British anthropologist Ernest Gellner writes of the Scythian society of the first millennium B.C. that every man was a shepherd, bard, soldier, and senator. Nomadic society has an aversion to specialization, and political participation is widely diffused. This extends to women as well. Nomadic societies are of course clearly patriarchal, but it is inconvenient to seclude women because the exigencies of daily life require(d) them to have an economic role. Generally speaking, then, nomadic women had and have more power than their sedentary counterparts.[39]

Within nomadic society, a balance is struck between the private (family) ownership of herds and the communal ownership of (or right to) pasture. The former can lead to varying degrees of social differentiation, yet mutual aid is part of the pastoral ethos. Nomadic leaders have no interest in depriving other tribesmen of access to the means of production. Economic inequality, when it does arise, tends to be the result of continuous war and trade; it is not inherent in the internal functioning of the nomadic economy. Centralized accumulation of livestock, says Khazanov, is practically impossible.[40]

Similarly, leaders do not (and did not) form a closed stratum. As in the case of HGs, the role of a nomadic chief can be great in military situations, but he does not retain his position once the conflict is over. Under normal circumstances, the leader wields no coercive power. Furthermore, when stratification appears among agricultural populations, it changes the structure of the society, whereas among nomads, tendencies toward centralization are eventually followed by a reversion to communal organization. Leadership is normally diffuse and decentralized, and oscillation, not "progress," is the rule.[41]

Fluidity of organization permeates nomadic society down to the smallest detail. As in the case of HGs, one has units of a few households, but members do not move or live together permanently. The different families in a nomadic community don't always pasture together; the normal tendency is to break up and regroup. As in the case of HGs, a combination of low population density and high mobility inhibits the development of hierarchy or political centralization.[42]

Nomad political organization is governed by a principle known as "segmentary lineage," which includes the practice of complementary opposition and which amounts to a kind of ordered anarchy.

Basically, local groups are organized in lineages or descent groups, and each of these gets subdivided (segmented) into smaller groups. These then compete with each other and have different degrees of importance in different contexts (economy, religion, government, etc.). Any one group, furthermore, can subdivide in one context and yet retain its corporate identity in another. So we might find a segment being autonomous in one type of situation and merged with other segments in other situations. A famous Bedouin proverb captures the principle of complementary opposition concisely:

> I against my brother
> I and my brother against our cousin
> I, my brother and our cousin against the neighbours
> All of us against the foreigner.[43]

This type of unorganized organization was first described by E. E. Evans-Pritchard for the Nuer of southern Sudan and by Meyer Fortes for the Tallensi of the Gold Coast; but it has since been verified as fairly typical of nomadic peoples in general. I. M. Lewis saw it among the northern pastoral Somali, for example, who have no centralized government and no instituted positions of leadership. The key to their politics, he found, lay in kinship, that is, lines of male ("agnatic") descent. Affiliation, writes Lewis, is highly elastic, and political status rapidly changes with context. Every man has a direct say in governance. He goes on to say that one cannot really speak of "tribes" as such; nothing so stable as that exists in this case. However, lest we start to romanticize the situation, Lewis points out that Somali nomads are heavily engaged in banditry, that governance is characterized by guile and strategy, and that there are considerable variations in wealth within this society.[44]

The final point I wish to make regarding nomadic social structure is one on which virtually all anthropologists and historians agree: nomadic societies develop hierarchy and institutionalized social inequality due to their interactions with sedentary states, not from their own internal dynamics. The *potential* for this is there because some families own more livestock than others; but there are cooperative tendencies within nomadic society—systems of reciprocity and distribution—that act as leveling mechanisms to this. Furthermore, says Khazanov, property differences in themselves are not capable of turning the system into one of stable social stratification. This occurs in cases in which nomads are incorporated into a sedentary state, but no state has ever emerged as a result of the internal development of a nomadic society. The key factor in generating social inequality among nomadic societies, he writes, is that of external links to sedentists. We see this in the case of centralization that developed among Bedouin, and even then, says Khazanov, there was no essential differentiation between aristocratic and ordinary nomads with respect to ownership of key resources. The same thing happened among nomads of North Africa and among the Somali as soon as they got involved in agriculture. The Maasai, who lived near agriculturalists and began raiding them, wound up institutionalizing social inequalities and developing a hereditary priesthood. When agriculture became important to the Nandi nomads, a supreme priest arose in their midst. A study of the Shammar nomads of northern Arabia revealed that in the late nineteenth and early twentieth centuries, interaction with the state consolidated power in the hands of their own *amir*, due to his role as distributor of surplus, which he got from tribute. Philip Salzman also concluded from his own survey of nomadic tribes that incorporation into a state, or even increased dependence on agricultural resources over pastoral ones, broke down the usual leveling mechanisms and put significant power into the hands of the chiefs. And on and on. Plainly put, sustained interaction with sedentists leads to the beginnings of a class situation.[45]

It is also likely that, as in the case of the tribes discussed by Pierre Clastres (above, chapter 2), nomadic peoples are fully aware of what is at stake, especially since their interaction with sedentary agricultural society is normally unavoidable. Akbar Ahmed, who studied nomadic tribes living along the Gomal River in Pakistan in the late 1970s, claims that their nomadism was not motivated by ecological necessity but was "part of a political strategy which expresses explicitly a desire to live freely." To these nomads, the state, which is highly centralized in South Asia, represents power and corruption, and they wish to avoid it at all costs. Migration is less a response to herding needs than a way of slipping between the cracks (political zones). The Gomal nomads are acephalous and egalitarian and pick an *amir* to lead them during migration, after which his leadership ends. All members of the tribe have roughly the same standard of living. The Gomal understand that were they to get enmeshed with the state, all of this would go by the boards.[46] As in the case of HGs, nomads are not "failed sedentists," just waiting for the right moment to settle down. Some do settle, of course, as we have seen, and historically, some have even formed states. The majority, however, see the choice as being one of flux or death. They may not be as "pure" as HGs, but when all is said and done, they (and a handful of surviving HGs) remain the bearers of the paradoxical way of life.

And yet there is a strange twist to this story because, historically speaking, nomadic peoples inadvertently proved to be a major
factor in the creation of the Axial civilizations. I have already suggested that nomadic/sedentary relations took a new turn sometime
after 1500 B.C., when mounted nomadism began to appear on the
Eurasian steppes in the form of the war machine. This was the migration of the Indo-Europeans, and the world hasn't been the same
since. It was at this point that the fluctuating symbiosis of enclosed
nomadism finally broke down, and war became the norm.

The Coming of the Aryans

On Marija Gimbutas' theory of the "goddess culture" of Old Europe,
a date such as 1500 B.C. is hopelessly late. Following the work of Gordon
Childe (*The Aryans*, 1926), which in turn was partly based on the Aryan/
Semitic dichotomy proposed by the German Indologist Max Müller in
the nineteenth century, Gimbutas holds that "kurgan" invasions (briefly
referred to in chapter 4) came in three waves, beginning circa 4500 B.C.
and ending around 2500 B.C. This "traditional" view goes something
like this:
    Horse domestication and the use of wheeled vehicles arose on
the Russian steppes sometime before 4000 B.C., and the horse-drawn
chariot appeared several centuries later. This technology was developed by Aryan people who were patriarchal and warlike. In a series
of three invasions, they overran the peaceful farming communities
to the west and southeast. They spoke a proto-Indo-European language, which was the parent of Sanskrit, Latin, Greek, and their de-
rivatives; and their invasions led to the spread of this language
group across the globe. From Neolithic times, these societies were
divided into priests, warriors, and farmers/herders. Scythians and
other warrior peoples that appeared on the Russian steppes after 900
B.C., speaking an Iranian language, were part of this general process.
Nomadic pastoralism was thus (on this theory), almost from its in-
ception, a war machine. This is how "goddess culture" got destroyed
and the Indo-European languages dispersed.[47]
    What is the evidence for this? Not very good, as it turns out.
Scholars such as the British archaeologist Colin Renfrew, who are
skeptical of the kurgan thesis, point out that the rule of parsimony
in scientific explanation (relying here on archaeological and linguistic evidence) won't allow for such early dates. Thus, for example,
the Irish archaeologist and Gimbutas disciple J. P. Mallory points to
cheek pieces for horses (made from bone and·antler) dating from the

fourth millennium as evidence for horse riding at that time, whereas Renfrew notes that (a) we cannot be sure these really *are* cheek pieces; (b) such pieces do not, in any case, constitute proof of horse *riding*; that is, the horses were more likely used as pack animals or for traction; and (c) even if horses *were* ridden, we have no evidence that they were ridden in armed conflict.[48] Or Mallory argues for the presence of the word *ekwos in the proto-Indo-European language (cf. *equus* in Latin, "equestrian" in English), whereas Renfrew points out that the word did not necessarily mean a *domesticated* horse, and Robert Coleman shows that the word for horse was not limited to the Indo-European languages.[49] I take the trouble to provide the reader with this level of detail because recent research makes it clear that if one sticks to the archaeological and linguistic evidence actually available and eschews wishful extrapolation, the kurgan thesis falls apart. Even scientific studies of genetic drift among Indo-European peoples conducted in the early 1990s have demonstrated that the world of Gimbutas and the early Childe is largely invented.[50] It is also instructive that by 1950 Childe had repudiated his early writings on the Indo-Europeans, while Max Müller, for his part, had blasted the simplistic preoccupation with Aryans that followed in the wake of his work as a "species of lunacy."[51]

What *is* the historical record? As far as developments in mounted nomadism go, the domestication of the horse may have occurred somewhere around 3000 B.C., in (present-day) Russia, but we have no evidence that the animal was actually ridden at this time. The earliest evidence of that on the steppes comes sometime during the second millennium B.C. The riding of horse-drawn chariots occurs among Indo-Aryan groups sometime before 2000 B.C., and chariot warfare was involved in the supposed Indo-European colonization of Indus valley civilization (it's a controversial point) sometime after that date. The horse-drawn chariot makes its appearance in Mesopotamia circa 1800 B.C. and comes into general use on the Eurasian steppes and in the Near East after 1600 B.C. True military mounted nomadism, which dates from after 1400 B.C. on the Chinese frontier, begins to appear in the areas of Iran, Mesopotamia, and Syria only toward the end of the second millennium. On the southern Russian steppes (present-day Ukraine), Scythians and Sakas gave up steppe farming and began breeding horses, and (along with the Cimmerians) emerged as full-blown military horse-riding cultures during the ninth century. The first depiction we have of mounted warriors dates from about 800 B.C., in Scythian and late Mesopotamian art. And at some point after 1000 B.C., the peoples of Kazakhstan, northern Mongolia, and southern Siberia made a radical transformation to an economy based entirely on animals dependent on changing pasture.[52]

The ninth century also saw important technical innovations. Horse riding became more controlled due to the saddle and improved bits and bridles, and mounted archery made its appearance. A few centuries later, in the Middle East, the problem of how to fight from atop a one-humped camel without falling off was solved by the construction of a frame (saddle) around the hump. All of this was important because the riding of horses, in and of itself, which probably dates from about 1400 B.C. in the Middle East, does not constitute mounted nomadism. Pastoral peoples did not yet ride as a general habit in the fourteenth century; this latter development required techniques of attack and defense.[53]

In other words, mounted warrior nomadism of the proto-Genghis-Khan variety is largely an Iron Age (first millennium B.C.) phenomenon; neither it nor a certain type of warrior society can be projected backward onto a proto-Indo-European culture of the fourth or fifth millennium or even onto Indo-Aryan or Iranian society of 2000 B.C. As Renfrew succinctly puts it, "the dream-world of Indo-European mythology . . . finds virtually no support from a critical examination of the archaeological record."[54] In addition, the lateness of these developments coincides pretty clearly with everything said above regarding enclosed nomadism and nomadic/sedentary symbiosis. Hard lines don't really show up prior to 1500 B.C. or later, when mounted horse nomadism (not just chariots, which are clumsy for nomadic people to drag around) begins to spread. We have to remember that pastoralism starts in the Neolithic with animal husbandry, occasional herding, and transhumance; and even much later, in the third millennium, the Amorites are more often citizens and (by marriage) kinsmen of the Mesopotamians than they are raiders and enemies. The war machine, the sharp ideological difference between ways of life, is a later development and is coincident with a certain type of technology.

But why do these changes occur at this particular time? Why not one thousand years earlier, for example? Of course, it is easy to point to certain technological developments, as Lynn White did many years ago in his study of the impact of the stirrup during the Middle Ages;[55] but my own view is that technology is not, of itself, a sufficient explanation for social change. The more likely scenario is that technological developments are evoked by certain needs and cultural dispositions; they don't just fall out of the sky. Although there is always a long, slow development internal to the technology itself, there is also a set of cultural pressures, conscious as well as unconscious, that impinges on that development, spurring it on. (This is why the breakthrough that occurs with respect to any given invention often proves to be part of a wider pattern of simultaneous discovery.) So, for example, it took millennia for the techniques of stock breeding to get to the point of breeding a horse large enough and strong enough to carry a rider for long periods of time; but there was very likely a strong need for such an animal in the first place.[56]

In the case of mounted nomadism, we might speculate that the desire for movement was itself gaining momentum. We have already seen how the nomadic/sedentary opposition was in place from very early times, despite (or because of) the mutual need that existed between the two groups. Identities, ways of life, had already crystallized around these differences, and as the centuries wore on, the tendency toward polar opposition alternately waxed and waned, but it increased as an overall pattern. By 1500 B.C. or later, the sedentary/nomadic tension that had simmered for millennia boiled over into full-blown ideological opposition. But what evoked this? Why didn't the tension just continue to simmer? I really have no answer; what we *can* say is that at some point in the second millennium, something "systemic" occurred, a convergence of changes that led to the formation of the Axial civilizations and their severely dualistic world view. Roughly, these changes are from the use of bronze to that of iron; from horse-drawn chariot to mounted warfare; from the SAC to unitive trance practice (i.e., from "given" religion to revealed religion); from an accessible realm of the gods to a transcendent, virtually unattainable one; from a relative acceptance of death to a search for immortality; from an "embedded" self to a harshly alienated, objectified one (Julian Jaynes); and so on. By the time the Scythian scourge has run its course and Plato is making a pitch for the examined life, we are living in a very different sort of world.

Where do genetic patterns, the knowledge of eons, go when such information falls into disuse? Does the knowledge of mobility and everything that accompanies it simply disappear when HGs are superceded by agriculturalists? I don't believe it, myself. I believe the information goes underground, as it were, and then resurfaces in a different form. We were mobile for 99 percent of our history; is it any wonder that civilization—the repression of our mobile genetic heritage—slowly began to spawn ways of life based on movement once again, until these finally crystallized as warrior nomadism, that is, as *anti*-civilization? Why this took from about 9000 B.C. to roughly 1000 or 1500 B.C. to accomplish is unclear, but we might conclude that it took seven to eight millennia for the genetic repression to hit critical mass and finally explode. Then we get the true hosts of Gog and Magog, the ultimate Other, emerging from the deep human disposition toward flux that could not be contained forever. And because it resurfaced in a distorted, war machine form, the nomadic phenomenon had unanticipated consequences that altered the face of civilization.

I shall say more about that in a moment. For now, we need to conclude this part of the discussion, on the identity of the Aryans, by saying that finally scholars are not entirely certain who these people were. Renfrew believes they were farmers living in Anatolia (Turkey), but the argument is farfetched, and the genetic evidence does not bear him out.[57] The best guess is that they were, at least by the second millennium, farmers/herders who used horse-drawn chariots and had a priestly class. In terms of language groups (leaving the issue of a theoretically reconstructed proto-Indo-European language aside), we have the Indo-European languages, with the Indo-Iranian languages as a subgroup and the Indo-Aryan (or Indic) languages as a subgroup of that. The earliest Indo-Aryan works are the hymns of the *Rigveda* (composed sometime between 1500 and 1000 B.C.), the language of which is the parent of Sanskrit and closely related to Old Iranian. In terms of genealogy, we have a trunk that is proto-Indo-Iranian (groups living on the Russian steppes) that splits, by 2000 B.C., into Iranians and Indo-Aryans. Both seem to be pastoral peoples, the former being more settled than the latter.[58]

The traditional view, based on the *Rigveda* (RV), is that of an Indo-Aryan invasion of India around 1500 B.C. The RV, in other words, is a literary corpus that can be interpreted as the artifact of a seminomadic pastoral people who migrated from Iran into the Punjab, riding chariots and driving herds of cattle. These Indo-Aryans eventually settled and took up agriculture, although cattle remained their primary source of income. The brahmins, or priests, composed the Vedic (Old Sanskrit) hymns celebrating all of these events. In the RV, the Aryans are described as fair skinned, and the defeated indigenous people, the Dāsas, as dark skinned. The text tells how Indra, the god of war, was on the Aryan side, enabling their conquest of horses, cattle, and pasturage.[59]

Was there really an invasion? This has been the traditional view, but as in the case of Gimbutas' argument for "kurgan" invasions and subsequent destruction of a "goddess culture," it has fallen apart on closer scrutiny. Archaeologist George Dales points out that there has been a kind of delight "in being able to boo and hiss the evil villain, the murderous invader, the barbarian hordes . . . descending upon the once great and proud cities of the Indus civilization," but that the archaeological evidence does not support the occurrence of any such event. What we have learned in recent years is that this was not an event but a *process*, one involving the slow disintegration of Harappan civilization and accompanied by gradual Aryan coexistence and takeover, and that the reasons for the disintegration seem to have been internal to the Indus valley civilization itself. There was no sudden collapse, in short; rather, a complex cultural dynamic was at work. The decline was prolonged and irregular and caused by different factors in different areas, including changes in climate and the decay of economic and administrative structures.[60]

Of course, this poses problems for the linguistic evidence, for if a major invasion did not take place, the RV would seem to be a gigantic fantasy. Inasmuch as this is very unlikely and that a war between Aryans and Dāsas *did* take place, the Finnish scholar Asko Parpola was led to posit that the battle between the two groups took place in Bactria (northern Afganistan) and Margiana (modern Merv, in Turkmenistan), that is, outside of India; and that the Dāsas may have been a different group of Aryans! Parpola has been roundly criticized for this, and with good reason; but he can at least be credited with the attempt to reconcile the RV with the archaeological record.

In terms of our own concerns, however, these academic disputes may not matter. The crucial point, with respect to the rise of Axial civilization and a transcendent ideology, is the nature of the Vedic religion, its influence on the later Iranian religion of Zoroastrianism, and the relationship of all this to a dramatic increase in the opposition between nomadic and sedentary ways of life.[61] With these developments, the SAC is transformed, and the vertical structure of religion/ideology that characterizes the non-HG way of life enters its most intense phase, which is where we still are today—certainly in the West, Zoroastrians all.

The reader will recall, once again, that the religions of the great theocracies were not shamanic; there was no ecstatic practice or fusion with the godhead in Egypt and Mesopotamia. Ecstatic practice starts to show up at Mari—an outpost of settled pastoralists, interestingly enough—around 1800 B.C., and after that it becomes more common, gaining ground with the Eleusinian and Mithraic mysteries, Gnosticism (later on), and the rise of salvationist cults. It turns out that the Indo-Aryans were major contributors to this development, and the Iranian religions are centered around individual and collective salvation. The central ritual of the Vedic religion was the ingestion of a liquid that was pressed out of what was probably a hallucinogenic plant, *soma* in Vedic Sanskrit, or *haoma* in Avestan, the closely related (and earliest known Iranian) language spoken by

Zarathustra (Zoroaster) a few centuries later. (If you are picking up Nietzschean echoes here, you are not off the mark.)[62]

Whoever the Aryans and the Dāsas were, however, this much we know from the RV: the latter possessed a different religion from the former, at least initially, and did not use soma. The hymns say that Indra, the god of war, "exists only for the Soma-presser." Soma is said to be Indra's favorite drink, and he is described as insuperable in his fury when under its influence. By ingesting it before battle, the Aryan warriors were said to receive his help and also his fury. The Dāsas apparently did not have this advantage. It was the Aryans, according to Parpola, who brought the soma religion to Iran and India, and who may have also introduced a goddess cult into India as well.[63]

Soma, in any case, was said to create ecstasy, and the Vedas describe it in poetic terms. The entire ninth book of the RV, in fact, consists of hymns dedicated to this plant, hymns that may have been composed under its influence. It was said to bestow "divine power" on those who took it and to work warriors up into rage for battle. The RV also speaks of a superhuman knowledge that was and is always available, which was "seen" by sages of old in an ecstatic state. Soma, says the RV, reveals heavenly secrets.[64]

The Zoroastrian Revolution

It was in this context that, at some point around 1200 B.C. (although the dating is rather labile), a priest named Zoroaster arose as a religious figure among the Aryans. As Mary Boyce writes in *Zoroastrians*, this is the oldest of the revealed world religions, it dominated the Near and Middle East for centuries, and it set the pattern for the religions that were to follow. The seventeen hymns composed by Zoroaster, known as the *Gathas*, are inspired utterances, and Zoroaster himself believed that God had chosen him to be His special messenger. According to the British historian Norman Cohn, he was the earliest example we have of a millennarian prophet, promising a total transformation of existence. In the *Gathas*, Zoroaster refers to himself as an initiate possessed of divinely inspired wisdom. Walking down to the river to fetch water for the haoma ceremony when he was thirty, he supposedly had a vision of a being called Ahura Mazda, whom Zoroaster proclaimed to be the one uncreated god. As in the case of the Vedas, the core of the *Gathas* is mystico-ecstatic religious experience, and haoma was regarded by the Indo-Iranians as an elixir of immortality. Zoroaster thus adopted the soma ritual of the older, Vedic religion, and it became the central sacrament of the new one.[65]

What was this new religion, and how did it differ from its predecessor? Basic to all Indo-European ideology is the notion of dualism, or binary opposition. The Vedic religion, for example, espoused a split in the human world between those who upheld the fundamental notion of *ṛta*, truth (or order) and those who did not. Thus, when Zoroaster supposedly had a vision of Ahura Mazda, he also saw the evil spirit Angra Mainyu; these two represented, respectively, the forces of life and not-life. In this important sense, his teaching was continuous with the older Indo-Iranian religion and with the antithesis of Truth versus Lie limned in the RV. Zoroaster "knew no spirit of compromise," according to the historian R. C. Zaehner; the world was a battleground between Black and White, and "Black" included those who supported the traditional religion. Since the new religion seems pretty similar to the old one, we are still left with the question of what Zoroaster was fighting against.[66]

The key difference between the world view of the RV and the teachings of Zoroaster is that the former states that the cosmos would never change, whereas Zoroaster believed that it would and must. In this sense, Vedism is ideologically continuous with the SAC. The RV speaks of a world free of chaos in the *afterlife*, but this entry into heaven for a privileged few had no bearing on the future of the world itself. For the Vedic Indians, as for the Egyptians and Mesopotamians before them, the world was held in timeless equilibrium. The SAC sees the cosmos as a field of combat, to be sure, but problems and struggles just go on; there is no apocalypse or watershed, at which time God will triumph and all will be resolved. The SAC, in short, is not a utopian vision, nor is its dualism (when it exists) utterly stark. The Vedas, for example, describe a world of many gods and goddesses; they don't sort themselves into two basic categories.[67]

Before we examine Zoroaster's doctrinal innovation more closely, it will be necessary to say just a few words about the social context of all this because it is at this point that the story of nomads versus sedentists, as developed in this chapter, comes to a climax and impinges so heavily on Western civilization at large. In the world circumscribed by the SAC, the world of sedentary states and ambivalent relations with Amorites, nomadic raiders—who traveled on foot—were a chronic aggravation, but not much more. Human behavior, and history, is oscillatory here. The nomadic raider in this era may, in fairly short order, settle down, marry your sister, and become an artisan or a farmer. The nomad is a nuisance, a "tent dweller who eats uncooked meat," but his identity is not fixed, and lines are not so sharply drawn.

Within a few centuries, all of this changed. Not that technology was the determinant, but the emergence of mounted horse riding, and the extensive use of bronze and (later) iron, coincided with the Iranian "heroic age" of pillage. Zoroaster lived during this time and saw the breakup of a settled pastoral society, which he describes in the *Gathas*. Within the ranks of herdsmen themselves, a type of warrior arose who was no longer herding, but raiding. The *Gathas* reflect a point in Indo-Iranian history when this settled society was coming under attack from marauding warriors, men who possessed a new and dangerous mobility. In other words, farmer and herdsman had basically melded by this time. The settled life was based on cattle, not sheep or goats, and these did not move so much and were used in plowing fields. All of this was in stark contrast to groups who would be the ancestors of the Scythians. Zaehner writes:

> On the one side [Zoroaster] found a settled pastoral and agricultural community devoted to the tilling of the soil and the raising of cattle, on the other he found a predatory, marauding tribal society which destroyed both cattle and men, and which was a menace to any settled way of life.

So the moral dualism of the *Gathas* is in fact the universalization of a concrete political and social situation, namely, that of peaceful pastoralists constantly being threatened by fierce nomadic tribes. These latter are, in Zoroaster's words, "followers of the Lie," men who would subvert the peaceful order of a sedentary community that had once been nomadic itself. The plight of the ox in the face of this new nomadic violence is the subject matter of an entire Gatha, and Zoroaster speaks of "the evil-doer who cannot earn a livelihood except by doing violence to the husbandman's herds." Such people are agents of chaos, who must be defeated in order for Good to prevail.[68]

It is with Zoroaster that the dichotomy between settled and nomadic not only reaches its apogee but is transformed into something very different: the ancient combat myth of the Vedas and the Near Eastern mythologies now elevated to the level of apocalyptic faith. Nomads are no longer merely a nuisance. Unless armageddon occurs and they are completely defeated, the now-settled community of pastoralist farmers will not survive. So things are no longer oscillatory but linear, and as Mary Boyce tells us, Zoroaster's concept of history having an end was wholly original. Zoroaster proclaims a new order, one in which the prevailing violence will be replaced by peaceful pastoral communities. Whereas the older religion admired warrior raiders and compared them to *daevas* (gods), Zoroaster preached that the *daevas* of the RV were in fact demons. The new religion promised protection of cattle and would be a means of cementing a settled pastoral life. Zoroastrian dualism thus becomes the ideology of settled peoples who were previously nomadic.[69]

What Zoroaster did, then, was to take the cosmic antagonism that can be found in the SAC and the RV and make it the defining structure of the world. The entire cosmos is now seen as defined by the conflict between the True and the False, and the goal of the new religion is to defeat the agents of the latter and/or convert them to the former. In true guru fashion, Zoroaster declared that he was the judge who would decide what was True and what False, for he had been chosen by God to do this. (Where have we heard this before?)[70]

It is, then, in Zoroaster's prediction of a perfect future of blissful immortality that we have the clearest break with the older religion and with the SAC in general. There is Evil, but it will be defeated. Cosmos will overcome chaos, and the divine plan will be realized. Nor can the common man and woman, as they could in Egypt or Mesopotamia, be uninvolved bystanders in religion. No, this new religion puts an obligation on each individual, and each must choose between the two gods. This injunction to purity weighs on us all, and the push to transcendence now permeates all of life. For Evil includes anger, sloth, sickness, old age, even death. All of this must be overcome; all existence must be totally transformed. In the final consummation, comments Norman Cohn, all will be "made wonderful," and history will be replaced by eternity. The grand eschatology of the Axial Age is upon us now: the Messiah, the Second Coming, the world of Righteousness vs. Evil, and of Absolute Truth. We have arrived at the threshold of the modern world.[71]

Although specific links between Zoroastrianism and ancient Judaism, early Christianity, Gnosticism, and other messianic or salvationist religions cannot be unequivocally established, the coincidence of doctrine here is remarkable. Zaehner points out that the Dead Sea Scrolls, for example, reproduce quite closely the so-called Zurvanite heresy within Zoroastrianism, in which Good and Evil are seen to have a common father. Zoroastrianism did, centuries later, become the official religion of the Persian Empire, and the Jews were very likely exposed to it when they came under Persian rule. Iranian religion, it is now generally believed, strongly influenced Judaism, the Hellenistic mystery cults (including Mithraism), and, eventually, Islam. The general world view was that of a supreme creator God;

an evil power opposed to Him; the belief that this world, in its present state, would eventually come to an end; and that that development would usher in the kingdom of God, forever. All of these ideas were adopted by various Jewish sects in the post-Exilic period (i.e., after 586 B.C.), if not before. In the days of the monarchy (circa 1000 B.C.), Judaism was similar to the religion of the Canaanites: there was a divinely appointed order that would never change. In addition, despite the central importance of Yahweh, Israelite society was *de facto* polytheistic and included the worship of Ba'al and Asherah. With the emergence of the prophetic tradition and "revealed" knowledge, Yahweh becomes the one true god; and after 600 B.C., the view was that of a radically different future, in which all things would be made right. The world would be transformed, and the followers of Yahweh would have a glorious position in it. In certain oracles (described in various passages in Joel and Isaiah), the new age is seen to be one of visionary ecstasy. There may have even been a nomadic warrior influence here, as chapters 38 and 39 of Ezekiel tell how the hosts of Gog and Magog will come to plunder the Israelites, but that Yahweh will overthrow them, and this will be the extermination of ultimate evil. The books of Daniel, Jubilees, and I Enoch talk of revelations and ecstatic visions, and the world view becomes increasingly dualistic and eschatological. The Qumran sect of the Dead Sea Scrolls, and the early Christians, emerge as apocalyptic groups along these lines between 200 B.C. and 100 A.D. Again, the similarity to Zoroastrianism is remarkable, and historians of religion now assume a strong and obvious influence, although it cannot be proven beyond a doubt.[72]

All of this, to my mind, bespeaks a progressive loss of spiritual intelligence. We start with paradox among HGs, in which the sacred is the secular and the aliveness of the world is all that needs to be "worshipped." We lose our mobility, form into sedentary communities, and find ourselves caught in a vertical SAC. With the Aryans and the Vedic religion, we add in soma, shamanism, and dualism, though still not on an Axial, transcendent scale; and then with the settled pastoralists of Iran, we get a clear case of an Axial split. There is a curious parallel, that the nonuse of trance or fusion with God in the SAC is accompanied by an absence of sharp vertical dualism and that the introduction of ecstatic practice among the Aryans eventually leads to a sharp division of worlds (transcendent versus mundane orders). An equally important parallel is that of the now harsh boundary between sedentary and nomadic, between "in here" and "out there," and the equally strict division between heaven and earth. Add to this the irony, already stated, that nomadic life is about flux, and that that very flux, in the form of the war machine, generates the severe religious dualism and rigid ideological "certainty" that characterizes Zoroastrianism and the three surviving monotheisms. It is as though sedentary society, through its loss of movement, were eventually trumped by what it repressed, as a distorted form of nomadic life arose to force civilization into the no-win situation of opposing camps and absolute beliefs.

I also cannot help thinking how all of this must be part of the child-rearing practices described in chapter 3. As we have seen, all human beings, presumably even in the Upper Paleolithic, come to conscious awareness and have to deal with the dualism of Self vs. Other; this is the stuff of Object Relations. Yet how different must those Object Relations have been forty thousand years ago, even seven thousand years ago, compared to the severity reflected in the Iranian world view! Donald Winnicott's duality of the True versus False Self, Melanie Klein's dichotomy of good versus bad breast—all of this is the product of the late Axial world; save for its nascent form, it is simply not the human condition. That the Other is dangerous, or that anything outside my True Self or My Group is evil, is the heart of pathology; and yet this, from the Axial Age on, is the way the modern psyche gets wired up. This could be the deeper meaning of that famous film about the !Kung Bushmen of some years ago, *The Gods Must Be Crazy*. It might be more to the point to say that people who have these kinds of gods must be crazy.

I have called this chapter "The Zone of Flux"; "Ambivalent Legacy" might be closer to the mark. In one of those messy twists that is so endemic to human history, nomads turn out to be agents of "certainty" (ideological rigidity) and of paradox, lived uncertainty, at one and the same time. They are the Basseri Bedouin whose "religion" is the sky and the wind; and they are—in the very same part of the world—the Aryans of the *Rigveda*, who drink soma to generate battle fury and whose descendents terrorize settled pastoralists to the point that the latter finally produce a religion of total cosmic and moral certitude. They are, in short, a rejection of civilization's fixed forms and Ozymandian obsessions and—by "accident," as it were—a cause of greater verticality and rigidity than Ramses II ("Ozymandias") ever imagined.

Yet the nomadic commitment to movement and fluidity as the key to life and consciousness remains. Despite the reality of the war machine, there is a psychic continuity with HG life that nomads have, that may be their ultimate legacy to *our* life: the persistence of paradox. Nomadism is the continuation of the HG impulse in a different form, a response to sedentism that says, This doesn't work.

Thus Gilles Deleuze makes the distinction between the tree and the rhizome. Trees are vertical; the structure of root, trunk, and branch forms a hierarchy. The rhizome, on the other hand, is the tuber with horizontal roots, "a multiplicity of interconnected shoots going off in all directions," the "segmentary lineage" of nomadic life. Whereas power is inevitably arborescent, says Deleuze, generating schools of thought, leaders, and manifestoes, the rhizome is not about following a path. His colleague, Claire Parnet, writes:

> Nomads are always in the middle. The steppe always grows from the middle, it is between the great forests and the great empires. The steppe, the grass and the nomads are the same thing. The nomads have neither past nor future, they have only becomings, woman-becoming, animal-becoming, horse-becoming: their extraordinary animalist art. Nomads have no history, they only have geography.

The tree, in short, is based on a first principle, and first principles only can produce "huge sterile dualisms." Creativity, however, only occurs on a "line of flight." "Things do not begin to live," says Deleuze, "except in the middle."[73]

The oak tree, of course, conjures up grand images; it is heroic. Rhizomes, with their lateral and circular taproot systems, are a lot less romantic: potatoes, weeds, crabgrass. But their power lies precisely in being *anti*-Platonic, *anti*-Jungian, *non*transcendent, for the heart of rhizomatic patterning is immediate interconnection and heterogeneity, dialects and argots, not a universal language. This patterning is not composed of centers of significance and subjectivization, as arborescent systems are. And whereas the tree, which has dominated Western thought, is about transcendence, the rhizome, the steppe, is about immanence. "Don't sow," declare Deleuze and Guattari; "forage!"[74] In our penultimate chapter, I wish to explore what this kind of foraging looks like when it finally burrows its way into the intellectual awareness of the twentieth century.

6

WANDERING GOD: THE RECOVERY OF PARADOX IN THE TWENTIETH CENTURY

No "answer" can offer man a possibility of autonomy. An "answer" subordinates human existence. The autonomy—sovereignty—of man is linked to the fact of his being a question with no answer.

—Georges Bataille, *Guilty*

An honest religious thinker is like a tightrope walker. He almost looks as though he were walking on nothing but air. His support is the slenderest imaginable. And yet it really is possible to walk on it.

—Ludwig Wittgenstein, *Culture and Value*

We have come a long way since our early discussions of hominid biocultural evolution and the nature of hunter-gatherer politics. I hope it is a journey the reader has found rewarding. Before bringing this to a conclusion and discussing the fate of nomadism and the likely shape of future civilization, I have to ask the reader to indulge me in one more discussion, that of the emergence of nomadic consciousness in some of the philosophical work of the twentieth century. For if there *is* such a thing as genetic memory (conceived in terms of our sociobiology, rather than as "archetypes"), it is not surprising that the nomadic world view would inevitably find its way into our most sophisticated sedentary musings. Our genetic mobile heritage, as I said above, does not simply vanish with the advent of sedentism. Rather, it takes other forms; and one of these forms is in our thinking processes, such that a "rogue element" shows up, a mocking rhizome to our established tree. In my view, this is not the trendy (and hopefully soon-to-be passé) intellectual fashion of postmodern deconstructionism, much of which is really nihilism and despair dressed up as radical chic. Rhizomatic thinking is something else, something very affirmative, namely, spiritual nomadism, which, if it is "not going anywhere," is doing so because it understands that, in the most fundamental sense, there is really nowhere to go. ("Without a destination," said the twelfth-century Zen master, Hakuin, "I am never lost.")

Actually, there are a number of interesting detours we could take at this point, because nomadic consciousness has shown up in a few literary figures who are very famous, but who have not, for the most part, been viewed through the lens of spiritual nomadism presented in this book. These include Franz Kafka, who represents the dark side of paradox; Heinrich von Kleist, whose analysis of doubt could not get much of a hearing in a world dominated by Goethe's archetypal certainties; and the literary giant Virginia Woolf, whose confrontation with paradox finally exploded in her later novels (in particular, *Between the Acts*, 1941), which probed a world that lay beyond stories and plots. A discussion of the nomadic aspects of just these three writers could fill a book of its own, and even summarizing their work is a temptation I am going to have to resist. I do wish, however, to take a brief look at one twentieth-century figure, the Austrian philosopher Ludwig Wittgenstein (1889–1951), one of the greatest thinkers of modern times and one whose work has been consistently misunderstood. For it is in Wittgenstein that "rhizomatic thinking" and the nomadic world view discussed in previous chapters presents itself in what is probably the starkest form to date. In terms of his own life, in both social and philosophical terms, Wittgenstein seemed to slip between the cracks of civilization, and he was at one point led to remark that the "philosopher is not a citizen of any community of ideas; this is what makes him into a philosopher."[1]

Ludwig Wittgenstein (Figure 18) was nineteen years old when he enrolled at the University of Manchester in 1908 with the purpose of studying the fledgling science of aeronautics. This was largely at the behest of his father, the wealthy Viennese industrialist Karl Wittgenstein, who regarded engineering as a suitable career for his youngest son. But the latter had previously shown a disposition toward philosophical questions, and he found himself attending lectures on the theory of mathematical analysis. As discussions with fellow students led him to the question of the logical foundations of mathematics, Wittgenstein ultimately was introduced to Bertrand Russell's recent work, *The Principles of Mathematics*. This proved to be a decisive event in his life. By 1911, he outlined a book he wished to write on philosophy and traveled to Jena to discuss it with the great mathematician Gottlob Frege. Frege suggested he go to Cambridge and study with Russell, which he subsequently did.

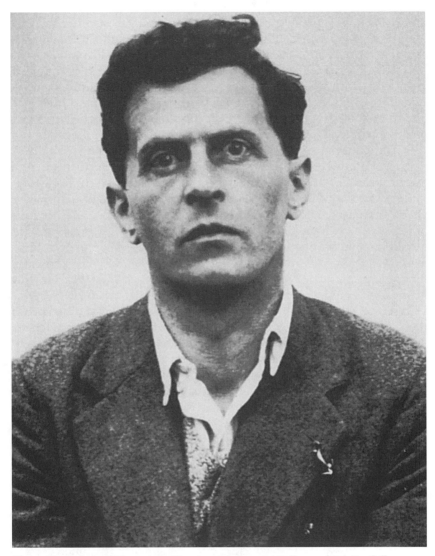

Figure 18. Ludwig Wittgenstein. Courtesy Master and Fellows of Trinity College Cambridge.

Russell's mentorship effectively launched Wittgenstein's career. By the end of 1915, he had completed most of what would become one of the greatest philosophical works ever written, the *Tractatus Logico-Philosophicus*, an analysis of the foundations of logic. It was the epitome of the vertical transcendent tradition, a Platonic-intellectual version of the sacred authority complex, if you will, in which the explanation of the world (i.e., its fundamental laws) is seen as lying not in the world but somewhere outside of it. Of this classical, analytical model, the British philosopher David Pears has written: "The *Tractatus* has the kind of aloof beauty which is admired from a distance, like ancient Egyptian architecture." The propositions of the *Tractatus*, said Wittgenstein, were the steps of a ladder that one must ascend in order to climb beyond them. Through pure logic, one attains the Ideal.

The book, in fact, is Plato taken to its logical conclusion; and like Plato's work, it is a curious hybrid of the intellectual and the mystical. As Eric Dodds demonstrated in his classic study *The Greeks and the Irrational*, Plato's epistemology is the intellectualization of the Greek mystery religions, in which ecstasy and revelation are the core of *gnōsis*, direct knowledge of the world. Through an initiation, the would-be "philosopher-king," in Plato, leaves the cave, the world of shadows, and climbs the noetic ladder to a place of pure knowing, now conceived of not as an encounter with the Great Mother, but with the Ideas, the Forms that underlie all material things.[2] Wittgenstein's concluding sentence—"Whereof one cannot speak, thereof must one be silent"—was for many years misinterpreted as a statement of logical positivism when it was actually something very different: the declaration that certain (vertical, intuitive) experiences are ineffable. This mystical material was not in the 1915 version of the manuscript, so it behooves us to ask what happened between then and 1922, when it finally appeared in print.

What produced this shift in Wittgenstein, this eleventh-hour crossover from logic to *gnōsis*, was a near-death experience he had in 1916 while active on the front lines. Serving in the Austrian army, Wittgenstein records an "encounter with God" that changed his life, and led to corresponding changes in the *Tractatus*. Although his religious tendencies were well underway from early youth, it was the experience of war that pushed him in a mystical direction and led him to add, at the end of the book, a series of remarks on the soul, the meaning of life and "that which cannot be spoken." In June of 1916, Russia launched a major offensive, and Wittgenstein's regiment (among others) faced the brunt of the attack. "It was precisely at this time," writes his most recent biographer, Ray Monk, "that the nature of Wittgenstein's work changed." He began to make notes on the nature of God, and the meaning of life, which turned out to be the same thing, in his view: "To pray is to think about the meaning of life . . . To believe in God means to see that the facts of the world are not the end of the matter." Two months later, he wrote that his work had "broadened out from the foundations of logic to the essence of the world."

The Austrian army had to retreat under the pressure of the Russian attack, and Wittgenstein was courageous in the face of death. He kept to his post under heavy fire, was recommended for decoration, and was quickly promoted. The terror he felt in these situations made the question of the self, the "philosophical I," a question of utmost importance. Wittgenstein concluded that the meaning of the world lay outside the world, that logic and mysticism sprang from the same root. In 1919, Russell wrote in a letter to Lady Ottoline Morell that his former student had become a complete mystic.

The war over, the book finished, Wittgenstein didn't know what to do with himself. In the preface to the *Tractatus,* he stated that he had solved all of the problems of philosophy, but that he was not impressed with this. The work, wrote Wittgenstein, finally showed "how little is achieved when these problems are solved."

The story doesn't end there, of course; it turns out that there are two Wittgensteins. The first was the logician-turned-mystic, who spoke for spiritual verticality, Platonic essence, and—in effect—unitive trance. Knowledge was a ladder, and the truth of the world lay outside the world. The second Wittgenstein was a very different creature, but this took time to mature and did not really get going until 1928. (This gap between vertical and horizontal experience is not atypical; St. Teresa of Avila, for example, records in *The Interior Castle* that it took her about ten years.) In effect, Wittgenstein had to "fall off the ladder," both socially and intellectually. He gave away his inheritance (which was a fortune) to his siblings and began working as a schoolteacher in small villages in Lower Austria, an "irrelevant" occupation that proved to be a fateful choice, as he wound up absorbing a philosophical outlook that would shape the second half of his life. The "lost years" of the 1920s, as many biographers have regarded them, were in fact not as lost as one might think.

Wittgenstein's entry into the public schools coincided with the Austrian school reform movement, as it was called, the movement that shaped educational policy in Austria after the Great War. The socialist and egalitarian ideals of the movement were alien to Wittgenstein's religious outlook, yet his teaching methods shared some of these basic principles, in particular the notion that education was not a matter of rote learning but of individual student initiative based on genuine curiosity and active participation. Thus, practical exercises were central to Wittgenstein's pedagogy; he was, in fact, steeping himself in the philosophy that one knows the world not through abstract essences (as he had held in the *Tractatus*), but by contextual awareness. To that end, Wittgenstein compiled a

Figure 19. Duck/Rabbit Figure. From Joseph Jastrow, *Fact and Fable in Psychology.*

spelling dictionary for use in the schools (*Wörterbuch für Volksschulen*) that attempted to teach German grammar by means of concrete, situational examples that were often presented in local Austrian dialect. This is exactly the sort of technique he would use as an instructor and professor at Cambridge in the 1930s and 1940s, when he would draw examples from his favorite pulp detective story magazine, a technique that became central to his later work.

It is also noteworthy that the Austrian school reform movement had its philosophical roots in the new Gestalt psychology of Karl Bühler, which was antireductionist and argued that context determined meaning. Hence, as a Cambridge lecturer, Wittgenstein was fond of reading from Wolfgang Köhler's *Gestalt Psychology*, and his most famous example of "aspect-seeing" was that of the ambiguous "duck/rabbit" figure (Figure 19), taken from a psychology text by Joseph Jastrow, and which is really another version of Köhler's well-known "cup/faces" diagram.[3] In both of these cases, the object depicted changes dramatically depending on how it is viewed; and in his later work, Wittgenstein would repeatedly hammer home the point that meaning was context-dependent rather than essential (inherent) and that the precision and rigor of language did not necessarily improve communication or understanding. It was a posture of total horizontality, a complete reversal of the vertical argument of the *Tractatus*. The British philosopher A. J. Ayer was led to label the later work "therapeutic positivism," and I think it fair to say that this is a partial reflection of the influence on Wittgenstein of the new educational psychology.

Another influence was the Dutch mathematician L. E. J. Brouwer, father of the so-called "intuitionist" school of mathematics, whose ideas Wittgenstein may have first come across in a lecture given by the latter in Vienna in 1928. In contrast to Russell and the whole "rationalist" school, Brouwer rejected the idea that mathematics needed to be grounded in logic, or the notion that there was a "mind-independent mathematical reality about which mathematicians make discoveries." For Brouwer, writes Monk, "mathematics is not a body of facts but a construction of the human mind." It is precisely this direction, which one might call "psychological" or even "anthropological," that is evident in Wittgenstein's later work, and that contributed so heavily to his "nomadization."

Yet another individual who had a significant—indeed, enormous—impact on this drift toward "anthropology" was the Italian economist Piero Sraffa, a colleague of Wittgenstein's at Cambridge. Sraffa effectively demolished the vertical tree of Wittgenstein's earlier *Weltanschauung*. They had many discussions along these lines, but the most famous example is a conversation in which Wittgenstein insisted that a proposition and the thing it describes must have the same "logical form." Sraffa made the classic Italian gesture of brushing the underside of the chin with the fingertips—*me ne frego*, "I don't give a hoot"—and asked Wittgenstein: "What is the logical form of *that*?" Note that Sraffa did not counter Wittgenstein's logic with more logic, but presented him with an emotional fact, a fragment of "tribal" behavior. It left the latter speechless.[4]

We see the shift that Wittgenstein was undergoing in the so-called *Blue Book* (like the later *Philosophical Investigations*, this was published posthumously, from his notes and lectures). He begins by questioning the tendency to believe that a substantive in language— "Time," "Knowledge," and so on—corresponds to an actual thing, or that for any given concept there exists an essence. This was the old, Platonic Wittgenstein. In contrast, the *Blue Book* argues for things or ideas having resemblances, like members of the same family. Thus, he attacks the (vertical) search for essence as an example of a misguided scientific "craving for generality"—such as can be found in the *Tractatus*. The new philosophy, writes David Pears, "has an extraordinary leveling effect." Ideas of reality are, as Sraffa showed, "tribal"; they are determined by daily use. Monk writes that "concept-formation . . . is not something fixed by immutable laws of logical form (as he had thought in the *Tractatus*) but is something that is always linked with a custom, a practice." Hence, pulp detective magazines can teach one more, if one knows how to look, than articles in philosophy journals. Depths are on the surface, Wittgenstein was saying; what you see is what you get. Instead of "truth," we should speak of "grammar," the syntax of use.[5]

It was for this reason that Wittgenstein came to admire Freud, for the latter's way of thinking—using fragments from myth or from dreams, for example—was one that depended on contexts, on the "feel" of a situation. It broke, said Wittgenstein, with rigid scientific thinking and allowed us to move in a noncausal yet (inexplicably) clearer direction. But Wittgenstein rejected Freud's notion that all dreams were about wish fulfillment because this is the same old "craving for generality" that gets us into trouble. What we need is a way of seeing, not doctrines. This is why his later work proceeds in an almost anecdotal fashion, like his German grammar book. It requires a personal involvement on the part of the reader, a sense of immediacy. This is paradox at its best, it seems to me.

"Was ist dein Ziel in der Philosophie?" Wittgenstein asks himself in the *Philosophical Investigations*; What is your aim in philosophy? "Der Fliege den Ausweg aus dem Fliegenglas zeigen"; To show the fly the way out of the fly bottle—that is, to shift conceptualization from essence to aspect (context). In "seeking to change nothing but the way we look at things," writes Monk, "Wittgenstein was attempting to change *everything*." True philosophy is willing to change its own pet notions, willing to change direction if the occasion warrants it, a "position" reflected by the fact that he published almost nothing after the *Tractatus* but instead kept filling and revising notebooks. For nomads, truth is a verb, something you live. No sooner are you at one point than an elaboration or revision suggests itself. "Incompetence," wrote Flaubert, "consists of wanting to reach conclusions."[6]

Of course, Wittgenstein was fully aware that what he was doing could be made into a "story," or a doctrine, as much as anything else. On a visit to Cornell University in 1949, two years before he died, he remarked to Oets Bouwsma, who was teaching in the Philosophy Department at the time, that he thought his teaching had probably done more harm than good. Like Freud's teachings, he said, it had made people drunk; they didn't know how to use the ideas soberly. Bouwsma said it for him: "They had found a formula."[7]

"The only seed I am likely to sow," Wittgenstein said on another occasion, "is a certain jargon." He was not far off the mark.

Students and colleagues imitated Wittgenstein's gestures, adopted his expressions, and did "Wittgensteinian philosophy," thereby missing the entire point of what he had been trying to teach. For Wittgenstein had no wish to found a school, a cult of Wittgensteinism. "All philosophy can do," he wrote in one of his notebooks, "is to destroy idols. And that means not creating a new one—for instance as in the 'absence of an idol.' "[8]

Wittgenstein's Legacy

What *is* Wittgenstein's legacy, then? In the case of the *Tractatus*, the book had an enormous impact by virtue of being completely misunderstood. That is to say, it gave a great impetus to the philosophical school known as logical positivism, which incorrectly saw Wittgenstein as one of its own; as saying, in effect, that "metaphysics was bunk" because it could not be empirically validated, when Wittgenstein was actually saying that it was only those things that lay beyond scientific scrutiny that were really important in life. Wittgenstein tried, on a number of occasions, to correct this misunderstanding in very candid and explicit terms, but without success. The philosophical community heard what it wanted to hear, and that did not include things like the ultimate value of mystical experience. In this convoluted way, by 1939 Wittgenstein was "recognized as the foremost philosophical genius of his time."[9]

For our purposes, of course, it would have made little difference if the philosophers *had* understood him. For whether the insight is scientific or mystical, it is still vertical in structure, and in that sense the two traditions are not terribly different (see Table 2, below). More important is the impact of the later, horizontal Wittgenstein; and here the verdict has been rather mixed. Bertrand Russell was among the harshest judges, stating that the later work was not philosophy at all, but only an attempt to escape thinking itself. "It was not by paradoxes that [Wittgenstein] wished to be known," he wrote, "but by a suave evasion of paradoxes." Russell Nieli, in a recent biography, agrees with this assessment, charging that Wittgenstein had "abandoned his true genius." A. C. Grayling, as late as 1988, felt (as Wittgenstein feared) that the legacy was one of a host of clever imitators and that philosophy was largely left untouched by the later work. Grayling's assessment is, in fact, tinged with contempt, and at one point his description of the man is reminiscent of Sumerian attitudes toward the Amorites, who eat raw meat and have no fixed abode:

[Wittgenstein] was, in truth, a nomad, a rootless wanderer, trailing from one country to another and one place to another, varying longer stays with many restless shorter travels . . . His sojourns in one place rarely lasted more than a few years . . . His was . . . a fragmented and displaced life.

How could we learn anything from such a person? is the implication here. Russell, in his autobiography, asserted that Wittgenstein was schizoid and paranoid, and the same theme was picked up as recently as 1991 in the pages of *Nature*, in which a British neurologist argued that Wittgenstein's work was not philosophy but rather "schizophrenese," a kind of insane German poetry.[10] One can only wonder who is crazy here, but the more significant point is the replay of the nomadic/sedentary antagonism. When the proponents of "fixed truth" come up against a spokesman for a variable, nomadic truth—in particular, one who declines to enshrine the latter as the new "fixed" truth—they simply cannot tolerate it.

However, this negative assessment does not only come from hostile quarters. Norman Malcolm, who was one of Wittgenstein's most devoted followers, candidly comments that the direction of philosophical work did not sharply alter after the publication of the *Philosophical Investigations* in 1951. Philosophers did not stop looking for universals any more than novelists, in the wake of Virginia Woolf, stopped telling stories. As Malcolm says, books on the "theory" of art, language, ethics, whatever, continue to roll off the presses; and such writers would regard Wittgenstein's contention that philosophy should simply *describe* the usage of words or concepts, and eschew explanations, as ridiculous. As it is still practiced, says Malcolm, philosophy remains the attempt to get at the "essential nature of things."[11]

Yet this is not entirely true. There is a whole body of work that argues for the primacy of "thought communities" in determining facts and that has clear Wittgensteinian echoes. I am thinking, for example, of *The Structure of Scientific Revolutions*, in which Thomas Kuhn used Wittgenstein to say that every "language-game," every form of discourse (system of meaning), stands or falls on paradigmatic evidence.[12] Indeed, contemporary discussions of the sociology of science tend to focus on the "tribal" habits of the knowledge community, not on the inherent truth (or lack thereof) of the ideas under debate.[13] In Richard Rorty (*Philosophy and the Mirror of Nature*) and Michel Foucault, no less than in Kuhn and Wittgenstein, we have an outlook that says that "truth is whatever satisfies the rules obtaining in a given speech-community." Thus, Wittgenstein was able to say that science and religion were in some sense epistemologically equivalent, "forms of life" (*Lebensformen*) that do not require justification. Central to Kuhn's work is the idea/possibility that different paradigms are just different, not better (more accurate) than one another.[14]

That branch of philosophy known as hermeneutics, or interpretation, also seems to bear a Wittgensteinian stamp. The idea of the "hermeneutic circle" is that answers are prefigured in the questions being asked. In other words, all we can finally get is the consensus of a given community, and each community is a closed system, which now has epistemic authority and which cannot be measured by the standards of another community (this is the "incommensurability" about which Foucault would later write).[15] This cultural relativism inevitably slides toward deconstruction as well, and one can see obvious similarities to Wittgenstein in the attack on essences, for example, or in Rorty's announcement (explicitly citing Wittgenstein as his authority) of the "end of philosophy." Rorty effectively takes the history of philosophy as an *imitatio Wittgensteini*, a pilgrim's progress from belief in essential truths to a description of "language games" ("tribal" knowledge) to, perhaps, a repudiation of philosophy altogether. And Henry Staten has compared Wittgenstein to the major theorist of deconstruction, Jacques Derrida, who argues that all reality is a "text" (language game) and that all texts are somehow equivalent. It all dissolves in "mind"; we have to give up the philosophical project of the mind as the "mirror of nature," that is, as representative of the outside world, as being able to know anything about the outside world.[16]

My own feeling is that some of this is true, but that it also misunderstands Wittgenstein's later thought, perhaps no less than the logical positivists misunderstood his early thought. To see this, we need to consider two issues in Wittgenstein's life and work: first, the role of God (also known as the "foundational" issue); and, second, the relationship between the *Tractatus* and what came after that, that is, between vertical and horizontal outlooks. I believe this will make his brand of "nomadism" clearer to us. For unlike so many of the postmodernists and radical relativists, Wittgenstein was no nihilist. If his philosophical career was partly born in despair, it certainly didn't wind up there, as even his dying words make abundantly clear ("Tell them I've had a wonderful life"). Deconstructionism is nomadism without content; there is no hunter-gatherer truth, no sense of "presence" that it carries—something that it explicitly denies as even possible.[17] Wittgenstein's "end of philosophy" issued out into something else; and if the later work pointed to a certain kind of emptiness, it had a function analogous to the tribal arrangements described by Pierre Clastres, which paradoxically celebrate the power of nonpower. Clastres' Indians, it suffices to say, were not deconstructionists.

Insofar as the role of God (or better, "God") is concerned, consider the second epigraph to this chapter: the honest religious thinker, said Wittgenstein, can walk on air. Deconstructionists, to say the least, are not religious thinkers. But the real point is, Is there a safety net here? For Wittgenstein, the answer was yes, but this "God" was largely manifest in experience itself. We are not talking about the SAC, or unitive trance, and during the 1920s Wittgenstein was well on his way to abandoning "encounters with God." Thus, when he asked colleagues and friends, on one occasion, to listen to a written confession of what he regarded as his dishonest behavior, he was undertaking to undo his own personality structure (pride and ego). Similarly, several years after he left the Austrian village of Otterthal, where he had, as a schoolteacher, struck some children and then lied about it in a court hearing in 1926, he returned to apologize personally to the children he had hurt. The courage involved in being willing to undergo such humiliation can well be imagined, but in the world of his own spiritual nomadism, you couldn't speak the truth if you didn't live it. The same thing is true of his willingness to listen to Brouwer, or Sraffa, to the point that he was led to reject the whole of the *Tractatus*, which had been his entire life's work up to that point. He was not holding onto it as a child does a T.O. "The solution to the problem of life," he remarked in later years, "is to be seen in the disappearance of the problem."

Real philosophy, Wittgenstein wrote to Rush Rhees in 1944, involves a willingness to change one's own pet notions, as well as one's life. As such, it is nasty and disagreeable. (Note that we are not, à la Joseph Campbell, "following our bliss" here or making our lives into heroic dramas; quite the opposite.) "And when it's nasty," he wrote to his American colleague, Norman Malcolm, "then it's most important." "You can't think decently," said Wittgenstein, "if you don't want to hurt yourself." It is not, then, that reality is no more than a text and can be made, in the manner of Derrida, to disappear in this way; that would just be cheating, in Wittgenstein's view. Rather, you make reality "disappear" by merging into it; by living in such a way that the problems of that reality cease to be problematic. "In a way that is centrally important but difficult to define," writes Ray Monk, "he had lived a devoutly religious life."

The other issue is that of the relationship between the early and the later work, which deserves some discussion because it goes to the heart of Wittgenstein's nomadism, which is not that of a pure

Deleuzian rhizome (see the end of the previous chapter). Rather, it is more akin to what one might call "grief," though this has nothing in common with postmodern nihilism or despair. Let me explain what I mean.

On the surface of it, we have a man who lived the first half of his life in a severe, totally vertical, scientific-mystical/transcendental world and the second half in a horizontal, rhizomatic, contextual/ hermeneutic one. The *Tractatus* is about universal knowledge and transcendent truth, the *Philosophical Investigations* about language games and local/tribal reality systems. There is a quality of a sharp *volte-face* here, and Russell's remark regarding Wittgenstein's "schizoid" character would seem to have some validity.

It is also the case that this bipolar odyssey is not, in the twentieth century, so atypical. It may even go back to the (possible) conflict between Plato and the Sophists, which was the subject of Robert Pirsig's immensely popular book of twenty-odd years ago, *Zen and the Art of Motorcycle Maintenance*, whose author went mad from an inability to integrate vertical and horizontal reality. As already noted, Richard Rorty regards this odyssey, in Wittgenstein, as paradigmatic of the "progress" of Western philosophy.

According to Ernest Gellner, however, this vertical/horizontal duality has very specific historical roots. Wittgenstein, says Gellner, was a product of the closing years of the Hapsburg Empire, which was torn between the cosmopolitan liberalism (universalism) of the upper middle class and the nationalism (tribalism) of various ethnic groups. The philosophical expression of the former was *Gesellschaft*, the legal-contractual world of Karl Popper's "open society" and Friedrich von Hayek's free-market economy (von Hayek was, interestingly enough, a distant cousin of Wittgenstein); whereas for the latter groups it was *Gemeinschaft*, the romantic ideal of "a closed community suffused by intimate [a]ffective relations" and delimited by an idiosyncratic culture. The *Tractatus*, says Gellner, was about *Gesellschaft*, about universal truth and language, not about ethnic subworlds and cultural idiosyncracies. This latter was the world of the children's grammar book and the *Philosophical Investigations*, the world of *Lebensformen*, in which meaning is possible *only* in community. Platonic/Cartesian transcendence, essences, and universals are now seen as pathological, and the local language of a closed community as the road to health. ("If you believe that," comments Gellner sarcastically, "you'll believe anything.")[18]

Now Gellner has captured something that is true of all of those who have gone the route from "transcendent truth" to "all paradigms are equal." As he says, anthropologists in particular have escaped from culture blindness, arguing that our particular Western scientific life form is just one among many. This insight, he adds,

> is liable to have a very special potency for them, to be wildly exciting, intoxicating, and utterly vertiginous. It will be addictive and constitute a revelation. It will acquire the same luminous authority as that which previously surrounded [their own] local culture.

The idea that the world is a cultural artifact, says Gellner, is exciting and disturbing to those who have lived with the notion of universal truth, and something of this vertiginous quality clearly captured Wittgenstein in the late 1920s and 1930s. "Meanings," what Clifford Geertz calls "thick description," take on a mystical quality. One abandons the cosmopolitan globe-trotting of Vienna and Cambridge and "puts down roots" in Otterthal. One gives up transcultural truth and falls prey "to the Hermeneutic plague, the reification and fetishism of idiosyncratic and varied Systems of Meaning." The danger is that what started out as an attempt to refute scientific dogmatism turns into a hermeneutic dogmatism, a dogmatism about these "forms of life."

So there is something valid in Gellner's characterization of Wittgenstein, in that when the twentieth century's foremost representative of the vertical mindset tried to escape it, he could only do so by swinging the pendulum 180 degrees and declaring that his entire life and all of Western philosophy were an error. ("Anything that I might reach by climbing a ladder," he now wrote, "does not interest me.") At this time, Wittgenstein was searching for a meaningful way out of verticality. The problem was that when he tried to find horizontality in practical terms, it disappointed him badly. Hence, the romance of Austrian village life went sour when he discovered that these simple peasant folk were rednecks, stubborn anti-intellectual provincials who regarded the schoolmaster from Vienna as more than a little weird. Wittgenstein's notebooks and letters from these years reflect his bitterness at their "stupidity" and "unteachability," and it is a sad irony that the school reform idealist wound up hitting the children who were less than precocious in logic and mathematics.[19]

All of this may have cooled Wittgenstein's ardor for horizontal truth; it is hard to say. But what *is* clear is that he did understand, as cultural relativists and deconstructionists apparently do not, that there finally is no way of jettisoning the transcendent, that is, the vertical/universal, without drifting into incoherence (at least, not

within the world of civilization). This is, in my view, his real nomadism, the real living of life "between the acts," and a position that
can best be captured by the word "grief." The British director Derek
Jarman, in his marvelous film *Wittgenstein*, put it this way:

> There was once a young man who dreamed of reducing the
> world to pure logic. Because he was a very clever young man,
> he actually managed to do it [in the *Tractatus*]. And when he'd
> finished his work, he stood back and admired it. It was beau-
> tiful. A world purged of imperfection and indeterminacy.
> Countless acres of gleaming ice stretching to the horizon. So
> the clever young man looked around the world he had cre-
> ated, and decided to explore it. He took one step forward and
> fell flat on his back. You see, he had forgotten about friction.
> The ice was smooth and level and stainless, but you couldn't
> walk there. So the clever young man sat down and wept bitter
> tears. But as he grew into a wise old man, he came to under-
> stand that roughness and ambiguity aren't imperfections.
> They're what make the world turn. He wanted to run and
> dance. And the words and things scattered upon this ground
> were all battered and tarnished and ambiguous, and the wise
> old man saw that that was the way things were. But some-
> thing in him was still homesick for the ice, where everything
> was radiant and absolute and relentless. Though he had come
> to like the idea of the rough ground, he couldn't bring himself
> to live there. So now he was marooned between earth and ice,
> at home in neither. And this was the cause of all his grief.[20]

Several decades later, it is perhaps possible to *choose* this grief
and to do so without quite so much torment as Wittgenstein suffered. For inasmuch as the latter was a pioneer in all this, he had
to sort it out as best he could by himself. But my point here is that
to live with any degree of reason at all—that is, both from a logical
and from a human point of view—the transcendence of the *Tractatus*
(or any similar vertical/rationalist outlook) is absolutely unavoidable.
For without some degree of verticality or objectivity, the language
games and the tribalism of various thought communities cannot even
be discussed because one would not be able to get outside of them
to discuss them. Hence Wittgenstein's remark to Oets Bouwsma,
when they met in Oxford in 1950 less than a year before he died, that
the "sense of the world must lie outside the world. In it there is no
value, it must lie outside all happening and being-so. It must lie outside the world."[21] This, too, is part of the "later work."

This is why Gellner's critique of Wittgenstein is a bit unfair, because Wittgenstein would have finally agreed with Gellner's assessment of the problem (albeit grudgingly, perhaps). "Cultures," writes Gellner,

> are not cognitively equal, and the one in which alone anthropology is possible cannot really be denied a special status. The nature and justification of that pre-eminence is a deep and difficult matter. But it springs from something far more important than the arrogance of an imperial class. It is linked to the very possibility of *reason*.[22]

Otterthal may be nice, but Vienna it ain't.

At the risk of belaboring a point, let me put this another way, so the reader clearly understands what I am saying here. As Michael Hodges points out, any assertion of "truth" is necessarily a transcendent activity, whether that truth is "Tractarian," later-Wittgensteinian, or anything else. There has to be an external foundation. Hence Wittgenstein's explicit remark that "a language-game is only possible if one trusts something," or his comment that if one is playing chess, one can't be having doubts as to whether the pieces might be changing positions by themselves. "Doubt itself," he wrote in *On Certainty*, "rests only on what is beyond doubt." Every language game presupposes that the communicating partners in the game take numerous facts for granted. All examination or discourse takes place within a system, and this is not arbitrary; it belongs to the essence of argument. In short, says the German philosopher Karl-Otto Apel, criticism presupposes a transcendental framework in order to have a critical discussion at all. "Forms of life evidently play the role of a metaphysical ultimate in terms of which the functioning of language itself is to be understood."[23]

It is for this reason that Wittgenstein cannot really be regarded as a phenomenologist. As Nicholas Gier says in *Wittgenstein and Phenomenology*, a number of passages in his work, in which he talks about phenomenology directly, make it clear that his own phenomenological method—the description of "forms of life" or language games—is really a transcendental one. Wittgenstein distinguishes between the world of facts that, say, physics deals with and the world of frameworks within which these facts have meaning. One can clearly identify a science of essences, that is, an investigation of the formal conditions that make the experience of facts possible. But then, one has stepped outside the phenomena and into a transcendental perspective.[24]

Wittgenstein never left the framework of the *Tractatus*; at least, not completely. Indeed, within civilization, no intelligent person can. It comes back to Object Relations, in many ways, and Wittgenstein even spoke of the "two godheads: the world and my independent I."[25] What rationalists (or many scientists) want to do, on the one hand, and the deconstructionists wish to do, on the other, is to collapse the tension that is involved in living between Vienna and Otterthal (if I may put it metaphorically). But it is not possible, if one has any reflective capabilities, to opt for a world of pure universals (Jarman's "ice") or one of pure local tribalism (Jarman's "friction"). So the postmodernists tend to exalt the mind as the creator of reality, and this gives them a Nietzschean sense of freedom and power. The result, says the Canadian philosopher Charles Taylor, is a flattened world devoid of any crucial issues. But as I said before, this is nihilism, not nomadism, and it doesn't correspond to what Wittgenstein believed. It was his "grief" to have to "walk on air," walk the tightrope between the local and the universal. My own feeling is that we can now, as an act of spiritual nomadism, choose that high-wire act and find it, if not exactly a barrel of laughs, at least OK, maybe even occasionally fascinating. And at least on the individual level, the problem disappears because we are living in a way that turns it into a nonproblem.[26]

But there is more than this, for it takes on a whole new meaning when we subsume it under the discussion of power and authority as they exist in HG society versus agricultural civilization. This the philosophers have *not* done, and I hope to show (chapter 7) that when we bring this present discussion and our earlier discussion (chapter 2) face to face, the results are quite startling in terms of what we can learn about the nature of knowledge and power in and out of civilization. For now, I want to close the present chapter by providing the reader with a schematic overview of the nature of Western thought, one that gives us a picture of where nomadic consciousness, or the paradoxical legacy, fits in. Consider, then, the columns indicated in Table 2, below.

Western Categories of Knowing

To the left of the double line, we have a skeleton summary of the dominant (intellectual) tradition in the West. In this tradition, that which is true and unchanging is a set of rules or laws that constitute the forms underlying phenomenal appearances. These forms may be different in different eras—Ideas for Plato, for example, or atoms for

Table 2: The Search for Truth in Western Civilization

DOMINANT TRADITION: (Primacy of Logic and Form)	THE THREE MAJOR COUNTER-TRADITIONS: COUNTER-TRADITION (1) (Primacy of Spirit, or Process)
Pythagoras	Oracular prophecy
Parmenides	Zoroaster Mystery cults
Plato	Empedocles
Aristotle	Some alchemists, Gnostics, heretics; Hildegarde of Bingen, St. Francis
Medieval church philosophy (e.g., Aquinas)	Renaissance magicians, Giordano Bruno; the early St. Teresa of Avila; Neoplatonists
Descartes Newton Locke Kant	English and German Romantics: Wordsworth, Shelley, Goethe, Hölderlin, Rilke (partly)
Freud Marx Einstein	Hegel Nietzsche Order of Golden Dawn, Theosophists
Lévi-Strauss	Jung, Campbell, Eliade A. N. Whitehead Rudolf Steiner
The early Wittgenstein	The later Heidegger The later Gregory Bateson The early Wittgenstein
—————— Here truth consists of the underlying form, or laws. *Governing motif:* Parable of the Cave.	—————— Here laws exist, but they are of a different kind of law than in the dominant tradition and experienced in a nonrational way. *Governing motif:* Evolution of the Soul (world seen as a personal reflection).

Table 2: The Search for Truth in Western Civilization *(continued)*

THE THREE MAJOR COUNTER-TRADITIONS:

COUNTER-TRADITION (2) (Primacy of Matter as Vehicle for the Spirit)	COUNTER-TRADITION (3) (Paradox: Truth Emerges Only When It Is Not Pursued)
Ancient atomists?	Do ancient forms of this exist, beyond hunter-gatherers?
Some mystery cults, Gnostics, heretics, alchemists	Sophists?
	Meister Eckart?
Giordano Bruno	The later St. Teresa of Avila
William Blake	Heinrich von Kleist John Keats
Georges Bataille, Marquis de Sade (perverse form of argument)	Rilke (partly) Kafka (perverse form of argument)
Body workers: F. M. Alexander, Wilhelm Reich, K. von Dürckheim	The early Heidegger Gurdjieff (partly)
Isadora Duncan	Virginia Woolf The later Wittgenstein The early Gregory Bateson
Merleau-Ponty, phenomenologists; existentialists	Gilles Deleuze Umberto Eco Bernadette Roberts
Certain aspects of feminism	
Here truth is in matter; spirit *is* matter; "laws" are an illusion. *Governing motif:* Immersion in Experience.	Here laws exist, but not in a fixed form. *Governing motif:* Rilke's "Live in the Question."

Newton and Locke—but the schema is always one of "what you see is not what you get." The governing motif here is from Book VII of Plato's *Republic*, the Parable of the Cave, in which the deluded masses sit in a cave staring at shadows on the wall, not realizing that these *are* shadows and that what is real is the light behind them, casting the shadows. Hence, for Plato, material phenomena are illusions; it is the Ideal Type in each case—the perfect circle, for example—that somehow causes the material manifestations, for example, a cup or a ring. Or, in the case of Newtonian physics, one might mistakenly think that the cup is the real thing, when in fact it is composed of atomic particles. Thus, reason "knows better" than the evidence of the senses, on this schema—something that is generally held to be true for science since the seventeenth century (e.g., the evidence of our senses tells us that the earth is stationary). In a similar way, it would be an error to take human behavior at face value, when it is really repressed sexuality (Freud) or the mode of production (Marx) that is running the show. In the dominant tradition, truth consists of invisible, underlying laws, and knowing the truth consists of *analysis*, breaking down the larger complex phenomena into their constituent parts.

To the right of the double line, we have three "underground," or counter-traditions, that got buried by the dominant tradition but that have survived in one form or another. The first counter-tradition is not, in my view, really at odds with the DT (though it appears to be), but it says that the DT is too limited and needs to be situated within a larger spiritual context, one that sees spirit as the primary determinant in the operation of reality. This is the world of unitive trance, ecstasy, and revealed religion. It includes the oracular prophecy at Mari, the soma ritual of the Aryans, and the mystery cults of antiquity. It also includes some alchemists and heretics of the Middle Ages, the Romantic poets, and comparative mythologists such as Jung and Campbell.

Dreams, magic, Hermeticism, the occult tradition—these are all part of this category, which privileges intuition over analysis, and whose governing motif is the Evolution of the Soul. Life is a Mystery; through some sort of (heroic) initiation, one enters the Holy of Holies and attains wisdom. As in the DT, laws are said to exist, but they constitute a different type of law, an esoteric type, which is experienced in a nonrational way.

The second counter-tradition occasionally overlaps with the first, but its theoretical orientation is very different. In this tradition, it is not that spirit is primary and matter the expression of it, but rather that the two are virtually indistinguishable; spirit *is* matter, or matter is seen to possess a kind of intelligence or sentient awareness.

"Optimistic" Gnostics, as they have been called, and some heretics, lie in this tradition; William Blake was a foremost exponent of it ("energy is eternal delight"). In a sexual context, Bataille and de Sade represent the dark or perverse pole of this tradition, and Wilhelm Reich the healthy one. For these thinkers, it was only through direct bodily (erotic) experience that one had any real grounding in the world, any knowledge of it. In a larger physical sense, Maurice Merleau-Ponty and the whole school of phenomenology argued that underlying "laws of nature" were an illusion. Immediate perception, rather than being epiphenomenal or derivative, was primary. The governing motif in this case is knowledge through Immersion in Experience.

Finally, in the third counter-tradition, with which I have been concerned in this book—the tradition of paradox—the truth is seen to emerge only when it is *not* pursued, and this requires the ability to play with empty space, the Void. This is a pattern-challenging tradition, one that only hints indirectly that underlying laws exist, but not in a fixed sense, and not at all in the sense of the Holy of Holies (Umberto Eco makes fun of CT no. 1 in *The Name of the Rose* and *Foucault's Pendulum*). Hence, Wittgenstein's notion that "depths are on the surface." It takes a certain shift of perception to recognize how extraordinary this "ordinariness" really is. From the viewpoint of the DT and the first two CTs, this tradition seems like nothing, but it is a very full sort of nothing—Clastres' power of nonpower, Keats' "negative capability." If you just sit with it, your consciousness eventually issues out not into ecstasy or "wisdom" (CT no. 1), or into bodily experience (CT no. 2), or into simple emptiness (a misunderstanding of CT no. 3), but into the remarkable awareness that reality *as is* was the "mystery" you were seeking all along. The governing motif here is the line from Rilke, "Live in the Question." "Perhaps you will then gradually, without noticing it," he wrote, "live along some distant day into the answer."[27]

Comparisons with Eastern traditions are perhaps obvious. As the British historian Joseph Needham once argued, the East "failed" to develop Galilean science because it had no belief in underlying laws of nature.[28] Certain forms of Buddhism postulate an evolution of the soul, while the Tantric tradition most closely corresponds to CT no. 2, and Taoism and Zen Buddhism have affinities with CT no. 3. Western philosophy is very rich for having all four traditions, though there has been such an overvaluing of the Dominant Tradition and of CT no. 1, that our civilization has suffered from not allowing the two horizontal CTs, nos. 2 and 3, to have much of a say. In terms of our discussion of Wittgenstein, we can now see that the *Tractatus* was a hybrid of the DT and CT no. 1, and that the later work quite clearly falls into CT no. 3. But as indicated, he never completely left the DT because it is this form of intellectual transcendence that makes any rational discourse and analysis (including the present book) possible.

I do not mean, of course, for this chart to be even mildly exhaustive or accurate in any strict sense. The reader will undoubtedly find all kinds of overlaps and crossovers among the categories, as well as inevitable errors, and that is fine. It is only meant heuristically, as a sketch or suggestion, to clarify the intellectual/spiritual orbit of Western urban/agricultural civilization. All four of these traditions have enriched us; taken in isolation, all of them have misled us (CT no. 1 especially). The first two columns represent the supremely vertical, the last two, the explicitly horizontal. In this book, in particular, I am dealing with the horizontality of nomads and HGs, with a "rhizomatic" consciousness that I believe has largely been lost since our HG days came to an end, but which is derivative from our animal ancestry, deeply rooted in our brain structure and our evolutionary history. As sedentism got going, verticality overwhelmed us. We got caught up in a spirituality that was heavily distorted, and our earlier paradoxical heritage of alertness and immediacy faded into a dim memory. But nomads, and even a few HGs, are still around to keep it alive, and we do have a few "oddball" spiritual nomads who keep rediscovering it on a mental level.

As I shall indicate in chapter 7, the paradoxical tradition by itself, when it reappears within civilization, is no guarantee of anything wonderful. Heidegger started out in CT no. 3, fell from there into CT no. 1, and finally became a Nazi, so let's not get too excited here.[29] In order to understand how the paradoxical tradition can go wrong, we have to examine what happens to it when it becomes a societal phenomenon, and intersects with the orbit of power. Once we do this, the various threads of this book—evolution of mind, emergence of political and religious verticality, cross-cultural child rearing, delayed versus immediate-return economies, agriculture and the Great Mother, to name but a few—come together to show what is really possible for us in terms of psyche and culture at this point in the history of civilization. The real question for us now, I believe, is whether nomadic consciousness is something that can exist at more than just an individual level. Is there a way that the insight of thinkers such as Virginia Woolf and Ludwig Wittgenstein can be made to operate institutionally? What would it mean, *in civilization*, to reconnect with this precivilized legacy? Or is nomadic spirituality, by definition, a kind of oblique, highly individual experience? This will be the subject of our next, and final, chapter.

7

THE OTHER VOICE

We suffer from an addictive weakness for large illusions . . . Power in our civilization is repeatedly tied to the pursuit of all-inclusive truths and utopias . . . The unshakeable belief that we are on the trail to truth—and therefore to the solution to our problems—prevents us from identifying this obsession as an ideology.

—John Ralston Saul, *The Unconscious Civilization*

Do not become enamored of power.

—Michel Foucault, preface to the
American edition of Deleuze and Guattari, *Anti-Oedipus*

Se hace camino al andar.
(We make the road by walking it.)

—Antonio Machado

If I am going to be true to the ideas discussed in this book, I can't really be "going anywhere" with it. As the above quotation from the Canadian philosopher John Ralston Saul suggests, we need to get beyond what might be called "paradigm-shift addiction," the (apparently) unending and desperate search for mental theme parks that have their origins in the sacred authority complex and its connection to the orbit of power. My "goal" has not been to come up with yet another goal for society to pursue, but rather to see through this kind of behavior and to understand why it is so hard for human beings in civilization (in particular, in Axial civilization) to stop doing it.

That hierarchical tendencies existed even in the Paleolithic might suggest that at least to some extent, we are a flawed species. Perhaps we are. But this is not the sum total of it. If we didn't have other abilities—ones that persist even in the context of civilization—

we wouldn't be able to generate characters such as Virginia Woolf or Ludwig Wittgenstein. We wouldn't have a Michel Foucault telling us to avoid—as he himself was not able to do—falling in love with power, or a poet like Antonio Machado saying that we build the road as we travel. So my only purpose here has been to take the reader on a tour of a few "pastures," as it were—the evolution of the mind, our HG past, cross-cultural child rearing, the emergence of vertical power arrangements, and the nomadic rejection of agricultural civilization—so that he or she can get some idea of what has happened to us and what we are up against as a result. If there *is* any way out of our current dilemma, it seems to me, knowing the "civilizational terrain" is surely the first step.

We have seen, in any case, the conditions under which the relative egalitarianism and horizontal, embodied spirituality of HG life got transmuted into power politics and vertical sacrality. This momentous shift in our cultural evolution—the greatest we have had, really—represents an immense loss. It is not that the HG life was without its problems, and I am not romanticizing an existence that contained a great deal of hardship and early death. A hunter-gatherer with a toothache, let alone appendicitis, was probably not a pretty sight. Pain, some degree of hierarchy, aggression, and conflict are part of the human condition.

That being said, I do believe that HG life was more congruent with the multiple aspects of human Being—spiritual, political, somatic, environmental, and sexual (and perhaps even intellectual)—than the civilized form of life that followed it. The irony of civilization is that the SAC promises a better life yet delivers one that is probably worse. Vertical power politics and the belief in God or some Gnostic, transpersonal reality are ultimately palliatives; they address the pain of the human condition only to keep us trapped in it, in a morass. Individually or collectively, we struggle for a way out; and largely because of the ingrained habits of the last ten to twelve thousand years, we find ourselves more tightly enmeshed. We *think* we are solving problems with the latest fashion in paradigm shifts, whether they consist of holism, ecology, systems theory, altered consciousness, revivals of mythology, Gnostic "insight," "third waves" of postindustrial society, postmodernism, information highways—you name it—but the basis of this merry-go-round remains untouched because the whole shebang moves within the orbit of authority, of "solutions." As one wag put it, we think we are seeing light at the end of the tunnel when what we are actually seeing is the light of an on-coming train. If you live in the world of what I have called counter-tradition (1), of the SAC and Axial civilization, then lurching from one ism to the next seems normal, when it is really a kind of religious and Zoroastrian pathology. Some of these current postmodern ideas undoubtedly will be helpful to our situation, but much of it is a magic lantern show, for the "solution," if it exists at all, is far more modest: it lies in the ability to live in paradox and to move from there, without any utopian expectations. As world population continues to swell (a possible 11 billion estimated for the year 2050), the most likely scenario is that of Ridley Scott's *Blade Runner*, or Jacques Attali's prediction (in *Millennium*) of even greater social inequality for the twenty-first century. In this context, phrases such as "holism" or "emerging planetary culture" are shallow and deceptive. For that culture, if and when it does arrive, could easily prove to be quite oppressive—a new Dark Age.

Now since we are not going to get out of civilization in any great hurry (an attempt that would be fraught with disaster in any case), it may be that damage control is the best we can expect. But let me leave that aside for the moment and get down to what *does* lie at the root of being *Homo sapiens sapiens* (*Hss*). It seems to me that some conclusions about who we are need to be drawn from the discussion of the last two hundred pages.

Hss: A Flawed Species?

Evolutionarily speaking, the genus *Homo* came into a "mind" something like forty thousand to one hundred thousand years ago (if not somewhat earlier), in the Jaynesian sense of the awareness of awareness. By the time of the Late Paleolithic, *Hss* is decorating itself with various objects and engaging in symbolic representation. Through its technology, it demonstrates a sudden new level of planning depth. Most of its life is present awareness, but something else has occurred, such that *Hss* can create an internal narrative that can move the mind into past or future time. With this existential self-recognition comes the problem of the Self and the Other. The psyche is not a seamless whole; to live with other beings who have their own self-recognition makes conflict, (some degree of) alienation, and negotiation part of the human (*Hss*) condition. And this means that fear is part of that condition as well. It is not that fear is the *essence* of being human, but only that some degree of alienation from others and the world is as basic as sexuality, creativity, death, and what I have called "paradox." Boundaries are real; *Hss* life is a package deal.

Symbolic systems come into being for a variety of reasons, but one of these is to manage the fear and alienation that are intrinsic to Self/Other awareness. This occurs even in small Paleolithic societies with groups of less than five hundred, living in face-to-face contact. Hence, we see evidence of ranking even in the Middle Paleolithic. Men are often ranked above women; some individuals are endowed with greater prestige than others. Under conditions of population pressure and circumscription, ranking systems get exacerbated to insure social coherence and control. More often than not, it is probably the frightened and the insecure who come forward to claim leadership.

Yet if we are a flawed species, we also have ways of making things better (or worse). Sedentism and population density make them worse, but then there are also leveling mechanisms, fission-and-fusion patterns, and certain child-rearing practices that make infants feel more secure in the world. Paradox is also about less self-preoccupation and a greater sense of presence and immediacy. Death, above all, can be seen by a culture as just a part of life—which (life) then can be experienced as a miracle, a gift. It is in this sense, that HG life did not know a great deal of social stratification or alienation, or a SAC that took them out of an immediate horizontal relationship with the world, that we can reasonably speak of a "Golden Age." Subsequent Neolithic developments did not *create* the conditions of misery, as Rousseau would have it, but rather multiplied the negative potential that was already present. The impulse for mastery, vertical organization, religion, and the like gradually took over. It produced great civilizations with brilliant and inspiring aspects to them, but—as Freud said—at an increasingly high price. The result is what confronts us in the daily newspapers. On page 1, we read about who won the Nobel Prize in literature; on page 2, about the latest massacre in the Balkans or the latest episode of mass starvation in Africa. Reviews of a Cézanne exhibit in Paris vie with an Amnesty International report that torture is routine in Mexico City (as it was in Paris during the Algerian conflict); and so on.

Should I then tell you that we need: (a) sharp controls on population growth; (b) more loving, somatic child-rearing practices; (c) a more relaxed attitude towards death; (d) horizontal political arrangements, and the ability to see the will to power as an expression of insecurity; (e) greater gender equality; (f) an immediate-return economy; (g) the abandonment of religion and ideology in favor of trust and paradox? Well, some of this would undoubtedly improve our situation (I would put item (a) at the top of the list), and knowing this might be the major legacy that HG civilization has bequeathed to us. But much of it would get badly distorted in the context of civilization, to the point that it could be quite destructive; and movements designed to promote these sorts of causes easily turn into self-righteous "microfascisms," complete with hierarchies and party lines. You know it; I know it; and we've seen far too much of it.

The crucial issue, of course, is not what we "should" do, but what is likely to happen. It is not likely, for example, that Newt Gingrich (remember him?) or some "new paradigm" guru will suddenly (or even gradually) recognize the sadness that is driving his power-hungry life; this does not happen in the real world. In the real world, men and women run their power trip until it collides with someone else's power trip, and then it's *ricominciare da capo*. All of this is to say that as mass society and global civilization play their dramas out over the next millennium, the best we can probably hope for *is* some form of intelligent damage control and the occasional breakthrough. After all, rigid empires (USSR) do collapse, and old enemies (Rabin and Arafat) do shake hands. Civilization is not a monolith; there is better, and there is worse.

On the individual level, however, a lot is possible, though the results are usually very mixed, and people do not so much change as evolve. And socially, certain local experiments are possible that may move us in a healthy direction. Before I talk about all this, however, I want to say a bit more about the problem of civilization as our framework and the value of the nomadic/horizontal insight as an available reality, for these things will surely condition what is possible for us. In other words, I believe that it is our duty to be optimistic, but that "realistic optimism" is an even greater duty and that this cannot be formulated without having a good sense of our socioeconomic and religious context. David Orr, in his discussion of the contemporary interest in "sustainable societies" (*Ecological Literacy*), says something similar, emphasizing the need for the

> explicit recognition of persistent and otherwise inexplicable tragedy and suffering in history, and in history to come—even in a world that is otherwise sustainable. This realism can provide deeper insight into human motives and potentials, and an antidote to giddy and breathless talk of new ages and paradigm shifts. Whatever a sustainable society may be, it must be built on the most realistic view of the human condition possible.[1]

So before we can talk about what Octavio Paz calls *la otra voz*—the other voice—we need to delineate the elements of an unconscious civilization.

Dérapage: The Modern SAC

In essence, unconsciousness means mechanically doing the same damn thing over and over again without the slightest awareness that this is going on. This is especially characteristic of civilization in terms of two crucial features: vertical power relations and vertical religious experience. When the latter of these two takes the form of paradigms and ideologies, we have the situation John Ralston Saul describes: power tied to the pursuit of truth and utopia. It is this configuration that prevents the other voice, a certain historical alternative—what might be called "antihistory"—from ever coming forward; as the American poet Charles Olson recognized some years ago:

> History itself . . . can be shown to be of two kinds, and that of these two kinds, one is negatively capable and the other is power. Men can and do wilfully set in motion egotistical, sublime events. They have effect which looks like use. But in the schema here presented, these are power, and history as primordial and prospective is seen to demand the recognition that the other history, what I would call anti-history, is not good enough.[2]

This other history, or voice, is what vertical power arrangements and the SAC are able to bury as inferior, or render invisible. We cannot rest in paradox or negative capability and find out what might *naturally* emerge. No, empty space must be forever filled up with "egotistical, sublime events" that are primordial and prospective ("going somewhere"). It is this peculiar configuration that generates paradigm-shift addiction and the subsequent blindness it entails.

The best modern (secular) equivalent I have found for the SAC is that of *dérapage*, a term introduced (into English, anyway) by *New York Times* reporter Richard Bernstein in his trenchant and desperately needed critique of the new political correctness movement and the ideology of multiculturalism (*Dictatorship of Virtue*), but which applies to much else besides. The word, which literally means "slipping," in French, has been used by a number of French historians to describe the point at which the revolution of 1789 shifted from a concern with the rights of man to what is called the "Reign of Terror." This is the move to dogmatism, "that familiar skid into ideological excess," says Bernstein, and is typically endowed by its proponents with what Robespierre (by 1794) called "an emanation of virtue." Thus, for example, one aspect of what began as the civil rights movement in the United States with Martin Luther King, Jr.

ended up as the racism and so-called "multiculturalism" of Louis Farrakhan. In the process, Bernstein points out, the original movement "slipped from its moorings and turned into a new petrified opinion of the sort it was supposed to transcend." A messianic program, multiculturalism is really *mono*culturalism, a cloak for *dérapage*; "it does not take kindly to true difference." In many institutions now, as Bernstein is easily able to document, the new ism has generated a kind of thought police, who can easily frighten those who are scared of being labeled "racist" or "sexist." Its alleged diversity is thus a fraud, because it imagines a world of enforced identical opinions. It denigrates notions of objectivity and achievement and celebrates the postmodern slogan that everything is socially constructed. White European males are now seen as the "bad guys," often required (if they wish to hold onto their jobs) to attend insensitive "sensitivity sessions" or "diversity training" that tell(s) them how to think and feel, and in which opinions different from those of the trainers are not tolerated. "Respect for difference," which is obviously a very good idea, has slipped into a secularized religion that will be imposed on everybody, and group affiliation is made into an ultimate principle. "Virtue" is big here, says Bernstein; the attitude is one of rooting out sin. In many institutions across the United States, including those of higher education, the result has been to shut down the free exchange of ideas. And all of this in the name of freedom.

Thought proceeds in terms of slogans, in this multicultural Brave New World. (In my own experience, this is especially true of so-called "alternative" institutions.) It is a Manichaean world, that of oppressor and oppressed, and its proponents frequently adopt the jargon of Michel Foucault: "dominant discourse," "marginalized other," "hegemonic curriculum," and so forth. The result is a terrifying loss, for as Bernstein points out, "We are unwilling to defend complicated truths." Indeed, nuance and complexity of thought become impossible in such a climate; to raise objections to the new regime is not regarded as a healthy diversity of opinion, but quite simply as evil. Education turns into a cult. "Multiculturalism," writes Bernstein, "is an ideology that is unaware of itself as an ideology."[3]

This last point is crucial: paradigms move within the orbit of hierarchy, of power relations, and that is why the New Truth becomes the Old Story in fairly short order. "Revolution" here is never a *seeing-through* of paradigm addiction and the power relations game. As a result, rebellion against one orthodoxy only leads to another orthodoxy. "The object of power is power," wrote George Orwell in *1984*; and in the case of the political correctness movement, this means membership in the rising "club." "It takes no bravery to be a multiculturalist," writes Bernstein. Grants are typically awarded if the writer promises a "radical transformation of the dominant paradigm." If she simply says, "This work might make a modest change in our way of thinking," she had better look for other sources of support.[4]

Of course, there is a curious parallel between the multiculturalism of today and the communism of an earlier age. As Doris Lessing pointed out in 1992, it is no accident that the political correctness movement arose at the very same time that the Soviet Union and the Communist experiment fell apart. Indeed, much of what Bernstein and other critics correctly identify as the pathology of the p.c. movement today was said of communism a few decades earlier. Recalling his days in the Party, Arthur Koestler commented: "Not only our thinking, but also our vocabulary was reconditioned." Certain words became taboo; others met with official approval. (The same thing occurs today in "sensitivity training," where one is taught a "correct" vocabulary.) The Italian ex-Communist Ignazio Silone remarked on the complete incapacity of his Russian comrades to discuss opinions that conflicted with their own: "The adversary, simply for daring to contradict, at once became a traitor, an opportunist, a hireling ... To find a comparable infatuation one has to go back to the Inquisition."[5]—or, we might add, to the sacred authority complex itself.

New Paradigm Worship

Dérapage, however, is hardly confined to deconstruction or multiculturalism or to the communism of a previous era. Bernstein refers to a "normal human propensity toward a foolish zealousness," and the British historian, Noel Annan, states that "nothing will ever stop people [from] demanding large-scale explanations of the world."[6] But I think we need to be clear that this propensity, this demand, is "normal" only for people conditioned to a form of thinking that moves within the orbit of sacred authority (especially of the Zoroastrian variety) and vertical power relations. The problem is not that certain ideas are not valid but that sedentary, population-dense cultures are driven to fetishizing these ideas, turning them into total explanations. In our own time, this tendency has reached a kind of apogee in the frenzy over finding a "new paradigm," a new consciousness that will celebrate myth and ritual, ecology and transpersonal psychology, and leave the dull and ugly world of science, history, and partriarchal/industrial society behind in the dust. Now some of this is clearly desirable, inasmuch as the scientific breakthrough of Descartes and others actually turned into another ism (truth content notwithstanding); but as framed by its proponents, the new paradigm is typically presented as a Zoroastrian/utopian scheme, a choice of either/or. The religious banner here (for that is what it is) is "machine to green." Mechanistic science, the ultimate evil, will now be replaced by an "emerging planetary culture," the ultimate good. I shall say a bit more below on why sedentary cultures are compelled to think in terms of these manic-depressive mood swings; but for now, the words of Arthur Koestler, on his own experience of how conversion to communism affected his life, provides an important clue to the fetishism involved in the new paradigm movement or indeed any movement that promises tortured souls such as we all are existential clarity:

> To say that one had "seen the light" is a poor description of the mental rapture which only the convert knows . . . The new light seems to pour from all directions across the skull: the whole universe falls into pattern like the stray pieces of a jigsaw puzzle assembled by magic in one stroke. There is now an answer to every question: doubts and conflicts are a matter of the tortured past.[7]

"New paradigm" literature seems to arrive in my mailbox almost every week, proclaiming the inevitable triumph of the new over the traditional. For example, one recent letter I received sets up a series of sharp dichotomies, extolling "pattern recognition skills" over "information," "context" over "specialization," "lay science" over "expertise," and the "relativeness of truth" over the "laws of nature." In another case, a "new paradigm" journal tells me how education will be totally revamped along the lines of an "alchemical circus." "The future of our species," it declares, "depends on physical ecstasy" (no, I'm not kidding). This new doctoral program(!) will demonstrate the limits of rationalism and "techno-addictive thinking," plus teach the "technology of the sacred," along with "ancestral worship," "whole systems politics," and "political pharmacology." For some strange reason, there are no courses in new-paradigm addiction in the syllabus, or in critical thinking and analysis, or in the basic elements of the social sciences.

This kind of literature reminds me of an incident that occurred at a lecture I attended in London in October 1975, given by the cultural anthropologist Gregory Bateson. The talk was chaired by R. D. Laing, and when I arrived, the large auditorium was overflowing. The mood of the crowd was somewhat strange and more than a bit charged: people in search of a new paradigm, might be the best way to describe it. For the most part, I came away from that evening with a conviction, which I still hold, that Bateson was onto something significant. But one event in particular, a question from someone in the audience, sticks in my mind, inasmuch as it proved to be uncannily prescient. "What," said this man, candidly and without any hostility, "is to prevent this new way of looking at things from becoming, in its turn, the next new set of tricks, with a different group of people managing the reality for the rest of us?" The man was clearly, I realized, a goat in a world of sheep. As for Bateson, he had no answer and was only able to mumble something about Zen masters replacing each other based on integrity. It was not very convincing.

A major problem with all of these crusades for change-via-consciousness is that they do not have any sense of genuine historical, dialectical process. On a fundamental level, they just don't get it: they don't understand that the mechanical paradigm of the seventeenth century was embraced with the same type of zeal that is now fueling the new holistic one. There is no speculation on the possibility that this new paradigm could become tyrannical and obscurantist. If our model of paradigm shift is, for example, the disintegration of the Roman Empire or the Middle Ages, we have to remember that verticality, rule by elites, and the use of religion (secular or otherwise) as legitimation all survived intact. As Bateson's questioner was suggesting, they will undoubtedly survive the next paradigm shift intact as well, as will ideology and sloganeering. So what kind of change are we talking about? If these things remain intact, then shifts in consciousness are mere window dressing. It's all "groovy" now, in the mind of the new paradigm crowd, but the essential structures, the essential problems, remain the same.

In point of fact, when the holistic paradigm *does* get institutionalized, we get a learning atmosphere that is cultish, zealous, and dogmatic. We now have large groups of people running around who can think systemically but not analytically; who rave about "the sacred," but haven't a clue as to the nature of scientific research; who chatter on about the "tyranny of experts" when they have no expertise themselves. Cultural relativism is passed off as sophistication, when it is little more than sophistry; "diversity" becomes a slogan, repeated with a kind of hypnotic grunting; quantum mechanics is held up as a new philosophy, even though most of its proponents can't do a single freshman physics problem. In an apt bit of satire of this kind of self-deception, the American psychologist S. I. Shapiro writes of the "incredible beliefs" endemic to the field of transpersonal psychology, whose "more advanced members," he assures us, "would of course never harbor such astonishing assumptions." These include: "It's all in the mind"; "Everything is perfect"; "Modern physics confirms transpersonal psychology"; "The planet is undergoing a transformation in consciousness"; and "Transpersonal psychology will save the world."[8] And Shapiro is right: there is literally no awareness whatsoever among the crowd he satirizes that this kind of blind mythologizing is politically disastrous. Of course, if you point any of this out to them, you are obviously a cultural dinosaur, for (as in the case of thirties Marxism) "the truth" will prevail, and you are either on the bandwagon or you are not. One can only hope that we can set up a few halfway houses or twelve-step programs over the next few decades, to help these folks break the grip of new paradigm addiction that, like drugs or alcohol, provides them with short-term ecstasy while it is robbing them of their real life.

A dramatic example of this kind of thinking can be found in Richard Tarnas' book, *The Passion of the Western Mind*. In many ways, it is actually a fairly decent summary of European intellectual history, written in a lucid and accessible style. The strange bend in the road comes during the last fifty pages, when the author suddenly turns history into archetypal psychology and takes hermeneutics (the science of interpretation) and postmodernism to be the new truth. Ignoring all contemporary critiques of deconstructionism, Tarnas declares authoritatively that "no interpretation of a text can claim decisive authority." He claims "to refuse the tyranny of wholes" and the "escapism" of cults and ideologies. He then concludes by adopting Jungian archetypes, Stanislav Grof's LSD research, and the need for all of us to embrace the Great Mother and undergo "dissolution of the ego in ecstatic unity with the universe." In his own adaptation of Hegel, Tarnas argues for a biological mysticism, in which "the human mind is ultimately the organ of the world's own process of self-revelation." (What in the world does he think could be the *proof* of this? one might ask.) All of Western history, since its alleged destruction of a supposed (in fact, nonexistent) matriarchy, has been moving toward a particular destiny, which is to reunite with the repressed feminine. "Man is something that must be overcome," writes Tarnas, "—and fulfilled, in the embrace of the feminine." Presumably, with this *conjunctio oppositorum*, this *hieros gamos* and Hegelian *Aufhebung*, we shall come to the end of history; our restless search for paradigm will be dissolved in a final synthesis of ecstatic realization. (Come to Mommy, she will make you whole again.)[9]

I dealt with much of this Jungian/gaian foolishness in chapter 4, but I hope the reader finds this transpersonal tyranny as scary as

I do. That someone obviously intelligent could come to such a pass is nothing less than terrifying. Tarnas pays no attention to the numerous critiques of deconstruction that now abound in the scholarly literature; does not see that his uncritical embrace of cultural relativism inevitably drives him into the arms of "gaia," an absolute haven in an uncertain world; is unaware that matriarchal cultures never existed; adopts Stanislav Grof as a guru, when the LSD work was performed on contemporary, middle-class individuals living in a heroic/Axial culture, whose "archetypal psyches" are not likely to be representative of the human race stretching back to the Paleolithic;[10] and fails to grasp that his new-found biological mysticism is precisely the sort of "escapism" (regression, in fact) that he just finished condemning two pages earlier. The totalitarianism embedded in such a reading of history, complete with an unconscious, deterministic destiny literally leaps off the page. As Hannah Arendt once commented, the presupposition of any great, hidden purpose in history that is ineluctably working itself out and that must inevitably lead to some specified outcome (good or bad) "is one of the most virulent and dangerous diseases of the modern age."[11] Tarnas' vision is only one more example of what Norman Cohn describes as the Zoroastrian/utopian impulse, the belief that all conflict will be resolved and that Western civilization will finally come to "rest." It is a child's view of the world, really, the ache for its mother; what Albert Camus once referred to as "nostalgia for the absolute," the frenzied wish to be cured. Like Cohn, Arendt, Karl Popper, and Camus, I can't imagine a more deluded way of thinking.[12]

Versions of Tarnas' world view seem to abound these days. In *The Architecture of the Jumping Universe*, Charles Jencks tells us that "the universe is a single, unfolding, self-organizing event," a "truth" to which chaos theory, complexity theory, the gaia hypothesis, and quantum mechanics all supposedly point. "We know truths that have been revealed to no other generation," he declares.

> Fundamentally [writes Jencks], this new understanding of reality overturns the four great enslaving "isms" of Modernity: determinism, mechanism, reductivism, and materialism. The new concepts which have replaced them are emergence, self-organization, evolution by punctuated equilibria, and cosmogenesis—creativity as basic in the universe.
>
> They refute the nihilistic view, developed because of Modern determinism and materialism, that our place in the universe is accidental, tangential, absurd, and discontinuous with the rest of nature . . . Mind, consciousness, and sentient

creatures with intelligence are not alien to but *central* to the cosmogenic process.[13]

I find it remarkable that Jencks does not see assertions such as these as addictive, or at the very least, ideologically naive. Here is a presumably intelligent human being telling us that we have finally overcome our previous, enslaving isms for—what? A new ism! which he cannot see as *merely the next ideology*. (Who was it that said that "ism" stands for "incredibly short memory"?) Instead, he is telling us that these "new concepts" are radically different—the "truth." When I read these paragraphs, Fritz Perls' concept of "introjection" (see above, chapter 4) came immediately to mind. Like an infant, without discrimination, Jencks has swallowed this supposed new paradigm whole. By way of contrast, consider the reaction of Brendan Gill, in his review of Jencks' book in the *New Yorker*:

> How is one to deal with so vehement a lover's declaration of war? What does Jencks imagine he has succeeded in conveying to his readers when he employs the words "know" and "truths" as if they required no qualifying? What is his "know" compared to mine—his "truth" to my "truth"? As an old-fashioned enslaved nihilist, I might believe and assert that the universe is accidental, tangential, and absurd, but I would certainly never claim that I *knew* this, or that it was a truth.

I am reminded of a speech I heard more than thirty years ago, by the radical activist Saul Alinsky, in which he said, "To me the man who stands up and says he has the truth, wears the mask of the Inquisition." Once again, we dance around the SAC and call it liberation.[14]

As in the case of multiculturalism, it is not, of course, that things such as chaos theory or complexity theory have no validity. There are surely some good ideas here. But we can only know this through empirical testing, experiential reality. The problem with Jencks is that he doesn't seem to be terribly concerned about such verification (let alone falsification); his quest is a religious one. He cannot see, any more than Tarnas, that jazzing ourselves up with chaos theory, gaia, paradigm shifts, and archetypes is the voice of the SAC, the next phase of our "unconscious civilization." We need this sort of Perlsian "introjection" like a *loch in kop*, as my mother would say—a hole in the head.

"We have suffered from this 'either-or' sickness for a long time," writes John Ralston Saul: "With the stroke of an intellectual argument, the planet is put in its place. Terrifying. Only the bravest and most foolish of individuals would not become passive before such awe-inspiring destinies." Where, he goes on, does this desperate need come from? It is the need of a child who refuses to grow up. The need to believe in single-stroke solutions, says Saul, is rooted in a fear of reality[15]—and, I suspect, a fear of one's self. One escapes into future scenarios and avoids the immediate and uncomfortable difficulties of one's daily life.

The Causes of Dérapage

This brings us, then, to the causes of *dérapage*. The structure of it seems fairly obvious:

1. Map a partial truth onto all of reality;
2. Reject all disagreement as a "failure to understand";
3. Build your whole identity around the new "truth."

This last item is, in many ways, the key to the whole business. In the context of the SAC and a Zoroastrian way of thinking, it becomes almost inevitable. As Doris Lessing once put it, referring to the Marxism of an earlier era, the hidden agenda always seemed to be, "I-make-Revolution-and-Therefore-I-Am."[16] So now we can make the New Paradigm Revolution, and thereby get our identities validated, qualify for a place in the (civilized) world. This is a sad situation: instead of life being enough, as it was for HGs, we have to qualify for it. Contrast this desperation with the relaxed intelligence of someone like Albert Einstein: "Where the world ceases to be the scene of our personal hopes and wishes," he wrote, "where we face it as free beings, admiring, asking and observing, there we enter the realm of art and science."

The desperate need for a cause, for obtaining existential clarity by organizing the psyche along binary-Zoroastrian lines (which produces a unitary belief system), is another version of what the psychologist Heinz Kohut calls the "idealized parental imago," one of two basic narcissistic configurations. In the other, less complex configuration, known as the "grandiose self," the person's unconscious assumption is, "I am perfect." In the case of the idealized parental imago, the disciple looks at the guru and says to himself, "You are perfect, but I am a part of you."[17] If we substitute "cause" or "paradigm" for guru here, we unravel the sources of *dérapage*: it is nothing more than Fritz Perls' "introjection" writ large. It is socially what introjection is psychologically. This is why thirties Marxists needed to explain not merely social inequality with the theory of dialectical materialism, but also the rings of Saturn, or why systems theory or chaos theory cannot be allowed simply to be useful in some situations, but are instead elevated into total explanations of the universe. The problem is that Einstein was right: the world is *not* a stage for our personal (or transpersonal) schemes and desires; that is the childish dream of the narcissist. Einstein's remark echoes that of Charles Olson, that the historical record is one of power, of "egotistical, sublime events," but this record forecloses the option of "antihistory," of paradox, in which we live as free beings, not hooked into proving that we exist, are OK, whole.

"A revolution," wrote Immanuel Kant, "will never produce a true reform in ways of thinking. Instead, new prejudices, like the ones they replaced, will serve as a leash to control the great unthinking mass." Kant's point is a crucial one, and the whole process of paradigm merry-go-round is lucidly captured in his remark. For the "aggressive subgroup" that I described in chapter 2 need hardly be limited to those who seek political and economic power. As the Italian sociologist Antonio Gramsci pointed out, hegemony is more often a case of *symbolic* control. If I espouse some particular paradigm and manage to impose it on society, then I not only reap the "benefits" of my narcissism, but I get to control the beliefs and thought processes of others as well. In this sense, Isaac Newton became hegemonic for the modern era; and the historian Frank Manuel, in his biography of the British scientist, lays bare the sadness and alienation that underlay Newton's need to do this. It is a reasonable guess that this situation has not changed much and is as true of the early twenty-first century as it was of the early eighteenth. We certainly don't lack for hegemonic wannabes these days; that seems obvious enough. Nor is it likely that the dynamic driving them is much different than it was in previous eras. New bottles, same wine, I suppose.[18]

Noting that postmodern society is a fountainhead of new "noble lies," Walter Truett Anderson points to the "new paradigm story" as a classic case of this, an ideology driven by a dubious logic: "The message," he says, "is essentially millen[n]arian prophecy, older than history, but stated in ways that suggest the coming of the millennium is practically a scientific fact." Thus, we are told that feminism will replace patriarchy, ecology will replace control of nature, and so on, as though these things will necessarily prevail, and soon, as part of a major historical discontinuity. The ideas, says Anderson, are "cited as zealously as redneck preachers quote the Bible." In reality, the new paradigm story is a "rigid prediction of historical inevitability" and quite linear in its outlook: there is a paradigm, then a revolution, then another paradigm. "The paradigm is dead, long live the paradigm." Omitted in the new paradigm story is Thomas Kuhn's declaration that his theory did not apply to social change and the fact that many scholars don't even believe it applies to science. Like many other postmodern "stories," the new paradigm version of history is basically a story of the conflict between good and evil. Anderson predicts it will be a force for divisiveness rather than for unification—as we are already seeing in the case of multiculturalism and deconstruction.[19]

If social *dérapage* corresponds to individual introjection, the sad restlessness described by Object Relations theory—"I feel empty, but once I get *x*, then I'll be happy"—has a social counterpart in the new paradigm game. In other words, the following diagram of the "Wheel of Suffering" as it operates for individuals (when one finally gets *x*, one then wants *y*, ad infinitum) can easily be seen to be the underlying mechanism of paradigm-shift addiction and of Zoroastrian utopianism in general.[20] Here, we start on the left with our hope or dream ("a new job/relationship will change everything," e.g.) and translate it into action. We go for it. Let us say that we then get what we want ("You're hired!"); what happens next? Well, it is no longer a fantasy: the perfect job proves to be rather mundane, after a while, or the perfect dream partner all too human. Elation over, I go into depression (the Wheel of Suffering has an interesting similarity to the pattern of caffeine addiction); I feel hopeless, defeated. It is at this point that I could sit with the feelings, live with them in my body and see what comes up. But living in the present, outside of fantasy, is too painful to contemplate, so I generate another dream ("I'll get a promotion"; or "I'll get a new partner"), and I'm off and running once again. Like a hamster on a treadmill, I never see that this is a game without an end. The only "end" is to experience my life as it actually is, as it presents itself; to really grasp the fact that "there" is not necessarily going to be very different from "here."

The same logic applies on a cultural scale. We live with a certain paradigm that we once endowed with salvationist promises. But it went sour; a few centuries down the road, it failed to deliver the goods and actually created a number of severe, unexpected problems. Now we see it as evil, oppressive; we need a new paradigm that will liberate us from the negative aspects of the old one. Gurus arise who offer to take us to the promised land; they found institutes, hold workshops, get everybody mobilized and excited. Eventually, perhaps, we succeed: we get our new culture, our New Jerusalem. But

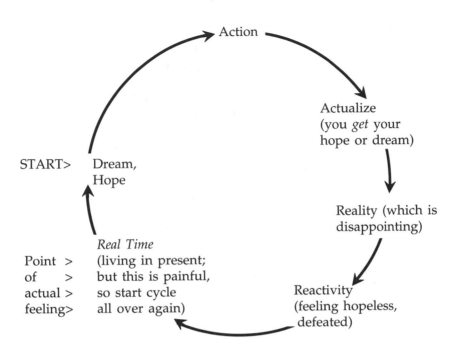

as time passes, guess what? We discover that the reality has fallen short of the promise, and, in addition, we now have a number of new, very serious problems we never anticipated. Hmm . . . what we need is a new paradigm! All of this is a bid for immortality, really; the denial of the body, and of death. It is also part of the panorama of cultural distraction.

However, there is an alternative to this paradigm-shift addiction, but because it is not addictive, it is much less exciting. This is to recognize that what we need is not a dramatic transformation of reality and culture, but simply the willingness to live in *this* culture and reality as we work on the intelligent repair of present problems, without hype or bombast, and let the future take care of itself. For that future, when it arrives, will have *its* problems, and we shall have to deal with *them*. Thus, commenting on the goddess craze and the dubious arguments of Riane Eisler (see chapter 4), Walter Anderson asks:

> Can we work toward equality of the sexes without believing that it is going to fix up all our problems? Or do we need to swallow whole [i.e., introject] another shakily assembled story about the past and another glib promise about the future?[21]

Much the same could be said of environmental pollution, population control, racial tensions, and probably all of the challenges facing us. We don't *have* to behave like infants, go the route of introjection and *dérapage*; in a rational sense, it's just not necessary. The British mathematician G. Spencer Brown captured the possibility of an alternative to the mechanical, unconscious game of paradigm shifting in a poem he published some years ago under the pseudonym of James Keys. The poem is called "The Opening":

> Once every 500 years
> The gates of heaven are opened
> Just a little way
> Just a little light
> Just a little
> Just enough
> Soon
> They will close again
> Bang
> Clang
> Missed it
> Ah well
> Another 500 years[22]

I should add, however, that I am not arguing that progress of various sorts, scientific or otherwise, does not occur in history; nor am I saying that this is a bad thing. My view is rather that it cannot be fetishized without doing violence to reality and to ourselves. It is, for example, progress to have Galileo's laws of motion instead of Aristotle's; the former predict that arrows fired into the air hit the earth at an angle (which they do) while the latter claim they fall straight down to earth in a perpendicular path (which they don't). But as important (I believe) as modern science is for a democratic society, it cannot "save" us; it can't create a better world for all, and it would appear that it hasn't (though it has improved the lot of many). Similarly, certain aspects of systems theory describe, let us say, some types of human interaction better than traditional social or behavioral science, and that is fine. But systems theory also cannot save us, and mapped onto all of reality at large, it becomes a kind of idiocy.[23] The difference between "useful notions" and the slavery of *dérapage* was captured perfectly by Noel Annan when he wrote: "It is not wrong to see progress in history; but history does not *consist* of progress."[24]

Well, I trust I have made my point. I have talked extensively about what it means to live in an unconscious civilization; now let us consider the possibility of a conscious one.

The Elements of Conscious Living

On the individual level, there are two things that strike me as integral to HG civilization that we moderns can adopt, though the process of making these things a part of our lives would be a slow and difficult one. The first is the cultivation of silent spaces; the second, the radical acceptance of death. Both of these contribute greatly to the ability to experience paradox.

Of course, the issue of population density has a lot to do with this. Following the discussion of chapter 2, I am convinced that this is an overriding factor in the shaping of different ways of life. Some time ago, I had the opportunity to visit Australia, a country that is roughly the same physical size as the United States but with a mere 17 million people—less than 7 percent of the American population. Now this is hardly a perfect society, by any means; the history of white-Aboriginal relations during the last two hundred years, in particular, has left a terrible wound that the country is only now beginning to address. But the presence of vast, quiet spaces is quite striking, and means that silence is easily available. This physical fact even filters into city life. From the vantage point of the "antipode," the United States appears to be one big Woody Allen movie. Australian society seems to be much less caught up in a vortex of intensity, chasing one new cultural trend after another. Discussions of the need for the healing of black/white relations, which I was privy to, at least, were not couched in the language of frenzied multicultural hype. There was also a healthy public conversation regarding the drawbacks of getting too deeply drawn into the microchip revolution because there is some understanding that this could deluge the country with tons of useless information (it's only *information*—something Americans tend to lose sight of). In short, it is impossible for individuals in most of Europe and North America to find silence and the state of mind it engenders as a cultural norm, outside of a monastery or perhaps small village life. The result is that desperation and a kind of hysteria are not perceived by those living in Euro-American culture because this is what we "northerners" live in all the time. It is also why most books must have slogans and "target populations" (whom publishers presumably "fire" upon) in order to see the light of day; why, more generally, *everything* has to be couched in terms of a sales pitch, with a hidden promise of salvation behind it, in order to get a hearing at all. Snorkeling at the Great Barrier Reef, watching the exquisite fish move silently past me, a mere six inches from my nose, or looking down and seeing the purple coral spiraling up toward me, I thought: What religion do I possibly need, beyond this? What other evidence of "the sacred" could possibly be necessary?

I need to say a few words about the work of Bernadette Roberts here, which I have mentioned only in passing.[25] Roberts is someone who slowly moved through the unitive experience of the sacred—what I have called counter-tradition (1)—to the state of mind I am talking about. In CT no. 1, we discover a new self, which functions as a divine center. But, eventually, there is a movement to a life without a self, divine or otherwise, in which we can recognize the "experience of God" as a useful stepping-stone, but finally empty. This movement Roberts calls a "quiet explosion." "I quit wandering around looking for life," she writes; "—obviously it's everywhere, we're in it; it's all there is." The Jungian cultivation of a Higher Self finally reveals itself as a defense against having to live a life without God. This is the "false expectation that some ultimate reality lies hidden somewhere behind, beneath, or beyond what is." Hence the error of the transcendent or transpersonal search for "the ground of Being," when we cannot grasp that Being *requires* no ground. "How many," she writes,

> can honestly appreciate the triumph of being common and ordinary? Who can understand what it means to learn that the ultimate reality is not a passing moment of bliss, not a fleeting vision or transfiguration, not some ineffable, extraordinary experience or phenomenon, but instead . . . as simple as a smile?

Clinging to God, she says, "may be a great mistrust and the ultimate expression of disbelief."

Some of this may sound like Buddhism, in particular the *satori* experience of Zen practice; but in fact, *satori* is the falling away of ego or ego perspective, not the falling away of a divine, mythic, transpersonal center. According to Roberts, however, there is one reference in the Buddhist literature (in the *Dhammapada*) to the perception she is talking about, a brief commentary made by Buddha on his own experience. In this discussion, Buddha compares the self to a house and says that the ridgepole collapsed, taking the house with it. Roberts takes "ridgepole" to be a metaphor for the divine center, not the ego center, for Buddha says:

House-builder! I behold thee now,
Again a house thou shalt not build.

"Again" implies that the house had fallen down before and been re-
built around a new center, the divine one. This is the shift from the
dominant tradition I spoke of to CT no. 1, from ego/intellect to "cosmic consciousness," or Gnostic/mythic insight. But when this latter
collapses, she says, there is nothing left with which to rebuild the
house. This is CT no. 3, the experience of paradox (at least for moderns):
what we know as Truth falls away, and we make no attempt to recon-
struct the temple.

Some time ago I received a letter from a friend describing what
the experience was like for her. "Passion," she wrote,

> perhaps, is a prelude to something else, some "new life," some
> otherwise, not yet experienced kind of existence. Passion is so
> easy to understand, to be involved in, to feel alive with. It is
> so acceptable as proof of right living. Feeling, being passion-
> ate, says "I am alive" (as we know it), a kind of pat on the
> back, the best evidence that we exist. However, I'm beginning
> to perceive that at some point passion gives way to something
> akin to a tremendous letting go, a "going nowhere" ... I see
> passion as a "self" involvement ... [Absence of it] is no longer
> to me an indication of lack, quite the contrary, it indicates
> something very mysterious.[26]

Another way—perhaps—of describing Bernadette Roberts' journey and the evolution to paradox is something like this: for many
years of one's life, especially in youth, one is identified with ego,
and that ego has a particular goal: "I will do this or that," which is
the process of going from A to B. "A" here is not good enough; "B"
is "arrival." One does this for many years and may or may not arrive at B, or perhaps get there some of the time. But there comes a
point when the whole structure of going from A to B finally seems
like a drag. It is tedious; it is not worth it, one doesn't want to live
like that any more.

Then begins a process, perhaps, of spiritual work, often
identified with counter-tradition (1), when one's consciousness has
changed and one seems to be on a larger path, a path of great energy. One does this for years, and there are various results, many
of them positive; but one finally sees that the structure is the same
as before: I am at A (which is unworthy), but with enough effort, I

shall arrive at B (which will be worthy). This too now seems to be tedious, predictable.

Slowly, one begins to float; one has no direction because one has stopped believing in "direction." The ego now seems largely irrelevant; it feels like a small lump of yolk in an omelette, as it were. You don't really know where you are going, but you do have the feeling that the "omelette" will take care of that; it will take you wherever you are supposed to go—or nowhere, as the case may be. And then one day you realize that regardless of *where* it takes you, the state of mind that is letting the "omelette" do the work is paradoxically the place at which you were trying to arrive all along. So at the same time that you don't know where you are going—you're there.

As in the case of Kleist or Woolf or Wittgenstein, I can't imagine that such a spiritual odyssey could ever catch on; there is no glory in it. As Roberts herself says, "there is nothing to show for having taken this journey."[27] This is, of course, Pierre Clastres' "nothing," or Wittgenstein's "disappearance of the problem." Very few people will opt for this, and in any case, there is no formula here: it would necessarily be a different process for each person. But it remains significant, at least to my mind, that this ancient HG legacy remains open to us, and it is certainly possible that an awareness of it could spread. For what this legacy enables us to do, if we wish to do it, is to *see through* religion and leave it behind; not on the basis of a simple return to atheism (for those that had left it), but on the basis of an understanding that religion, "God," and vertical spirituality *are* the "fall from grace," grace being "nothing more" than the experience of paradox. What a different type of world *that* would be!

Reflecting on this whole issue in a different context, the Swiss psychotherapist Alice Miller offers the following trenchant commentary:

> It is easier to search for a way out in mysticism, whereby the person can close his eyes and conceal the truth in eloquent symbolic images. Yet sometimes this approach becomes virtually intolerable too because the power of the quite prosaic truth, the truth of the "little self" so disdained by the mystics, can be inexorable. Particularly for people who at some point in their childhood experienced loving care, this truth won't allow itself to be silenced completely, even with the help of poetry, philosophy, or mystical experiences.[28]

Institutionalized Paradox?

This brings me to the question I raised at the end of the last chapter: Can paradox be anything more than an individual experience or a private way of life? Let's have a look at the social possibilities.

To my mind, any change that seeks to institutionalize paradox has to work against social inequality and any kind of duplication of the SAC (which frequently shows up in secular form). As long as political hierarchy or "religious" tendencies are present (sloganeering, fetishizing, the cult of personality, etc.), we move within the orbit of power, and this will perpetuate the same mindset and structures of agricultural civilization. There also has to be an avoidance of large-scale organization, the sort of bureaucratization that encourages vertical outlooks.

One of the most remarkable experiments in this direction (indeed, I am hard-put to find another) is that of the town of Mondragón in the Basque region of Spain, which initiated a worker-owned, industrial cooperative of twenty-three people in 1956. The original salary differential, top to bottom, was 3 to 1. By 1987, Mondragón comprised nearly twenty thousand people in one hundred cooperatives, with a salary differential of 6 to 1—still remarkable, given the severe economic inequality of European and American corporations.[29]

However, the story of Mondragón goes back much earlier than 1956. In the aftermath of the Spanish Civil War, a student priest named José María Arizmendiarrieta (or Arizmendi, for short), who had worked as a journalist on the Republican side, returned to his studies, hoping to find a middle path between socialism and individual property rights. This was interrupted by the bishop, who felt his talents could be better employed as a priest in the parish of Mondragón, to which Don José went in 1941. After years of teaching, preaching, and developing his philosophy of cooperative economics, Arizmendi started a factory with five other villagers. It was called Ulgor, and it began to manufacture paraffin heaters and cookers. The establishment of a workers' savings bank followed soon after, and in 1966 a training school, which included women (Arizmendi spoke out for women's rights as early as 1964). After a strike occurred at Ulgor in 1974, largely because it had grown to three thousand members, it was decided to limit membership in any of the co-ops to five hundred people, since this was recognized as the upper limit for having face-to-face interactions. Although the co-ops followed the principle of verticality when it came to expertise (which

I would regard as healthy inegalitarianism), they preserved a horizontal political structure of one person, one vote. As Keith Bradley and Alan Gelb put it, the system is "almost classless."

As for Arizmendi, he appears to have been almost egoless. We all know how founders of institutions invariably try to perpetuate their ideas or organizations even beyond the grave, which is a variation on the narcissistic configuration described by Kohut. Arizmendi, as the grand old man of Mondragón, could have easily thrown his weight around. Instead, he deliberately stayed out of the strike at Ulgor and away from later attempts at organizational redesign. He also resisted any attempts to honor him and to personalize the movement he founded. (This did occur after his death, with plaques and icons springing up everywhere, a trend he would have deplored.) Arizmendi cannot be located ideologically; his favorite quote was the one from Machado: we build the road as we travel. One biographer wrote that he was "allergic to all isms . . . including cooperativism." "Isms imprison and oppress us," he wrote, but "to live is to renew one's self."

As to the success of the operation, Mondragón has outperformed its larger capitalist environment by a considerable margin. In 1986, when unemployment in the Basque region exceeded 25 percent, the Mondragón co-ops added five hundred new jobs.

However, the Mondragón experiment is no panacea, no ultimate solution. It has always existed in a state of "grief" (à la Wittgenstein), in a tension between horizontal and vertical relations. Expertise is recognized and honored; there is no fashionable American b.s. about how "we are all co-learners," for it is clear to educators with any degree of common sense that apprenticeship is a vertical arrangement, and it is via apprenticeship that we learn. Conflict and dissatisfaction within the co-ops is real and requires frequent negotiation. A strike did occur there, much to everyone's surprise. Arizmendi, in short, did not found a utopia and did not believe in such a thing in any case.

It is also doubtful whether the experiment could be exported to the large capitalist societies of (the rest of) Europe and North America. After all, the degree of homogeneity in Mondragón is very high. The town is in a mountainous region, relatively isolated, and the labor market is not fluid. Few visitors (beyond American sociologists!) come in from the outside. Basque nationalism provides a very strong ethnic glue, and the Basques speak a distinct language of their own (Euskera). All of this suggests a great dependence on regional peculiarities, and in addition, the region has a history of cooperative experiments going back to 1870 (of which Arizmendi was perfectly aware). So before we start the usual "conversion" trip described by Arthur Koestler (above) and turn Mondragón into the latest version of the SAC, we need to recognize the limitations of this model as something that can be generalized or exported.[30]

That being said, I remain impressed by a man whose "sainthood" lay in his insistence on being down-to-earth; who eschewed Platonic/transcendent principles in favor of a "road under construction"; who was free of hype and the need for self-perpetuation; and who saw the work in terms of the immediate task at hand, not in terms of ideology or slogans. I am equally impressed, regardless of the regional or ethnic limitations, by an experiment in paradox— vertical expertise, horizontal politics—that has actually worked, in a world in which Mexico, India, Brazil, and so on economically resemble the pyramidal structure of pharaonic Egypt, with the United States slowly drifting in the same direction.[31] As in the case of counter-tradition (3) and Bernadette Roberts' spiritual journey, it is a path very few will embrace. But it exists; it is on record. "The people I admire most," wrote E. M. Forster, "are those who . . . want to create something or discover something, and do not see life in terms of power."[32]

What, then, would it take for our civilization to become conscious? What I am arguing here is that we would have to integrate certain aspects of HG society, but that to a great extent we cannot do this without triggering a whole series of problems, some of them worse than what we had to begin with. Nevertheless, this is the challenge, and we need to examine what this would involve. In addition to the cultivation of silence and the easier acceptance of death, let us consider the elements of HG society that we have identified in the course of our discussion.[33]

Most of these elements, of course, are unavailable to us: an immediate-return economy (no storage or accumulation); low population numbers and population density; nomadic lifestyle and the fission-and-fusion pattern; band society (basic socioeconomic groups of twenty-five to thirty people); and so on. None of this is going to happen, and most of us wouldn't want it anyway. However, there are some things that we can surely do better with: greater economic equality; greater gender equality; a much closer relationship with the environment; a different pattern of child-rearing practices (including gentler birthing practices); organizational groups of five hundred or less; and, above all, keeping world population growth in check, as much as is politically possible. The trouble is that most of these elements cannot be neatly abstracted from HG society and imported into modern situations without getting seriously distorted. Even leaving our tendency to fetishize aside, we have to keep in mind that the road to hell is paved with good intentions. An easier acceptance of death, discussed above, could easily get institutionalized in a callous way: neglect of the elderly, for example, or the Spartan custom of allowing deformed infants to die. The same thing could be true of multiple mothering, which, as we saw in the case of the kibbutz experiment, generated individuals with a "flat" affect who could relate to a larger group but who had very little sense of individual autonomy (which HGs in fact *do* have).

As for social egalitarianism, this is valuable as long as we don't confuse a legitimate hierarchy of expertise with vertical political power. This mistake was not made at Mondragón, but I have seen this kind of misplaced egalitarianism render so-called alternative educational institutions, for example, little more than a joke: virtually everyone can get a degree; rule by putative "consensus" (on a supposed Native American model) stifles any form of dissent; "group process" enables alleged "nonleaders" to manipulate others and hide from their selves (what might be called "cutthroat cooperation"); and all of this goes on while the institution fetishizes itself as the "education of the future." My point here is that we cannot mechanically adopt the components of a vastly different way of life and assume a beneficial result. We don't really know what will happen; just the opposite could occur.

The "problem" is that civilization will remain civilization; both it and HG society are package deals, and we are reasonably not willing or able to take on the down side of HG life (infanticide, for example). As I stated in the introduction, the job of civilization is to do civilization well; we cannot radically transform ourselves into something else. But it is crucial, in my opinion, to open a dialogue between trees and rhizomes, as it were, to see what a relationship between these might be about. If our culture does have a future, it may well depend on the development of the dialectical possibilities that can exist *between* horizontal and vertical aspects of life. For it would seem that we have a horizontal or paradoxical heritage that we have to come to terms with, no matter how deeply it got buried, and that within civilization, certain problems can never get solved, but only improved upon. Nevertheless, there is some relief in just knowing this.

Thus, certain things may be desirable, but they are going to be extremely difficult to achieve. World population will not drop during the next fifty years; just the opposite. It will be anywhere between 8 and 11 billion by the year 2050, an almost unthinkable situation for the planet. In such a context, the best any nation can do is follow the Chinese example of legislating penalties for having more than one child per family. Greater population means that hierarchy and complexity will increase. Along with this, we can expect increasing economic inequality, which presages a very ominous situation. With the failure of the Soviet experiment, the gloves are now off for the unlimited development of global corporate hegemony (assisted by the very "information highway" that so many foolishly regard as liberatory), and this will be a disaster for the majority of the world's population. Local experiments such as Mondragón are clearly necessary, but the larger fight for a general economic safety net and greater distribution of wealth—democratic socialism, in short—will remain the touchstone of a humane civilization.

Ideally, gentler child-rearing practices and a kind of "ontological education" regarding the human drivenness for power and its roots in early infancy would be ideal, but I am skeptical as to how much society can or should be "therapized." I have personally observed spiritual groups designed to work on early Object Relations turn into hierarchical cults, in which "love" becomes a code word for power, manipulation, and the creation of even more inflated egos. (The self-deception here is breathtaking, and dissent from groupthink triggers a very hostile response.) As Ernest Becker remarked in *The Denial of Death*, if we want to avoid being perfect fools, we need to reject the Berkeley, California, sort of world view that says that our own little psychological experiments can or should save the world. All of this is not as titillating as the rosy promise of some "emerging planetary culture," but it is at least in touch with reality, rosy or not.[34]

The issue of an *embodied* culture is an important contribution that an understanding of HGs can make to civilization and corresponds to counter-tradition (2), as listed in Table 2 (chapter 6). I have not said much about CT no. 2 in this book because I have dealt with it elsewhere at some length;[35] but embodiment is quite important to paradox, for without it, the practice of nonformula easily turns into one more formula. This is the greatest con of all, the conversion of nomadic consciousness into a position, a philosophy; instead of being lived (embodied), it just becomes the paradigm-of-no-paradigm. Gurus in this category are the creepiest of the bunch. They talk of "living in process," "nonoppositional thinking," and so on, but beneath the facade of openness one senses an enormous rigidity and authoritarianism: the commitment to their own influence or power as the real bottom line. This is finally their deepest value, and it often shows up in a kind of strange and incongruent body language. Whereas Wittgenstein's purpose was precisely to *break* the hold that discipleship (whether to a living person or to a mode of thought) had over people,[36] the goal of modern-day "no-paradigm" gurus is basically to *extend* the grip of the idealized parental imago, in another form. In this effort, they do not lack for followers.

That branch of holistic thinking known as systems theory is the most blatant example of this pseudonomadic position, in which the concept of avoiding a fixed point *becomes* the fixed point. The systems paradigm is really an attempt to dress up what Aldous Huxley called the "perennial philosophy" in a kind of scientific garb, to sneak religion (or self-transcendence) in through the back door, as it were, which is why its proponents are typically zealots and why the theory, which certainly does contain some useful insights, is heavily caught up in a game of smoke and mirrors.[37] There is a great similarity here between systems theory and ethical theory, in fact, in the sense that a theory of ethics finally tells us nothing at all. As Bernard Williams points out in his brilliant and much-needed book, *Ethics and the Limits of Philosophy*, "thick concepts" such as honor, mercy, and honesty derive from actual situations that occur in the world, that is, are grounded in character and human nature, and no theory of ethics (or set of communal rituals) is likely to make us behave decently. All of this, as in the case of systems theory, is a bit like losing your child by trying officially to adopt it.[38]

The problem of trying to capture Being, or "no-paradigm," in a paradigm goes to the heart of the potential danger of CT no. 3. All of the traditions listed in Table 2 have their drawbacks, and paradox—at least in the world of civilization—is no exception. For paradox generates an empty space, one that band society (or even a small chiefdom, as Clastres showed) knows how to deal with. In the context of power politics and the SAC or its modern secular equivalents, however, the empty space becomes a vacuum, and the ache to fill it is too great. This is why Heidegger slipped from CT no. 3 to CT no. 1, replacing Being with the spirit of the Third Reich. (Which is why embodiment is so important. As someone once said of Heidegger's philosophy, "*Dasein* never had an orgasm.") Thus, there is probably no way of maintaining the wisdom of the empty center that Wittgenstein stumbled onto, on a communal level. Mondragón is not typical of local groups; the rule is that the space gets filled with someone's ego, such that we get what Gilles Deleuze calls the "microfascism of the avant-garde."

It is for this reason that Deleuze, after extolling rhizomes as opposed to trees, points out that horizontality can become a tyranny of its own. Figures such as Heinrich von Kleist and Antoinin Artaud, he says, themselves end up as models to be copied; and this is far more insidious than the other copies. Within civilization, he maintains, the "tribe" needs to remain the underdog; it must never become dominant. Ironically enough, this was the position of that great Enlightenment figure Gotthold Ephraim Lessing: "If my opinions were to become too general," he wrote, "I should be the first to abandon them for the opposite view . . . I cannot believe that truth can ever be common; as little, indeed, as that there could ever be daylight on the whole globe at one and the same time." Or as Pierre Clastres put it, "Thought is loyal to itself only when it moves *against the incline.*"[39]

Rhizomes versus trees, after all, can easily become the latest incarnation of Zoroastrian dualism. There are, says Deleuze, anarchic deformations in trees and nodes of arborescence (i.e., power) in rhizomes. Wittgenstein's "grief" was, as we have seen, the attempt to balance the two.[40]

The problem is that pure rhizomatic thought can be its own form of tyranny, except perhaps in an HG world. In the context of civilization, this mode of consciousness not only is potentially disintegrating of world and psyche, but also (in pure form) wrong. HGs live locally. For better or worse, we do not. As a result, universals, whether in story lines (Woolf) or atomic propositions (Wittgenstein), become necessary. The key to true spontaneity here is Deleuze's remark that our job is "teaching the soul to live its life, not to save it." This, above all, is the great difference between HGs and ourselves.[41]

All in all, then, we cannot simply pretend we are HGs, jump into CT no. 3, and imagine that the other traditions don't exist. In *The Gutenberg Elegies*, Sven Birkerts shows how the Internet and World Wide Web effectively mimic the world of the "eternal present" by creating a purely horizontal mindset, and how destructive this is to the self, to the experience of meaningful depth and vertical understanding. To the extent that HG consciousness is mimicked by the computer addict (with severe disembodiment thrown in for good measure), such an importation of horizontality into modern society only results in shallowness and a kind of mass idiocy. Birkerts thus talks of a drift toward a situation in which we become "creatures of the hive, living some sort of diluted universal dream in a perpetual present." He also points out how easily the new horizontal technology and outlook mesh with multiculturalism, deconstruction, chaos theory, and the abolition of history itself, as everything disappears into "hypertext," freeing us from the supposed "domination" of the author, and finally, from any belief in truth at all. "The future belongs to crowds," he says, quoting the American novelist Don DeLillo; we may be moving from a

culture of depth to the "ersatz security of a vast lateral connectedness." It is a chilling thought.[42]

It is for this reason also that we cannot dispense with the dominant tradition, science and history in particular. Commenting on the
postmodern position that science is just another myth, to which
many people cling out of fear and desperation, Bernard Williams asserts that this is open to the charge of *tu quoque* (you also), that com-
fort is no less sought by the postmodernists, who derive enormous
relief from their belief that science is merely another set of rituals
or is only dealing with another set of texts. To these folks, says Williams, the "idea that modern science is what absolute knowledge
should be like can be disquieting." And insofar as the human world
is concerned, he continues, "we need to have some reflective social
knowledge, including history, that can command unprejudiced assent
if the better hopes for our self-understanding are to be realized." This
is why the postmodernist/multiculturalist attack on such understanding is so off the mark. As Birkerts puts it, "To challenge repression
is salutary. To challenge history itself, proclaiming it to be simply
an archive of repressions and justifications, is idiotic." No, we need
to take the dominant tradition with us into the twenty-first century.[43]

The Role of Unitary Consciousness

What about counter-tradition (1), the Gnostic/transcendent tradition?
This has taken a bit of a beating in this book, as I have tried to restore
the role of paradox to its rightful evolutionary position and to suggest
that much of what we regard as issues of depth psychology, "mythic
substrate," and so on is Neolithic in origin, not the "human condition." But here again, such issues cannot be dealt with by ignoring
them or dismissing them as Neolithic. For *we* are Neolithic; unitive
trance and the SAC are not going to go away by fiat. Most of us have
had the sort of one-on-one child rearing that involved the "hallowed
presence" of the mother and its concomitant imprinting of the psyche
for ecstasy. The way out of this is through, not around. If we are going
to have a dialogue between rhizomes and trees (hopefully avoiding
the establishment of institutes for this purpose), then the phenomenon
of unitary consciousness and all that entails has to be engaged in a
way that is honorific as well as cautionary; nothing less will do. (I
realize I might be shocking the reader at this point, but give me some
credit: Did you really expect me to make a monolith out of paradox?)

One of the best discussions of this issue is Joel Whitebook's
study, *Perversion and Utopia*, which is sensitive to both the creative

and the destructive potential of CT no. 1. Whitebook takes his cue from the psychologist Hans Loewald, who, like Jung, argued that the quest for boundary loss, for the merger of Self and Other, lies very deep within us and contains its own kind of truth. Freud, says Loewald, underestimated the oceanic urge; he did not explore "alternative destinies for it in a postreligious world." A fulfilled life, Whitebook points out, requires a "robust notion of the unconscious."

The conundrum is that great creativity, including major achievements of reason, can come out of that search for merger, but so can a lot of nonsense and complete irrationality. Hence, in our time, we have the legitimate desire to rediscover the maternal voice in the context of an overly scientific society that seems bent on destroying its environment *and*, at the same time, a strong regressive aspect to this, the attempt to contact the primitive mother and the potential for barbarism that this effort contains. The desire to make connections—what Cornelius Castoriadis calls "the monster of unifying madness"—underlies much science and philosophy, but also psychosis, religion, and political totalitarianism. "The most monstrous and the most sublime," writes Whitebook, "have their origins in the same source." The result, he adds, is that "we are compelled to pursue something whose attainment would be undesirable; *to achieve these goals would be just as inhuman* [I would say, non-Neolithic] *as not to strive after them*." Hence, Whitebook argues for a dialogue between rhizomes and trees. Political wisdom, he says, requires "the proper tension between the utopian urge toward completeness and the diffuseness of experience."

According to Whitebook, this dialogue was something Freud did not understand because his equation of pleasure with tension reduction did not let him see the extent to which tension (bound energy) itself can produce stability. But as Jung observed, the vitality of the self is proportional to the extent that it has integrated disavowed parts of the psyche; fantasy itself is a primary source of the critical function of the mind. In a similar vein, the German philosopher Hans-Georg Gadamer has argued that play, a kind of "sacred involvement," is part of the generation of all theory; and Marianna Torgovnick, in *Primitive Passions*, adds that probably no culture "can deny oceanic sensations with impunity," even though the cultivation of these, she says, necessarily involves the courting of complicated dangers. It is no accident that the Eleusinian mysteries were practiced in the ancient world for nearly two thousand years, and George Mylonas argues that they addressed the deepest longings of the human heart, "imparted a modicum of truth to the yearning human soul." Indeed, Cicero, who was reputed to have been an initiate, wrote that they were Athens' greatest gift to the world. He had, apparently, momentarily forgotten about democracy; but the point is that these impulses, at least in civilization, have to be preserved as well as surpassed. The trick, in terms of pursuing such experiences, is to remember that despite their intensity, they are not the "end of the road." Thus, the Greek poet Pindar, four centuries before Cicero, was led to write: "Strive not, O my soul, at immortal life, but use to the utmost the means within thy power" ("exhaust the limits of the possible" would be an alternative translation). Both of these ancient writers, it seems to me, have a valid point.[44]

For the foreseeable future, then, our job will be to work with all four traditions outlined in Table 2. We really can't do without any of them, for they need each other in order to function sanely; at least, as I have said, within civilization. However, I wish to conclude with an appeal to paradox in a context that may be very different, although there is no way of knowing what that might be. But the phase of "global economy" and transnational corporate hegemony that we entered upon when the twentieth century effectively ended in 1989 simply cannot last forever; *no* civilization does. To submerge the entire planet in a business culture is demeaning to human beings and inimical to life itself; and if there are enormous forces pushing us toward a *Blade Runner* world, I am convinced that there is a life force that knows beyond a doubt that a life circumscribed by commercial values and video display terminals is no life at all. (Those excluded from this way of life will undoubtedly create their own forms of resistance.) Sadly, I don't think we shall be able to escape the magnetic attraction of power; things are just too far gone for that. But there is at least the possibility of *knowing* about the "other voice," the antihistory of which Charles Olson speaks, the one not driven by "egotistical, sublime events." "At the core of every human being," wrote D. H. Lawrence, "there is a revolt against that which is fixed."[45] The wandering life is just too deep a part of our genetic memory for us to forget it completely.

It is hard for me to say where my own nomadic tendencies came from, and, frankly, I have spent a great deal of time wishing they would go away. On those rare occasions (but sometimes lasting weeks or even months) when I have felt the fly slip out of the fly bottle, as Wittgenstein was wont to say, and I had the sense of a Wandering God around me or within me, and every day was like a golden coin, as though I were out at the Great Barrier Reef all the time, I would think: yes, it's worth it; you can't put a price on this type of security. But most of the time, there's no romance in it; it's just a hard slog, of putting one foot in front of the other and praying that you'll land on solid ground. There is no salvation on this path, only questions, indications, possibilities. But for the past ten years or so, at least, I haven't been able to live any other way.

Perhaps Octavio Paz, that great Mexican poet, said it best. In the following quotation, he is talking about poetry; but as the HGs he refers to did not write poetry, I have substituted the word "paradox" instead. See if you agree that this is a better reading:

> The relationship between man and [paradox] is as old as our history: it began when human beings began to be human. The first hunters and gatherers looked at themselves in astonishment one day, for an interminable instant, in the still waters of a [moment of paradox]. Since that moment, people have not stopped looking at themselves in this mirror. And they have seen themselves, at one and the same time, as creators of images and as images of their creations. For that reason I can say, with a modicum of certainty, that as long as there are people, there will be [paradox]. The relationship, however, may be broken. Born of the human imagination, it may die if imagination dies or is corrupted. If human beings forget [paradox], they will forget themselves.[46]

And so we come to the end of our story, the story of the Other Voice. *Somebody* has to live the message; maybe—*you*?

NOTES

Introduction: The Experience of Paradox

1. Pierre Clastres, *Society Against the State*, trans. Robert Hurley (New York: Zone Books, 1989; orig. French ed. 1974). My definition of the state is taken from Robert L. Carneiro, "A Theory of the Origin of the State," *Science, 169* (21 August 1970), 733. For a discussion of Clastres' work, see below, chapter 2.

2. The following tripartite schema was first suggested to me by Paul Shepard in a somewhat different form. I found it necessary to modify it rather extensively in this book, based on my own research, but I am very grateful to Dr. Shepard for discussions we had on the subject.

3. I discuss this at length in *Coming to Our Senses* (New York: Simon & Schuster, 1989), some of which is summarized in chapter 1 below (along with the question of whether Object Relations can be applied to the Paleolithic).

4. Berman, *Coming to Our Senses*, chs. 4–8, and below, chapter 1.

5. Julian Jaynes, *The Origin of Consciousness in The Breakdown of the Bicameral Mind* (Boston: Houghton Mifflin, 1976). In general, Jaynes' dating of the origins of self-conscious awareness, about 1000 B.C., cannot possibly be correct. The proliferation of items such as grave goods and personal ornamentation in the Late Paleolithic, that is, after 40,000 B.C., strongly suggests that the existence of such an awareness was already present. See the discussion of this issue in chapter 1, below.

6. E. R. Dodds, *The Greeks and the Irrational* (Berkeley: University of California Press, 1951); Morris Berman, *The Reenchantment of the World* (Ithaca, NY: Cornell University Press, 1981), chs. 3 and 4.

7. From Percy Bysshe Shelley, "Ozymandias," in Thomas Hutchinson (ed.), *Shelley: Poetical Works* (London: Oxford University Press, 1967), p. 550.

8. On omnivalence see John Briggs, *Fire in the Crucible* (Los Angeles: Jeremy Tarcher, 1990), pp. 114–15.

9. Joanna Field [Marion Milner], *A Life of One's Own* (London: Virago, 1986; orig. publ. 1934), *passim*.

247

10. Hugh Brody, *Maps and Dreams* (Vancouver: Douglas and McIntyre, 1981), p. 43.

11. The passage from Ortega y Gasset is quoted in the *New York Times Book Review*, 27 April 1986, p. 43. For the essay by Ong, see "World as View and World as Event," *American Anthropologist*, 71 (1969), 634–47.

12. Tony Hiss, *The Experience of Place* (New York: Vintage Books, 1991), pp. 20–21 and 34.

13. Ibid., pp. 3–4.

14. Galway Kinnell, *The Book of Nightmares* (Boston: Houghton Mifflin, 1971), pp. 51–52.

15. Guillaume Apollinaire, "Le Pont Mirabeau," in Marcel Adéma and Michel Décaudin (eds.), *Apollinaire: Oeuvres poétiques* (Paris: Gallimard, Bibliothèque de la Pléiade, 1956), p. 45; from *Alcools*, originally published by Gallimard in 1920.

16. Cited in Stanley Diamond, *In Search of the Primitive* (New Brunswick, NJ: Transaction Books, 1974), p. 194.

17. Jean-Paul Sartre, *Nausea*, trans. Lloyd Alexander (New York: New Directions, 1964; orig. French ed. 1938), pp. 114–15; Bertrand Russell, *Autobiography*, vol. 2: *1914–1944* (Boston: Little, Brown, 1968), pp. 4–6. See also Noel Annan, *Our Age* (London: Fontana, 1991), p. 93.

18. On this see S. N. Eisenstadt, "Heterodoxies and Dynamics of Civilizations," *Proceedings of the American Philosophical Society*, vol. 128, no. 2 (1984), pp. 104–13; Norman Cohn, *Cosmos, Chaos, and the World to Come* (New Haven: Yale University Press, 1993); and the discussion in chs. 4 and 5, below.

19. I am translating from a German translation of the original Akkadian, an excerpt taken from a brochure published by the Museum für Vor– und Frühgeschichte in Berlin, no. 1121–15, entitled "Frühe Haus- und Siedlungsformen in Vorderasien." The excerpt, in turn, comes from Albert Schott and Wolfram von Soden (eds. and trans.), *Das Gilgamesch-Epos* (Stuttgart: Reclam, 1958), p. 29. English versions include those of E. A. Speiser in James B. Pritchard (ed.), *Ancient Near Eastern Texts Relating to the Old Testament* (2d ed., corrected and enl.; Princeton: Princeton University Press, 1955), p. 77, and Thorkild Jacobsen in *The Treasures of Darkness* (New Haven: Yale University Press, 1976), pp. 198–99.

20. Bruce Chatwin, *The Songlines* (New York: Penguin Books, 1988).

21. Ray Monk, *Ludwig Wittgenstein* (New York: Free Press, 1990); Bernadette Roberts, *The Experience of No-Self* (rev. ed.; Albany: State University of New York Press, 1993). See also below, chs. 6 and 7.

22. Walter Ong, "World as View and World as Event," pp. 634 and 637.

23. James L. Peacock and A. Thomas Kirsch, *The Human Direction* (3d ed.; Englewood Cliffs, NJ: Prentice-Hall, 1980), pp. 294–95.

1. The Writing on the Wall

1. Mircea Eliade, *Shamanism: Archaic Techniques of Ecstasy*, trans. Willard R. Trask (rev. ed.; Princeton: Princeton University Press, 1972; orig. French ed. 1951), pp. xiv, xvii, 8, and 265.

2. On the following, see Peter J. Ucko and Andrée Rosenfeld, *Paleolithic Cave Art* (New York: McGraw-Hill, 1967), pp. 129–33 and 177–78; Horst Kirchner, "Ein archäologischer Beitrag zur Urgeschichte des Schamanismus," *Anthropos*, 47 (1951), 244–86, esp. 254ff.; Steven L. Kuhn, *Mousterian Lithic Technology* (Princeton: Princeton University Press, 1995), pp. 54–57; and Demorest Davenport and Michael A. Jochim, "The Scene in the Shaft at Lascaux," *Antiquity*, 62 (1988), 558–62.

3. This viewpoint dates in particular from an article published by Salomon Reinach in 1903 entitled "L'art et la magie," published in *L'Anthropologie*, vol. 14, pp. 257–66. In *Paleolithic Cave Art*, Ucko and Rosenfeld note (p. 125) that Reinach's influence was enormous and that all subsequent magical interpretations of Paleolithic art are little more than elaborations of his ideas.

4. Erika Bourguignon, *Religion, Altered States of Consciousness, and Social Change* (Columbus: Ohio State University Press, 1973), esp. pp. 9–17 and appendix; David Lewis-Williams and Thomas Dowson, *Images of Power* (Johannesburg: Southern Book Publishers, 1989). Bourguignon's representative sample of 488 societies was taken from the 862 societies listed in George P. Murdock, *Ethnographic Atlas* (Pittsburgh: University of Pittsburgh Press, 1967).

5. For example, André Leroi-Gourhan developed a structural theory of sexual dualism by which to classify Paleolithic art, which for a time enjoyed a great deal of popularity. He held that this complementary opposition could explain the content and topographical locations of cave images. It didn't, however, and he ultimately abandoned it. See his *Treasures of Paleolithic Art* (New York: Abrams, 1965) and "The Evolution of Paleolithic Art," *Scientific American*, 218 (February 1968), 58–74; Randall White, "The Earliest Images," *Expedition*, vol. 34, no. 3 (1992), p. 49; and Ucko and Rosenfeld, *Paleolithic Cave Art, passim*.

6. Jane Harrison, *Prolegomena to the Study of Greek Religion* (3d ed.; Meridian Books, 1955), p. 380; Felicitas D. Goodman, *Ecstasy, Ritual, and Alternate Reality* (Bloomington: Indiana University Press, 1992), p. xii. For an astute indictment of this kind of comparative mythologizing, mounted by the great sociologist of religion, Emile Durkheim, see Robert Nisbet, *The Sociology of Emile Durkheim* (New York: Oxford University Press, 1974), pp. 70–71 and 166–67.

The question of the nature of comparison, when it is methodologically valid and when it is not, is a complicated one and has been debated by anthropologists for more than a century. Franz Boas, one of America's greatest anthropologists, addressed the issue in a famous lecture he gave to the American Anthropological Association in 1896, in which he argued against the then popular notion that "the sameness of ethnological phenomena found in diverse regions is proof that the human mind obeys the same laws everywhere." It is more likely, he asserted, that different historical developments can lead to the same results, that the same phenomena can have a multitude of developmental pathways. Thus, anthropologists must demand that the causes from which a phenomenon developed be examined and that "comparisons be restricted to those phenomena which have been proved to be the effects of the same causes." Otherwise, the comparisons are unjustified. The true scientific presumption (he went on) is in favor of a *variety* of historical or developmental pathways; the burden of proof is on those who wish to argue "that there is one grand system according to which mankind has developed everywhere." The starting point in each case has to be local and historical, before we can attempt to argue—inductively—for general laws or uniformity of underlying patterns.

In 1953, Fred Eggan, in *his* address to the AAA, returned to the question, noting that Boas' lecture had a chilling effect on comparative studies (which was not Boas' intention; it was only to tighten the criteria on the basis of which comparisons might be made). This, he said, was unfortunate, because science is about general explanations, and that necessitates the use of comparisons. The task at hand is to find a methodological balance between the general and the particular that is trustworthy, by generating "controlled comparisons" that are small-scale and do not range over the entire planet. He gave some examples of fieldwork that was successful in this regard, but ultimately was not able to come up with a methodological rule as to when an apparent parallel was a true one.

More recently, the comparative question received a mature and extended treatment by Jonathan Smith, who lays out a paradigm of four major modes of comparison which he calls "ethnographic," "encyclopedic," "morphological," and "evolutionary." Of these, he says, only the morphological approach, which assumes the existence of a few original elements (archetypes) from which complex systems are generated, has any validity (in his view), but most scholars have been wary of it because it contains romantic or Neoplatonic presuppositions designed to exclude historical dimensions. (Eliade clearly falls into this category.) The question thus becomes, Can we have a morphological mode that does justice to history? For it is easy, he points out, simply to weave patterns. The problem is, So what? How do I know that my pattern is really valid, actually present in the world, and not just in my head? It is also the case, says Smith (following Karl Popper), that you cannot use enumerative arguments to establish certainty. No matter how many instances of human religiosity we might observe, this does not justify the conclusion that human beings are fundamentally religious.

All in all, Smith is not able to do much better, methodologically speaking, than Boas or Eggan, except to add an important caveat, taken from Morris Jastrow, Jr. (*The Study of Religion*, 1901), that in the search for a balance between the general and the particular, the subjective and the objective, we must be "as much concerned with determining where comparisons should not be made as with drawing conclusions from comparisons instituted."

On such a basis—that of reasonable scholarly restraint or skepticism—writers such as Eliade and Campbell fail miserably, as Smith, among others, is able to demonstrate quite convincingly (in the case of Eliade; for Campbell, see below, chapter 4, notes 2 and 14). Smith's examination of one particular case, that of Eliade's completely erroneous interpretation of an aboriginal myth, is paradigmatic of the whole Eliadean approach. In *The Sacred and the Profane*, Eliade describes an Australian myth of the Achilpa (or Tjilpa) tribe, about climbing a sacred pole and then disappearing into the sky. Eliade claimed that the Tjilpa carried the pole as a "sacred axis," and if it broke, there was reversion to chaos (death of the ancestors). The message: man must live with a sacred center that enables him to communicate with heaven.

Now this formulation owes much to the research of the so-called Pan-Babylonian school on Near Eastern temples. Cuneiform texts tell of the *Dur-an-ki*, or bond between heaven and earth, which Eliade made central to his ideas. The problem is that the term refers to the "scar" left when heaven and earth got separated during the creation, i.e., it emphasizes *disjunction*, not connection. In addition, the Tjilpa do not *actually* wander around with such a pole; the story occurs only in the "Dreamtime," the mythical time of the ancestors (Eliade later cleared this confusion up). It also turns out that the tale is, in one important respect, atypical of aboriginal (Aranda) traditions. The usual mode of ancestral disappearance is via a return to earth, e.g., turning into rocks and trees. I.e., the typical pattern is terrestrial—horizontal—not celestial, and it involves continued presence. Hence, there would be no need for a pole to connect sky to earth. Eliade chose to read this tale as one of vertical shamanism, which is terribly unlikely. Shamanic traditions depend on a celestial "High God," says Smith, rather than on terrestrial ancestors. Eliade wanted to assimilate the aboriginal world into the shamanic pattern, so he found an anomalous story onto which he could project this.

Part of the problem is that Eliade's source was *The Native Tribes of Central Australia*, by Spencer and Gillen, published in 1899 and then reissued, with some revisions, as *The Arunta* in 1927. Eliade relied on this latter version, which was in fact marred by a native/Christian syncretism, i.e., was a Christianized reinterpretation of Arandan myth. As it turns out, T. G. H. Strehlow (author of the classic work *Aranda Traditions*) discovered that the myth was concocted by Charlie Cooper, a police tracker in Alice Springs who was having Spencer on; hence its "anomalous" nature. Yet even leaving all of this aside, it is clear that Eliade did not concern himself with what was the pervasive ethos of aboriginal culture; in addition, his reading of this particular tale is untrustworthy. He focuses on nine elements in the myth, but only one of them can be verified in the Spencer-Gillen text. Three of these items do not occur in the text at all, and Eliade conveniently misread the other five. Thus, there is no statement of the pole being a cosmic axis; the aborigines do not get their direction from the pole; and the breaking of the pole is not given as the reason for the death of the ancestors. The break is in fact about a loss of status (the ancestors are embarrassed because their broken pole is not as splendid as other poles), not a loss of orientation to the sacred, and is nowhere regarded as an apocalyptic event or reversion to chaos. The pole story, says Smith (minus the disappearance of ancestors into the sky, I presume), is actually a common form of ancestral narrative in Australia, and the elements of the story that Eliade elevates to cosmic significance are commonplace events within typical myths. By ignoring the specific context—the history and anthropology of the situation—Eliade missed the entire structure of the narrative; something he does in his work again and again. (As already noted, he also adds details to the myth that are not in the Spencer-Gillen text at all.) The ancestral narratives stress a man-made world, an environment derived from human beings. Rupture in this world does not occur by breaking poles allegedly linking heaven and earth, but by simple human forgetfulness.

We come back, then, to the question of what constitutes a valid comparison, something Eliade never really worried about in terms of rigorous criteria. In this particular case, he chose to read the Tjilpa text in terms of a pattern that exists in ancient Near Eastern and Indic materials—the symbolism of the "Center" (one of Eliade's basic preoccupations). But the comparison is not valid; it can't be legitimately made except in a *negative* sense (things that at first glance seem to look alike turn out to be fundamentally different). Eliade, says Smith, claims to find elements of this shamanic pattern in HG and nomadic peoples from around the world, but the Tjilpa story constitutes his sole (inaccurate) example of the Center motif among truly "primitive" peoples. Unlike sedentary agriculturalists, the Tjilpa do not build (vertical) temples and shrines; rather, it is the (horizontal) landscape that is sacred to them, and sacred objects get hidden in trees or under rocks. Eliade, as Smith points out, consistently collapsed the crucial distinction between these two types of sacrality. In fact, the language of the Center is primarily political, not cosmological; it is a vocabulary that stems from ideologies of kingship and is not a universal or even a dominant pattern. The Aranda language is not one of edifices, but of "tracks," "paths," "traces," and "prints." In effect, Eliade had no real understanding of the differences between the Paleolithic and the Neolithic, and this collapsing of categories, says Daniel Noel, was central to his shaping of our own (Western) misunderstanding of shamanism. The American anthropologist Michael Taussig argues that shamanism is a modern, made-up Western category, and that indigenous visionary experiences do not proceed according to a traditional narrative pattern, as Eliade claimed. (In particular, he says, they do not have a heroic/cathartic structure, which was how Joseph Campbell chose to read them.)

A similar example of Eliade's distortions (whether willful or conveniently unconscious) and his attempt to convert horizontal traditions into vertical ones is discussed by Richard Gombrich, who takes on Eliade's book, *Yoga: Immortality and Freedom*. In chapter 5 of this book Eliade attempts to make the Buddha into a shaman, which he does by misreading a Pali text as referring to the "symbolism of ascent." At one point, says Gombrich, Eliade cites in his defense a passage about early Buddhist meditation producing a sensation of heat. The only problem is, the Buddha was describing the *wrong way* in which he meditated, before he attained enlightenment(!) Initiation, mystical death, and resurrection are all imposed by Eliade on texts that he apparently did not understand ("one hopes," writes Gombrich, "that the proofs of the next edition will be read by someone who knows Sanskrit and Pali.")

Examples of this sort, I trust, make my point, that "Eliadean scholarship" is a bit of an oxymoron, and that the notion of human beings being intrinsically religious, and everywhere the same, is nothing more than an a priori assumption. A significant number of leading scholars and anthropologists have shown that Eliade's methodology is flawed to the core, and I refer the reader to discussions and bibliographies of this provided by Edmund Leach, Guilford Dudley, Ivan Strenski, and Robert Brown, below. Bryan Rennie attempted an extended defense of Eliade a few years ago, which to my mind finally falls apart, relying (among other things) on a postmodern critique of notions of evidence and on what can be called special pleading. (See also the review of Rennie by Russell McCutcheon.) Especially instructive is the article by Robert Brown, who attempts a comprehensive methodological review of Eliade and seeks to defend him in some ways, yet finally cannot avoid calling his approach "simplistic and uncritical." In particular, Brown argues that much or perhaps most (I suspect, all) of what Eliade calls "religious behavior," "archaic vestiges," and so on has perfectly naturalistic explanations. Thus, Eliade argues for the sacred meaning of aquatic symbolism because of its universality, whereas Brown points out that considering the fact that the natural properties of water are everywhere the same in their bearing upon human life and its ecosystems, "Why then should we expect aquatic symbolism to be anything other than fairly uniform?" Human behaviors such as attachment to one's birthplace, or secular initiation rituals, are probably simply *human*, he says, by virtue of our psychological constitution; why label them "religious"? Why indeed. To my mind, writers such as Jung, Campbell, and Eliade are themselves exemplars of Neolithic distortion, in which what is simply naturalistic and secular has to be inflated with vertical sacrality so that they can feel life is meaningful. That life might be meaningful without all of this symbolic hoopla appears to have escaped their understanding. Despite all of this, the shamanistic interpretation of Paleolithic art persists (see the discussion of the work of Jean Clottes and David Lewis-Williams below, n. 21).

Concomitant with all this, and (I believe) fueling much of it, is the contempt these thinkers have for history and historical time; for them, only the transcendent is "really" real. Thus, Dudley quotes a passage Eliade wrote in 1934: "Suppress every trace of sentimental memory, suppress evanescent contemplations, memories of infanc[y], autumns, pressed flowers, nostalgia." (How sad!) And here is Eliade, twenty years later: "My essential preoccupation is precisely the means of escaping History, of saving myself through symbol, myth, rites, archetypes" (Dudley, pp. 70 and 72). All well and good; but let us not pass off a literary interpretation of the world as an historical or anthropological description of it.

See Franz Boas, "The Limitations of the Comparative Method of Anthropology," *Science*, n.s., vol. 4, no. 103 (18 December 1896), pp. 901–8; Fred Eggan, "Social Anthropology and the Method of Controlled Comparison," *American Anthropologist*, 56 (1954), 743–63; Jonathan Z. Smith, *Imagining Religion* (Chicago: University of Chicago Press, 1982), pp. 19–38, *Map is Not Territory*

(Chicago: University of Chicago Press, 1993; orig. publ. 1978), pp. 240–64, *Drudgery Divine* (Chicago: University of Chicago Press, 1987), p. 28, and *To Take Place* (Chicago: University of Chicago Press, 1987), pp. 1–21, 122, 124, 126–27, and 130–31; Daniel C. Noel, *The Soul of Shamanism* (New York: Continuum, 1997), pp. 29–40; Michael Taussig, "The Nervous System: Homesickness and Dada," *Stanford Humanities Review*, vol. 1, no. 1 (1989), pp. 57–63; Richard Gombrich, "Eliade on Buddhism," *Religious Studies*, 10 (1974), 225–31; Edmund Leach, "Sermons by a Man on a Ladder," *New York Review of Books*, 20 October 1966, pp. 28–31; Guilford Dudley III, *Religion on Trial: Mircea Eliade and His Critics* (Philadelphia: Temple University Press, 1977); Ivan Strenski, *Four Theories of Myth in Twentieth-Century History* (London: Macmillan, 1987), pp. 70–128; Robert F. Brown, "Eliade and Archaic Religions: Some Old and New Criticisms," *Sciences Religieuses*, vol. 10, no. 4 (Fall 1981), pp. 429–49; Bryan S. Rennie, *Reconstructing Eliade* (Albany: State University of New York Press, 1996); and Russell T. McCutcheon, review of Rennie, in *Religion*, 28 (1998), 91–110.

7. Eliade, *Shamanism*, pp. 481, 481n, and 503; Kirchner, "Ein archäologischer Beitrag"; Ucko and Rosenfeld, *Paleolithic Cave Art*, p. 186; N. K. Sandars, *Prehistoric Art in Europe* (2d ed.; New York: Viking Penguin, 1985), p. 134; see also p. 78. The "other scholar" referred to by Eliade is Johannes Maringer (*Vorgeschichtliche Religion*).

8. Ucko and Rosenfeld, *Paleolithic Cave Art*, pp. 129–33; Paul G. Bahn and Jean Vertut, *Images of the Ice Age* (New York: Facts on File, 1988), pp. 42–44 and 142–52. Ucko and Rosenfeld (*Paleolithic Cave Art*, p. 204) note that some of the details shown in Breuil's rendition may have conceivably existed and then been damaged between the time of his drawing and the time the cave wall was first photographed. However, it is unclear what might have caused such hypothetical damage (oxidation?); as they point out, damage by visitors is unlikely since the "sorcerer" is very difficult of access. Exactly what happened is hard to say, and I am not sure what one should make of Nancy Sandars' statement (*Prehistoric Art in Europe*, p. 136) that Breuil's copy work at Trois Frères is an "astonishing achievement," inasmuch as his "maze of lines and superpositions defeats the camera." Her own bias here (see pp. 64–66) is one of shamanism and hunting magic; perhaps, in consequence, she does not see Breuil's difference from the camera as the product of an overactive imagination. Instead, she writes that his work "show[s] the figure in all its strangeness," despite the fact that "all the visitor of today can make out, or the camera record, of the 'god' today are staring eyes and an indistinct shape."

9. Bahn and Vertut, *Images*, p. 142; Monica Wilson, "The Hunters and Herders," in Monica Wilson and Leonard Thompson (eds.), *The Oxford History of South Africa* (2 vols.; Oxford: Oxford University Press, 1969), 1, 48; George W. Stow, *The Native Races of South Africa* (London: Swan Sonnenschein & Co., 1905), pp. 82–84 (the ostrich figure is facing p. 82). The quote from Graziosi occurs specifically in reference to the Trois Frères figure, on p. 33 of his *Paleolithic Art* (London: Faber and Faber, 1960).

While I do feel that the shamanistic interpretation of the Trois Frères "sorcerer" is a modern projection, Harald Pager's research on the rock art of southern Africa casts some doubt on George Stow's ethnography. In particular, says Pager, there is not a lot of evidence to show that Bushmen frequently used animal heads or skins when stalking game, and there are numerous hunting scenes in which the hunters are not wearing any animal disguises. The interpretation by contemporary Bushmen (when interviewed) of these paintings that show hunters wearing animal heads is that these are depictions of mythological creatures (e.g., sorcerers or spirits of the dead). However, San rock art is part of a known (and relatively "recent") shamanic culture, whereas Paleolithic culture is not (except in the popular imagination) known to be shamanic—so why assume it is? In addition, even if Figure 5 is exceptional, frequency of practice over the last few hundred years does not tell us much about frequency of practice in the Paleolithic. My point in reproducing the Stow illustration is to give the reader a clear example of a much simpler, and therefore more likely (less theory-laden), possibility. While hunting and shamanism are hardly exclusive activities, the point remains that we have (obviously) extremely good evidence that Paleolithic hunters hunted and very little (or no) evidence that they practiced shamanism. And even in "modern" times, the shamanic ratio (so to speak) is terribly small: Pager notes that among the thousands of rock art figures he examined in the Ndedema Gorge (in the Natal Drakensberg Mountains, RSA), only 210 could be identified as being mythological creatures; and (see text, below) only 13 trance-dance scenes occur in a survey of more than 3,900 individual paintings.

See Harald Pager, "The Antelope Cult of the Prehistoric Hunters of South Africa," in Emmanual Anati (ed.), *Les Religions de la préhistoire* (Capo di Ponte: Centro Camuno di Studi Preistorici, 1975), pp. 401–11.

10. Kuhn, *Mousterian Lithic Technology*, pp. 54–57.

11. Ucko and Rosenfeld, *Paleolithic Cave Art*, pp. 177–78; White, "Earliest Images," p. 45. There are many more examples we could provide. Cave walls sometimes have representations of hands on them, for example, which have been taken to mean a supplication of spirits. Why not assume it was done for amusement, or to leave a "signature"? (Ucko and Rosenfeld, *Paleolithic Cave Art*, p. 158). As for the "phalli," it has now been pretty well demonstrated that these were bits of clay that were kneaded by sculptors in advance, to determine the material's plasticity (see p. 63 of Jean Clottes and David Lewis-Williams, cited in n. 21, below).

12. The "one exception," according to Benjamin Ray, is El Juyo (see his review of Bruce Dickson's *Dawn of Belief* in *History of Religions*, vol. 23, no. 3 [February 1993], pp. 303–6). See also Lawrence Krader, "Shamanism: Theory and History in Buryat Society," and Å. Hultkrantz, "Ecological and Phenomenological Aspects of Shamanism," in V. Diószegi and M. Hoppál (eds.), *Shamanism in Siberia*, trans. S. Simon (Budapest: Académiai Kiadó, 1978), pp. 226 and 52, respectively.

13. The quotation is from Robert Gargett, "Grave Shortcomings," *Current Anthropology*, vol. 30, no. 2 (April 1989), p. 177; see also Francis B. Harrold, "A Comparative Analysis of Eurasian Paleolithic Burials," *World Archaeology*, 12 (1980), 195–211.

14. Lewis-Williams and Dowson, *Images of Power*; D. F. Bleek, "Bushmen of Central Angola," *Bantu Studies*, 3 (1928), 124–25, and "Beliefs and Customs of the /Xam Bushmen, Part VII. Sorcerers," *Bantu Studies*, 9 (1935), 1–47. It must be noted that decorated stones that go back twenty-six thousand years, and some paintings of animals and geometric forms that go back six thousand years, have been found, but that rock art per se cannot be dated to much before five hundred years ago. See also chapter 2, n. 25, below.

15. Peter J. Wilson, *The Domestication of the Human Species* (New Haven: Yale University Press, 1988), p. 44.

16. I. M. Lewis, *Religion in Context* (Cambridge: Cambridge University Press, 1988), ch. 5. John Whitney was kind enough to run a statistical analysis of Bourguignon's data for me. He concluded that her study is peculiarly constructed: her analysis is skewed by a mushy overlap of categories, such that one cannot obtain a valid breakdown of them (e.g., matching trance with subsistence patterns) from her work. However, the 90 percent figure for the presence of some ASCs still holds.

17. Ucko and Rosenfeld, *Paleolithic Cave Art*, pp. 122, 156–58, and 231. On the problem of using Australian aborigines as the prototype for HGs, see chapter 2, n. 12, below.

18. "Behold the Stone Age," *Time*, 13 February 1995, p. 60, and Jean-Marie Chauvet et al., *Dawn of Art: The Chauvet Cave*, trans. Paul G. Bahn (New York: Henry N. Abrams, 1996). And yet, those committed a priori to the shamanistic thesis are going to find shamanism regardless of evidence to the contrary. Thus, on p. 124 of this book, Jean Clottes refers to "the spirits and gods [the people of Chauvet] worshipped" and calls the animal representations "artistic manifestations of the Paleolithic religion."

19. In addition, trance practice among *any* contemporary tribe has to be checked against the recent history of that tribe before we can start extrapolating backward in time. Syncretistic tendencies can be very powerful, especially among those HG societies that are very open to outside influences. Thus, when the anthropologist Kirk Endicott went to live with the Batek Negrito pygmies of Malaysia, he discovered that they engaged in trance practice and believed in spirits (which they call *hala'*, which also refers to shamans), as well as in superhuman beings (*nabis*). If we want to extrapolate backward, we can project all of this onto our Paleolithic forebears. Before we do that, however, it might be useful to note that these sorts of beliefs, which involve the notion of a radical separation between heaven and earth, more properly belong to the "Axial" religions, those that arose or took on strong gnostic tendencies after 1000 B.C. Such religions, which include Christianity and Islam, have the expe-

rience of an "encounter with God" at their core, at least in the early stages. Should we be surprised to learn that the Malay peoples were heavily influenced by their Islamic neighbors? That the two major *nabi*s (*nabi* is Arabic for "prophet") are called Allah and Allah the Younger? That these peoples also refer to a *nabi* Adam and a *nabi* Noah (associated with a flood story), and frequently utter the words "*Allah ta'ala'* "—"God most high"? That in gnostic fashion, they regard the body as a shell, with the soul trapped in it, released to the afterworld only upon death? None of this is HG stuff, and Endicott concludes his study by pointing out that primitive religions are not really primitive but have a history that has included a great deal of change and the wholesale absorption of outside influences. "As a result," he writes,

> few of the notions that compose Batek religion are distinctively Negrito and likely to have come down directly from their ancient ancestors . . . It is likely . . . that Batek religion has been less stable over time than the religions of the more "advanced" peoples who fix, record, and defend their religious conceptions. Paradoxically, we can probably learn more about ancient religion from the modern religions with written traditions . . . than from a hunting and gathering people like the Batek, who are foragers of ideas as well as foragers of food.

See Kirk Endicott, *Batek Negrito Religion* (Oxford: Clarendon Press, 1979), pp. 23, 52, 58–59, 82–93, 128, 145, and 220–21.

20. S. N. Balagangadhara, "The Origins of Religion: Why Is the Issue Dead?" *Cultural Dynamics*, 3 (1990), 281–316 and Nicholas Thomas and Caroline Humphrey, "Introduction," in Thomas and Humphrey (eds.), *Shamanism, History, and the State* (Ann Arbor: University of Michigan Press, 1994), p. 2.

21. I need to mention here the most recent and most sophisticated reworking of the shamanistic interpretation of Paleolithic art, viz., Jean Clottes and David Lewis-Williams, *The Shamans of Prehistory: Trance and Magic in the Painted Caves*, trans. Sophie Hawkes (New York: Henry N. Abrams, 1998). The text itself, which is by Jean Clottes, is essentially a reworking and extrapolation of an essay by Lewis-Williams and Thomas Dowson entitled "The Signs of All Times: Entoptic Phenomena in Upper Paleolithic Art," *Current Anthropology*, vol. 29, no. 2 (April 1988), pp. 201–45. Since it is the best case to date for the shamanistic thesis, a few words regarding the argument and its possible validity are perhaps in order.

To start with the article by Lewis-Williams and Dowson (hereafter LWD), the authors argue that the nervous system is a human universal, the same in the Upper Paleolithic as it is today. It is wired up to generate geometrical visual percepts or "entoptic phenomena," and the authors select six basic ones for examination: grids, lines, dots, zigzags, curves, and webs. When an individual undergoes an altered state of consciousness (ASC), he goes through three stages. In stage 1, he sees the entoptic phenomena; in stage 2, these are elaborated into iconic forms (e.g., curved lines become the tusks of animals); in stage 3, the imagery turns into hallucinations (e.g., human/animal combinations). The presence of all six entoptic categories in U.P. art suggests that a significant component of the art originated in shamanic practice. And if, as is the case, some signs occur that are not entoptic, this actually strengthens the argument because it renders invalid the criticism that virtually any mark can be interpreted as an entoptic phenomenon.

By way of ethnographic comparison, say the authors, we can see evidence of all three stages in the (recent) shamanic rock art of the San people as well as the Shoshonean Coso. Much of U.P. art occurs in dark caves because the isolation of these places would have induced an ASC. But the images also occur in more accessible areas (e.g., outside) and on mobile art and artifacts, as reminders of the large body of shamanic lore. These images were mental ones, already in the mind, and then projected onto the walls. In this sense, Paleolithic artists were marking what was "already there"; they probably did not suppose the images stood for real animals.

As noted, Jean Clottes develops the argument further and makes clear in his preface what he and Lewis-Williams assumed from the start: "[W]e set out to encounter the shamans of the caves" (p. 9). "At all times and in all places," he asserts on the second page of the text (p. 12), "people have entered ecstatic or frenzied altered states of consciousness and experienced hallucinations." How do we know this? Through neuropsychology. Because people of the U.P. had the same nervous system as we do, current research on the brain and ASCs provides the principal access to their mental and religious experience. Although (says Clottes) we must not uncritically project the present onto the past, it is the "deep neurologically generated commonalities" (p. 19) between ancient and more recent shamanism that enable us to understand Paleolithic religion. Thus, the ubiquity of shamanic beliefs regarding descent into the earth can be explained by a transitional "vortex" (or "tunnel") phase that occurs between stages 2 and 3 posited by LWD; entry into the cave reenacts this neuropsychological experience. For the shamanic cosmos, says Clottes, consists of tiered levels (usually, three), and we can see this in San rock art, which "illuminates" the art of the U.P. and shows how the neuropsychological experience is always expressed but unique to each culture.

Toward the end of the book, Clottes develops his own theory, that the Paleolithic cave itself should be seen as an ensemble of spaces differentiated by the performance of different rituals. At Enlène (which is physically connected to Les Trois Frères), we find about sixty bone objects thrust into the floor of the cave or into cracks in the walls, and there are also instances of the walls being touched. This (he says) can be explained by the tiered shamanic cosmos: clearly, our ancestors were trying to get to the underworld, and the artists were using the surfaces of the walls in their work to create a sense of the images coming out from behind the walls. The images float independently of background of scenery because this is characteristic of stage 3 of ASCs. Even *untouched* passages in caves were part of this process because they were "liminal, transition spaces between areas that were visibly defined by images and different kinds of activities" (p. 107).

What is one to make of these arguments? The British anthropologist Robert Layton, in the "Comments" section of the LWD article (p. 226), is led to ask,

"In what way is their use of ethnographic analogy less simplistic than Breuil's?" In fact, Breuil and Eliade (and Clottes cites the latter a number of times) claimed much the same thing, except that their "constant" was God, whereas for LWD and Clottes, it is the human nervous system. The problem with focusing on the nervous system as a fixed universal is that this fails to distinguish between capacity and consciousness (or behavior) or allow for the likelihood that even if the brain has been anatomically the same for the last forty thousand years, human consciousness has evolved during that time. The absence of personal adornment among Neanderthals does not prove that they had a more primitive brain that Cro-Magnons, for example. The fact that the brain is wired up to do something doesn't mean that it actually did it, and recent trance behavior could reflect modern developments (cf. n. 36 below, comment of Paul Mellars, that potential for culture should not be equated with expression of culture). There is no evidence that trance behavior was actually triggered during the Paleolithic, in other words. As John Halverson writes ("Art for Art's Sake in the Paleolithic," *Current Anthropology*, vol. 28, no. 1 [February 1987], p. 83), the human species "has shared the same cognitive capacities throughout time, but not the same cognitive achievements. The brain is the same, but what the brain does has a history of development." Nor does the existence of a universal nervous system mean that San/Shoshonean symbolism and U.P. symbolism have the same meaning. Given the time span involved, it seems more likely that they do not and that the burden of proof is on those who wish to assert that they do. As Robert Bednarik ("Comments" section of LWD article, p. 219) puts it, "Trance hypothesis is no panacea for the immense complexities facing us in prehistoric art."

By the same token, comments Paul Bahn (LWD article, p. 217), how do we know that the entopic signs are universal? Have they been recorded in every human population? And even if universal today, the LWD thesis requires that we assume that the people of 30,000 B.C. had the same hallucinations as modern people. In addition, he says, the theory here can never fail because regardless of the source, there are very few basic shapes one can draw: dots, lines, grids, squiggles, etc. We do not have to assume ASCs to find these signs in U.P. contexts. It is not that any mark can be interpreted as entoptic, but that in any collection of nonfigurative art, there are bound to be lots of marks that look like some or all of the six entopic categories. Robert Bednarik also notes (LWD article, p. 218) that scientific examination of prefigurative markings has been able to account for these phenomena without reference to ASCs or shamans, but these studies are conveniently omitted by LWD.

What about the data base? LWD rely on only two "recent" cultures, San and Shoshonean Coso, and apparently there is some debate as to whether the latter is truly shamanic in nature. What is more significant, as Bednarik points out (LWD article, p. 218), the Franco-Cantabrian area represents .03 percent of the world's surviving rock art, hardly a basis for arguing for universal trends with profound implications. LWD reply (p. 235) that this is not true because the universality they propose derives not from the art but from neuropsychological research; but this is to confuse the matter: LWD do use the .03 percent for the (attempted) *verification* of that universality, and that is what rightly troubles Bednarik.

Finally, LWD tend to make their argument immune to criticism, claiming, for example, that weaknesses in it are actually strengths or insisting, in the face of the fact that U.P. art contains very few human/animal combinations (which are fairly common in ASCs), that paucity does not count against a shamanistic explanation. What *would* disconfirm their hypothesis, in their eyes? The truth is that they are unwilling to consider the possibility that these effects might be produced by other causes or that more parsimonious explanations might be available. (How likely is it, for example, that Paleolothic artists were recording mental images or hallucinations and not real animals? This stretches the boundaries of all credibility.) LWD produce a Kuhnian sort of argument on how data can never tell us anything, how all facts and observations are theory-laden, how ideas come strictly from the researcher and never from the data, and so on. This genre of philosophy of science is by now a bit passé and much too subjective; one still has to deal with Karl Popper's argument regarding falsifiability, it seems to me, and LWD wish to avoid this at all costs. They claim that "best fit" (plausibility) is the issue, not "proof"; but it is questionable whether they have provided this. Do we have tons (or even more than a very few examples) of Paleolithic cave art showing human/animal combinations? Do we have U.P. cave paintings—even *one*—depicting dancers in trance, blood gushing out of their noses? The answer to both is a resounding *no*, so what are we talking about?

As for Jean Clottes, critique here would be along a fortiori lines. Despite his disclaimer, he does, like Breuil and Eliade (and Campbell and Frazer), uncritically project the present onto the past, lumping all shamanic behavior together under the rubic of a universal nervous system. He argues for a "complex link between the caves and altered states" (p. 29), and then admits (p. 33) that there are no deep caves in the most densely painted rock art areas of southern Africa. As for his thesis that the cave itself represents an ensemble of ritual space, which can be understood by U.P. shamanic cosmology (about which, in fact, we know zilch), this strikes me as pure projection, similar to David Macaulay's satire, *Motel of the Mysteries* (a future archaeologist digs up a Holiday Inn in the American Midwest and "proves" it was a sacred ritual site, with the toilet being a throne of the high priestess, etc.). Is it really parsimonious (or even commonsensical) to argue that the use of parietal surfaces indicates an attempt to reach the underworld or that a lack of background scenery for painted animals demonstrates that the art is shamanic in nature or that *lack* of cave paintings constitutes evidence of shamanic activity? This is complicated to the point of being baroque. Clottes did not enter the caves in a spirit of investigation, it seems to me. Rather, he, and presumably Lewis-Williams and Dowson, "knew" what Paleolithic art was in advance, and, unsurprisingly, they found what they were looking for.

22. On the following, see Sandars, *Prehistoric Art in Europe*, pp. 76, 83, 92, 117, 126, and 129–30, and Ucko and Rosenfeld, *Paleolithic Cave Art*, p. 181. Naturalism is Sandars' predominant orientation, yet in a few cases she gets strangely drawn into the religious orientation she so deftly criticizes (cf. above, n. 8).

23. The reader should be aware that my argument for Paleolithic art as being an appreciation of vitality and expression of paradox is not a resurrection of an old argument that such art was simply "art for art's sake," in which the activity was regarded as having no purpose at all beyond simple representation. While I appreciate many of the points made by John Halverson in his article on the subject (see n. 21), I find it unlikely that all of that magnificent cave art is finally meaningless, a kind of stimulus-response reaction to the environment.

24. Wilson, *Domestication*, p. 5. On field dependence and so on, see the discussion in chapter 5, below, as well as Joseph C. Berland, *No Five Fingers Are Alike* (Cambridge: Harvard University Press, 1982), pp. 28, 34–38, and 42, and H. A. Witkin and J. W. Berry, "Psychological Differentiation in Cross-Cultural Perspective," *Journal of Cross-Cultural Psychology*, vol. 6, no. 1 (March 1975), pp. 4–87.

25. On the following, see Morris Berman, *Coming to Our Senses* (New York: Simon & Schuster, 1989), chapter 1.

26. Julian Jaynes, *The Origin of Consciousness in the Breakdown of the Bicameral Mind* (Boston: Houghton Mifflin, 1976), p. 9; A. Irving Hallowell, "Self, Society, and Culture in Phylogenetic Perspective," in Sol Tax (ed.), *Evolution after Darwin*, vol. 2: *The Evolution of Man* (Chicago: University of Chicago Press, 1960), pp. 310, 324, 327, 352–56, and 361, and "Personality, Culture, and Society in Behavioral Evolution," in *Contributions to Anthropology* (Chicago: University of Chicago Press, 1976), p. 238.

27. Jaynes, *Origin of Consciousness*, pp. 59–66.

28. Sources for this chart include Gary G. Tunnell, *Culture and Biology: Becoming Human* (Minneapolis: Burgess, 1973), p. 16 (a bit dated, however); John Eccles, *The Human Mystery* (Berlin: Springer-Verlag, 1979), pp. 74, 79, and 98–103; C. Loring Brace, *The Stages of Human Evolution* (2d ed.; Englewood Cliffs, NJ: Prentice-Hall, 1979), p. 53; Harry J. Jerison, *Brain Size and the Evolution of Mind* (New York: American Museum of Natural History, 1991), p. 74; Erik Trinkaus and William Howells, "The Neandertals," *Scientific American*, *241* (December 1979), 118–33; Paul Shepard, *The Tender Carnivore and the Sacred Game* (New York: Scribner's, 1973), pp. 282–83; Elwyn Simons, "Human Origins," *Science, 245* (22 September 1989), 1343–50; and Randall White, "Thoughts on Social Relationships and Language in Hominid Evolution," *Journal of Social and Personal Relationships, 2* (1985), 95–115. I am also grateful to Erik Trinkaus for reviewing the chart with me.

29. Lewis R. Binford, "Isolating the Transition to Cultural Adaptations: An Organizational Approach," in Erik Trinkaus (ed.), *The Emergence of Modern Humans* (Cambridge: Cambridge University Press, 1989), pp. 19–21.

Jaynes argues that one can have intent, and even thought in general, without self-conscious awareness, and he cites things such as driving a car or playing a piano as examples, for which self-conscious awareness actually would be a hindrance—like the centipede who couldn't move because she thought about which leg to lift first. Thus, Jaynes envisions civilizations building pyramids or whatever in a state of bicamerality or automatic pilot. The problem with this argument is that it is true once the activity has been mastered, but not before. In the learning process itself, one is constantly thrown back on the self; "flow" is constantly being interrupted. Planning depth necessarily involves self-consciousness. But once the activity has been mastered and sinks to unconscious levels, automatic behavior takes over, self-consciousness disappears, and intent is no longer a conscious consideration. It is for this reason that a significant level of p.d. can be equated with self-objectification.

30. Peter Reynolds, *On the Evolution of Human Behavior* (Berkeley: University of California Press, 1981), pp. 141 and 150–64. See also Michael Corballis, *The Lopsided Ape* (New York: Oxford University Press, 1991), pp. 60–63. However, I have to say that we probably do not know for certain what apes can or cannot do with generic face cut-outs since (to my knowledge) the phenomenon has not been the subject of careful study. I am also ruling out instinctive construction here—mud dauber wasps building an elaborate nest, for example—because, presumably, no futurizing, or conscious mental template, is involved.

31. Lewis Binford, *Working at Archaeology* (New York: Academic Press, 1983), p. 431, and "Isolating the Transition," pp. 19–21; Randall White, *Dark Caves, Bright Visions* (New York: American Museum of Natural History, 1986), pp. 16–19. On curation, also see Molly R. Mignon, *Dictionary of Concepts in Archaeology* (Westport, CT: Greenwood Press, 1993), p. 121.

"Mousterian" and "Middle Paleolithic" refer to a cultural tradition and are used interchangeably. "Mousterian" is used especially in Europe and derives from an early discovery of tools at Le Moustier, in southwest France. The "industry" consists of flakes, points, and biface tools, dating from between one hundred eighty thousand to thirty thousand years ago, and generally regarded as the work of Neanderthals.

Flakes are small cutting tools that are chipped out of amorphous rough cuts of stone, which are in turn removed from large globular chunks of stone known as "cores." Blades are more sophisticated. They are also stone flakes, but they are twice as long as they are wide, not amorphous, and retouched to obtain different forms of tools. They are frequently found in Cro-Magnon assemblages, rarely in Neanderthal ones.

32. Binford, "Isolating the Transition," pp. 27 and 33; Milford H. Wolpoff, "The Place of the Neandertals in Human Evolution," in Trinkaus, *Emergence of Modern Humans*, p. 123; White, "Thoughts on Social Relationships," pp. 95, 107–8, and 112, and *Dark Caves*, p. 78; Kuhn, *Mousterian Lithic Technology*, pp. 8ff.; and Paul Mellars, "Cognitive Changes and the Emergence of Modern Humans in Europe," *Cambridge Archaeological Journal*, 1 (1991), 66.

33. Binford, "Isolating the Transition," pp. 29–31; Kuhn, *Mousterian Lithic Technology*, pp. 9ff. and 174–83; White, *Dark Caves*, p. 43. However, large animals can be brought down without projectiles, e.g., by means of drive-and-trap techniques or by what Grover Krantz calls "persistence hunting," in which an animal is pursued until it finally drops from exhaustion. This latter tech-

nique is one level of p.d. and has been practiced by the Tarahumara and Shoshonean Indians in recent times. In general, however, it was replaced by a deeper level of p.d., which involved the use of projectiles and the elaborate organization of hunting expeditions (Grover Krantz, "Brain Size and Hunting Ability," *Current Anthropology*, vol. 9, no. 5 [December 1968], p. 450, and C. Loring Brace, *Stages of Human Evolution*, pp. 72–73).

At one time, it was believed that evidence (large animal bones) found at Torralba, in Spain, showed that the drive-and-trap technique (e.g., setting fire to plains and then driving the animals into swamps, where they were trapped) went back four hundred thousand or five hundred thousand years. Lewis Binford was later able to show that the tools found at the site were manufactured on the spot from local materials, used to carve up the carcasses, and then finally discarded (expedient technology). This was not, then, actual hunting and involved very little p.d. (See Lewis Binford, "Were There Elephant Hunters at Torralba?" in Matthew and Doris Nitecki [eds.], *The Evolution of Human Hunting* [New York: Plenum Press, 1987], pp. 47–105. Also relevant to this discussion are the articles by M. Nitecki, R. G. Klein, Erik Trinkaus, and L. G. Straus in the same volume. See also William Howells, *Evolution of Genus Homo* [Reading, MA: Addison-Wesley, 1973], p. 130; John McCrone, *The Ape that Spoke* [New York: William Morrow, 1991], pp. 46–47; Tunnell, *Culture and Biology*, p. 16; and Binford, "Isolating the Transition," pp. 30–31.)

Paul Mellars, however, argues that Binford may be wrong in his contention that Mousterian "hunting" was inevitably scavenging, and he says there is evidence to show that there was some deliberate hunting of large game on the part of Neanderthals, though it was less logistically organized than in the Upper Paleolithic ("Major Issues in the Emergence of Modern Humans," *Current Anthropology*, vol. 30, no. 3 [June 1989], pp. 349–85, esp. pp. 356–57). One of the oldest hunting implements known to us is a curved wooden (yew) spear, nearly eight feet long, hardened in fire, and found between the ribs of an elephant skeleton in the village of Lehringen, Niedersachsen (Lower Saxony), in 1948. The original is preserved in the Landesmuseum in Hanover; a display in Berlin's Museum für Vor- und Frühgeschichte dates it to about –100,000 years. (See Hallam L. Movius, Jr., "A Wooden Spear of Third Interglacial Age from Lower Saxony," *Southwestern Journal of Anthropology*, 6 [1950], 139–42, as well as V. I. Kochetkova, *Paleoneurology*, trans. under the editorship of H. J. and Irene Jerison [Washington: V. H. Winston, 1978], p. 264.) However, Binford (in "Isolating the Transition," p. 35), says that the nearby tools were expedient, suggesting that this was an encounter with a corpse. (See also his reply in Randall White, "Rethinking the Middle/Upper Paleolithic Transition," *Current Anthropology*, vol. 23, no. 2 [April 1982], pp. 177–81; Richard G. Klein, "What Do We Know About Neanderthals and Cro-Magnon Man?" *American Scholar*, 52 [1983], 386–92; and Paul Shepard, "A Post-Historic Primitivism," in Max Oelschlaeger [ed.], *The Wilderness Condition* [Washington: Island Press, 1992], pp. 40–89). In general, the lateness-of-hunting thesis has recently received independent confirmation from Steve Churchill, who did a study of upper-arm-bone cross-sections among Neanderthals and Cro-Magnons, showing a shift in strategy toward more planning and the development of spears that could be thrown. (Report in *Science, 268* [21 April 1995], 364–65)

The whole issue of the evolution of hunting, and the tendency to make it central to human development, has come under fire from feminist scholars over the last twenty years, and, for the most part, I find their arguments convincing; though I would still maintain that prior to war, hunting was the premier goal-oriented activity. Intent *is* involved in gathering and catching small prey, of course, and Nancy Tanner and Adrienne Zihlman point out that the cognitive processes here involve remembering where the likely places are to obtain food and what environmental cues are relevant to particular kinds of food sources. Yet this doesn't have the "keen edge" provided by the hunt, and as Zihlman points out, hunting became a "dramatic" part of Western European culture only during the last thirty thousand years. Along with the logarithmic increase in intent, it is important to see hunting as an extension of gathering, as well as an outgrowth of a number of complex changes, such as food sharing, child rearing, social organization, and perhaps even cortical development. Otherwise, as Sally Slocum notes, we are unable to explain the evolution of food sharing, and hunting remains a discontinuous phenomenon that can't explain its own origin. All of these authors refer to Richard Lee's 1968 article ("What Hunters Do for a Living," in the *Man the Hunter* volume, based on the 1966 Chicago conference of the same name, and cited below), which shows that female gathering among foragers accounted for something like 60 percent to 80 percent of the diet (Arctic hunters are the main exception to this). Gathering is a kind of safety net; with these calories assured, the riskiness of the hunt (i.e., the hunter can easily return empty-handed) is mitigated. Finally, in terms of the archaeological record, the data are probably skewed because intent leaves more of a mark than other cognitive activity. Flint arrowheads and animal bones tend to last, whereas wooden digging tools and plant refuse tend to decay (Lee also made this point at the "Man the Hunter" conference). As in the case of social organization and the human relations that surround hunting, the "soft" data do not endure ("behavior does not fossilize," as Tanner and Zihlman cogently put it).

Nevertheless, among surviving HGs, hunting remains a prestige activity, and good hunters are often more highly desired as lovers (*Women Like Meat*, as Megan Biesele put it in the title of one of her books). In addition, a study by Carol Ember (using George Murdock's *Ethnographic Atlas*) revealed that in 83 percent of the sample cases of HGs, men contribute more to primary subsistence than women do; in only 8 percent do women contribute more than men. On this basis, Ember says that gathering is *not* the dominant pattern among HGs. Yet it is hard to know whether this can be legitimately extrapolated backward to the Paleolithic. Hunting is often tied to male identity; and a number of authors believe that when meat becomes a significant food source, it triggers a sharper division of labor between the sexes, with men and women more likely to be caught in what are now called "traditional" roles. But all of this is a late development. The "notion that early 'man' was primarily a hunter," writes Zihlman, "and meat the main dietary item, has become more and more dubious." Paul Shepard, however, believes (personal communication, June

1993) that hunting has multiple motives, including protein (certain amino acids are available only from meat), taste, predatory psychology, perceptual fascination with animals, the excitement of the ludic or contest aspects of hunting, and the gratification of sharing.

See R. B. Lee and Irven DeVore (eds.), *Man the Hunter* (Chicago: Aldine, 1968), articles by Lee and by Sherwood Washburn and C. Lancaster; Ernestine Friedl, "Sex the Invisible," *American Anthropologist*, 96 (1994), 836; Nancy Tanner and Adrienne Zihlman, "Women in Evolution. Part I: Innovation and Selection in Human Origins," *Signs*, 1 (1976), 587, 598, 601, and 608; Adrienne Zihlman, "Women in Evolution, Part II: Subsistence and Social Organization among Early Hominids," *Signs*, 4 (1978), 5, 7, 13, and 18–19; Susan Kent, "Cross-Cultural Perceptions of Farmers as Hunters and the Value of Meat," in Susan Kent (ed.), *Farmers as Hunters: The Implications of Sedentism* (Cambridge: Cambridge University Press, 1989), pp. 4, 5, 7, and 11–16; Sally Slocum (Linton), "Woman the Gatherer: Male Bias in Anthropology," in R. R. Reiter (ed.), *Toward an Anthropology of Women* (New York: Monthly Review Press, 1975), pp. 40–48; Linda M. Fedigan, "The Changing Role of Women in Models of Human Evolution," *Annual Review of Anthropology*, 15 (1986), 25–66; and Carol R. Ember, "Myths about Hunter-Gatherers," *Ethnology*, vol. 17, no. 4 (October 1978), p. 441.

34. Sally R. Binford, "A Structural Comparison of Disposal of the Dead in the Mousterian and the Upper Paleolithic," *Southwestern Journal of Anthropology*, 24 (1968), 139–53.

Walter Goldschmidt writes: "There is no evidence of any non-pragmatic cultural items (burial and burial artefacts) prior to the late Mousterian and even they are suspect. . . . Culture as we know it . . . seems to have appeared late on the scene" ("On the Relationship between Biology and Anthropology," *Man* [n.s.], *28* [1993], 343).

As in the case of n. 30, above, distinctions need to be made between instinctive behavior and conscious existential awareness. Thus, when I write that status differentiation must reflect a distinction between Self and Other, I would be hard put to defend this as it applies, let us say, to chickens. Human beings seem to create cultural devices to accomplish things that occur on a purely biological level among animals, as sociobiologists would argue, but, obviously, there is strong *dis*continuity here as well. Arguing that human hierarchy is as biological or inevitable as the pecking order among chickens strikes me as being too reductionistic.

35. Randall White, "Toward a Contextual Understanding of the Earliest Body Ornaments," in Trinkaus, *Emergence of Modern Humans*, p. 229; "Thoughts on Social Relationships," pp. 97–98 and 103–6; and *Dark Caves*, pp. 7, 30, 81, and 138.

36. White, "Thoughts on Social Relationships," pp. 108–11 and Mellars, "Cognitive Changes," p. 65.

However, there is an objection to this argument, viz. the relationships between the evolution of the brain, of the mind, and of culture. Randall White's argument that this dramatic cultural transformation presupposes "a modern grade of neurological complexity and organization" (White, "Toward a Contextual Understanding," pp. 211–31) is a view shared by some archaeologists and anthropologists (e.g., Richard Klein, "What Do We Know"), but certainly not all. Thus, Paul Mellars says that the argument that increased complexity of culture must reflect a shift in neurological capacities is fallacious because it mistakenly equates the *expression* of culture with the *potential* for culture. On this reasoning, he adds, we would have to conclude that nineteenth-century European thinkers were less intelligent than twentieth-century ones since they lacked knowledge of nuclear physics, computers, and space travel. Capacity and activity, in other words, are not the same thing. Similarly, Fred Smith and Steven Paquette concede that White is *probably* correct in saying that art and personal adornment reflect a modern level of neurological organization, but they add that the absence of this behavior among Neanderthals is not evidence for a more primitive brain (Fred H. Smith and Steven P. Paquette, "The Adaptive Basis of Neadertal Facial Form, with Some Thoughts on the Nature of Modern Human Origins," in Trinkaus, *Emergence of Modern Humans*, pp. 205–7). In general, behavioral differences do not prove the existence of cognitive differences, and Mellars says that if Neanderthals had not gone extinct, they might have had time to develop more complex technology, art, and so forth. (The alternative argument, of course, is that they went extinct precisely because Cro-Magnons edged them out due to mental superiority.) Mellars himself, however (see J. M. Lindly and G. A. Clark, "Symbolism and Modern Human Origins," *Current Anthropology*, vol. 31, no. 3 [June 1990], p. 246) wavers on the issue, for he claims that there is a large amount of evidence from Central and Western Europe that "there were in fact fundamental changes in human behaviour that can be shown to correlate remarkably closely with an equally abrupt transition from anatomically archaic to anatomically modern forms."

The reader will note that I deliberately omitted inserting a column in Table 1 for the evolution of brain size. *Australopithecus* starts out at around 350 cc. in volume; by the time we reach the Neanderthals, we are looking at 1500 cc. As far as Harry Jerison is concerned—and he is the leading researcher in this field—the fossil record of brain size, as computed from (usually, latex) endocasts, is direct evidence for the evolution of mind, in that brain size is a good estimator of total information-processing capacity. For the growth of the brain means the growth of the neocortex, specifically, the frontal lobes; and it is here that the most "human" functions—planning depth, self-awareness, rational-analytic thought, the ability to symbol, "personality," the ability to establish a context for behavior beyond immediate stimuli—seem to be located. Thus, paleoanthropologist Dean Falk notes that when the prefrontal lobes are damaged or removed, the person loses the ability to plan. And it is this area that, in evolutionary terms, is the most precociously and recently developed. Even leaving hominids aside, says Jerison, endocasts clearly show that encephalization, i.e., the enlargement of the brain in mammalian evolution beyond that associated with body size, was driven by neocortical expansion. With the appearance of *Homo sapiens*, and even before, the frontal lobes become the focus of maximum growth; and the "higher" one goes up the evolutionary scale, the larger is the frontal region of the neocortex. That is to say, this part of the brain is a proportionately larger fraction of the entire brain in humans than it is in other primates. As the British psychologist R. E. Passingham explains it, selective pressures have operated on the neocortex more than on any other part of the brain. The human neocortex, for example, is 3.2 times as large as would be expected in comparison with a nonhuman primate matched for body size, whereas the medulla oblongata (brain stem) hardly changed at all. Such a shift would point to the emergence of a new way of knowing, one that conferred a selective advantage. That selective advantage was social, interactive, and discriminatory, related to the abilities peculiar to the frontal lobes and discontinuous with pure animal awareness. We get, then, some sense of how important brain size—in particular, the size of a certain *region* of the brain—may be for the discontinuous cultural developments discussed above.

However, this is not the end of the story. Both the "brain size" school and the "localization of function" school have their critics, who argue that this schema is simplistic. How crucial can size be, asks Ralph Holloway, if the French writer Anatole France—no slouch intellectually—was a microcephalic, with a brain 1000 cc. smaller than that of the Russian writer Ivan Turgenev? Apparently, this staggering lack of gray matter did not get in the way of France's literary abilities, nor did Turgenev's rather large brain serve to make him a better writer than France. In and of itself, says Holloway, size is of no real consequence.

As for localization of function, the problem here is whether specific functions of the brain really can be restricted to specific sites in it. Opponents of this way of thinking argue that the brain is too interconnected (holographic) to make such specific distinctions, that virtually all of it is engaged in whatever brain function comes up. Thus, while the frontal lobes are designated by the first school as the locus of rational-analytic thought, proponents of the second school point out the close relationship this area has to the limbic system, which regulates sexuality and aggression. Sir John Eccles, who has taken an intermediate position in this debate, claims that although the prefrontal lobes are probably the principal sites of memory storage (for example), the structural basis of memory nevertheless is encoded in neuronal connections. I.e., the relevant neural pathways run through the prefrontal lobes, the orbital cortex, the limbic system, and the hippocampus; they are not just located in one place. It would seem that the human ability to break with the present tense, and live in a private mental world, required a dramatic expansion not only in size, but in neural interconnectedness as well. Jerison is also in agreement that the various categories of the mind that we try to localize in the brain never can function independently of one another; symbolic activity and self-conscious awareness for example, are too "rich" for this not to be the case. Thus, he says, localization does exist, but the "wiring diagrams" for all of this are quite diffuse. Thus, causal correspondences are thus present, but things are fairly systemic (holistic) in terms of actual operation.

Holloway's argument is that it is the way things are *organized* in the brain that is the crucial point, not how large the brain is or where it houses the function of memory (or whatever). What we have to look for in the evolution of the brain, if we are to learn anything about the evolution of mind, is neural reorganization. This, says Holloway,

> means that quantitative shifts between components or substructures of the brain, as measured in terms of area or volume, have taken place under natural selection such that the outputs of the systems are different between the species. By shifting interactions between components in quantitative ways, the product of the whole is altered.

This is undoubtedly right; the problem is, there is no way to prove it. Endocasts are not, in the most profound sense, really "endo"; they cannot tell you what went on *inside* the brain of our Paleolithic ancestors. Categories such as memory or symbolism, says Holloway, cannot be correlated with the surface configurations of the endocasts. To do so would be "a species of phrenology." Yet there is a certain amount of indirect evidence for reorganization and "shifting interactions." For example, Erik Trinkaus notes that there was a shift in neurocranial shape with the emergence of modern *Homo sapiens*; the cranium is higher and more rounded, and he takes this to imply a shift in information processing.

We also know something about how *living* brains function, and research in this area increasingly points to the great *plasticity* of the brain. It appears to be the case that the brain is quite dynamic and fluid in its organization—even in adults—and that organizational changes can occur without much difficulty. In a word, morphological changes are relatively minor, evolutionarily speaking. Large changes would include the shift from an earbone to a jawbone, or from fins to limbs, or the development of vertebrae. Changes in the size of the prefrontal lobes—adding more of the same material—is, within limits, no big deal. Breeders effect this type of change with plants in a few generations, as Darwin himself observed and as one can see from a visit to an annual tulip festival. However, even though adding more gray matter is relatively minor, the *consequences* of this change can be major, involving, as they do, changes in neural density and interconnection, synaptic complexity, dendritic branching, and, in short, what we call "neural reorganization." The explanation here, once again, is systemic rather than linear: incremental, continuous differences can suddenly precipitate large qualitative effects.

It is here that the debate between Jerison and Holloway becomes more complementary than bipolar. For if size alone cannot account for an increase in cognitive abilities, it does increase the probability of neural reorganization and complexity. The total number of neurons, says Jerison, is bound up with their connectedness; everything we know tells us that an increase in size means an increase in the density and interconnectivity of neural concentrations and relationships. Even if endocasts can't show such reorganization, we are forced to conclude that it occurred in the course of hominid evolution because it is implicated in increased brain size; the density of neural interconnections is quite simply higher in large brains. Thus, Eccles points out that qualitative changes occurred as a function of the proportion of the total brain occupied by the neocortex, especially those areas involved in speech, memory, and cognition. Jerison agrees that the evidence suggests that small quantitative changes in brain size can result in major shifts in neural control and organization, and recent research on phantom limbs in monkeys and human beings, and on visual impairment in kittens, has provided evidence for the sort of plasticity that could make this possible. Apparently, the brain will dramatically rewire itself in response to environmental influences; one doesn't have to be a Lamarckian to see that this is so.

We are still left with two problems. The first is, as Sir John Eccles pointedly remarks, that no one has solved the question of how mental events, including intentions, interact with events occurring in the brain. How the brain actually possesses consciousness, says Eccles, remains a mystery. Thus, he feels obliged to postulate the existence of what he calls a "liaison brain," a "leak" in the material world that includes the mental state of self-awareness. This is very good speculation, but it is speculation nonetheless.

The second problem is that even if specific cognitive functioning, such as ego-awareness, *could* be tied to neocortical development, we still cannot prove that culture is implicated in this. Humans could have possessed Self/Other differentiation for a very long time, without "acting" on it. Again, capacity is not equivalent to behavior, and theoretically at least, Object Relations could go back a million years. But how likely is this? Our standards, after all, may be getting a little too severe here. As Table 1 shows, we have evidence for only the faintest degree of planning depth prior to *Homo sapiens*. It seems reasonable that some sort of coalescence is involved and that changes in brain, mind, and culture cannot seriously be kept in three watertight compartments. Cultural activity from the Middle/Upper Paleolithic transition, and certainly from -35,000 years, reflects, at the very least, a different kind of *psychological* orientation, a new type of personality organization, especially if the brain does have a fair degree of plasticity, as already discussed. *Something* discontinuous with respect to the phenomena of intent and self-awareness, finally, can be assumed without stretching scientific credulity, it seems to me.

See Mellars, "Major Issues in the Emergence of Modern Humans," pp. 377–78; Jerison, *Brain Size*, esp. pp. 1, 8, 20, 26–29, and 50; Tunnell, *Culture and Biology*, pp. 36–37; Kochetkova, *Paleoneurology*, p. 79 and *passim*; Philip Lieberman, *Uniquely Human* (Cambridge: Harvard University Press, 1991), pp. 20–25 and 161; Dean Falk, *Braindance* (New York: Henry Holt, 1992), pp. 63 and 180; R. E. Passingham, "Changes in the Size and Organisation of the Brain in Man and His Ancestors," *Brain, Behaviour, and Evolution*, 11 (1975), 73 and 83–87; Ralph L. Holloway, Jr., "Cranial Capacity and the Evolution of the Human Brain," in Ashley Montagu (ed.), *Culture* (New York: Oxford University Press, 1978), pp. 172–75, 178, and 182–82; Holloway, "On the Meaning of Brain Size," *Science*, *184* (10 May 1974), 677–79; Eccles, *Human Mystery*, pp. 74, 180–201, and 210–34; Harry Jerison, "Fossil Evidence of the Evolution of the Human Brain," *Annual Review of Anthropology*, 4 (1975), 30–35, 42, and 51; McCrone, *Ape that Spoke*, 172; Ralph Holloway, "The Evolution of the Primate Brain," *Brain Research*, 7 (1968), 135–36; Erik Trinkaus, "The Upper Paleolithic Transition," in Trinkaus, *Emergence of Modern Humans*, p. 61; Sandra Blakeslee, "Missing Limbs, Still Atingle, Offer New Clues to Changes in the Brain," *New*

York Times, 10 November 1992, pp. B5 and B7; Douglas J. Besharov, "Getting Wise With IQ," *Washington Post National Weekly Edition*, 31 October–6 November 1994, p. 24; and Michael S. Gazzaniga, *Nature's Mind* (New York: Basic Books, 1992), pp. 36 and 51–52 (a list of more technical references is provided on p. 206); and Dieter Kruska, "How Fast Can Total Brain Size Change in Mammals?" *Journal für Hirnforschung, 28* (1987), 59–70. For corroboration from a different direction, see Gerald Edelman, *Bright Air, Brilliant Fire* (New York: Basic Books, 1992), pp. 3, 6–7, 49, 80–85, 112, and 119–35.

37. Colin M. Turnbull, *The Forest People* (New York: Simon & Schuster, 1961), and *Wayward Servants* (Garden City, NY: Natural History Press, 1965). See also the discussion in chapter 2, below.

38. On the following, see Harry F. Harlow and Robert R. Zimmerman, "Affectional Responses in the Infant Monkey," *Science, 130* (1959), 421–32; Mary D. Salter Ainsworth, "Object Relations, Dependency, and Attachment: A Theoretical Review of the Infant-Mother Relationship," *Child Development, 40* (1969), 970–81 and 999–1000, and "The Development of the Infant-Mother Attachment," *Review of Child Development Research*, vol. 3: *Child Development and Social Policy* (1973), pp. 54–55, 65–66, and 77; Charles M. Super, "Behavioral Development in Infancy," in Robert H. Munroe et al. (eds.), *Handbook of Cross-Cultural Human Development* (New York: Garland, 1981), p. 235; John Bowlby, *Attachment and Loss*, vol. 1: *Attachment* (New York: Basic Books, 1969), and "The Nature of the Child's Tie to His Mother," *International Journal of Psycho-Analysis, 39* (1958), 350–73; William McKinney, "Separation and Depression: Biological Markers," in Martin Reite and Tiffany Field (eds.), *The Psychobiology of Attachment and Separation* (Orlando: Academic Press, 1985), p. 208.

The enduring mother-offspring bond, in fact, is the core of almost all mammalian social life. See Linda M. Fedigan, "The Changing Role of Women in Models of Human Evolution," *Annual Review of Anthropology, 15* (1986), 40.

In terms of biological foundations, there is some research to indicate that bonding is part of the brain functioning of all mammals, human or otherwise. In their article on "Brain Opioids and Social Emotions," Jaak Panskepp and colleagues argued that emotional bonding seemed to be an addiction, in a neurochemical sense, functioning in much the same way that opium did. Christopher Coe and his group, working with squirrel and Rhesus monkeys, discovered that in the former, maternal loss was extremely stressful, generating prolonged and heavy pituitary-adrenal activity. In general, write Coe et al., the presence of familiar social partners can ameliorate the distress, but the most overt and effective caregiving comes from an adult female. Finally, one of Harry Harlow's students, Stephen Suomi, found that separation was much more traumatic for peer-raised monkeys than mother-reared ones and that a brief separation from the mother early in life predisposed monkeys to a heightened response to separation (protest and despair) two to three years later, even without any intervening stress. "What would appear to be a modest social stress," writes psychiatrist Peter Kramer, "produces a minor but long-standing change in personality style, and a vulnerability to separation that is highly reminiscent of rejection-sensitivity in humans."

See Jaak Panskepp et al., "Brain Opioids and Social Emotions," in Reite and Field, *Psychobiology*, pp. 6–7 and 25; and Christopher Coe et al., "Endocrine and Immune Responses to Separation and Maternal Loss in Nonhuman Primates," in the same volume, pp. 164 and 195–96. Stephen Suomi's work is discussed by Peter Kramer in *Listening to Prozac* (New York: Penguin, 1994), pp. 119–22.

39. On the following, see Erik H. Erikson, "The Development of Ritualization," in Donald R. Cutler (ed.), *The Religious Situation: 1968* (Boston: Beacon Press, 1968), pp. 713–15.

40. Quoted in Edith Weigert-Vorwinkel, "The Cult and Mythology of the Magna Mater from the Standpoint of Psychoanalysis," trans. F. M. von Wimmersperg, *Psychiatry*, 1 (1938), 347.

41. Thomas and Humphrey, "Introduction," p. 11, and Humphrey, "Shamanic Practices," in *Shamanism, History, and the State*, p. 197.

2. Politics and Power

1. V. Gordon Childe, *The Dawn of European Civilization* (New York: Knopf, 1925; 6th ed., Vintage, 1957).

2. Mark N. Cohen, *The Food Crisis in Prehistory* (New Haven: Yale University Press, 1977), pp. 2–3 and 5.

3. Alain Testart, "Significance of Food Storage among Hunter-Gatherers: Residence Patterns, Population Densities, and Social Inequalities," *Current Anthropology*, vol. 23, no. 5 (October 1982), pp. 525 and 530.

4. Alain Testart, "Some Major Problems in the Social Anthropology of Hunter-Gatherers," *Current Anthropology*, vol. 29, no. 1 (February 1988), p. 3; Gary A. Wright, "Origins of Food Production in Southwestern Asia: A Survey of Ideas," *Current Anthropology*, vol. 12, nos. 4–5 (October/December 1971), p. 447.

5. Cohen, *Food Crisis*, pp. 6–9, 15, and 19–24; Allen W. Johnson and Timothy Earle, *The Evolution of Human Societies* (Stanford: Stanford University Press, 1987), p. 63; John E. Pfeiffer, *The Emergence of Man* (3d ed.; New York: Harper & Row, 1978), p. 226. See also Wright, "Origins of Food Production," and the discussion in n. 8, below.
On the pattern of semisedentary HGs sporadically experimenting with agriculture over long periods of time in the New World, see John Noble Wilford, "Corn in the New World: A Relative Latecomer," *New York Times*, 7 March 1995, pp. B5 and B8.

6. Marshall Sahlins, *Stone Age Economics* (Chicago: Aldine, 1972); Testart, "Significance of Food Storage," p. 525; and Lewis R. Binford, "Post-Pleistocene Adaptations," in Sally R. Binford and Lewis R. Binford (eds.), *New Perspectives in Archeology* (Chicago: Aldine, 1968), p. 329.

7. Robert L. Carneiro, "A Theory of the Origin of the State," *Science, 169* (21 August 1970), 734.

8. Barbara Göbel, "The Beginnings of Agriculture in Mesoamerica and South America: A View from Decision Theory," *Cultural Dynamics*, 4(2), 1991, pp. 142 and 146–49; Colin Renfrew, as quoted by Robert Carneiro in "The Chiefdom: Precursor of the State," in Grant D. Jones and Robert R. Kautz (eds.), *The Transition to Statehood in the New World* (Cambridge: Cambridge University Press, 1981), p. 46; Cohen, *Food Crisis*, p. 4; and especially the survey provided by Gary Wright in "Origins of Food Production." As the reader will appreciate, studies of the origins of agriculture, and of domestication in general, are numerous enough to fill several large warehouses and cannot be listed here. However, Wright's article is very good in this regard, discussing the so-called Flannery-Binford model of the evolution of agriculture and Kent Flannery's concept of the "Broad Spectrum Revolution" in food production that began about 20,000 years ago. (Lewis Binford's contribution was primarily to show the crucial importance of population growth and density for this whole process.) The evidence for this model is quite good and discussed at length in Wright's essay.

Finally, although there is a general evolutionary pattern from hunting and gathering to agriculture, increasingly we find evidence of nonlinear developments and local exceptions. Recent excavations in southeastern Turkey, for example, turned up a settlement filled with pig bones rather than traces of grain. Dating here goes back 14,000 years and suggests that the transition from foraging to farming did not, in this case, involve the cultivation of wild cereals, but the domestication of the pig. Cultural factors, rather than environmental or technological ones, seem to have been the key issue. See John Noble Wilford, "First Settlers Domesticated Pigs Before Crops," *New York Times*, 31 May 1994, pp. B5 and B9.

9. Alan Barnard, "Contemporary Hunter-Gatherers: Current Theoretical Issues in Ecology and Social Organization," *Annual Review of Anthropology, 12* (1983), 204–6; James Woodburn, "Hunters and Gatherers Today and Reconstruction of the Past," in Ernest Gellner (ed.), *Soviet and Western Anthropology* (London: Duckworth, 1980), p. 97. Woodburn worked among the Hadza from 1958 through 1960. In 1964, a government settlement scheme radically altered their way of life, so descriptions provided in the text are of a way of life that is probably a thing of the past. See Woodburn, "Ecology, Nomadic Movement and the Composition of the Local Group among Hunters and Gatherers: an East African Example and Its Implications," in Peter J. Ucko et al. (eds.), *Man, Settlement and Urbanism* (Cambridge, MA: Schenkman, 1972), p. 206.

10. Woodburn, "Minimal Politics: The Political Organization of the Hadza of North Tanzania," in William A. Shack and Percy S. Cohen (eds.), *Politics in Leadership* (Oxford: Clarendon Press, 1979), pp. 244–48 and 257–58. Cf. n. 37, below.

11. Woodburn, "Hunters and Gatherers Today," pp. 98 and 104; "Egalitarian Societies," *Man*, n.s., *17* (1982), 444.

12. Woodburn, "Minimal Politics," pp. 258–60; "Hunters and Gatherers Today," p. 98; Barnard, "Contemporary Hunter-Gatherers," pp. 107–8. For more on power relations among Australian aborigines, see John Bern, "Ideology and Domination: Towards a Reconstruction of Australian Aboriginal Social Formations," *Oceania, 50* (1979), 118–32.

Australian aborigines are sometimes taken as the exemplar of HGs since they effectively had the continent to themselves until very recently and hence would seem to represent the only group of HGs among HGs. As Kenneth Maddock points out, however (*The Australian Aborigines* [London: Allen Lane, 1973], pp. 21–22), the view that studying present-day aborigines necessarily gives us accurate information about their Paleolithic ancestors is no longer widely held. For one thing, beliefs are very different among different aboriginal groups. Some, for example, believe in reincarnation, while others do not, so "reconstructing the Paleolithic" becomes problematic. Regions in Australia are also very ecologically distinctive; we don't have a situation such as exists in southern Europe or the Near East. Finally, the severe isolation of the continent itself, says Maddock, makes it difficult to argue that the aborigines are representative of anything but themselves. "Aborigines," he writes, "typify neither early men nor modern hunters and gatherers. They are properly to be regarded as having a distinctive and specialized culture."

13. Woodburn, "Hunters and Gatherers Today," p. 113; "Egalitarian Societies," p. 431. In his Malinowski Memorial Lecture, delivered at the London School of Economics in 1976, Maurice Bloch told his audience:

> The fundamental nature of the challenge brought by such data explains the extraordinary reactions of disbelief when Woodburn first presented his Hadza data in the early 1960s in seminars in Cambridge and London.... He showed that the Hadza had practically no concepts of permanent roles categorically binding people or sets of people together and gave little attention to supernatural beings.

See Maurice Bloch, "The Past and the Present in the Present," *Man,* n.s., *12* (1977), 288.

14. Woodburn, "Egalitarian Societies," pp. 433–35 and 447 (most of the information here is based on male society among the Hadza and the !Kung); "Ecology, Nomadic Movement, etc.," pp. 202–5; and "Minimal Politics," pp. 250–53. For more information on the fission-and-fusion pattern and its role in conflict resolution, see David Fabbro, "Peaceful Societies: An Introduction," *Journal of Peace Research,* vol. 15, no. 1 (1978), pp. 69–71 and 80.

15. Discussed in Barnard, "Contemporary Hunter-Gatherers," pp. 206–7. For Testart's major work, see *Les chasseurs-cueilleurs ou l'origine des inégalités* (Paris: Société d'ethnographie, 1982).

David Spain makes the important point, however (personal communication, July 1996), that viewing Northwest Coast groups, or fishers in general, as HGs may be an ethnocentric error, in that they may really be "harvest" people. I.e., migration of fish is seasonal, and they are "harvested" in a pattern quite similar to that of farming.

16. Testart, "Significance of Food Storage," pp. 524–27. His data base, compiled on pp. 529–30, is dramatically convincing. The quote from Barnard is in Peter M. Gardner, "Forager's Pursuit of Individual Autonomy," *Current Anthropology*, vol. 23, no. 5 (December 1991), p. 559. Cf. Barbara Bender, "The Roots of Inequality," in Daniel Miller et al. (eds.), *Domination and Resistance* (London: Unwin Hyman, 1989), p. 87: "Farming of itself does not create the necessary surplus to underwrite more hierarchized positions; surplus is relative and is initiated by society."

Marvin Harris, in *Our Kind* (New York: Harper & Row, 1989), pp. 378–82, comments that the drift toward social inequality gained momentum from storage since resource abundance gave "big men" power over others. In the case of the Trobriand Islanders, for example, the storage of yams produced chiefs who served to redistribute the food. They had hereditary status and wore shell ornaments to signify their rank. This pattern, says Harris, occurs on several continents (cf. the Cherokee during the eighteenth century). Warfare, he goes on, brought the power relations inherent in the functions of storage and redistribution to fruition.

Equally stimulating is the work of Olga Soffer, who examined evidence from the Late Paleolithic in Europe and concluded that permanent storage spelled the end of mobility and thus the end of HG egalitarianism. The whole thing, she says, increases the number of people who have to interact regularly, necessitating new social strategies, such as hierarchy and the manipulation of surplus. (See Olga Soffer, "Storage, Sedentism and the Eurasian Palaeolithic Record," *Antiquity*, 63 [1989], 719–32.)

On the issue of storage and distrust, Heribert Adam points out (personal communication, January 1997) that the shift to storage may more prosaically come about due to the kind of goods stored. Thus, he says, among Northwest Coast Indians (see above, n. 15), salmon and berries are stored because they are not available at all times of the year. So storage might reflect an experience of seasonal cycles, not necessarily a distrust of nature or of other human beings, although hierarchy among Northwest Indians is quite prominent (see below, n. 55).

17. For Testart's critics, see "Significance of Food Storage," pp. 531–33, and Testart, "Some Major Problems," pp. 14–25. Other information can be found in "Some Major Problems," p. 6, and "Significance of Food Storage," p. 533.

18. Eleanor Leacock and Richard Lee (eds.), *Politics and History in Band Societies* (Cambridge: Cambridge University Press, 1982), pp. 7–8; Woodburn, "Egalitarian Societies," pp. 431 and 444–45. However, issues of gender constitute an important exception. See below, n. 49.

19. Gardner, "Forager's Pursuit," pp. 543, 549–54, 557, 561, and 568.

20. Richard Lee, "Is There a Foraging Mode of Production?" *Canadian Journal of Anthropology*, vol. 2, no. 1 (Spring 1981), pp. 15–18.

21. Pierre Clastres, *Society Against the State*, trans. Robert Hurley (New York: Zone Books, 1989; orig. French ed. 1974).

As it turns out, a number of scholars and field workers had already reported, prior to Clastres, that HG politics was frequently egalitarian. Thus, John Pfeiffer says that "big chiefs" were typically nonexistent among foragers, and Carleton Coon remarks that priesthoods are also very rare among them. Paul Radin observed that when chiefs do exist, they have very little power; and in any case, that such cultures have a noted absence of any centralized authority. Sometimes "chiefs" do exist, but the title moves around from person to person. In effect, "the law" is diffused throughout the group, and it is largely equivalent to custom. "Primitive" law is thus public law, deferred and decentralized.

See Pfeiffer, *Emergence of Man*, p. 205; Carleton S. Coon, *The Hunting Peoples* (New York: Nick Lyons Books, 1971), p. 284; Paul Radin, *The World of Primitive Man* (New York: H. Schuman, 1953), pp. 11–15, 183, 189, 202–3, 221ff., and 244–45; and Stanley Diamond, *In Search of the Primitive* (New Brunswick, NJ: Transaction, 1974), pp. 135–36.

22. The discussion that follows is from Clastres, *Society Against the State*, esp. pp. 11–23, 29–32, 37–47, 189, and 199. As far as I could determine, most of the societies Clastres studied were sedentary—in some cases, having large villages—and pursued a mixture of hunting and agriculture. Movement was still a major part of their way of life, however. The leaders he identifies would seem to fall into what is called the "Big Man" pattern or "ranked" society; yet in those societies Clastres lived with (see discussion below), these Big Men had no real power.

For a brief critique of Clastres' analysis, see John Gledhill, *Power and Its Disguises* (London: Pluto Press, 1994), pp. 32 and 39–40.

23. Morton H. Fried, *The Evolution of Political Society* (New York: Random House, 1967), p. 13.

24. Clastres is following the schema here of Robert H. Lowie in "Some Aspects of Political Organization Among the American Aborigines. Huxley Memorial Lecture, 1948," *Journal of the Royal Anthropological Institute of Great Britain and Ireland*, vol. 78, parts 1 and 2 (1948), pp. 11–24.

25. David Lewis-Williams and Thomas Dowson, *Images of Power* (Johannesburg: Southern Book Publishers, 1989), p. 12. The authors' source for this is material collected by W. H. I. Bleek and L. C. Lloyd in the 1870s among the /Xam Bushmen and edited for *Bantu Studies* by Dorothea Bleek in the 1920s and 1930s.

26. Richard Lee, "Eating Christmas in the Kalahari," *Natural History*, vol. 78, no. 10 (December 1969), pp. 14–22 and 60–63.

27. Woodburn, "Egalitarian Societies," p. 440; Clastres, *Society Against the State*, pp. 129–50 and 177–88.

28. Mark N. Cohen, "The Ecological Basis of New World State Formation: General and Local Model Building," in Grant Jones and Robert Kautz (eds.), *The Transition to Statehood in the New World* (Cambridge: Cambridge

University Press, 1981), pp. 110–11, 114–18, and 120–22; *Food Crisis*, pp. 12 and 14.

29. Mark N. Cohen, "Archaeological Evidence for Population Pressure in Pre-Agricultural Societies," *American Antiquity*, vol. 40, no. 4 (1975), pp. 471–72. Cf. Michael Corballis, in *The Lopsided Ape* (New York: Oxford University Press, 1991), p. 74, who gives the following estimates for world population growth: from 1 million years ago to –25,000 years, an increase in numbers from 125,000 to 3 million; a figure of 5 million for –10,000 years; and an increase from 5 million to 80 or 90 million between –10,000 and –6,000 years.

30. Cohen, "Archaeological Evidence," pp. 473–75; "Ecological Basis," pp. 107–10. Note that Cohen is a "Boserupian," as opposed to a Malthusian; i.e., his work follows that of Ester Boserup, who argued for the impact of population pressure on food supplies rather than the reverse (*The Conditions of Agricultural Growth* [Chicago: Aldine, 1965]).

Studies of skeletal pathology suggest that agriculture was accompanied by an increase in stress (which shows up as malnutrition and infection). See Cohen, "Prehistoric Hunter-Gatherers: The Meaning of Social Complexity," in T. D. Price and J. A. Brown (eds.), *Prehistoric Hunter-Gatherers* (Orlando: Academic Press, 1985), p. 113, and M. N. Cohen and G. J. Armegalos (eds.), *Paleopathology at the Origins of Agriculture* (New York: Academic Press, 1984).

Climatic shifts won't work as a nonlocal explanation because periods of interglacial warming occurred prior to 11,000 B.C. without resulting in agriculture.

31. Victor A. Shnirelman, "Complex Hunter-Gatherers: Exception or Common Phenomenon," *Dialectical Anthropology*, 17 (1992), 183–96; Cohen, "Prehistoric Hunter-Gatherers," pp. 104–11.

32. Brian Hayden, "Research and Development in the Stone Age: Technological Transitions among Hunter-Gatherers," *Current Anthropology*, vol. 22, no. 5 (October 1981), pp. 519–48; Göbel, "Beginnings of Agriculture." See also George L. Cowgill, "On Causes and Consequences of Ancient and Modern Population Changes," *American Anthropologist*, 77 (1975), 505–25, and "Population Pressure as a Non-Explanation," in Alan C. Swedlund (ed.), *Population Studies in Archaeology and Biological Anthropology: A Symposium*, issued as *American Antiquity*, vol. 40, no. 2, part 2 (April 1975), pp. 127–33.

33. Robert Carneiro, "On the Relationship between Size of Population and Complexity of Social Organization," *Southwestern Journal of Anthropology*, 23 (1967), 234–41.

34. Carneiro, "Theory of Origin of the State," esp. pp. 734 and 737, and also Carneiro, "The Circumscription Theory," *American Behavioral Scientist*, 31 (1988), 498–99 and 505.

35. Susan Kent (ed.), *Farmers as Hunters: The Implications of Sedentism* (Cambridge: Cambridge University Press, 1989), p. 10; "And Justice for All: The Development of Political Centralization Among Newly Sedentary Foragers," *American Anthropologist*, 91 (1989), 708.

36. Lee, "Eating Christmas in the Kalahari"; Leacock and Lee, *Politics and History*, p. 9; and Lorna Marshall, "Sharing, Talking, and Giving: Relief of Social Tensions," in *The !Kung of Nyae Nyae* (Cambridge: Harvard University Press, 1976), pp. 287–312.

37. Woodburn, "Minimal Politics," pp. 250–53 and 258–60, and "Egalitarian Societies," pp. 435 and 438; Johnson and Earle, *Evolution of Human Societies*, pp. 104, 121, 126, 150, and 323.

I do not mean to suggest by this (nor, I am sure, do Johnson and Earle) that HGs pursue the isolated way of life common to Western industrial societies. As the British anthropologist Tim Ingold has observed, the IR economy has a spiritual mechanism behind it, which he calls "sharing in." "Sharing out," says Ingold, is fairly obvious, being merely a form of distribution, e.g., of meat after an animal is killed. Sharing in is a principle of collectiveness and central to HG social relations. It is trust, really, a mode of relatedness or sociality. Although HGs are very good with respect to questions of autonomy and boundary relations, their individualism (which is very different from the modern bourgeois form, i.e., the individualism of inequality) depends on a commitment to the whole; for example (in the case of the Mbuti Pygmies), to the forest, to their way of life. In this sense, says Ingold, HGs "share" one another, belong to one another. In (agricultural) tribal life, one derives a sense of belonging, of identity, from excluding others. HG identity, by contrast, is based on *in*clusion, on sharing in, which nevertheless preserves personal freedom and fluidity and avoids relationships of specific dependency. This principle gets strained when population figures exceed that of band-level society, but it exists as a principle nonetheless, along with the pattern of fission and fusion. See Tim Ingold, *The Appropriation of Nature* (Manchester: Manchester University Press, 1986), pp. 223–24 and 236–39.

38. Kent, "And Justice for All," p. 704; Richard Lee, "Population Growth and the Beginnings of Sedentary Life among the !Kung Bushmen," in Brian Spooner (ed.), *Population Growth: Anthropological Implications* (Cambridge: MIT Press, 1972), pp. 346–47.

39. On the following, see Margaret Power, "The Cohesive Foragers: Human and Chimpanzee," in M. R. A. Chance (ed.), *Social Fabrics of the Mind* (Hillsdale, NJ: Lawrence Erlbaum, 1988), pp. 75n, 76, 79 and n. 80, and 85–86, and also Chance's introduction, p. 13; "The Foraging Adaptation of Chimpanzees, and the Recent Behaviors of the Provisioned Apes in Gombe and Mahale National Parks, Tanzania," *Human Evolution*, 1 (1986), 252–54, 257, and 260; and *The Egalitarians—Human and Chimpanzee* (Cambridge: Cambridge University Press, 1991), *passim*.

40. John A. Price, "Sharing: The Integration of Intimate Economies," *Anthropologica*, n.s., vol. 17 (1975), pp. 4–7.

41. Joseph B. Birdsell, "Some Environmental and Cultural Factors Influencing the Structure of Australian Aboriginal Populations," *American Naturalist*, vol. 87, no. 834, Supplement (May/June 1953), pp. 171–207; "On Population Structure in Generalized Hunting and Collecting Populations,"

Evolution, 12 (June 1958), 189–205; "Some Population Problems Involving Pleistocene Man," in Katherine B. Warren (ed.), *Cold Spring Harbor Laboratory Symposium on Quantitative Biology* (Cold Spring Harbor: Cold Spring Harbor Laboratory Press, 1957), vol. 22, pp. 47–70; "Some Precedents for the Pleistocene Based on Equilibrium Systems among Recent Hunter-Gatherers," and "The Magic Numbers '25' and '500': Determinants of Group Size in Modern and Pleistocene Hunters" (discussion with Lewis Binford et al.), in Richard B. Lee and Irven DeVore (eds.), *Man the Hunter* (Chicago: Aldine, 1968), pp. 229–40 and 245–48; "Local Group Composition among the Australian Aborigines: A Critique of the Evidence from Fieldwork Conducted since 1930," *Current Anthropology*, vol. 11, no. 2 (April 1970), pp. 115–42.

42. Birdsell, "Some Precedents for the Pleistocene," p. 232; Richard B. Lee, "The Intensification of Social Life among the !Kung Bushmen," in Spooner, *Population Growth*, p. 343; Fekri A. Hassan, "Determination of the Size, Density, and Growth Rate of Hunting-Gathering Populations," in Steven Polgar (ed.), *Population, Ecology, and Social Evolution* (The Hague: Mouton, 1975), pp. 27–52; Ulf Hannerz, *Cultural Complexity: Studies in the Social Organization of Meaning* (New York: Columbia University Press, 1992), pp. 1–47; Krisztina Kosse, "Group Size and Societal Complexity: Thresholds in the Long-Term Memory," *Journal of Anthropological Archaeology*, vol. 9, no. 3 (September 1990), pp. 275–303; Martin Wobst, "Boundary Conditions for Paleolithic Social Systems," *American Antiquity*, vol. 39, no. 2 (1974), pp. 147–78; Anthony Forge, "Normative factors in the settlement size of Neolithic cultivators (New Guinea)," in Ucko et al., *Man, Settlement and Urbanism*, pp. 373 and 375.

43. George P. Murdock, *Ethnographic Atlas* (Pittsburgh: University of Pittsburgh Press, 1967). For more on the number five hundred, see Pfeiffer, *Emergence of Man*, pp. 312–15.

44. Cohen, "Prehistoric Hunter-Gatherers," p. 101. This and the discussion that follows is taken from Johnson and Earle, *Evolution of Human Society*, pp. 19–22, 207–11, 256, 270, and 314–19, and Kent V. Flannery, "The Cultural Evolution of Civilizations," *Annual Review of Ecology and Systematics*, 3 (1972), 401–2. The reader should note that reference to "band" society here is not that of the old typology originally drawn up by Julian Steward and Elman Service, who saw such societies as patrilineal or patrilocal, i.e., tightly organized and male-centered. This model was discredited in the sixties and seventies. Societies of small communities exist, of course, but their social organization is/ was one of flux and fluidity. (See Barnard, "Contemporary Hunter-Gatherers," pp. 195–96.)

45. Harris, *Our Kind*, p. 358. In his "Chiefdom" article, Carneiro argues that this step, i.e., from local (Big Man) autonomy to chiefdom ("an autonomous political unit comprising a number of villages or communities under the permanent control of a paramount chief"), is the crucial qualitative jump. The chiefdom embodies features of permanence and centralized political control, and this sets it apart from all previous forms of organization. To go from this to the state, he says, is basically a quantitative development.

See also Molly R. Mignon, *Dictionary of Concepts in Archaeology* (Westport, CT: Greenwood Press, 1993), pp. 72–75; and Henry T. Wright, "Prestate Political Formations," in William Sanders et al. (eds.), *On the Evolution of Complex Societies* (Malibu: Undena Publications, 1984), pp. 41–77.

46. Fried, *Evolution of Political Society*, pp. 113–14, and "On the Evolution of Social Stratification and the State," in Stanley Diamond (ed.), *Culture in History* (New York: Columbia University Press, 1960), pp. 722 and 724; Robert Carneiro, "Further Reflections on Resource Concentration and Its Role in the Rise of the State," in Linda Manzanilla (ed.), *Studies in the Neolithic and Urban Revolutions* (Oxford: BAR International Series 349, 1987), p. 250; Johnson and Earle, *Evolution of Human Society*, p. 270; and Testart, "Significance of Food Storage," p. 535. In his comments on this last article (p. 531), Canadian archaeologist Richard Forbis argues that no culture has become a "civilization" without agriculture.

For further discussions of the rise of the state, see Henry T. Wright, "Recent Research on the Origin of the State," *Annual Review of Anthropology*, 6 (1977), 79–97, and "Toward an Explanation of the Origin of the State," in James N. Hill (ed.), *Explanation of Prehistoric Change* (Albuquerque: University of New Mexico Press, 1977), pp. 215–30; Malcolm Webb, "The State of the Art on State Origins?" *Reviews in Anthropology*, vol. 11, no. 4 (Fall 1984), pp. 270–81; and Morton H. Fried, "State," in David L. Sills (ed.), *International Encyclopedia of the Social Sciences*, vol. 15 (New York: Macmillan, 1968), pp. 143–50.

47. Jacqueline S. Solway and Richard B. Lee, "Foragers, Genuine or Spurious?" *Current Anthropology*, vol. 31, no. 2 (April 1990), p. 141.

48. Chance, *Social Fabrics*, pp. 2–31.

49. Francis B. Harrold, "A Comparative Analysis of Eurasian Paleolithic Burials," *World Archaeology*, 12 (1980), 195–211. Harrold's evidence consists of thirty-six M.P. burials and ninety-six U.P. burials from Europe and Asia, i.e., all the known Paleolithic burials from those continents. The former date from –75,000 to –35,000 years (and are mostly of Neanderthals); the latter date from –35,000 to –10,000 years. In the U.P., excluding those few cases where association with grave goods was unclear, fifty-nine of sixty-seven subjects were buried with grave goods, whereas only thirteen of the thirty-three Mousterian subjects were. The discrepancy comes, again, from female subjects: in both eras, female subjects are found in smaller numbers than males, but only in the M.P. were females less likely than males to be buried with grave goods. Necklaces and other items of adornment were found in thirty-three out of sixty-six cases (where information is available), but in none of the Mousterian cases. In both the M.P. and the U.P., we find fewer women buried than men.

On possible gender differentiation with respect to the hunt, see above, chapter 1, n. 33.

In the case of gender inequality among contemporary HGs, the evidence is, of course, much more forthcoming; although there is no way of projecting what we know back onto the Paleolithic, and what we would be projecting appears to be a mixed bag anyway. Thus, in her study of sex and status among egalitarian societies, Elsie Begler was led to postulate the existence of two types of the latter, pure egalitarian societies and semi-egalitarian ones. So while there is a great deal of egalitarianism within some Australian societies, the use of force by a man against a woman is considered perfectly legitimate, and there will be a lack of kin support for a wife injured by her husband. Fathers have authority over daughters, and husbands over wives, by virtue of the sociocentric (role-defined, or ascribed) status of male over female. Eskimo, Begler says, also fit the Australian pattern. When we shift to the Mbuti Pygmies, however, we find that gender relations are at greater parity. For example, if a woman is struck by a man, both men and women come to her aid. Nor can a Mbuti husband compel his wife to return to his camp, as can be done in Australia. As for the !Kung, they fit this pattern as well: a woman can leave if she is unhappy with the marriage, or she can refuse to cook, and so on. What Begler concludes, à la *Animal Farm*, is that many contemporary foraging societies may be egalitarian, but some are more egalitarian than others. In some of these societies, relations between the sexes are characterized by differential ranking, by sociocentric status along gender lines. In others, the ability to fill a position of leadership is not sociocentric but based on personal influence, whether one is male or female. The issue of gender equality among contemporary HGs is thus a rather checkered picture. See Elsie B. Begler, "Sex, Status, and Authority in Egalitarian Society," *American Anthropologist*, *80* (1978), 571–88.

50. The view that we are looking at primitive lifeways that are, in their radical difference from us, a pointed reminder of "what we are not and what we could be" tended to underscore the Harvard Bushman project directed by Richard Lee between 1963 and 1974, as well as the "Man the Hunter" conference held in Chicago in 1966. As Thomas Patterson put it in 1990, these critiques of our own culture, and images of a more peaceful and just one, "afford a glimmer of hope in today's dangerous, fragmented, and crisis-ridden world; in the long run, these images may be anthropology's most significant contribution to humanity."

The challenge to this optimism has been most strongly mounted by the anthropological school of revisionism (also known as historical particularism), which argues that contemporary HGs can be understood only in the context of detailed historical experience. These peoples have hardly been immune to modern influences, in other words, sedentism and agriculture included. The most dramatic revisionist statement appeared in 1989 with the publication of Edwin Wilmsen's book *Land Filled with Flies*, which presented evidence that the !Kung Bushmen had been influenced by Iron Age culture for nearly fifteen hundred years and had been part of a colonial cash economy for centuries. Their current condition as subsistence foragers, Wilmsen maintained, reflects not an old way of life but, rather, contemporary poverty. The !Kung had been involved in pastoralism in the past, and now, under adverse economic conditions were not able to do any herding. In a follow-up article with James Denbow, Wilmsen brought forward a mass of historical and archaeological evidence that he claimed supported the argument "that 'Bushman' and 'San' are invented categories and 'Kalahari foragers' an ethnographic reification drawn from one of several subsistence strategies engaged in by all of Botswana's rural poor." Richard Lee, in short, had gone to Africa wearing rose-colored glasses and had found what he was looking for.

Lee's response to this is to point out that the revisionist argument hangs on the dubious theoretical position of what is called "postmodernist deconstruction" (most closely associated with the work of the French philosopher Jacques Derrida), that the study of any subject inevitably says more about the investigator than the investigated. On this view, everything is a "text," all texts are equivalent, and Otherness is finally a myth: everything, ultimately, is Us (see discussion of this in chapters 6 and 7, below). Applied to anthropology, says Lee, ethnography is converted to fiction; and the natives, who do not live in a pristine HG world and have been exposed to larger world patterns of hierarchy and exploitation, are really, on this view, Euro-Americans. The error of such a position, says Lee, should be self-evident. Either we rely on empirical evidence, or we dismiss all research and social science as illusion.

Second, Lee argues, Wilmsen et al. have created a monolith, whereby all primitive society is everywhere the same; and once part of it gets compromised by capitalism or whatever, *all* of it is seen as compromised. But history just doesn't work that way: what we always have is a diversity of locale and exposure. Some areas of the Kalahari desert have been "cannibalized" by European trade or neighboring pastoralism; others have not. In the particular region focused on by Wilmsen, the Dobe area of the Kalahari, most of the archaeological and historical evidence points to this region as being off the beaten track, thus corroborating the notion of long-term continuity of the foraging lifestyle.

Finally, as to the charge of "romanticizing" present-day HGs, this surely cuts both ways. For just as it is possible to idealize the primitive and get caught up in a "noble savage" kind of vision that is the bane of both past and present "New Age" mythologizing, it is equally possible to romanticize "the system," the world capitalist economy, regarding it as so powerful that nothing can ever be resistant to this juggernaut or to its values. This, says Lee, is no less a set of rose-colored glasses, through which ancient foraging lifeways are distorted into "contemporary, marginal subsistence tactics." The revisionists are thus trying to understand history with a shovel, when a scalpel would be more appropriate.

The truth, then, is a bit of this and a bit of that. Yes, the !Kung and other HGs have been strongly influenced by agropastoralist neighbors and an Iron Age economy; and yes, we see evidence of continuities of forager lifeways in regions that have escaped such influence, as well as a hanging-on to those lifeways in regions that have not. As Lee points out, we do see evidence of the ability of band societies to maintain non-wealth-accumulating behavior in the context of power-driven scenarios of world misery and hierarchical, class society, and this is no mean achievement. "The preponderance of evidence," writes M. G. Bicchieri, "suggests that hundreds of years of contact did not result in abandonment of autonomy by groups characterized by 'flexible egalitarian sharing.' "

The issue, finally, is where we wish to put our emphasis: on the internal dynamic of foraging relations, on agropastoralist influence, or on the loss of autonomy to a capitalist world system. As Lee says, the revisionists are preoccupied with the last two, whereas he has been exercised (though not exclusively) by the first. But beyond the debate over the Kalahari, it seems that we must push deeper into the archaeological record in our examination of the continuity (or noncontinuity) of forager lifeways. Does the record in fact support the hypothesis of a basic evolutionary trend from early band egalitarianism to subsequent statist hierarchy?

For Robert Carneiro's mentor, the eminent anthropologist Leslie White, there was no doubt that the social systems of peoples living in the Paleolithic were "characterized by liberty, equality, and fraternity [and] were unquestionably more congenial to the human primate's nature, and more compatible with his psychic needs and aspirations, than any other that has ever been realized in any of the cultures subsequent to the Agricultural Revolution, including our own society today." On such a model, Peter Gardner's figure of 22 percent of HGs being nomadic/nonstoring/egalitarian, discussed earlier in this chapter, would represent the residue, as it were, of those people who have been able to hang on to foraging Paleolithic lifeways in the context of an agricultural/industrial (and hierarchical) world system. But another model is also possible, according to which a figure such as 22 percent may *also* be true for, say, 20,000 years ago. Thus, Price and Brown, in *Prehistoric Hunter-Gatherers*, argue (contra Lee) that means of subsistence do not dictate levels of cultural complexity; that complex HGs may have actually been common in Paleolithic times; that we have archaeological evidence of sedentism, cultivation, social inequality, and differential treatment of the dead, from Late Paleolithic Czechoslovakia, California, and the Natufian region of Israel; and in short, that the "seeds of status differentiation are present in all groups of hunter-gatherers," presumably Paleolithic ones as well. So it's not so much that we have been evolving from egalitarianism to hierarchy, on this view, but that prehistoric HGs were diverse, and what we see is a modification of aspects.

The problem with this Paleolithic revision is that most of it is speculative; in terms of hard evidence (as in the case of their view of the !Kung), the revisionists have yet to make their case. "The neoevolutionist story has been criticized," writes Robert Paynter, "but no clearly superior single alternative has yet emerged." Despite the revisionist bias of the editors themselves, for example, a number of the contributors to *Prehistoric Hunter-Gatherers* come down firmly on the side of the evolutionary model. Thus, Donald Henry argues that evidence from the Levant during the Late Pleistocene shows a progression from simple HG society, to complex HG society, to agriculture. His study of Natufian sites leads him to assert that the "replacement of simple hunter-gatherer societies composed of small, highly mobile, materially impoverished, egalitarian groups by a society that was characterized by large, sedentary, materially rich and socially stratified communities represented a dramatic shift from an adaptive system that had enjoyed several million years of success." What the archaeological evidence in the Natufian and a number of other regions shows is increasing complexity, brought on by a variety of factors, such that complex hunting and gathering was fully in place before the emergence of agriculture. According to Henry, complex HG systems did arise in the Late Pleistocene, but they were of short duration, about two to three millennia, and transitional to agriculture. It would appear that simple HG societies and agricultural societies are relatively stable systems; complex HG societies are not. The Natufian evidence reveals a dramatic increase, in the early Holocene (8000 B.C.), in artifact densities, settlement patterns, population density and plant-processing techniques. Evidence of ranked society, including burial patterns that show status differentiation, and matrilocal residence patterns (typical of agricultural civilization), begin to show up at this time. In the same volume by Price and Brown, Mark Cohen notes that status, group boundary, formal leadership, and delayed-return economies all cluster at the *end* of the archaic record and that prior to that, episodes of sedentism and complexity were scarce and brief. It's as though there was a testing of the waters, so to speak, but nothing of lasting duration.

Similar evidence appears in Johnson and Earle's *Evolution of Human Society*. The archaeological evidence for all continents shows a basic pattern of cultural evolution: from the small-scale to the complex, with subsistence intensification and social stratification coming at the end. HGs adopt agriculture, villages coalesce, leaders come to dominate. On balance, then, the evidence is for an evolutionary trend toward increasing complexity. All of this would in turn suggest that generalizations backward into the past, based on the archaeological record as well as on the behavior of contemporary societies, have to be made carefully, but that the whole thing is hardly a futile exercise. A high degree of prehistoric egalitarianism would seem to be a likely scenario, with a change in this occurring toward the end of the Late Paleolithic.

See Donna J. Haraway, "Remodelling the Human Way of Life," in George W. Stocking (ed.), *Bones, Bodies and Behavior* (Madison: University of Wisconsin Press, 1988), pp. 206–59; Solway and Lee, "Foragers, Genuine or Spurious?" pp. 123, 133, and 141; Edwin N. Wilmsen, *Land Filled with Flies* (Chicago: University of Chicago Press, 1989); Roger Lewin, "New Views Emerge on Hunters and Gatherers," *Science*, 240 (27 May 1988), 1146–48; Edwin N. Wilmsen and James R. Denbow, "Paradigmatic History of San-speaking Peoples and Current Attempts at Revision," *Current Anthropology*, vol. 31, no. 5 (December 1990), pp. 489–524; Alan Barnard, *The Kalahari Debate: A Bibliographic Essay* (Edinburgh: Centre of African Studies, Edinburgh University, Occasional Papers No. 35, 1992); Megan Biesele (ed.), *The Past and Future of !Kung Ethnography* (Hamburg: Helmut Buske Verlag, 1986); Thomas N. Headland and Lawrence A. Reid, "Hunter-Gatherers and Their Neighbors from Prehistory to the Present," *Current Anthropology*, vol. 30, no. 1 (February 1989), pp. 43–66; Susan Kent, "The Current Forager Controversy: Real versus Ideal Views of Hunter-Gatherers," *Man*, n.s., 27 (1992), 45–70; Adam Kuper, "Post-Modernism, Cambridge, and the Great Kalahari Debate," *Social Anthropology*, 1 (1993), 57–71; Richard B. Lee and Mathias Guenther, "Problems in Kalahari Historical Ethnography and the Tolerance of Error," *History in Africa*, 20 (1993), 185–235; Carmel Schrire (ed.), *Past and Present in Hunter-Gatherer Studies* (New York: Academic Press, 1984); Carmel Schrire, "An Inquiry into the Evolutionary

Status and Apparent Identity of San Hunter-Gatherers," *Human Ecology*, vol. 8, no. 1 (1980), pp. 9–32; George Silberbauer, "Morbid Reflexivity and Overgeneralisation in Mosarwa Studies," *Current Anthropology*, vol. 32, no. 1 (February 1991), pp. 96–99; Daniel Stiles, "The Hunter-Gatherer 'Revisionist' Debate," *Anthropology Today*, vol. 8, no. 2 (1992), pp. 13–17; and Edwin N. Wilmsen, "On the Search for (Truth) and Authority: A Reply to Lee and Guenther," *Current Anthropology*, vol. 34, no. 5 (December 1993), pp. 715–21; Richard B. Lee, "Art, Science, or Politics? The Crisis in Hunter-Gatherer Studies," *American Anthropologist*, vol. 94, no. 1 (March 1992), pp. 31–54; Richard B. Lee, "The !Kung in Question: Evidence and Context in the Kalahari Debate," in Preston T. Miracle et al. (eds.), *Foragers in Context* (vol. 10 of *Michigan Discussions in Anthropology*, 1991), pp. 9–16; Richard Lee and Mathias Guenther, "Oxen or Onions? The Search for Trade (and Truth) in the Kalahari," *Current Anthropology*, vol. 32, no. 5 (December 1991), pp. 592–601; Leslie A. White, *The Evolution of Culture* (New York: McGraw-Hill, 1959), p. 278; Price and Brown, *Prehistoric Hunter-Gatherers*, pp. xii, xv, 4–5, 12, 16, and 100–101; Barnard, "Contemporary Hunter-Gatherers," p. 209; Robert Layton et al., "The Transition between Hunting and Gathering and the Specialized Husbandry of Resources: A Socio-ecological Approach," *Current Anthropology*, vol. 32, no. 3 (June 1991), pp. 255, 260, 263, and 269; Robert Foley, "Hominids, Humans and Hunter-Gatherers: An Evolutionary Perspective," in Tim Ingold et al. (eds.), *Hunters and Gatherers 1: History, Evolution and Social Change* (Oxford: Berg, 1988), pp. 215 and 219–20; Donald O. Henry, "Preagricultural Sedentism: The Natufian Example," in Price and Brown, *Prehistoric Hunter-Gatherers*, p. 365; Robert Paynter, "The Archaeology of Equality and Inequality," *Annual Review of Anthropology, 18* (1989), 373; and Johnson and Earle, *Evolution of Human Society*, p. 4.

51. Paul B. Roscoe, "Practice and Political Centralisation," *Current Anthropology*, vol. 34, no. 2 (April 1993), pp. 111–40. Fried is cited by Kent Flannery in "The Cultural Evolution of Civilizations," *Annual Review of Ecology and Systematics, 3* (1972), 414; his most important work is *The Evolution of Political Society* (see above, n. 23).

52. Testart, "Significance of Food Storage," pp. 528 and 531.

53. Cohen, "Prehistoric Hunter-Gatherers," p. 100, discusses Woodburn; Johnson and Earle, *Evolution of Human Society*, p. 96; and Fried, "On the Evolution of Social Stratification and the State," p. 727.

54. For the discussion below, see his reply to Testart in the latter's "Some Major Problems," p. 16.

55. The Northwest Coast of North America, in fact, is very fertile ground for studying social inequality among HGs since it seems to be the rule rather than the exception there. Tribes in this part of the world had hereditary elites, organized warfare, and even institutionalized slavery. Based on his own studies of this region, Herbert Maschner concluded that differentiated access to status, wealth, or leadership—i.e., social inequality—may be "the result of individuals striving for success at opportune moments in the history of that society." Imbalances occur between population and environment, and the

ensuing stressful conditions "allow certain individuals to take advantage of [those imbalances] in order to increase their wealth and status." See Herbert Maschner, "Resource Distributions, Affluence, Circumscription, and Stress: Social Inequality on the Northern Northwest Coast," *Sixth International Conference on Hunting and Gathering Societies* (CHAGS 6), University of Alaska, Fairbanks, May 27–June 1, 1990, vol. 1, pp. 457–60.

56. On the following, see Brian Hayden and Robert Gargett, "Big Man, Big Heart? A Mesoamerican View of the Emergence of Complex Society," *Ancient Mesoamerica*, 1 (1990), 3–20.

57. There is, however, one problem left over from this and other studies that advance the "aggressive subgroup" theory, namely, that all of these studies are of situations in which complexity already existed. Hayden and Gargett admit that they were not studying pristine HGs in the process of becoming complex. (Their defense of this approach, methodologically speaking, is very weak.) Once again, the line of argument in such cases assumes that an extrapolation into the past is reasonable; but it may not be. One is then arguing (which Hayden and Gargett are) that "human nature" is a particular thing, competitive; which may not be the case, as Margaret Power's comments on egalitarian chimpanzees suggest. So if such an argument can be made, it would have to depend on baseline child-rearing practices or on things such as brain chemistry. In other words, even assuming the existence of aggressive subgroups going back to the year dot (which were, then, possibly kept in check by leveling mechanisms), and the role of voluntarism and intention in the emergence of complexity, whence cometh this aggression, this intentionality? For if we stop our inquiry at this point, we really haven't explained all that much; we've "solved" the problem of social inequality by labeling it "inherent." This is why I believe that issues of Object Relations and comparative child rearing can no longer be ignored in other (macro) topics of anthropological inquiry.

58. Harris, *Our Kind*, p. 366.

59. James Woodburn, "Social Dimensions of Death in Four African Hunting and Gathering Societies," in Maurice Bloch and Jonathan Parry (eds.), *Death and the Regeneration of Life* (Cambridge: Cambridge University Press, 1982), pp. 187–88, 193–98, 202, 205–7, and 208n–209n; D. F. Bleek, "Bushmen of Central Angola," *Bantu Studies*, 3 (1928), 124–25. The !Kung do believe in an afterlife, but one has to wonder to what extent this is due to Bantu influence. Bushmen have been in contact with Bantu speakers for as much as eighteen hundred years. As for Australia, Woodburn maintains (as already indicated in the text) that aboriginal systems are actually DR because of male control over women, which means long-term economic control of dowries and estates through marriage brokering. On the problem of generalizing from Australia, see above, n. 12.

60. For the discussion that follows, see Colin M. Turnbull, *The Forest People* (New York: Touchstone Books, 1968; orig. publ. 1961), pp. 27, 32, 50, 80–81, 83, 92–93, 96, 107, 110, 124–25, 129, 137, 145, 223–24, 228, 260, and 286.

61. Colin M. Turnbull, *Wayward Servants* (Garden City, NY: Natural History Press, 1965), pp. 246 and 254.

Of course, as Maurice Bloch pointed out some years ago, the Balinese also live in a "timeless present" and yet are soaking in ritualistic behavior. The difference, he says, is that in Balinese culture "the present and the past are so fused that the present is a mere manifestation of the past," whereas among the Hadza and the Mbuti, there is an absence of the past as a subject matter of their discourse. They are not, in other words, concerned with the past in the present and hence have almost no rituals for birth, death, ancestor worship, and the like. See Bloch, "The Past and the Present in the Present," p. 288.

62. Turnbull, *Wayward Servants,* p. 14.

63. Susan Kent, "And Justice for All," p. 704; Richard Katz, "Education for Transcendence," in Richard B. Lee and Irven DeVore (eds.), *Kalahari Hunter-Gatherers* (Cambridge: Harvard University Press, 1976), pp. 285–89 and 294; Colin M. Turnbull, *The Mbuti Pygmies* (New York: Holt, Rinehart, and Winston, 1983), pp. 5–6, 123, and 128; and Charles Lindholm, *Charisma* (Oxford: Basil Blackwell, 1990), p. 165.

64. Peter J. Wilson, *The Domestication of the Human Species* (New Haven: Yale University Press, 1988), p. 44. In Richard Katz et al., *Healing Makes Our Hearts Happy* (Rochester, VT: Inner Traditions, 1996), the authors remark at various points that the *!kia* ritual serves to bind the community together in times of stress and that in those times, as well, the intensity of the trance increases, and certain trance dancers begin to acquire political leadership roles. For related discussions, see Brian Hayden, "Alliances and Ritual Ecstasy: Human Responses to Resource Stress," *Journal for the Scientific Study of Religion,* vol. 26, no. 1 (1987), pp. 81–91, and Johnson and Earle, *Evolution of Human Societies,* p. 200.

One of the best studies of the verticalizing process in religion is the work of the Soviet anthropologist A. F. Anisimov, who did fieldwork among the Evenks in the twenties and thirties. The Evenks, or Evenki, also go by the name of *Tungus,* and the word "shaman" is in fact a Tungus word. Strictly speaking, this example is perhaps not the most appropriate, since the Evenks are not HGs but nomads proper (see chapter 5), part of the Mongol family, who engage in reindeer herding as well as hunting and fishing. However, Anisimov has captured something that applies to other groups besides nomads, viz., the increasing exclusivity and verticality of religious functions that can occur over time under changing social and economic conditions. Among the Evenks, the progression was from totemism to shamanism. In the past, says Anisimov, religious functions involved the entire clan. As the economy began to change, Evenk communal social organization broke down, and the shaman became the specialist of a religious cult, which in turn formed the embryo of a priesthood. Individual clan totems became spirit lords and supreme deities, and the shaman's position turned into a hereditary office, associated with a particular family—one that would develop close ties to the new propertied "aristocracy." Finally, and most revealing for our purposes, these late religious developments were accompanied by a shift in spatial orientation. In the totemic stage, says Anisimov, the mythical clan did not move away spatially but stayed within the limits of the inhabited land. References were to East and West, not to up and down. "The horizontal orientation of the spatial concepts of the universe," he wrote, "preceded in time the vertical division into upper, middle, and nether worlds." In many ways, this single sentence epitomizes my entire argument.

See A. F. Anisimov, "The Shaman's Tent of the Evenks and the Origin of the Shamanistic Rite," trans. Ethel and Stephen Dunn, and "Cosmological Concepts of the Peoples of the North," trans. Barbara Krader, in Harry N. Michael (ed.), *Studies in Siberian Shamanism* (Toronto: Arctic Institute of North America, University of Toronto, 1963), pp. 84–85, 108–22, and 207.

65. Grant D. Jones and Robert R. Kautz, "Issues in the Study of New World State Formation," in Grant D. Jones and Robert R. Kautz (eds.), *The Transition to Statehood in the New World* (Cambridge: Cambridge University Press, 1981), p. 27; Richard S. MacNeish, "The Transition to Statehood As Seen from the Mouth of a Cave," p. 146, in the same volume; Malcolm Webb, "The State of the Art on State Origins?" *Reviews in Anthropology*, vol. 11, no. 4 (Fall 1984), p. 274; Robert McC. Netting, "Sacred Power and Centralization: Aspects of Political Adaptation in Africa," in Spooner, *Population Growth*, pp. 220 and 236–41; Ember and Ember, "Worldwide Cross-Cultural Studies," p. 104; and Carlo Levi, *Of Fear and Freedom*, trans. Adolphe Gourevitch (New York: Farrar, Strauss and Co., 1950), pp. 8–9. On charismatic leadership emerging under conditions of high population density, see Clastres, *Society Against the State*, pp. 189–218.

66. Cohen, "Prehistoric Hunter-Gatherers," pp. 106 and 111; Edward Shils, "Charisma," *International Encyclopedia of the Social Sciences*, ed. David Sills, vol. 2 (New York: Macmillan, 1968), p. 387; and Caroline Humphrey, "Shamanic Practices and the State in Northern Asia: Views from the Center and Periphery," in Nicholas Thomas and Caroline Humphrey (eds.), *Shamanism, History, and the State* (Ann Arbor: University of Michigan Press, 1994), p. 197.

67. Jones and Kautz, "Issues in the Study of New World State Formation," pp. 25–27; Roy A. Rappaport, "The Sacred in Human Evolution," *Annual Review of Ecology and Systematics*, 2 (1971), 23 and 39.

68. Bruce Chatwin, *The Songlines* (New York: Penguin Books, 1988).

69. Andrew Bard Schmookler, *The Parable of the Tribes* (Boston: Houghton Mifflin, 1984); William Poundstone, *Prisoner's Dilemma* (New York: Anchor Books, 1993).

70. Joseph A. Tainter, *The Collapse of Complex Societies* (Cambridge: Cambridge University Press, 1988).

71. Morris Berman, *Coming to Our Senses* (New York: Simon & Schuster, 1989), chs. 4–8.

72. Fried, "On the Evolution of Social Stratification and the State," pp. 719 and 727.

73. Testart, "Some Major Problems," p. 20.

74. Lindholm, *Charisma*, p. 156.

3. As the Soul Is Bent: The Psycho-Religious Roots of Social Inequality

1. Barbara Rogoff et al., "Cultural Variation in the Role Relations of Toddlers and Their Families," in Marc H. Bornstein (ed.), *Cultural Approaches to Parenting* (Hillsdale, NJ: Lawrence Erlbaum, 1991), pp. 173–74; Herbert Barry III and Leonora M. Paxson, "Infancy and Early Childhood: Cross-Cultural Codes 2," *Ethnology*, vol. 10, no. 4 (October 1971), pp. 466–508; and Mary D. Salter Ainsworth, "Attachment Theory and Its Utility in Cross-Cultural Research," in P. Herbert Leiderman et al. (eds.), *Culture and Infancy* (New York: Academic Press, 1977), p. 56. See also Michael Lewis, "Social Influences on Development," in Michael Lewis (ed.), *Beyond the Dyad* (New York: Plenum Press, 1984), p. 1; Saul Feinman and Michael Lewis, "Is There Social Life beyond the Dyad?" in the same volume, p. 14; and in particular, the work done by Coe and Suomi cited in chapter 1, n. 38 above.

2. On the Ajase complex, which is the rage and guilt that emerges from the mother/child dyad when the child discovers that it is not the sole purpose of its mother's life, see David H. Spain, "Oedipus Rex or Edifice Wrecked? Some Comments on the Universality of Oedipality and on the Cultural Limitations of Freud's Thought," in David H. Spain (ed.), *Psychoanalytic Anthropology after Freud* (New York: Psyche Press, 1992), p. 216 and n. The Japanese saying is quoted in Joy Hendry, *Becoming Japanese* (Honolulu: University of Hawaii Press, 1986), p. 17.

3. Hendry, *Becoming Japanese*, pp. 8, 19–20, 36, and 97–98.

4. William Caudill and Helen Weinstein, "Maternal Care and Infant Behavior in Japan and America," *Psychiatry*, 32 (1969), 12–16 and 30–31.

5. Ibid., pp. 15 and 29; Hendry, *Becoming Japanese*, pp. 97, 115, 163, and 175–76.

6. Mordechai Rotenberg, "Alienating-Individualism and Reciprocal-Individualism: A Cross-Cultural Conceptualization," *Journal of Humanistic Psychology*, vol. 17, no. 3 (Summer 1977), pp. 3–17.

7. Hélène Stork, *Enfances indiennes* (Paris: Centurion, 1986). Discussion that follows is taken from pp. 16, 36, 69, 75, 116, 139, 147–48, 177–81, 204, and 216–17.

8. Stanley N. Kurtz, *All the Mothers Are One* (New York: Columbia University Press, 1992), pp. 31, 41, and 53. On the general East-West pattern, Kurtz cites (pp. 251–52) the work of Robert LeVine ("Child Rearing as Cultural Adaptation," in Leiderman, *Culture and Infancy*, pp. 15–27), which notes that in Africa, Latin America, and much of Asia, one finds an "indulgent"

physical pattern of child rearing and a "nonindulgent" psychological or emotional one. There is no loving empathy in these cultures, says LeVine; what we find instead is a "simple, continuous physical presence." Which means: the infant is always on or near a caregiver's body; crying is quickly attended to, usually via the breast; and there is little attention given to the infant as an emotional individual, such as by eye contact or chatting. For a detailed study of this pattern and a comparison with the verbal/visual pattern found in the United States, see Robert A. LeVine et al., *Child Care and Culture* (Cambridge: Cambridge University Press, 1994), esp. pp. 247–56.

9. Annette Hamilton, *Nature and Nurture* (Canberra: Australian Institute of Aboriginal Studies, 1981), pp. 17, 31–32, 39, 65, and 194; Robert Munroe, personal communication (May 1996), using the data provided by Barry and Paxson (cited above, n. 1).

10. Melvin Konner, "Infancy Among the Kalahari Desert San," in Leiderman, *Culture and Infancy*, pp. 290, 297, 299, and 302; and Edward Tronick et al., "Multiple Caretaking in the Context of Human Evolution: Why Don't the Efe Know the Western Prescription for Child Care?" in Martin Reite and Tiffany Field (eds.), *The Psychobiology of Attachment and Separation* (Orlando: Academic Press, 1985), p. 298 (this draws on an earlier article by Konner).

11. Stork, *Enfances indiennes*, p. 30.

12. Konner, "Infancy Among the Kalahari Desert San," pp. 318–19; Hamilton, *Nature and Nurture*, pp. 166–67; and Jean Liedloff, *The Continuum Concept* (rev. ed.; Reading, MA: Addison-Wesley, 1977).

13. Charles M. Super, "Behavioral Development in Infancy," in Robert L. Munroe et al. (eds.), *Handbook of Cross-Cultural Human Development* (New York: Garland, 1981), pp. 235–39.

14. Mary Ainsworth, "Attachment Theory," in *Infancy in Uganda* (Baltimore: Johns Hopkins University Press, 1967), pp. 63–64, and "The Development of Mother-Infant Attachment," *Review of Child Development Research*, vol. 3: *Child Development and Social Policy* (1973), p. 81; and H. R. Schaffer and P. E. Emerson, "The Development of Social Attachments in Infancy," *Monographs of the Society for Research in Child Development*, 29 (1964).

15. Konner, "Infancy Among the Kalahari San," p. 290.

16. Melissa Heckler, "Oh Place Where We Have Played, Stay Well" (unpublished MS.). I am grateful to Ms. Heckler for making this essay available to me.

17. Hamilton, *Nature and Nurture*, pp. 27, 30, 46, 163–64, and 168.

18. Gilda Morelli and Edward Tronick, "Parenting and Child Development in the Efé Foragers and Lese Farmers of Zaire," in Bornstein, *Cultural Approaches to Parenting*, pp. 91–92; and Tronick et al., "Multiple Caretaking," pp. 294 and 314–16.

19. JoAnn F. Campbell, "Multiple Mothering and Separation-Individuation: Evidence from Some Nigerian Children," in Spain, *Psychoanalytic Anthropology after Freud*, p. 77; and Rogoff et al., "Cultural Variation," pp. 176–79.

20. On this and the discussion that follows, see Tronick et al., "Multiple Caretaking," pp. 315–16; Bruno Bettelheim, *The Children of the Dream* (London: Macmillan, 1969), pp. 72, 85–86, 97, 120, 124, 130, 246, 249, 276–78, 294, 306, and 317–20; and Melford E. Spiro, *Children of the Kibbutz* (new ed.; New York: Schocken Books, 1965; orig. publ. 1958), pp. 424–33.

21. Clyde Kluckhohn, "Some Aspects of Navaho Infancy and Early Childhood," *Psychoanalysis and the Social Sciences, 1* (1947), 37–86.

22. Hamilton, *Nature and Nurture*, pp. 80–81, 149, and 152–53. That multiple caregiving is no insurance against the development of dominance and hierarchy is surely clear from the case of Japan; and JoAnn Campbell, in her Nigerian study, found that in a diffuse mothering situation, children have a greater need for self-control and self-esteem to originate from the outside. In short, they have weaker internal defenses to cope with rivalry than, say, American children, and this makes it easier for Nigerian culture to maintain hierarchical relations in adulthood.

One of the pioneering research projects regarding cross-cultural child rearing is the famous "Six Cultures" study initiated a few decades ago under the aegis of John and Beatrice Whiting at Harvard. This research revealed the sort of pattern we are talking about. One culture was American (anonymized as "Orchard Town," New England); the other five were agricultural societies from various parts of the world. While the study did show that children reared in complex cultures tended to be more "dependent/ dominant" and less "nurturant/responsible" than children brought up in simpler cultures, the situation was not black and white. For example, children brought up in nuclear families proved to be less "authoritarian/aggressive" than children raised in extended ones. The study that Leigh Minturn and John Hitchcock did for the Whitings, of the Rājpūts of Khalapur (India), found that multiple mothering did not produce a happy society. Children were scolded rather than praised and tended to abandon tasks whenever they became difficult. Risk-taking and self-reliance were virtually unknown, and the culture was characterized by a great deal of hierarchy and social inequality. As part of the same project, Robert and Barbara LeVine worked with a Gusii community in Kenya—also a multiple caregiving situation—in which fear (i.e., threats of animals or strangers)—was used to control the infants. Not surprisingly, the culture turned out individuals who were dependent, generally timid toward the world, and obedient to authority.

Robert Munroe was also kind enough (personal communication, May 1996) to point out to me certain modifications with respect to monotropy, multiple caregiving, and HG/agricultural comparisons. Using the Barry-Paxson data (see n. 1, above), Munroe notes that for a sample of 186 societies that include 18 in the HG category, there seems to be the same degree of multiple caregiving among sedentary villagers as among HGs, although (a) degree of bodily contact is higher in early infancy among the latter, and (b) the principal contact HG infants have is with adults, whereas in agricultural societies, the principal contact is with children (often older siblings). This latter point might mean that in HG societies, there is a greater likelihood for the infant to experience itself as peripheral to adult activities, rather than become the mother's special focus. In the case of infants largely raised by other children, this may create a whole different configuration. Munroe's own fieldwork (with Ruth Munroe) among the Logoli of western Kenya (Bantu-speaking horticulturalists), where sibling caregiving plays a major role, revealed that the crucial factor for psychological purposes was *mother*-holding. That is to say, for an admittedly small sample of children studied over the period from one to twelve years of age, positive outlook on life and a sense of security correlated not with overall holding but specifically with the amount of holding done by the biological mother. At the same time, "high-density" households (ones with more caregivers) were more "indulgent" of Logoli infants, e.g., the infants were responded to more quickly when they cried. In short, it does become difficult to sort particular factors out in an area that is so subjective, and there remains the problem of what the implications are for Paleolithic child rearing.

See Campbell, "Multiple Mothering and Separation-Individuation," pp. 64, 78, and 86–87; Beatrice B. Whiting and John W. M. Whiting, *Children of Six Cultures* (Cambridge: Harvard University Press, 1975), pp. 128–29 and 176; Leigh Minturn and John T. Hitchcock, "The Rājpūts of Khalapur, India," in Beatrice B. Whiting (ed.), *Six Cultures* (New York: Wiley, 1963), pp. 327 and 359–60; Robert A. and Barbara B. LeVine, "Nyangsong: A Gusii Community in Kenya," in Whiting, *Six Cultures*, pp. 142–43, 147, and 181; and the following articles by Ruth H. and Robert L. Munroe: "Household Density and Infant Care in an East African Society," *The Journal of Social Psychology*, 83 (1971), 3–13; "Infant Experience and Childhood Affect Among the Logoli: A Longitudinal Study," *Ethos*, vol. 8, no. 4 (Winter 1980), pp. 295–315; "Infant Experience and Childhood Cognition: A Longitudinal Study Among the Logoli of Kenya," *Ethos*, vol. 12, no. 4 (Winter 1984), pp. 292–306; and (with Erika Westling and Jennifer Rosenberg), "Infant Experience and Late-Childhood Dispositions: An Eleven-Year Follow-up among the Logoli of Kenya," *Ethos*, 25 (1997), 359–72.

23. The discussion that follows is taken from Herbert Barry III, Irvin L. Child, and Margaret K. Bacon, "Relation of Child Training to Subsistence Economy," *American Anthropologist, 61* (1959), 51–63.

24. J. W. Berry, "Independence and Conformity in Subsistence-Level Societies," *Journal of Personality and Social Psychology*, vol. 7, no. 4 (1967), pp. 415–18.

25. Herbert Barry III, "Cross-Cultural Research with Matched Pairs of Societies," *Journal of Social Psychology, 79* (1969), 30; C. R. Badcock, *The Psychoanalysis of Culture* (Oxford: Basil Blackwell, 1980), pp. 83, 86–89, and 104.

26. Barry S. Hewlett, *Intimate Fathers* (Ann Arbor: University of Michigan Press, 1991), pp. 5, 11, 27–28, 32–35, and 44–46.

27. Richard B. Lee, "Population Growth and the Beginnings of Sedentary Life among the !Kung Bushmen," in Brian Spooner (ed.), *Population Growth: Anthropological Implications* (Cambridge: MIT Press, 1972), pp. 331 and 337–41. For a discussion of why lactation suppresses ovulation, see Richard B. Lee, "Lactation, Ovulation, Infanticide, and Women's Work: A Study of Hunter-Gatherer Population Regulation," in Mark N. Cohen et al. (eds.), *Biosocial Mechanisms of Population Regulation* (New Haven: Yale University Press, 1980), pp. 340–42.

28. Lee, "Lactation, Ovulation," pp. 344–45.

29. Linda M. Fedigan, "The Changing Role of Women in Models of Human Evolution," *Annual Review of Anthropology*, 15 (1986), 40.

30. R. V. Short, "Breast Feeding," *Scientific American*, 250, (April 1984), pp. 36–38. In a comparative study of women in Edinburgh, Melbourne, and among the !Kung, the first two groups weaned their infants within eighteen months, but the !Kung, after three and one-half years. The first two groups fed their babies less than eight times a day, whereas the !Kung fed them on an average of forty-eight times during the twelve hours of daylight.

Even more exact scientific studies now reveal that nipple stimulation affects the hypothalamus, releasing beta-endorphin in a complex chemical sequence that finally suppresses ovarian activity. The use of pacifiers erodes the contraceptive effect of nipple stimulation.

See Shyam Thapa et al., "Breast Feeding, Birth Spacing and Their Effects on Child Survival," *Nature*, 335 (20 October 1988), 679.

31. C. R. Badcock, personal communication, 1994.

32. Hamilton, *Nature and Nurture*, pp. 67–70, 78, and 100; Sudhir Kakar, *The Inner World* (2d ed., rev. and enl.; Delhi: Oxford University Press, 1981); and Konner, "Infancy Among the Kalahari Desert San," p. 290.

33. Lee, "Lactation, Ovulation," p. 333; David Fabbro, "Peaceful Societies: An Introduction," *Journal of Peace Research*, vol. 15, no. 1 (1978), pp. 73 and 75; Glenn Hausfater and Sarah Blaffer Hrdy (eds.), *Infanticide* (New York: Aldine, 1984), pp. xi, xvii–xix, and xxvi–xxix. For the Whiting study see "Infanticide," in *Society for Cross-Cultural Research Newsletter*, no. 5 (September 1977). Birdsell's comment can be found in "Some Predictions for the Pleistocene Based on Equilibrium Systems among Recent Hunter-Gatherers," pp. 227–40 of Richard B. Lee and Irven DeVore (eds.), *Man the Hunter* (Chicago: Aldine, 1968).

34. Marjorie Shostak, *Nisa: The Life and Words of a !Kung Woman* (New York: Vintage Books, 1983), pp. 19, 31–32, 51ff., 66–67, and 238. For further information on infanticide among the !Kung, see the references provided on p. 376 of her book.

35. Hausfater and Hrdy, *Infanticide*, p. xi; Susan Scrimshaw, "Infanticide in Human Populations: Societal and Individual Concerns," pp. 440 and 460–62 of the same volume; and Martin Daly and Margo Wilson, "A Sociobiological Analysis of Human Infanticide," p. 502 of the same volume.

36. Garrett Hardin, "The Tragedy of the Commons," *Science, 162* (1968), 1243–48; Margaret Mead, "A Cultural Anthropologist's Approach to Maternal Deprivation," in John Bowlby (ed.), *Maternal Care and Mental Health* (New York: Schocken Books, n.d. [1951]), pp. 240–42.

37. Marvin Harris, *Our Kind* (New York: Harper & Row, 1989), pp. 359–60.

38. On serotonin and dominance behavior, see some of the articles in Roger D. Masters and Michael T. McGuire (eds.), *The Neurotransmitter Revolution* (Carbondale, IL: Southern Illinois University Press, 1994). The single most important study of the "Soni" phenomenon discussed above—what might be called "secondary narcissism"—is contained in Heinz Kohut, *The Analysis of the Self* (New York: International Universities Press, 1971).

39. Jessica Benjamin, *The Bonds of Love* (New York: Pantheon Books, 1988).

40. The quote is from Brant Wenegrat, *The Divine Archetype* (Lexington, MA: Lexington Books, 1990), p. 140.
The following is a story told to me (personal communication, January 1995) by Jean MacGregor, who lived for a time with the !Kung Bushmen. Jean was walking along with some !Kung women, and she asked them if they were afraid of snakes (which can be particularly lethal in the Kalahari Desert). They said no because they were able to see them at very great distances. (Jean was not able to see with binoculars creatures that these women could see with the naked eye.) "However, there is one kind of snake," said Jean, "that buries itself in the sand. Aren't you afraid you might accidentally step on it, get bitten, and die?" "Well," one of the women replied, "if that happens, then that was the day that I was supposed to die." (End of discussion)

41. Wenegrat, *Divine Archetype, passim;* Arther Ferrill, *The Origins of War* (London: Thames and Hudson, 1985).

42. See above, chapter 1, n. 33, and the speculation of Ehrenberg in n. 51, below.

43. Galway Kinnell, *Mortal Acts, Mortal Words* (Boston: Houghton Mifflin, 1980), pp. 42–43 and 45.

44. Sigmund Freud, *New Introductory Lectures on Psychoanalysis*, trans. W. J. H. Sprott (New York: W. W. Norton, 1933), p. 182.

45. Philip E. Slater, *Footholds* (New York: E. P. Dutton, 1977), pp. 68, 79, 81, 87–88, and 144.

46. Philip E. Slater, *The Glory of Hera* (Boston: Beacon Press, 1968), pp. 33, 413 and n., and 439.

47. Ibid., pp. 462–65.

48. Quoted in Carole Klein, *Mothers and Sons* (Boston: Houghton Mifflin, 1984), p. 96. The following discussion is taken from pp. 72, 94, 225, and 228.

49. Clara M. Thompson, "Cultural Pressures in the Psychology of Women," in Maurice R. Green (ed.), *Interpersonal Psychoanalysis: The Selected Papers of Clara M. Thompson* (New York: Basic Books, 1964), pp. 229 and 236.

50. Dorothy Dinnerstein, *The Mermaid and the Minotaur* (New York: Harper & Row, 1976), p. 176.

51. Ibid., pp. 19 and note, 203, and 279–89. Cf. above, chapter 1, n. 33. In his essay "The Origins of the Family," Friedrich Engels argues that the amount of labor women put into subsistence is directly proportional to their power in society. This was borne out by the work of Patricia Draper, in her research among the !Kung Bushmen. She found that women derived a lot of esteem from their gathering activities; had control over the distribution of the food they gather; did not stay home at camp—i.e., were not valued less in comparison to men, "the adventurers," and so on. But she found that when the !Kung were forced to become sedentary, problems of gender inequality reared their head, and sex roles became more rigidly defined. Whereas in the nomadic situation, men often were willing to cross gender lines in terms of work (gather plant foods, collect water, etc.), in the sedentary situation such work came to be regarded as "unworthy"; men lost face if they did it. The women became more homebound, whereas the men now left home frequently, traveled widely, and began to carry an aura of authority that set them apart from women and children—fertile ground for the "Dinnerstein syndrome."

According to Margaret Ehrenberg, however, this constellation does not apply to horticulture, or the early stages of agriculture. She speculates that women start to play a subsidiary role later on, when the plow is introduced and when animals are kept on a large scale. The volume of work then needed to maintain the community, she believes, jumped exponentially; and women, who were involved in child rearing, got left behind. Their primary role became that of mothering; economically, they were relegated to secondary tasks. However, Heribert Adam says (personal communication, January 1997) that in all African subsistence economies, women do hard physical work in the fields and that in West Africa they even sell the products independently at the market. Hence, agriculture does not *necessarily* introduce a greater socioeconomic role for men, but I believe Ehrenberg is right in asserting that, for the most part, this eventually became the dominant historical pattern.

(See Fedigan, "Changing Role," pp. 30–31; Patricia Draper, "!Kung Women: Contrasts in Sexual Egalitarianism in Foraging and Sedentary Contexts," in Rayna Reiter [ed.], *Toward an Anthropology of Women* [New York: Monthly Review Press, 1975], pp. 82–87, 96, 103, and 109; and Margaret Ehrenberg, Women in Prehistory [London: British Museum Publications, 1989], pp. 77, 81, 99–107, and 173.)

Dinnerstein's belief that the syndrome could be resolved if men shared the caregiving with women is plausible, but the evidence for it is unclear. There are desultory references in the anthropological literature to how male parenting and gender equality leads to much healthier individuals, less war and social violence, etc.; but the only comprehensive study I know of is Barry Hewlett's work *Intimate Fathers* (see above, n. 26), which is a report on the Aka Pygmies of central Africa, among whom male parenting is the norm. The group is small: about three hundred nomadic HGs who live in the tropical forest regions of the Central African Republic. The Aka have no chiefs, and no relationship of command/obedience is in force. Gender relations are egalitarian. Husbands and wives both contribute to the diet and go out together for gathering and hunting, the latter being done with nets (an important issue; Colin Turnbull found that among the Mbuti, net-hunting fathers were more involved with their children than bow and arrow users, who excluded women from this form of hunting). Women have a big say in the distribution and exchange of food, and while Aka men hold the status positions, such as those of tribal leadership, women can challenge this authority and are influential in the decision-making process. Violence against women is virtually nonexistent.

The infants in Hewlett's study demonstrated strong attachment behavior toward their mothers, but they also sought out the attention of their fathers. As far as Hewlett could observe, the Aka do not have stronger feelings for their mothers than for their fathers. In fact, he found that 47 percent of the father's day (of twenty-four hours) was spent holding the infant or having it within arm's reach.

Hewlett argues that when resources are not stored or accumulated, and men are not the primary contributors to subsistence, they spend more time involved in child rearing. Thus, he points out that in a 1981 article Richard Katz and Melvin Konner did on the role of fathers, the authors discovered that father-infant proximity (both emotional and physical) was greatest in gathering-hunting societies, that is, ones in which meat was of secondary importance in the diet, and least in agropastoralist societies (which accumulate and store food). Katz and Konner also found that father-infant proximity was low in societies in which hunting by men was the primary mode of subsistence; and (notes Hewlett) the Whitings (*Children of Six Cultures*; see above, n. 22) further discovered that husband-wife intimacy was greatest in cultures that did not accumulate resources.

Hewlett's study is, moreover, borne out by the Barry-Paxson data (see above, n. 1), which indicate that fathers are closer to infants and young children in HG societies than in agricultural ones; but, as always, it is difficult to extrapolate backward in time, and Hewlett does not believe his work proves that it is universal or natural for fathers to be active caregivers. Furthermore, he argues that the assumption of Dinnerstein and Chodorow, that dominance patterns and misogyny would disappear if men were active in child rearing, is problematic because things such as less competition are found among the !Kung and other HGs where the fathers are *not* heavily involved in child rearing. It may be, then, that gender equality, rather than male caregiving per se, is the crucial factor.

See Hewlett, *Intimate Fathers*, pp. 5, 11, 27, 38–41, 47–48, 101, 109, 126, 134–35, 164, and 174–75.

4. Agriculture, Religion, and the Great Mother

1. A. Leo Oppenheim, *Ancient Mesopotamia* (rev. ed.; Chicago: University of Chicago Press, 1977), p. 183.

2. I have already dealt with Eliade and the problem of comparative mythology above (chapter 1, n. 6). Much that can be said of Eliade applies to Joseph Campbell as well. Thus, Robert Segal, for example, shows how Campbell constructs a composite hero pattern and then takes things that do not truly conform to it as examples. Campbell, says Segal, "is content to merely assert universality rather than bother to document it." Not only are many of his case studies wrong, or forced, but it is also the case that "every example he cites is interpretable in one or more of the other ways he arbitrarily rejects."

Campbell's methodology can be seen in any of his works. In her review of his *Way of the Animal Powers* (in the *New York Times Book Review*, 18 December 1983), Wendy Doniger notes that Campbell draws his examples from cultures that have no known links or contacts between them, and he provides no discussion of how a myth develops as it moves from one region to another. He is only interested in essences, repeatedly succumbing to "the siren song of the archetypes." The work, she concludes, is good art, but not good science. (Cf. below, n. 14)

We can see this artistic or even rhapsodic approach to the past in a book such as Campbell's *Primitive Mythology*. From an Apache tale of how birds were created, Campbell goes on to discuss designs on Mesopotamian pottery and the supposed universality of swastika symbolism. These images appear, he says, on Chinese drawings of the Buddha; and although there was no influence of Buddhism on Apache mythology, the notion expressed by both Calderón and Shakespeare, that life is a dream, was a basic theme of Hindu philosophers, and ancient yogic statues show the development of this trance-inducing exercise . . . etc. etc. Campbell concludes:

> What I am now suggesting, therefore, is that in this Apache legend of the creation of the bird we have a remote cognate of the Indian forms, which must have proceeded from the same neolithic stock; and that in both cases the symbol of the swastika represents a process of transformation: the conjuring up (in the case of the Hactcin), or conjuring away (in the case of the Buddha), of a universe that because of the fleeting nature of its forms may indeed be compared to the substance of a mirage, or of a dream.

What are we to make of such an "argument"? Campbell is obviously a great storyteller, and his narrative itself moves like a dream, enfolding the reader in a wonderful set of comforting associations. As art, it is high stuff. But Campbell does not, any more than Eliade did, intend this as a species of poetry; instead, he is claiming real anthropological connections. But there are no footnotes here and no substantiation of any of this. What, indeed, does "remote cognate" really mean? As with Eliade, this is pure fiction passed off as fact. At another point he relates a tale of the Blackfoot Indians of Montana (circa 1870), "The Legend of the Buffalo Dance," and then argues that something similar can be seen in the caves of Trois Frères. We then move on to Persephone and Demeter, and finally we are told: "One may hear in the chant of the dancing buffalo . . . a paleolithic prelude to the great theme of the Hindu *Bhagavad Gītā*."(!) As Wendy Doniger points out, Campbell was unwilling to do the real work of learning what myths actually say, to recognize that different variants of the "same" myth are *not* the same. "He cooked up the TV dinner of mythology so that everything tastes the same," she writes; this was "easy listening religion, Muzak mythology. He reduced great books to slogans."

See Robert A. Segal, "Joseph Campbell's Theory of Myth," in Alan Dundes (ed.), *Sacred Narrative* (Berkeley: University of California Press, 1984), pp. 256–57 and 263–68; Joseph Campbell, *Primitive Mythology* (rev. ed. 1969; New York: Penguin Books, 1991), pp. 232–34 and 282–93; Wendy Doniger, "Origins of Myth-Making Man," in Daniel C. Noel (ed.), *Paths to the Power of Myth* (New York: Crossroad, 1990), pp. 181–86, and "A Very Strange Enchanted Boy," *New York Times Book Review*, 2 February 1992, pp. 7–8.

3. It should be clear, in what follows, that I am attacking Jung's psychohistory, or historical methodology, not his legacy for psychology or psychotherapy, which obviously has many worthwhile aspects. For example, it was Jung who came up with the idea that all psychoanalytic trainees should be analyzed themselves. Concepts such as extraversion and introversion, as well as Jung's own brand of dream analysis, have been important contributions to human understanding. While the notion of archetypes cannot be validated for all human beings ever existing (the theory of a collective unconscious), these are images that can be very helpful heuristically, in a therapeutic context, so long as they are understood as metaphors and not reified into objective realities.

For a balanced assessment of Jung's strengths and weaknesses (which does not, however, deal with the problem of historical methodology discussed below), see Anthony Storr, *Feet of Clay* (New York: Free Press Paperbacks, 1997), pp. 85–105.

4. On the following, see Richard Noll, *The Jung Cult* (Princeton: Princeton University Press, 1994), pp. 21ff., 96ff., 105, 124–29, 163–64, 169–74, 202–4, 213, and 256.

5. Walter Burkert, *Ancient Mystery Cults* (Cambridge: Harvard University Press, 1987), pp. 6 and 98; Franz Cumont, *Textes et monuments figurés relatifs aux mystères de Mithra* (2 vols.; Brussels: H. Lamertin, 1896 and 1899).

6. Discreditation of the "Persian thesis" can be found in David Ulansey, *The Origins of the Mithraic Mysteries* (New York: Oxford University Press, 1989).

In some versions of the initiation, apparently, the holiest moment was the unveiling of the image of Mithras killing a bull.

I should add that I am not arguing that Jung was the only figure in the history of psychotherapy to set himself up as the head of a "priesthood"; indeed, this sort of cultishness seems endemic to the entire profession. Freud, as is well known, cultivated this kind of zealous loyalty to himself and his ideas. (For a recent, and amusing, look at this, see Daphne Merkin, "Freud Rising," in the *New Yorker*, 9 November 1998, pp. 50–55, as well as the scholarly treatment of it by François Roustang, *Dire Mastery*, trans. Ned Lukacher [Baltimore: Johns Hopkins University Press, 1982], *passim*.) Human failings aside, however, there is a difference between a doctrine that by its very nature seems to cultivate dependence and one that tries to resist it. Thus, Richard Wolin writes: "Jungian analysis would serve the ends of re-enchantment and myth rather than the Freudian ends of maturity and autonomy." (See "Prometheus Unhinged," *New Republic*, 27 October 1997, p. 32)

7. Noll, *Jung Cult*, p. 190; Walter Goldschmidt, "An Open Letter to Melford E. Spiro," *Ethos*, vol. 23, no. 2 (June 1995), p. 247. On Thomas and Humphrey see above, chs. 1 and 2, *passim*.

The quote from Jung is in Noll, *Jung Cult*, pp. 258–59, and occurs in an essay Jung wrote in 1928, "The Relations between the Ego and the Unconscious." The meaning is a bit ambiguous, however, because Jung also discusses the psychology of cults in the same essay, deploring the whole phenomenon of discipleship and guru worship, which he regards as a failure to individuate, as the Jungian scholar, Sonu Shamdasani, points out (*Cult Fictions* [London: Routledge, 1998], pp. 81–82). Nevertheless, Shamdasani overlooks Jung's 1910 correspondence with Freud, in which he tells the latter of his desire to use myth to found a new religion and so bring Christian Europe back to its "ecstatic instinctual forces," to "infinite rapture and wantonness," adding that by creating a new elite, they might usher in a golden age. Freud responded that he had no intention of doing any such thing, and he subsequently published (along with Ernest Jones) articles on the nature of narcissism. (See Noll, *Jung Cult*, pp. 188–90 and 204.)

8. Noll, *Jung Cult*, pp. 182–86. On Pauli, see Robert S. Westman, "Nature, Art, and Psyche: Jung, Pauli, and the Kepler-Fludd Polemic," in Brian Vickers (ed.), *Occult and Scientific Mentalities in the Renaissance* (New York: Cambridge University Press, 1984), pp. 212–20 and 228–29. For more on Noll's accusations of Jung's dishonesty, see Dinitia Smith, "Scholar Who Says Jung Lied Is at War with Descendants," *New York Times*, 3 June 1995, pp. 1 and 9; see also p. 18.

The case of the Solar Phallus Man involved a patient at the Burghölzli hospital in Zurich who, according to Jung, had a fantasy in 1906 of a sun with an erect phallus that generated wind when it moved. Jung saw this as evidence for a collective unconscious because a similar image occurs in a book by Dieterich, *Eine Mithraslithurgie*, published in 1910. As it turns out, however, the first edition of this book actually appeared in 1903, and in any case the patient was not Jung's, but Jung's assistant's, Honneger, who joined the hospital in 1909. The Solar Phallus Man could thus not have reported the dream in 1906, and even then, could have had access to Dieterich's work. According to Sonu Shamdasani, "The Solar Phallus Man, together with other figures, carried on his shoulders the weight and burden of proof of the Collective Unconscious." ("A Woman Called Frank," *Spring*, 50 [1990], 40.)

9. Noll, *Jung Cult*, p. 294. However, Noll's work is not without its problems, and Shamdasani, in *Cult Fictions*, is able to show that Noll is more than a little overzealous in arguing that Jung's explicit purpose was to establish a cult, or "Jungian church" (cf. Anthony Storr, in *Feet of Clay*, p. 96). Nevertheless, Shamdasani's own evidence doesn't rule out such a possibility; and for our own purposes, the issue is neither here nor there since the heart of the matter is the falsification of data in cases such as that of the Solar Phallus Man (see previous note), and this Shamdasani chooses not to address. Despite the rather aggressive approach of Noll's study, it does make the crucial point that what Jung claimed had emerged spontaneously from the unconscious of his patients came from his, and their, participation in the secular religious ideologies of the day, and therefore that what Jung claimed was universal and transcendent was in fact local and historical. (See the review of Noll by John Toews in *Central European History*, vol. 29, no. 2 [1996], pp. 261–64.)

10. On the discussion that follows, see Erich Neumann, *The Great Mother*, trans. Ralph Manheim (2d ed.; Princeton: Princeton University Press, 1972), pp. xlii, 25, 43–44, 82, 89, 91–92, 94–119, and 330–31.

11. Marija Gimbutas, *The Goddesses and Gods of Old Europe* (new ed.; London: Thames and Hudson, 1982), pp. 9 and 236–38. See also *The Language of the Goddess* (San Francisco: Harper & Row, 1989), and *The Civilization of the Goddess* (San Francisco: Harper & Row, 1991).

12. Riane Eisler, *The Chalice and the Blade* (San Francisco: Harper & Row, 1987); Anne Baring and Jules Cashford, *The Myth of the Goddess* (New York: Penguin Books, 1991); Anne L. Barstow, "The Prehistoric Goddess," in Carl Olson (ed.), *The Book of the Goddess* (New York: Crossroad, 1983), pp. 7–15; and *Goddess Remembered*, dir. Donna Read, National Film Board of Canada, 1989.

13. Gimbutas, *Goddesses and Gods*, pp. 39, 69–70, 88–91, 113–14, and 159; *Civilization of the Goddess*, pp. 244–45.

14. Consider in this regard the astonishing foreword that Joseph Campbell wrote for *The Language of the Goddess*, in which he praises Bachofen for supposedly uncovering the existence of an underlying "matristic order" to civilization and goes on to compare Gimbutas' work to the deciphering of the Rosetta Stone. With the concept of the Great Mother, says Campbell, Gimbutas provided the key to understanding a whole host of images from the past. But surely, the comparison is fatuous: Thomas Young and Jean-François Champollion were able to construct glossaries of hieroglyphics not via some a priori archetype or mythological schema, but by means of the translation available, on the Rosetta Stone itself, of the Egyptian characters into a *known language*, viz., Greek. The Stone speaks for itself; no schema of what the ideograms *might* mean was imposed from without. It is nothing short of amazing that Campbell and (apparently) Gimbutas believed that what the latter was doing was really no different from what the two Egyptologists were doing; that the methodologies were actually identical. (See Joseph Campbell, in Gimbutas, *Language of the Goddess*, pp. xiii–xiv.)

Anthropologist Ruth Tringham, who did archaeological work in Opovo (a Late Neolithic village in Yugoslavia), seeks to demonstrate how various archaeologists, herself included, would interpret the results of her own excavations. To this end, she constructs an imaginary scenario in which a number of archaeologists are interviewed, and she shows how the very same physical evidence can generate a variety of interpretations. In the case of Gimbutas, what emerges is a set of mechanical, predictable responses quite consistent with her approach to Old Europe. Here are some examples:

Interviewer: *Here is a picture of the ground of House 2 at Opovo . . . What do you think of the "room"?*
MG [Marija Gimbutas]: A temple to the Goddess.
Interviewer: *Who built the houses of Opovo?*
MG: Men under women's (the Goddess's) direction.
Interviewer: *What did the women do at Opovo?*
MG: Everything.

One is tempted to call this a parody, but when we read Gimbutas' work or her interviews, it becomes obvious that this vignette is quite characteristic of her approach.

See Ruth E. Tringham, "Households with Faces: the Challenge of Gender in Prehistoric Architectural Remains," in Joan M. Gero and Margaret W. Conkey (eds.), *Engendering Archaeology* (Oxford: Basil Blackwell, 1991), pp. 93 and 113; and Mirka Knaster, "Raider of the Lost Goddess," *East West Journal*, December 1990, pp. 36–42 and 68–69.

15. Brian Hayden, "Old Europe: Sacred Matriarchy or Complementary Opposition?" in Anthony Bonanno (ed.), *Archaeology and Fertility Cult in the Ancient Mediterranean* (Amsterdam: B. R. Gruner, 1986), pp. 17–30. See also the discussions by Mary Lefkowitz in "The Twilight of the Goddess," *The New Republic*, 3 August 1992, pp. 29–33, and "The New Cults of the Goddess," *American Scholar*, vol. 62, no. 2 (Spring 1993), pp. 266–67, as well as Brian Fagan, "A Sexist View of Prehistory," *Archaeology*, vol. 45, no. 2 (March/April 1992), pp. 14–15, 18, and 66. According to Lefkowitz, the notion of a unitary goddess is a very late one and shows up in rudimentary form only in Hellenistic Judaism and Gnosticism.

16. Margaret Ehrenberg, *Women in Prehistory* (London: British Museum Publications, 1989), pp. 9, 23, 37, 63, and 68–75, and Catherine Hodge McCoid and LeRoy D. McDermott, "Toward Decolonizing Gender: Female Vision in the Upper Paleolithic," *American Anthropologist*, vol. 98, no. 2 (June 1996), pp. 319–26.

"In reality," writes Randall White, "there are single Magdalenian sites that contain more animal engravings/sculptures than there are female figures in all of the European Paleolithic!" (Review of Bruce Dickson, *The Dawn of Belief*, in *American Antiquity*, vol. 56, no. 3 [1991], p. 572) Cf. Paul Shepard, *The Others: How Animals Made Us Human* (Washington, DC: Island Press, 1996), p. 346: "The importance of the small and rare 'Venus figures' has been exaggerated by the desire in modern feminism for a prehistoric goddess. As

Paleolithic objects these number fewer than a couple dozen—insignificant compared to the vast number of animal figures. Even if they do represent sacred beings, there is no evidence of their primacy or proof of status as a queen of beasts or 'Earth.' Although sometimes referred to as 'pregnant,' in more objective terms they are fat." To his credit, James Mellaart (see below, n. 20) says something similar, pointing out that this kind of female body type is the result of a grain diet and typical of peasant women in Anatolia. (See "Roots in the Soil," in Stuart Piggott [ed.], *The Dawn of Civilization* [London: Thames and Hudson, 1961], p. 48.) Whether fat or pregnant (as McCoid and McDermott argue), there is no reason to jump to an elaborate, and unwarranted, religious interpretation, which is the least parsimonious explanation around.

17. In addition to Ehrenberg, *Women in Prehistory* (esp. pp. 68–75), see M. I. Finley, "The Feminine Mystique Goes Amok," *Book World*, 12 October 1968, p. 15, and Paula Fredriksen, "Thank Goddess!" *National Review*, 45 (1 March 1993), 56.

18. See Nanno Marinatos, *Minoan Religion* (Columbia: University of South Carolina Press, 1993), pp. 31, 38, 179, 185, and 243–44; Peter Warren, "Minoan Crete and Ecstatic Religion," in Robin Hägg and Nanno Marinatos (eds.), *Sanctuaries and Cults in the Aegean Bronze Age* (Uppsala: Almqvist & Wiksell, 1981), pp. 155–67; William A. McDonald and Carol G. Thomas, *Progress into the Past* (2d ed.; Bloomington: Indiana University Press, 1990), pp. 378–79 and 390–92; comments by David Anthony, in Knaster, "Raider of the Lost Goddess"; Hayden, "Old Europe"; and Colin Renfrew, *The Emergence of Civilization* (London: Methuen, 1972), pp. 383, 387, 390, and 394.

19. McDonald and Thomas, *Progress into the Past*, pp. 177, 285, and 416ff.; George E. Mylonas, *Mycenae and the Mycenaean Age* (Princeton: Princeton University Press, 1966), p. 214; and Renfrew, *Emergence*, p. 367.

20. Anthony quoted in Knaster, "Raider of the Lost Goddess"; Joseph Tainter, *The Collapse of Complex Societies* (Cambridge: Cambridge University Press, 1988), pp. 63–64.

Another problem with the "kurgan" theory is that it rests on the now-discredited work of the French mythographer Georges Dumézil, who, based on comparative mythology, argued for a Proto-Indo-European culture divided into farmers, priests, and warriors. As critics have noted, this is a classic case of projecting Iron Age configurations (i.e., first millennium B.C.) onto the early Neolithic. Gimbutas' "kurgan culture," writes the Russian authority on nomads, Anatoly Khazanov, "is only an artificial and speculative construction which unites under one heading many archaeological cultures which themselves are very different and are from different periods." Gimbutas herself, in later years, recognized the truth of this and tried to retain the argument by referring to a "kurgan tradition" or "kurgan horizon" in the same way that Dumézil would say that his tripartite scheme was true "in spirit," even if not *historically* accurate—the usual Jungian dodge. I shall say more about the Indo-Europeans in chapter 5.

(See Georges Dumézil, *Mythe et épopée* [3d ed.; Paris: Gallimard, 1981], *Mitra-Varuna* [Paris: Gallimard, 1948], and *L'idéologie tripartie des Indo-Européens* [Brussels: Latomus, 1958]; Colin Renfrew, *Archaeology and Language* [New York: Cambridge University Press, 1988], esp. pp. 251–60 and 286, "Archaeology and Language," *Current Anthropology*, vol. 29, no. 3 [June 1988], pp. 441 and 465, and "They Ride Horses, Don't They?" *Antiquity, 63* [1989], 843; J. P. Mallory, *In Search of the Indo-Europeans* [London: Thames and Hudson, 1989], p. 142; Anatoly M. Khazanov, *Nomads and the Outside World*, trans. Julia Crookenden [2d ed.; Madison: University of Wisconsin Press, 1994; orig. publ. 1984], p. 90; and David W. Anthony, "The 'Kurgan Culture,' Indo-European Origins, and the Domestication of the Horse: A Reconsideration," *Current Anthropology*, vol. 27, no. 4 [Aug./Oct. 1986], pp. 291–313.)

I haven't said much about Riane Eisler's study, *The Chalice and the Blade*, largely because it is so derivative from the work of Gimbutas. But, in addition, it relies quite heavily on works that also have been rightly criticized for making large intuitive leaps based on very slender evidence: James Mellaart, for example (see the reviews of his work by Robert Whallon, Jr., in *American Anthropologist*, vol. 70, no. 4 [August 1968], pp. 813–14, and Steven Diamant in *Classical World*, vol. 71, no. 3 [November 1977], p. 220), or Jacquetta Hawkes (*Dawn of the Gods* [London: Chatto & Windus, 1968]; see review by M. I. Finley in "Feminine Mystique Goes Amok"), in addition to Campbell, Neumann, etc. That scholars such as George Mylonas, Nanno Marinatos, and Colin Renfrew are absent from her sources is quite remarkable.

21. Martin P. Nilsson, *The Minoan-Mycenaean Religion and Its Survival in Greek Religion* (2d ed., rev.; Lund: C. W. K. Gleerup, 1950; orig. publ. 1927). He was not, of course, without important antecedents, such as Sir Arthur Evans, who was the first to reproduce these images. For a discussion of the history of the archaeological study of the Aegean, see McDonald and Thomas, *Progress into the Past.*

In *Minoan Religion*, p. 9, Marinatos points out a crucial drawback of Nilsson's work, namely, that it is "Whiggish." I.e., Nilsson was not interested in Minoan-Mycenaean religion per se, but only in its possible anticipation of later Greek religion.

22. Marinatos, *Minoan Religion*, pp. 13–37 and 147; William Taylour, *The Mycenaeans* (rev. ed.; New York: Thames and Hudson, 1983), pp. 43–44.

23. Marinatos, *Minoan Religion*, pp. 147, 162, and 165–66; Taylour, *Mycenaeans*, p. 62. The tablets written in what is called "Linear B" (early Greek language) show that by the thirteenth century most of the Homeric gods and goddesses (*inter alia*) were already worshipped. Taylour also says (p. 44) that the Minoan goddess was a composite character: mother of trees, the home, etc.

24. Samuel Noah Kramer, *The Sacred Marriage Rite* (Bloomington: Indiana University Press, 1969), pp. 3–7 and 16. On the discussion that follows, see pp. 48, 50, and 56–57, as well as J. N. Postgate, *Early Mesopotamia* (London: Routledge, 1992), *passim*. The reader should note that Mesopotamia consisted of Assyria (north) and Babylonia (south), with Babylonia further subdivided

into Akkad (north) and Sumer (south). Mesopotamian tablets, imprinted with cuneiform writing, are in the languages of Sumerian and Akkadian, the latter being a Semitic language. Although these were two distinct peoples, the degree of syncretism between them was high.

25. For an English translation of "The Curse of Agade," see Thorkild Jacobsen, *The Harp that Once* . . . (New Haven: Yale University Press, 1987), pp. 360–74.

26. On the discussion below, see Tikva Frymer-Kensky, *In the Wake of the Goddess* (New York: Free Press, 1992), pp. vii, 12, and 32–36.

27. Ibid., pp. 50–51; Kramer, *Sacred Marriage Rite*, pp. xiii–xiv, 17, 48, and 53. "Queen of all the *me*" occurs in "Enki and the World Order: The Organization of the Earth and Its Cultural Processes." In *Der numinose Begriff ME im Sumerischen* (Innsbruck: Sprachenwissenschaftliche Institut der Leopold-Franzens-Universität, 1963), Karl Oberhuber tries to make a case for the *me* as a numinous concept, but he admits that opinions on the subject are widely diverse. See also Thorkild Jacobsen, *The Treasures of Darkness* (New Haven: Yale University Press, 1976), pp. 32ff. and 85.

Portrayal of Inanna/Ishtar as a controller of destinies may be found in "The Greatness of Ishtar," in Benjamin R. Foster (ed.), *Before the Muses* (2 vols.; Bethesda, MD: CDL Press, 1993), 2, 586–87, and in the Hymn to Ishtar in 1, 66. Sumerian poetry identifying Inanna as "Lady of all the me's" may be found in William W. Hallo and J. J. A. van Dijk, *The Exaltation of Inanna* (New Haven: Yale University Press, 1968), pp. 15ff.; see also pp. 48–50.

28. Kramer, *Sacred Marriage Rite*, pp. 59, 70–73, and 148; see also Frymer-Kensky, *Wake of the Goddess*, p. 54, and Jacobsen, *Treasures*, p. 46. The original cuneiform tablet containing this poem is in the Istanbul Museum of the Ancient Orient and probably dates from circa 2000 B.C. In general, the earliest Sumerian poetry dates to circa 2500 B.C.

29. Frymer-Kensky, *Wake of the Goddess*, p. 56; Kramer, *Sacred Marriage Rite*, p. 62.

30. Frymer-Kensky, *Wake of the Goddess*, pp. 24–27, 47, and 56; E. O. James, *Prehistoric Religion* (London: Thames and Hudson, 1957), p. 188; Henri Frankfort, *Kingship and the Gods* (Chicago: University of Chicago Press, 1948), p. 4. Jacobsen argues that Inanna "is never depicted as a wife and helpmate or as a mother" (*Treasures*, p. 141), but see "The Greatness of Ishtar" (cited above, n. 27), in which she is addressed as "Mother-Matrix." The Akkadian word *mummu*, matrix, actually means "wisdom" or "skill" (Foster, *Before the Muses*, 1, 354n).

31. Weaving being the important exception; see E. W. Barber, *Women's Work* (New York: W. W. Norton, 1994), and *Prehistoric Textiles* (Princeton: Princeton University Press, 1991), ch. 13.

32. Quoted in "Die Mesopotamier im 3. Jahrtausend v. Chr.," publication No. 1127 of the Museum für Vor- und Frühgeschichte in Berlin; excerpted

from Adam Falkenstein and Wolfram von Soden (eds. and trans.), *Sumerische und akkadische Hymnen und Gebete* (Zurich: Artemis, 1953), pp. 235ff.

33. Kramer, *Sacred Marriage Rite*, p. 147. However, this may be a stretched interpretation on my part because the English translations do not specifically refer to feeding, although there does seem to be a mixture of caretaking and "voluptuousness." See Foster, *Before the Muses*, 1, 65–68, and "Hymn to Ishtar," trans. Ferris J. Stephens, in James B. Pritchard (ed.), *Ancient Near Eastern Texts Relating to the Old Testament* (2d ed., corrected and enl.; Princeton: Princeton University Press, 1995), p. 383.

In the case of Egypt, goddesses also are present, but they do not attain a significant role until Hellenistic times. Thus, the earth was a male god (Ptah or Geb), and it is Osiris, the brother/husband of Isis, who is identified with grain or barley. Isis later became the center of a mystery cult, especially in Greece and Rome.

34. On the following discussion, see Erik Hornung, *Conceptions of God in Ancient Egypt*, trans. John Baines (Ithaca, NY: Cornell University Press, 1982), pp. 182, 184, 207, and 253–56. See also Herman te Velde, "Theology, Priests, and Worship in Ancient Egypt," in Jack M. Sasson (ed.), *Civilizations of the Ancient Near East* (4 vols.; New York: Scribner's, 1995), 3, 1731–49, esp. p. 1744.

35. J. H. Breasted, *Development of Religion and Thought in Ancient Egypt* (New York: Scribner's, 1912), p. 290; Geraldine Pinch, *Magic in Ancient Egypt* (Austin: University of Texas Press, 1994).

36. Hornung, *Conceptions of God*, p. 191. The Dutch Egyptologist C. J. Bleeker tries to make a case for the existence of Egyptian mysteries of a noninitiatory sort, but his defense of this is not very convincing (*Die Geburt eines Gottes* [Leiden: E. J. Brill, 1956], pp. 63–66); but see Jan Assmann, *Egyptian Solar Religion in the New Kingdom*, trans. Anthony Alcock (London: Kegan Paul International, 1995), p. 17. Assmann notes (p. 22) that the Egyptian religious cult in general celebrates the communication between *gods*, not communication between gods and humans. This absolute separation is made clear in the famous Leiden Papyrus (Papyrus Leiden I 350), which dates from circa 1228 B.C. (toward the end of the reign of Ramses II) and which sounds to me eerily Mosaic in nature:

> . . . no one testifies to him accurately.
> He is too secret to uncover his awesomeness,
> he is too great to investigate, too powerful to know.
> Instantaneously falling face to face into death
> is for the one who expresses his secret identity, unknowingly or
> knowingly.
> There is no god who knows how to invoke him with it.
> Manifest one whose identity is hidden, inasmuch as it is inaccessible.

(Translated in James P. Allen, *Genesis in Egypt* [New Haven: Yale Egyptological Seminar, 1988], p. 53)

Insofar as the royal *ka* is concerned—the bearer of the Pharaoh's divinity—W. J. Murnane says (personal communication, April 1996) that it does not seem to fuse with the king's mortality but only to supercede it, temporarily.

37. Oppenheim, *Ancient Mesopotamia*, pp. 180–82 and 221–22, and J. J. Finkelstein, "The West, the Bible and the Ancient Near East: Apperceptions and Categorisations," *Man*, n.s., 9 (1974), 591–608. However, this may have been true of the region around Palestine as well. Oracles, for example, were popular in Canaan in the Late Bronze Age, as were fertility cults, but directly inspired revelation is mentioned only once in the Canaanite documents, circa 1100 B.C., which refer to a royal retainer having an ecstatic fit. See John Gray, *The Canaanites* (London: Thames and Hudson, 1964), pp. 125–26.

38. G. Rachel Levy, *Religious Conceptions of the Stone Age* (New York: Harper Torchbooks, 1963; orig. publ. as *The Gate of Horn*, 1948), p. 269. See also the brief but excellent discussion of this issue in A. S. Kapelrud, *The Ras Shamra Discoveries and the Old Testament*, trans. G. W. Anderson (Norman: University of Oklahoma Press, 1963), pp. 43–44 and 55. In terms of the later Canaanite context, the author comments (p. 56): "The conflict between Yahweh and Baal was more than an incidental historical episode. It was a conflict between principles and interpretations of life which in other forms is still being waged today."

39. On the following, see S. N. Eisenstadt, "Heterodoxies and Dynamics of Civilizations," *Proceedings of the American Philosophical Society*, vol. 128, no. 2 (1984), pp. 104–8, and his introduction (pp. 1–11) and commentary (pp. 291–93) in his edited volume, *The Origins and Diversity of Axial Age Civilizations* (Albany: State University of New York Press, 1986); Mark Elvin, "Was There a Transcendental Breakthrough in China?" in the same volume, p. 326; Hayim Todmor, "Monarchy and the Elite in Assyria and Babylonia: The Question of Royal Accountability," in the same volume, pp. 223–24; Adam Seligman, "The Comparative Study of Utopias," *International Journal of Comparative Sociology*, vol. 29, nos. 1–2 (January/April 1988), pp. 1–3 and 7; S. N. Eisenstadt, "The Axial Age: The Emergence of Transcendental Visions and the Rise of Clerics," *Archives européennes de sociologie*, 23 (1982), 307–10, and "Cultural Traditions and Political Dynamics: The Origins and Modes of Ideological Politics," *British Journal of Sociology*, vol. 32, no. 2 (June 1981), pp. 156–57 and 164.

40. Flinders Petrie, *Religious Life in Ancient Egypt* (New York: Cooper Square, 1972; orig. publ. 1924), pp. 77–78.

41. Ibid., p. 123.

42. Julian Jaynes, *The Origin of Consciousness in the Breakdown of the Bicameral Mind* (Boston: Houghton Mifflin, 1976), p. 324.

43. H. W. F. Saggs, *The Encounter with the Divine in Mesopotamia and Israel* (London: Athlone Press, 1978), pp. 140–41; H. Ringgren, "The Religion of Ancient Syria," in C. J. Bleeker and George Widengren (eds.), *Historia Religionum*, vol. 1: *Religions of the Past* (Leiden: E. J. Brill, 1969), pp. 213–14; and Johannes Renger, "Untersuchungen zum Priestertum der altbabylonischen Zeit.

2. Teil," *Zeitschrift für Assyriologie und vorderasiatische Archäologie, 59* (February 1969), 219–23. Renger notes that at Mari, the spelling of the term was *muḫḫûm* (an ecstatic). The *Assyrian Dictionary* (Chicago: Oriental Institute of the University of Chicago, 1977), vol. 10, part 1, p. 90, has a slightly different variant: *maḫḫû*, or in Mari, *muḫḫû*. On the Mari archives, see Robert M. Whiting, "Amorite Tribes and Nations of Second-Millennium Western Asia," in Sasson, *Civilizations of the Ancient Near East,* 2, 1231–42.

44. On this subject, see my *Coming to Our Senses* (New York: Simon & Schuster, 1989), chs. 4–8, and Norman Cohn, *Cosmos, Chaos, and the World to Come* (New Haven: Yale University Press, 1993).

45. John Ferguson, *Among the Gods* (London: Routledge, 1989), p. 105; George E. Mylonas, *Eleusis and the Eleusinian Mysteries* (Princeton: Princeton University Press, 1961), pp. 17, 31–32, and 49–50; Kevin Clinton, "The Sanctuary of Demeter and Kore at Eleusis," in Nanno Marinatos and Robin Hägg (eds.), *Greek Sanctuaries* (London: Routledge, 1993), p. 114–16 and 120; and John Chadwick, "Potnia," *Minos, 5* (1957), 126n. The part about a better lot in the next world, however, *could* apply to the palatial period on Minoan Crete, where, as we saw, rings and seals depict visionary epiphany occurring in the meeting with a goddess.

46. Joan C. Engelsman, *The Feminine Dimension of the Divine* (rev. ed.: Wilmette, IL: Chiron, 1994), pp. 48 and 55; Jane Harrison, *Prolegomena to the Study of Greek Religion* (3d ed.; Meridian Books, 1955), p. x; and Burkert, *Ancient Mystery Cults*, pp. 5 and 90–91.

47. On the following, see Harrison, *Prolegomena*, pp. x–xii, 155–59, 260–61, 404, 409, 425–26, 474, 476–77, and 561. Her definition of a mystery is as follows (p. 151, italicized in the original): "a rite in which certain sacra are exhibited, which cannot be safely seen by the worshipper till he has undergone certain purifications."

48. Mylonas, *Eleusis*, pp. 5, 259–60, and 319.

49. Mylonas, however, claims that Dionysus was not part of the Demeter/ Persephone cult (*Eleusis*, p. 238).

50. C. J. Bleeker, "Isis and Hathor, Two Ancient Egyptian Goddesses," in Carl Olson (ed.), *The Book of the Goddess* (New York: Crossroad, 1983), pp. 37–39.

51. Burkert, *Mystery Cults*, pp. 11, 90, 92, 97, and 99.

52. Edith Weigert-Vorwinkel, "The Cult and Mythology of the Magna Mater from the Standpoint of Psychoanalysis," trans. F. M. von Wimmersperg, *Psychiatry, 1* (1938), 351–53; Engelsman, *Feminine Dimension*, p. 47; and E. O. James, *The Cult of the Mother Goddess* (London: Thames and Hudson, 1959), p. 162.

53. From *The Golden Ass*, quoted in Engelsman, *Feminine Dimension*, p. 68; Burkert, *Mystery Cults*, p. 94. For a modern reconstruction of Eleusinian initiation (to the extent that it is possible), see Mylonas, *Eleusis*, pp. 237–85.

54. James, *Cult of the Mother Goddess*, pp. 156 and 160. His sources include Sophocles, Pindar, Plato, and Cicero.

55. Burkert, *Mystery Cults*, p. 114.

56. The Robbins and Anthony article is quoted in Felicitas Goodman, *Ecstasy, Ritual, and Alternate Reality* (Bloomington: Indiana University Press, 1992), p. 170.

57. For a detailed elaboration of how this works in Hindu culture, see Sudhir Kakar, *The Inner World* (2d ed., rev. and enl.; Delhi: Oxford University Press, 1981). A very different view of the same problematic is taken by Stanley Kurtz in *All the Mothers are One* (New York: Columbia University Press, 1982), although I do think the two books have a certain psychoanalytic overlap.

The issue of obedience and social inequality being closely linked to the SAC is, of course, a major part of my argument, and Marinatos (*Minoan Religion*, pp. 179, 185, and 243) argues the same thing for the goddess cult and the practice of visionary epiphany. She says there was a ruling class in Minoan Crete, and it probably expressed its status through religious office. Having an ecstatic vision put one among the priestly elite; the Minoan rings discussed earlier in this chapter were typically of high quality gold and could only have been in the possession of the wealthier members of the society.

58. Frederick S. Perls, *Ego, Hunger and Aggression* (New York: Vintage Books, 1969), pp. 128–33 and *passim*.

59. Discussed in Kent V. Flannery, "The Cultural Evolution of Civilizations," *Annual Review of Ecology and Systematics*, 3 (1972), 420.

60. Walter Truett Anderson, *Reality Isn't What It Used to Be* (San Francisco: Harper & Row, 1990), p. 11. Inventors of ideas, of course, are often very different in their attachments than disciples or devotees. Some years ago, Lovelock wrote me that Gaia was "inflating like a large balloon" and (he continued) threatening to carry him off with it (personal communication, 1987). I am reminded of Marx's comment in later life, that he wasn't a Marxist.

61. Perls, *Ego, Hunger and Aggression*, pp. 110–11.

5. The Zone of Flux

1. Anatoly M. Khazanov, *Nomads and the Outside World*, trans. Julia Crookenden (2d ed.; Madison: University of Wisconsin Press, 1994; orig. publ. 1984), p. xxxiii.

2. Despite the great number of studies, writes Neville Dyson-Hudson, "the simple if somewhat gloomy truth is that we really know extraordinarily little about human behavior in nomadic societies." ("The Study of Nomads," *Journal of Asian and African Studies*, vol. 7, nos. 1–2 [January and April 1972], p. 2.)

3. Stuart Piggott, introduction to E. D. Phillips, *The Royal Hordes* (London: Thames and Hudson, 1965), p. 6.

4. Gilles Deleuze and Félix Guattari, *Nomadology: The War Machine*, trans. Brian Massumi (New York: Semiotext(e), 1986).

5. C. P. Cavafy, "Waiting for the Barbarians," in C. P. Cavafy, *Collected Poems*, trans. Edmund Keeley and Philip Sherrard and ed. George Savidis (Princeton: Princeton University Press, 1975), p. 18.

6. Thomas J. Barfield, *The Nomadic Alternative* (Englewood Cliffs, NJ: Prentice Hall, 1993), p. 203.

7. On the following, see Deleuze and Guattari, *Nomadology*, pp. 45, 50–52, and *passim*.

8. Bruce Chatwin, *What Am I Doing Here* (London: Picador, 1990), p. 229.

9. Philip C. Salzman, "Political Organization among Nomadic Peoples," *Proceedings of the American Philosophical Society*, vol. 111, no. 2 (April 1967), p. 118; Khazanov, *Nomads*, pp. xl, 17, 86, and 89. By "nomadism" I shall be referring only to pastoral nomadism, which involves herding and the search for pasture. Quite obviously, there are other types of mobile peoples, including gypsies, traveling artisans and performers, people migrating on a unidirectional journey, and even (in modern times) hobos and the itinerant poor. But the historical phenomenon is associated with animal as well as human movement, and for the most part, that is what I shall be dealing with in this chapter. Cf. Khazanov, *Nomads*, p. 15.

10. Ofer Bar-Yosef and Anatoly Khazanov (eds.), *Pastoralism in the Levant* (Madison, WI: Prehistory Press, 1992), introduction, p. 4. For one exception, see the discussion of pig domestication in Ch. 2, footnote 8, above.

11. Kenneth W. Russell, *After Eden* (Oxford: BAR International, 1988), p. 157; Charles A. Reed, "Animal Domestication in the Prehistoric Near East," *Science*, 130 (11 December 1959), 1631–38; Juris Zarins, "Early Pastoral Nomadism and the Settlement of Lower Mesopotamia," *Bulletin of the American Schools of Oriental Research*, 280 (1990), 31, 39, 54, and 56; and Frank Hole, "The Prehistory of Herding: Some Suggestions from Ethnography," in M. T. Barrelet (ed.), *L'Archéologie de l'Iraq: du début de l'époque néolithique à 333 avant notre ère* (Paris: Editions du CNRS, 1980), p. 120.

12. Cf. Phillips, *Royal Hordes*, p. 10.

13. Gregory L. Possehl, "Pastoral Nomadism in Prehistoric Iran," M.A. thesis, University of Washington, 1966, pp. 3–4 and 129.

14. Thomas J. Barfield, "Inner Asia and Cycles of Power in China's Imperial History," in Gary Seaman and Daniel Marks (eds.), *Rulers from the Steppe* (Los Angeles: University of Southern California, 1991), p. 25. An old Mongol saying had it that "it is possible to create an empire on horseback, but it is

impossible to rule it from that position." (Quoted in Anatoly M. Khazanov, "Muhammad and Jenghiz Khan Compared: The Religious Factor in World Empire Building," *Comparative Studies in Society and History*, vol. 35, no. 2 [April 1993], p. 469.)

15. On the following discussion, see Khazanov, *Nomads*, pp. xxxii, 19–24, and 91–99, and Fred Scholz, *Nomadismus* (Berlin: Das Arabische Buch, 1992), pp. 14–16.

16. Roger Cribb, *Nomads in Archaeology* (Cambridge: Cambridge University Press, 1991), pp. 9 and 16.

17. Fuad Baali, *Society, State, and Urbanism* (Albany: State University of New York Press, 1988), pp. 2, 5, 43–48, and 95–100; Ibn Khaldun, *The Muqaddimah*, trans. Franz Rosenthal (abgd. ed.; London: Routledge and Kegan Paul, 1967); Philip C. Salzman, "Introduction: Processes of Sedentarization as Adaptation and Response," in Philip C. Salzman (ed.), *When Nomads Settle* (New York: Praeger, 1980), pp. 1–2, 7, and 13; and Dan R. Aronson, "Must Nomads Settle? Some Notes Toward Policy on the Future of Pastoralism," p. 173 of the same volume.

18. Allen Zagarell, "Pastoralism and the Early State in Greater Mesopotamia," in C. C. Lamberg-Karlovsky (ed.), *Archaeological Thought in America* (Cambridge: Cambridge University Press, 1989), pp. 287, 294, 296, and 300; and Brian Spooner, "The Status of Nomadism as a Cultural Phenomenon in the Middle East," *Journal of Asian and African Studies*, vol. 7, nos. 1–2 (January and April 1972), p. 126.

19. D. O. Edzard, "Mesopotamian Nomads in the Third Millennium B.C.," in Jorge Silva Castillo (ed.), *Nomads and Sedentary Peoples* (Mexico City: El Colegio de México, 1981), pp. 38 and 40–41; M. Liverani, "The Amorites," in D. J. Wiseman (ed.), *Peoples of Old Testament Times* (Oxford: Clarendon Press, 1973), pp. 102–12; Giorgio Buccellati, *The Amorites of the Ur III Period* (Naples: Instituto Orientale di Napoli, 1966), pp. 3–4, 9, 11, 235, and 336; Zarins, "Early Pastoral Nomadism," pp. 35 and 55; Alfred Haldar, *Who Were the Amorites?* (Leiden: E. J. Brill, 1971), pp. 67 and 82; and J.-R. Kupper, "Le rôle des nomades dans l'histoire de la Mésopotamie ancienne," *Journal of the Economic and Social History of the Orient*, vol. 2, part 2 (May 1959), pp. 121 and 124–26. Note that "not bending the knee" conceivably could refer to a refusal to farm, though the reference to (ir)religion seems more likely, inasmuch as they were accustomed to digging for mushrooms (see epigraph to this chapter).

On the Amorite wall, see Robert M. Whiting, "Amorite Tribes and Nations of Second-Millennium Western Asia," in Jack M. Sasson (ed.), *Civilizations of the Ancient Near East* (4 vols.; New York: Scribner's, 1955), 2, 1231–42.

20. M. B. Rowton, "Autonomy and Nomadism in Western Asia," *Orientalia*, 42 (1973), pp. 249 and 252. Lattimore's books include *Mongol Journeys* (New York: Doubleday, Doran and Co., 1941), *Nomads and Commissars* (New York:

Oxford University Press, 1962), and *Studies in Frontier History* (London: Oxford University Press, 1962).

21. M. B. Rowton, "Economic and Political Factors in Ancient Nomadism," in Castillo, *Nomads and Sedentary Peoples*, pp. 28 and 32; "Autonomy and Nomadism," pp. 253 and 255–57; "Enclosed Nomadism," *Journal of the Economic and Social History of the Orient*, 17 (1973), 19 and 29–30; and Buccellati, *Amorites*, pp. 235 and 339. Whiting, in "Amorite Tribes," pp. 1239–40, defines *nawû* as a "movable encampment of people and herds" and says that the Mari archives provide evidence of some Amorites living in villages and practicing agriculture.

22. Edzard, "Mesopotamian Nomads," p. 41; Haldar, *Who Were the Amorites?* pp. 51, 66, and 82; Liverani, "Amorites," pp. 104–5, 107, and 112–15; Buccellati, *Amorites*, pp. 336–40 and 358–59; and Victor H. Matthews, *Pastoral Nomadism in the Mari Kingdom* (Cambridge, MA: American Schools of Oriental Research, 1978), p. 156.

Perhaps even more remarkable is the fact that two outstanding rulers, Hammurabi of Babylon and Shamshi-Adad of Assyria, were of Amorite origin. See A. S. Kapelrud, *The Ras Shamra Discoveries and the Old Testament*, trans. G. W. Anderson (Norman: University of Oklahoma Press, 1963), p. 38.

23. Presumably in *The Muqaddimah* (see above, footnote 17), and quoted by Barfield in *Nomadic Alternative*, p. 210.

24. Khazanov, *Nomads*, pp. 160 and 221; and Joseph T. Hobbs, *Bedouin Life in the Egyptian Wilderness* (Austin: University of Texas Press, 1989), pp. 21 and 56. Cf. the following statement made by Ebrahim Konate, secretary of the Permanent Interstate Committee for Drought Control in the Sahel, 1973: "We have to discipline these people, and to control their grazing and their movements. Their liberty is too expensive for us. Their disaster is our opportunity." (Quoted in Khazanov, *Nomads*, introduction to second edition, p. l.)

25. I. M. Lewis, "The Dynamics of Nomadism: Prospects for Sedentarization and Social Change," in Theodore Monod (ed.), *Pastoralism in Tropical Africa* (London: Oxford University Press, 1975), pp. 426–27.

26. David Morgan, *The Mongols* (Oxford: Basil Blackwell, 1986), p. 35; Barfield, *Nomadic Alternative*, pp. 203–5; Amos Rapoport, "Nomadism as a Man-Environment System," *Environment and Behavior*, vol. 10, no. 2 (June 1978), pp. 220 and 223; and David C. Hopkins, "Pastoralists in Late Bronze Age Palestine: Which Way Did They Go?" *Biblical Archaeologist*, 56, 4 (1993), 200 and 204. The quote from Buber (which is from *Moses*) is in Bruce Chatwin, *The Songlines* (New York: Penguin, 1988), p. 186.

27. On the following, see Fredrik Barth, *Nomads of South Persia* (Oslo: Oslo University Press, 1961), pp. 1, 71, 135–37, and 147–53, and Mary Douglas, *Natural Symbols* (New York: Pantheon Books, 1982; orig. publ. 1970), pp. ix–xii and 9 (italics mine).

28. Chatwin, *What Am I Doing Here*, pp. 220–21.

29. Khazanov, *Nomads*, pp. 165 and 216; Hobbs, *Bedouin Life*, p. 55; and Walter Goldschmidt, "A General Model for Pastoral Social Systems," in *Pastoral Production and Society* (Cambridge: Cambridge University Press, 1979), p. 25.

30. Cited in C. R. Badcock, *The Psychoanalysis of Culture* (Oxford: Basil Blackwell, 1980), p. 102.

31. Khazanov, *Nomads*, p. 239 and note; Morgan, *Mongols*, pp. 40–41 and 44; and Khazanov, "Muhammad and Jenghiz Khan Compared." Walter Heissig, however, discusses the presence of an ecstatic shamanic tradition among the Mongols in *The Religions of Mongolia*, trans. Geoffrey Samuel (Berkeley: University of California Press, 1980). See also Vladimir N. Basilov and Natal'ya L. Zhukovskaya, "Religious Beliefs," in Vladimir N. Basilov (ed.), *Nomads of Eurasia*, trans. Mary Fleming Zirin (Seattle: University of Washington Press, 1989), pp. 160–81.

32. Herodotus, *The Histories*, trans. Aubrey de Selincourt (rev. ed.; Harmondsworth: Penguin, 1972), pp. 296–98; Renate Rolle, *The World of the Scythians*, trans. F. G. Walls (Berkeley: University of California Press, 1989; orig. German ed. 1980), pp. 125–26 and 129.

33. Badcock, *Psychoanalysis of Culture*, p. 111; I. M. Lewis, *A Pastoral Democracy* (London: Oxford University Press, 1961), pp. 1 and 26; and Richard Tapper, *Pasture and Politics* (London: Academic Press, 1979), p. 2.

34. Tapper, *Pasture and Politics*, pp. 15–16, 157, 163, 253–54, and 261, and also the foreword by Abner Cohen, pp. v–vii.

35. Badcock, *Psychoanalysis of Culture*, pp. 117–20; Robert B. Edgerton, *The Individual in Cultural Adaptation* (Berkeley: University of California Press, 1971), esp. pp. 264–99; and Walter Goldschmidt, "Independence as an Element in Pastoral Systems," *Anthropological Quarterly*, vol. 44, no. 3 (July 1971), pp. 132–35.

36. Joseph C. Berland, *No Five Fingers Are Alike* (Cambridge: Harvard University Press, 1982), pp. 28, 34–38, and 42; see also H. A. Witkin and J. W. Berry, "Psychological Differentiation in Cross-Cultural Perspective," *Journal of Cross-Cultural Psychology*, vol. 6, no. 1 (March 1975), pp. 4–87.

37. Berland, *No Five Fingers*, pp. 51, 53, 112–24, 137–42, and 156; H. A. Witkin and D. R. Goodenough, *Cognitive Styles: Essence and Origins* (Psychological Issues, No. 51; New York: International Universities Press, 1981); J. W. Berry, *Human Ecology and Cognitive Style* (New York: Sage Publications, 1976); J. W. Berry, "Ecology, Cultural Adaptation, and Psychological Differentiation: Traditional Patterning and Acculturative Stress," in Richard W. Brislin et al. (eds.), *Cross-Cultural Perspectives on Learning* (New York: Halsted Press, 1975), pp. 207–28; and D. R. Goodenough and H. A. Witkin, *Origins of the Field-Dependent and Field-Independent Cognitive Styles* (RM-77-9; Princeton: Educational Testing Service, 1977).

38. Ernest Gellner, foreword to Khazanov, *Nomads,* pp. xiii and xxii; and Brian Spooner, *The Cultural Ecology of Pastoral Nomads* (New York: Addison-Wesley, 1973), p. 15.

39. Gellner, foreword to Khazanov, *Nomads,* p. ix; and Thomas J. Barfield, *The Perilous Frontier* (Cambridge, MA: Basil Blackwell, 1989), p. 25.

40. Khazanov, *Nomads,* pp. 123, 131, 135, 137, and 155, and Gellner, foreword, pp. xii, xx, and xxiii.

41. Khazanov, *Nomads,* pp. 167–69, and Gellner, foreword, p. xxiv.

42. Khazanov, *Nomads,* pp. 132–34; Philip Burnham, "Spatial Mobility and Political Centralization in Pastoral Societies," in *Pastoral Production and Society* (see n. 29, above), p. 351; and William Irons, "Political Stratification among Pastoral Nomads," pp. 361–74 of the same volume.

43. John Middleton and David Tait (eds.), *Tribes Without Rulers* (London: Routledge and Kegan Paul, 1970; orig. publ. 1958), pp. 2–11. The Bedouin proverb is quoted by Chatwin in *Songlines,* p. 202. See also Barfield, *Nomadic Alternative,* pp. 41–42, and R.P. Lindner, "What Was a Nomadic Tribe?" *Comparative Studies in Society and History,* vol. 24, no. 4 (October 1982), p. 693. Middleton and Tait comment (pp. 7–8) that the principle of complementary opposition is not, of course, equivalent to fission and fusion. In a fission situation, a group ceases to exist as an entity. In segmentation, a group divides in certain contexts but retains a corporate identity in others. However, I am a bit confused by their study because most of the tribes they refer to are engaged in farming.

44. Meyer Fortes and E. E. Evans-Pritchard (eds.), *African Political Systems* (London: Oxford University Press, 1940), and Lewis, *Pastoral Democracy,* pp. 1–3, 27, 30, and 197. However, Lewis also notes (p. 196) that Somali political organization differs from the general character of segmentary lineage systems in some important respects.

45. Khazanov, *Nomads,* pp. 153–58, 162, 164, and 180–90; Madawi Al-Rasheed, "The Process of Chiefdom-Formation as a Function of Nomadic/ Sedentary Interaction," *Cambridge Anthropology,* 12 (1987), 32–40; Burnham, "Spatial Mobility," pp. 355–56; Philip C. Salzman, "Inequality and Oppression in Nomadic Society," in *Pastoral Production and Society* (see n. 29, above); and Spooner, *Cultural Ecology,* p. 34.

46. Akbar S. Ahmed, "Nomadism as Ideological Expression: The Case of the Gomal Nomads," *Contributions to Indian Sociology,* 17, 1 (1983), pp. 124–27 and 133.

47. Marija Gimbutas, "The Three Waves of the Kurgan People into Old Europe, 4500–2500 B.C.," *Archives suisses d'anthropologie générale,* 43 (1979), 113–37. See also J. P. Mallory, *In Search of the Indo-Europeans* (London: Thames and Hudson, 1989), for a comprehensive presentation of the traditional view. For problems with the argument, see (in addition to the discussion below) chapter 4, n. 20, above.

48. Mallory, *Search*, p. 199; Colin Renfrew, "They Ride Horses, Don't They?" (review of Mallory), *Antiquity*, 63 (1989), 845–46. See also Renfrew's major work on the subject, *Archaeology and Language* (New York: Cambridge University Press, 1988). Renfrew manages to sink the kurgan thesis pretty thoroughly, but his alternative hypothesis, that the Indo-Europeans were Anatolian farmers dating from 6500 B.C., is equally contradicted by archaeological evidence.

49. Mallory, *Search*, pp. 117ff.; and Renfrew, "They Ride Horses," pp. 844–45. Mallory concedes, however, that *ekwos* could be a wild horse. The asterisk in front of the word here indicates that we may not be dealing with a real word in a real language, but possibly with a hypothetical word from a reconstructed, proto-Indo-European language based on subsequent, presumably derivative languages. I.e., PIE, or proto-Indo-European language, may never have actually been spoken, and Renfrew, in *Archaeology and Language*, mounts a strong critique of the so-called paleolinguistic approach.

50. Zili Weng and Robert R. Sokal, "Origins of Indo-Europeans and the Spread of Agriculture in Europe: Comparison of Lexico-statistical and Genetic Evidence," *Human Biology*, vol. 67, no. 4 (August 1995), pp. 577–94. This also refutes Renfrew's "farming" hypothesis (see above, n. 48). A second study that rejects Gimbutas but is partly favorable to Renfrew is Guido Barbujani et al., "Indo-European Origins: A Computer Simulation Test of Five Hypotheses," *American Journal of Physical Anthropology*, 96 (1995), 109–32.

51. Mallory, *Search*, pp. 143 and 269.

52. Barfield, *Perilous Frontier*, pp. 28–29; Halder, *Who Were the Amorites?* pp. 27 and 49–50; H. von Wissman and F. Kussmaul, "Badw," in *The Encyclopaedia of Islam*, vol. 1 (new ed.; Leiden: E. J. Brill, 1960), pp. 878–79; Esther Jacobson, "Symbolic Structures as Indicators of the Cultural Ecology of Early Nomads," in Gary Seaman (ed.), *Foundations of Empire* (Los Angeles: University of Southern California, 1992), p. 1; Renfrew, *Archaeology and Language, passim*; and Mary Boyce, *Zoroastrianism* (Costa Mesa, CA: Mazda Publishers, 1992), pp. 42–43.

However, there was a military chariot, drawn by onagers (wild asses), in use in Sumer by 3000 B.C. Note also that the Scythians expelled (and also incorporated about half of) their predecessors, the Cimmerians, from the region north of the Black Sea in the eighth century.

53. Barfield, *Nomadic Alternative*, pp. 62 and 134; Phillips, *Royal Hordes*, pp. 46–47.

54. Renfrew, "They Ride Horses," p. 843; Norman Cohn, *Cosmos, Chaos, and the World to Come* (New Haven: Yale University Press, 1993), p. 241 n. 20; Mary Boyce, "Priests, Cattle and Men," *Bulletin of the School of Oriental and African Studies*, vol. 1, part 3 (1987), pp. 514–22; and chapter 4, n. 20, above.

55. Lynn White, Jr., *Medieval Technology and Social Change* (London: Oxford University Press, 1962).

56. Scythian horses, for example, were small by modern standards, but among the largest horses of the time (eighth century B.C.). See Rolle, *World of the Scythians*, p. 101, and Ward H. Goodenough, "The Evolution of Pastoralism and Indo-European Origins," in George Cardona et al. (eds.), *Indo-European and Indo-Europeans* (Philadelphia: University of Pennsylvania Press, 1970), p. 256.

Some historians believe that the period from 1200 through 500 B.C. was characterized by great aridity, making agriculture a less viable proposition than herding and pasturage.

57. See above, n. 48, and also the reviews of Renfrew's *Archaeology and Language* in *Current Anthropology*, vol. 29, no. 3 (June 1988), pp. 441–62.

58. Language groupings can be found in various encyclopedias of linguistics. On cultural groups and subdivisions, see Cohn, *Cosmos*, p. 57.

59. Walter A. Fairservis, Jr., *The Roots of Ancient India* (2d ed., rev.; Chicago: University of Chicago Press, 1975), p. 345; R. Champakalakshmi, "From the Vedic to the Classical Age, 1500 B.C. to A.D. 650," in Francis Robinson (ed.), *The Cambridge Encyclopedia of India* (Cambridge: Cambridge University Press, 1989), pp. 73–74.

60. On this and the following, see George F. Dales, "The Mythical Massacre at Mohenjo-Daro," *Expedition*, vol. 6, no. 3 (Spring 1964), pp. 36–43; articles by S. P. Gupta, Kenneth A. R. Kennedy, F. R. Allchin, and Robert H. Dyson, Jr., in Gregory L. Possehl (ed.), *Harappan Civilization* (New Delhi: Oxford & IBH Publishing Co., 1982); Mallory, *Search*, pp. 45 and 47; Asko Parpola, "The Coming of the Aryans to Iran and India and the Cultural and Ethnic Identity of the Dāsas," *Studia Orientalia*, 64 (1988), 195–302, and also published in a slightly different version in *International Journal of Dravidian Linguistics*, vol. 17, no. 2 (June 1988), pp. 85–229; Asko Parpola, *Deciphering the Indus Script* (Cambridge: Cambridge University Press, 1994), pp. 3–4 and 144–55; and the following reviews of Parpola's article: by Colin Renfrew, *Journal of the Royal Asiatic Society*, 3d ser., vol. 1, part 1 (April 1991), pp. 106–9; K. R. Norman, *Acta Orientalia*, 51 (1991), 288–96; and C. A. Winters in *International Journal of Dravidian Linguistics*, vol. 18, no. 2 (June 1989), pp. 98–127.

The most recent attempts to sort out the issues of Indo-European origins and the conflicts between archaeological and linguistic evidence can be found in George Erdosy (ed.), *The Indo-Aryans of Ancient South Asia* (Berlin: Walter de Gruyter, 1995); see esp. the articles by Erdosy (pp. 1–31) and Kenneth A. R. Kennedy (pp. 32–66). Among other things, Erdosy points out that while Indo-Aryan languages have an origin external to India, the Aryans of the RV were not their carriers into South Asia; he also points out that the Bactria-Margiana Archaeological Complex of circa 2000 B.C. and before (see discussion in the text, below) was a sophisticated civilization, so if migration did come from that quarter, we can rule out the popular view of an invasion of South India by a virile, barbaric race. (Erdosy, "Language, Material Culture and Ethnicity: Theoretical Perspectives," pp. 4 and 14.)

61. Richard Salomon informs me (personal communication, May 1996) that Zoroaster was probably rebelling against an early Iranian religion that was quite similar to the Vedic one but that cannot properly be termed "Vedic" because the Vedas are written in an Indian, not Iranian, language.

62. The botanical identity of soma/haoma has been the subject of some debate. Most scholars believe it is a plant of the genus *Ephedra*, and recent excavations at Margiana revealed a temple used by proto-Zoroastrians, in which the organic remains of this plant were found. Gordon Wasson, some years ago, argued that soma was the mushroom *Amanita muscaria*, but he was not able to prove it. See Parpola, "Coming of the Aryans," *Studia Orientalia*, p. 236; R. Gordon Wasson, *Soma: Divine Mushroom of Immortality* (New York: Harcourt Brace Jovanovich, 1968); John Brough, "Soma and *Amanita muscaria*," *Bulletin of the School of Oriental and African Studies*, 34 (1971), 331–62; Harry Falk, "Soma I and II," *Bulletin of the School of Oriental and African Studies*, 52 (1989), 77–90; and Harri Nyberg, "The Problem of the Aryans and the Soma: The Botanical Evidence," in Erdosy, *Indo-Aryans*, pp. 382–406.

63. Parpola, "Coming of the Aryans," *Studia Orientalia*, pp. 225–32, 237, and 265.

64. Mary Boyce, *A History of Zoroastrianism*, vol. 1: *The Early Period* (Leiden: E. J. Brill, 1975), pp. 156–58; Wasson, *Soma*, p. 3; Brough, "Soma and *Amanita muscaria*," pp. 339–40; and Cohn, *Cosmos*, pp. 58–59 and 69.

65. Mary Boyce, *Zoroastrians* (London: Routledge and Kegan Paul, 1984), pp. 1 and 17–20; Gherardo Gnoli, *Zoroaster's Time and Homeland* (Naples: Instituto Universitario Orientale, 1980), p. vii; and Cohn, *Cosmos*, p. 95. At one point, it was thought that Zoroaster lived ca. 550 B.C., but the general consensus today is that it was somewhere around 1200 B.C.

There is some unresolved confusion with respect to the use of haoma in the Zoroastrian religion. It seems to be as essential to the latter as it was to its Vedic predecessor, yet there are passages in the *Gathas* in which Zoroaster denounces its use and seems to be opposed to mystical practice (Gnoli, *Zoroaster's Time*, p. 188, and also his article, "Zoroastrianism," in Mircea Eliade [ed.], *The Encyclopedia of Religion*, vol. 15 [New York: Macmillan, 1987], p. 581). R. C. Zaehner, in *The Dawn and Twilight of Zoroastrianism* (London: Weidenfeld and Nicolson, 1961), puzzles over how the haoma ritual could have been the central rite of Zoroastrianism if it were condemned by the man who founded the new religion. No one has come up with a satisfactory answer, though Zaehner suggests a link to the Mithraic initiatory ritual of slaughtering a bull and says that the ecstatic killing of oxen was part of Vedic practice. Hence, says Zaehner, Zoroaster's condemnation was probably of the excesses of the ritual and its combination with ox or bull sacrifice, to which he was opposed (after all, he was guardian of the ox as the symbol of settled pastoral life; see below). (Zaehner, *Dawn*, pp. 15, 37–38, 78–85, and 90) Thus, in the *Gathas*, Zoroaster proclaims: "The Wise Lord has condemned those who take the life of the 'ox' with ecstatic cries!" (Quoted in George G. Cameron, "Zoroaster the Herdsman," *Indo-Iranian Journal*, vol. 10, no. 4 [1968], p. 280.) To this I would add, following the discussion below, that Zoroaster may have wanted to distance himself from the use of haoma to generate battle fury because it was the marauding raiders who pillaged pastoral settlements that he was defining as the incarnation of evil. At the same time, his own revelation of God came to him in the context of being a priest who performed this ritual, so he was caught in a contradiction. Thus, we have a confusion, in the historical record, of a religious leader trying to sort out the "correct" context for ecstatic experience. (He wouldn't be the last.)

66. Mallory, *Search*, p. 140; Boyce, *Zoroastrians*, pp. 8 and 19–20; and Zaehner, *Dawn*, pp. 35–40.

67. Cohn, *Cosmos*, pp. 60 and 76–77; and Zaehner, *Dawn*, p. 50.

68. Boyce, *Zoroastrians*, pp. 2–3, and *Zoroastrianism*, pp. 31–31 and 37–42, along with her "The Bipartite Society of the Ancient Iranians," in M. A. Dandamayer et al. (eds.), *Societies and Languages of the Ancient Near East* (Warminster, UK: Aris & Phillips, 1982), and "Priests, Cattle and Men," p. 512; Cameron, "Zoroaster the Herdsman," p. 265n; Zaehner, *Dawn*, pp. 34 and 40; and Cohn, *Cosmos*, p. 95.

69. Cohn, *Cosmos*, p. 114; Boyce, *Zoroastrians*, p. 67, and "Priests, Cattle and Men," pp. 513 and 524–25; Gnoli, *Zoroaster's Time*, p. 190; and Ninian Smart, "Zoroastrianism," in Paul Edwards (ed.), *The Encyclopedia of Philosophy*, vol. 8 (New York: Macmillan, 1967), p. 381.

70. Zaehner, *Dawn*, pp. 40–44; Cohn, *Cosmos*, p. 114.

71. Cohn, *Cosmos*, pp. 78, 82, 88, 91, and 99.

72. Zaehner, *Dawn*, p. 51; Smart, "Zoroastrianism," p. 381; Boyce, *Zoroastrians*, pp. 76–77; and Cohn, *Cosmos*, pp. 139–88 and 219–26.

73. Gilles Deleuze and Claire Parnet, *Dialogues*, trans. Hugh Tomlinson and Barbara Habberjam (New York: Columbia University Press, 1987), pp. x, xi (comment by Tomlinson), 25–31 (Parnet), and 54–55.

74. Deleuze and Guattari, *On the Line*, pp. 6, 10–13, 36, 40, and 57.

6. Wandering God: The Recovery of Paradox in the Twentieth Century

1. The crucial work of Kleist in this context is his *Über das Marionettentheater*, in *Der Zweikampf . . . und andere Prosa* (Stuttgart: Reclam, 1984), pp. 84–92. An English translation exists as *About Marionettes*, trans. Michael Lebeck (Mindelheim: Three Kings Press, 1970). For a sketch of Woolf that does justice to her nonideological outlook, see David Denby, *Great Books* (New York: Simon & Schuster, 1996), pp. 430–58. For the discussion of Wittgenstein below, see Ray Monk, *Ludwig Wittgenstein* (London: Vintage, 1991), pp. 18–42, 116–17, 134–50, 155, 182, 188–89, 195–95, 225–28, 237, 245–50, 256, 260–61, 276–78, 305,

338, 356, 367–72, 379, 415, 438, 446, 453–54, 468–77, 486, 490, 499, 508–16, 533, 555, 567–68, and 579–82. The following sources also were used: Ludwig Wittgenstein, *Tractatus Logico-Philosophicus*, trans. D. F. Pears and B. F. McGuinness (London: Routledge and Kegan Paul, 1969); *Philosophical Investigations*, trans. Rush Rhees and G. H. von Wright and ed. G. E. M. Anscombe (3d ed.; New York: Macmillan, 1958); and *Culture and Value*, trans. Peter Winch and ed. G. H. von Wright (2d ed.; Oxford: Basil Blackwell, 1980), pp. 7 and 73e; David Pears, *Wittgenstein* (New York: Viking, 1970), pp. 113–14 and 185; William Bartley III, *Wittgenstein* (2nd ed., rev. and enl.; LaSalle, IL: Open Court, 1985), pp. 71–114 and 126–131; A. C. Grayling, *Wittgenstein* (Oxford: Oxford University Press, 1988), pp. 10 and 112–19; and Russell Nieli, *Wittgenstein: From Mysticism to Ordinary Language* (Albany: State University of New York Press, 1987), pp. 239–45.

2. E. R. Dodds, *The Greeks and the Irrational* (Berkeley: University of California Press, 1951).

3. The duck/rabbit figure was not obscure; it had already appeared in the nineteenth century in a German jokebook. See Edmund Carpenter, "If Wittgenstein Had Been an Eskimo," *Natural History*, vol. 89, no. 2 (February 1980), p. 72.

4. The gesture of flicking the underchin with the back of the fingers differs in meaning from north to south. Both are expressions of disdain, but in northern Italy, it means something like, "I could care less," whereas in the south, it is much stronger, along the lines of "get off my back" or "don't bust my balls." Cf. Andrea de Jorio, *La Mimica degli antichi investigata nel gestire napoletano* (Naples: Associazione Napoletana, 1964; orig. publ. 1832), p. 207 and table 1, illustration 2.

5. Cf. Monk, *Wittgenstein*, p. 261: "One of the most striking ways in which Wittgenstein's later work differs from the *Tractatus* is in its 'anthropological' approach. That is, whereas the *Tractatus* deals with language in isolation from the circumstances in which it is used, the [*Philosophical*] *Investigations* repeatedly emphasizes the importance of the 'stream of life' which gives linguistic utterances their meaning: a 'language-game' cannot be described without mentioning their activities and the way of life of the 'tribe' that plays it."

6. Flaubert quoted in William Matthews, *Curiosities* (Ann Arbor: University of Michigan Press, 1989), p. 167. The Wittgenstein quote is from *Philosophical Investigations*, Book 1, Paragraph 309.

7. O. K. Bouwsma, *Wittgenstein: Conversations 1949–51*, ed. J. L. Craft and R. E. Hustwit (Indianapolis: Hackett Publishing Co., 1986), pp. 11–12.

8. From the "Big Typescript"; quoted in the epigraph to Hans-Johann Glock, *A Wittgenstein Dictionary* (Oxford: Blackwell Reference, 1996).

9. On this misreading of Wittgenstein, see Allan Janik and Stephen Toulmin, *Wittgenstein's Vienna* (New York: Simon & Schuster, 1973), chapter 7.

10. See the "Correspondence" section in *Nature*, *350*, 7 March 1991, p. 9; *351*, 2 May 1991, p. 10 and 16 May 1991, p. 179; *352*, 11 July 1991, p. 100; *353*, 17 October 1991, p. 598; and *355*, 6 February 1992, p. 490.

11. Norman Malcolm, *Wittgenstein: A Religious Point of View?* (Ithaca, NY: Cornell University Press, 1994), pp. 48 and 74.

12. Karl-Otto Apel, "The Problem of Philosophical Fundamental-Grounding in Light of a Transcendental Pragmatic of Language," trans. Karl Richard Pavlovic, *Man and World*, vol. 8, no. 3 (August 1975), p. 254; and T. S. Kuhn, *The Structure of Scientific Revolutions* (2d ed., enl.; Chicago: University of Chicago Press, 1970), pp. 44–46. The real "grandfather" of the discussion of facts and "thought-communities" is Ludwik Fleck, in *Genesis and Development of a Scientific Fact*, trans. Fred Bradley and Thaddeus J. Trenn, and ed. Thaddeus J. Trenn and Robert K. Merton (Chicago: University of Chicago Press, 1979; orig. German ed. 1935).

13. See, e.g., Bruno Latour, *Laboratory Life: The Social Construction of Scientific Facts* (Beverly Hills: Sage Publications, 1979), as well as the work of Steven Shapin and David Bloor, among others.

14. Peter Munz, "Philosophy and the Mirror of Rorty," in Gerard Radnitzky and W. W. Bartley III (eds.), *Evolutionary Epistemology, Rationality, and the Sociology of Knowledge* (La Salle, IL: Open Court, 1987), p. 349; Norman Malcolm, "The Groundlessness of Belief," in Stuart C. Brown (ed.), *Reason and Religion* (Ithaca, NY: Cornell University Press, 1977), p. 156.

15. Munz, "Philosophy and the Mirror of Rorty," pp. 361 and 363; Ernest Gellner, "The Stakes in Anthropology," *American Scholar*, *57* (Winter 1988), 17–30.

16. Munz, "Philosophy and the Mirror of Rorty," p. 383; Michael P. Hodges, *Transcendence and Wittgenstein's Tractatus* (Philadelphia: Temple University Press, 1990), pp. 18–19; and Henry Staten, *Wittgenstein and Derrida* (Lincoln: University of Nebraska Press, 1984). Wittgenstein also had a strong influence on Peter Winch's classic work, *The Idea of a Social Science* (1958).

17. For an excellent critique of deconstruction based on this point, see George Steiner, *Real Presences* (Chicago: University of Chicago Press, 1989).

18. On this and the following, see Gellner, "Stakes in Anthropology," pp. 18–19, 23–25, and 29. Peter Munz calls this "epistemological euphoria," the idea that knowledge is no longer a relationship between knower and the known, but only a state of mind ("Philosophy and the Mirror of Rorty," p. 363). The world of Werner Erhard's *est*, that all of reality is a mental creation, is strangely enough encountered even outside of California.

19. See Monk, *Ludwig Wittgenstein*, chapter 9, and Wittgenstein's *Letters to Russell, Keynes, and Moore*, ed. G. H. von Wright (Ithaca, NY: Cornell University Press, 1974), pp. 94 and 97.

20. Derek Jarman and Ken Butler, "Wittgenstein: The Derek Jarman Film," in *Wittgenstein* (London: British Film Institute, 1993), p. 142. This is a slight modification of the original text by Terry Eagleton, which can be found on p. 55.

21. Bouwsma, *Wittgenstein*, p. 68.

22. Gellner, "Stakes in Anthropology," p. 29.

23. Hodges, *Transcendence*, p. 196; Malcolm, "Groundlessness of Belief," pp. 147 and 188; W. W. Bartley III, "Non-Justificationism: Popper *versus* Wittgenstein," in Paul Weingartner and Johannes Czermak (eds.), *Epistemology and Philosophy of Science, Proceedings of the 7th International Wittgenstein Symposium* (Vienna: Hölder-Pichler-Tempsky, 1983), p. 257; and Apel, "Problem of Philosophical Fundamental-Grounding," pp. 252–53. The last quote is by H. R. Smart, as cited in Nicholas F. Gier, *Wittgenstein and Phenomenology* (Albany: State University of New York Press, 1981), p. 17.

24. Gier, *Wittgenstein and Phenomenology*, pp. 94–95.

25. Quoted in Hodges, *Transcendence*, p. 26.

26. Charles Taylor, *The Ethics of Authenticity* (Cambridge: Harvard University Press, 1991), pp. 66–68.

27. R. M. Rilke, *Letters to a Young Poet*, trans. M. D. Herter Norton (rev. ed.; New York: W. W. Norton, 1954; orig. German ed. 1929), p. 35.

28. Joseph Needham, "Human Law and the Laws of Nature," in *The Grand Titration* (Toronto: University of Toronto Press, 1969), chapter 8.

29. Victor Farías, *Heidegger and Nazism*, trans. Paul Burrell and Gabriel Ricci (Philadelphia: Temple University Press, 1989).

7. The Other Voice

1. David W. Orr, *Ecological Literacy* (Albany: State University of New York Press, 1992), p. 18.

2. Charles Olson, *The Special View of History* (Berkeley: Oyez, 1970), p. 16.

3. Richard Bernstein, *Dictatorship of Virtue* (New York: Vintage Books, 1995), pp. 3–10, 30, 36–38, 49, 89, 104ff., 226–29, 241, 278, and 355.

4. Ibid., pp. 343–44. There is by now a fair amount written on the rigidity and authoritarianism of multiculturalism and feminism—things that started off with very good ideas and evolved into dogmas. See Christina Hoff Sommers, *Who Stole Feminism?* (New York: Simon & Schuster, 1994); Lynne V. Cheney, *Telling the Truth* (New York: Simon & Schuster, 1995); Mary Lefkowitz, "Louis Farrakhan's Challenge to Rational Discourse," *Chronicle of Higher Education*, 1 December 1995, p. A60; Erik Lacitis, "White Guys Speak Out; Don't Color Them Optimistic," *Seattle Times*, 17 December 1995, pp. L1–2. For a very

thoughtful critique of "diversity" and political correctness, see David Rieff, "Therapy or Democracy?" *World Policy Journal*, vol. 15, no. 2 (Summer 1998), pp. 66–76.

5. Doris Lessing, "A Dying Ideology Bequeaths Us Its Deadening Way of Thinking," *International Herald Tribune*, 27–28 June 1992. Quotes from Koestler and Silone appear in Richard Crossman (ed.), *The God that Failed* (New York: Harper and Bros., 1949), pp. 45 and 101.

6. Bernstein, *Dictatorship of Virtue*, p. 343; Noel Annan, *Our Age* (London: Fontana, 1991), p. 404.

7. Quoted in Annan, *Our Age*, p. 243.

8. S. I. Shapiro, "Incredible Assumptions: Contributions from Transpersonal Psychology," *Journal of Humanistic Psychology*, vol. 23, no. 3 (Summer 1983), pp. 101–3.

9. Richard Tarnas, *The Passion of the Western Mind* (New York: Harmony Books, 1991), pp. 395–445.

10. Grof's work does raise interesting questions along the lines of exactly whose psyche is being explored in the LSD experience. He just assumes, as Jung did, the existence of an eternal structure, a universal and unchanging mythic substrate, and sees LSD as laying bare the world's mythologies, as it were. As with Eliade, Grof has no interest in context or historicity; the acid trip of death and rebirth is, for him, the shamanic experience, true for all time (pp. 195–203 of his *Human Encounter with Death*, for example, could have been written by Eliade).

To the extent, of course, that we are all "born broken," have creature anxiety and disturbed Object Relations, one might argue that the encounter with death, with the fear of separation from the world or the mother, is something that is universal and goes back to Paleolithic times. That is very likely to *some* degree, as I have said. But as I have tried to show in this book, the SAC, let alone unitive trance, may not go back very far at all; and we may not have been that "broken" in a Paleolithic context of child-rearing practices and Object Relations that were very different from what they are today. Certainly, the psychic encounter with spiritual death, whether triggered by LSD or anything else, can be very healing to those of us living in a painful, alienating context; but the whole notion of death/rebirth and subsequent heroism corresponds to a modern age in which these things have gotten exaggerated and distorted. A world in which T.O.s are not necessary is a very different one, psychologically speaking, from our own. The appreciation of immediate sensual detail that an acid trip or encounter with death or prolonged meditation experience, for that matter, can provide, was probably a given in a world defined by paradox rather than ecstasy.

As for heroism, even before Joseph Campbell, James Frazer was taken with the notion of a "dying god" and wrote that he hoped "to prove that these motives [motifs?] have operated widely, perhaps universally, in human society, producing in varied circumstances a variety of institutions specifically different but generically alike." Yet on Frazer's own analysis, says historian Henri Frankfort, the generic features of the "dying god" proved to be much less significant than the differences, culture for culture; and Frankfort shows this in detail for Tammuz, Adonis, and Osiris. In Frazerian fashion, Grof (pp. cited above) lumps all of these together and also assumes the existence of a shamanic experience that, as the evidence for Egypt and Mesopotamia seems to show, was not part of those religions (see above, chapter 4).

There is also the problem of what to make of one's mythic encounters, i.e., what validity to assign them. A friend of mine had the experience of birth while on an acid trip; he saw himself clearly making his way through the birth canal, struggling to be born, and so on. The next day, having come down from the drug, he remembered that he had been delivered by Caesarian section. One can of course say that he had had an experience of *symbolic* birth, but that was not *his* experience of it, as far as he is concerned. We can believe in Paleolithic shamanism or the collective unconscious or whatever based on drug experiences, but that doesn't prove they exist.

See Stanislav Grof, *Realms of the Human Unconscious* (New York: Viking, 1975), and (with Joan Halifax) *The Human Encounter with Death* (New York: E. P. Dutton, 1977); Henri Frankfort, *Kingship and the Gods* (Chicago: University of Chicago Press, 1948), pp. 287–91 and 405 n. 1.

11. Richard J. Bernstein, *Beyond Objectivism and Relativism* (Philadelphia: University of Pennsylvania Press, 1983), p. 211. See also the remarks by Stuart Hampshire quoted in John Gray, *Isaiah Berlin* (Princeton: Princeton University Press, 1996), pp. 88–89.

12. Albert Camus, *The Myth of Sisyphus and Other Essays*, trans. Justin O'Brien (New York: Alfred A. Knopf, 1969; orig. French ed. 1942), pp. 36 and 38.

It was only at the very end of writing this book that I discovered the similarity of Camus' views to the ones being expressed here, which caught me by surprise. Despite his enormous reputation and the winning of the Nobel Prize in 1957, Camus wound up having his ideas wrongly confused with those of Sartre and the Existentialist school, and he never got a real hearing. Thus, he did not believe in hope, especially the hope that some great idea would transcend life; he regarded this as a "fatal evasion," a betrayer of life (cf. the "Wheel of Suffering," below) and argued that while life had no meaning, this was hardly a cause for despair or even concern. In sharp contrast to someone like Joseph Campbell, or (in Camus' time) André Malraux, he had no interest in the cult of the heroic, and historian H. Stuart Hughes writes that "for Camus heroism was a bitter, unavoidable necessity, not a way of life to be sought out for its own sake." Camus repeatedly asserted the primacy of immediate sensual experience and rejected the Existentialist notion that the proper response to a meaningless world was to create meaning and impose it on the world. In his *Lettres à un ami allemand* (Letters to a German Friend, 1945), he wrote: "You aligned yourself with the gods . . . I chose . . . to remain faithful to this earth. I continue to believe that this earth has no superior meaning." Camus' "god" was "nothing more" than the natural world, the

Algerian sun, not as a transcendent symbol, but as actual physical warmth. Thus, in his autobiographical last novel, he says that "God" was a word "he never heard spoken throughout his childhood, nor did he trouble himself about it. Life, so vivid and mysterious, was enough to occupy his entire being." The inability to live without transcendent notions, Existentialist or otherwise (and he saw Existentialism as reifying the absurd), leads us to forge ideologies and then chain themselves down with them. Instead, wrote Camus, our job is to get along with the immediate evidence.

See Albert Camus, *The Myth of Sisyphus*, pp. 8, 32–38, 55, and 61, and *The First Man*, trans. David Hapgood (London: Hamish Hamilton, 1995), p. 129; Germaine Brée, *Camus* (rev. ed.; New York: Harcourt, Brace & World, 1964), pp. 46, 84, 230, and 236; and H. Stuart Hughes, *The Obstructed Path* (New York: Harper & Row, 1968), p. 245.

13. Charles Jencks, *The Architecture of the Jumping Universe* (London: Academy Editions, 1995), p. 125.

14. Brendan Gill, "Dear Darling Cosmos," *New Yorker*, 19 June 1995, p. 92. Jencks does say at one point (*Architecture of the Jumping Universe*, p. 15) that postmodernism has its dark side and is a "mixed blessing . . . not an ideology and movement to be accepted or rejected *in toto*." Unfortunately, this sensible qualification is nowhere developed and is in fact completely ignored. It constitutes only lip service to notions of balance and ambiguity, a half page of reason out of 160 pages of unqualified commitment to the new "truth."

15. John Ralston Saul, *The Unconscious Civilization* (Concord, Ontario: Anansi Press, 1995), pp. 20–21.

16. Doris Lessing, *The Golden Notebook* (New York: Bantam Books, 1973; orig. publ. 1962), p. vii.

17. Heinz Kohut, *The Analysis of the Self* (New York: International Universities Press, 1971), esp. pp. 25ff.

18. Immanuel Kant, "An Answer to the Question: 'What is Enlightenment?' " in Hans Reiss (ed.), *Kant: Political Writings*, trans. H. B. Nisbet (2d ed., enl.; Cambridge: Cambridge University Press, 1991), p. 55; Frank E. Manuel, *A Portrait of Isaac Newton* (Cambridge: Harvard University Press, 1968).

19. Walter Truett Anderson, *Reality Isn't What It Used To Be* (San Francisco: HarperCollins, 1990), pp. 11 and 244–50.

Here and elsewhere in the text I have been very critical of postmodernism, but I do not mean for my anecdotal remarks, or for a popular text such as Anderson's (competent though it is) to carry the weight of a full-blown critique. There are a number of trenchant critiques of postmodernism and deconstruction that leave the whole movement with not a leg to stand on, philosophically speaking. For starters, I refer the reader to James Miller, *The Passion of Michel Foucault* (New York: Anchor Books, 1994); J. G. Merquior, *Foucault* (Berkeley: University of California Press, 1987); and especially, Carl Rapp, *Fleeing the Universal* (Albany: State University of New York Press, 1998).

However, I do not mean to suggest that the postmodern critique of science, rationalism, and the Enlightenment tradition is without *any* value. Among other things, it served to shake the latter up, to take stock of itself, and that is always a good thing. In that sense, postmodernism might have a salutary effect, in the same way that the Dada, or "anti-art" movement of the early part of the twentieth century, forced a rethinking of the artistic enterprise. But just as anti-art is not art, so anti-epistemology is finally not epistemology, and neither Dada nor postmodernism had/have any place to go. We need now to go beyond postmodernism, hopefully with a new awareness of the problem of constructing narratives even as we construct them. If the worst of postmodernism argues for dismissing empirical evidence as "Western science" and a species of "imperialism," the best of it points to the need for honoring multiple narratives in the old-fashioned tradition of philosophical pluralism, something that John Dewey, *inter alia*, would have been perfectly happy with. Taken in this way, postmodernism becomes more acceptable, but also much less radical in nature.

20. Adapted from notes made by John Harper, from a lecture by A. H. Almaas.

21. Anderson, *Reality*, p. 10.

22. James Keys [G. Spencer Brown], *Only Two Can Play This Game* (New York: Bantam Books, 1974), p. 45.

23. For more on this, see Morris Berman, "The Shadow Side of Systems Theory," *Journal of Humanistic Psychology*, vol. 36, no. 1 (Winter 1996), pp. 28–54.

24. Annan, *Our Age*, p. 367.

25. On the following see Bernadette Roberts, *The Experience of No-Self* (rev. ed.; Albany: State University of New York Press, 1993), pp. 12–13, 30, 47, 70, 114, and 154; and *What is Self?* (Austin: Mary Botsford Goens, 1989), pp. 55 and 114–20. For a different interpretation of the quote from Buddha, see Mark Epstein, *Thoughts without a Thinker* (New York: Basic Books, 1995), pp. 75–77.

26. Pamela McGarry, personal communication, August 1994; excerpt reprinted by permission of Pamela McGarry.

27. Roberts, *Experience of No-Self*, p. 186.

28. Alice Miller, *The Untouched Key*, trans. Hildegarde and Hunter Hannum (New York: Anchor Books, 1990), pp. 59–60.

29. On this and the following, see Keith Bradley and Alan Gelb, *Cooperation at Work* (London: Heinemann Educational Books, 1983), pp. 12–17, 39, 51, 53, and 62–65; William F. and Kathleen K. Whyte, *Making Mondragón* (2d ed., rev.; Ithaca, NY: ILR Press, 1991), pp. xiv, 4, 9, 18, 28, 45, 124, 241, 253, 257, and 262; Ana Gutierrez Johnson and William F. Whyte, "The Mondragón System of Worker Production Cooperatives," *Industrial and Labor Relations Review*, vol. 31, no. 1 (October 1977), p. 25; and the review of Whyte and

Whyte by Gillian D. Ursell in *Organization Studies*, vol. 10, no. 4 (1989), p. 594. Also valuable is Henk Thomas and Chris Logan, *Mondragón: An Economic Analysis* (London: Allen & Unwin, 1982).

30. For an example of a text that fetishizes Mondragón, see Roy Morrison, *We Build the Road As We Travel* (Philadelphia: New Society Publishers, 1991). For a negative evaluation that sees the cooperatives as a way of discrediting labor unions and downplaying conflicts, see Sharryn Kasmir, *The Myth of Mondragón* (Albany: State University of New York Press, 1996).

There is also the potential danger that what I have called "healthy inegalitarianism," the legitimate recognition of differences in quality and expertise, will in practice tend to get translated into differential power at the expense of social equality. In a world of escalating population, less and less work for the mass of people, and a greater emphasis put on the cultivation of an educated elite, horizontal possibilities may prove to be increasingly difficult to maintain.

31. John Cassidy, "Who Killed the Middle Class?" *New Yorker*, 16 Oct 95, pp. 113–24.

32. E. M. Forster, "What I Believe," quoted in Janet Malcolm, "A House of One's Own," *New Yorker*, 5 June 95, p. 64.

33. On the issue of the recoverability of components, see also the insightful discussion provided by Paul Shepard in "A Post-Historic Primitivism," in Max Oelschlaeger (ed.), *The Wilderness Condition* (Washington, DC: Island Press, 1992), pp. 81ff.

34. Ernest Becker, *The Denial of Death* (New York: Free Press, 1973), p. 281. Becker's work remains a classic on this subject and is a good antidote to the sort of transpersonal heroism, and/or therapeutic shamanism, promoted by writers such as Tarnas, Campbell, and Grof. "If men could become noble repositories of great gulfs of nonbeing," he writes, "they would have even less peace than we oblivious and driven madmen have today."

35. Morris Berman, *Coming to Our Senses* (New York: Simon & Schuster, 1989).

36. Stanley Cavell, *Must We Mean What We Say?* (Cambridge: Cambridge University Press, 1976), p. 72.

37. Berman, "Shadow Side," esp. p. 36, and John Horgan, "From Complexity to Perplexity," *Scientific American*, 272 (June 1995), 104–9.

38. Bernard Williams, *Ethics and the Limits of Philosophy* (Cambridge: Harvard University Press, 1985), pp. 197ff.; Berman, "Shadow Side," p. 48.

39. Gilles Deleuze and Claire Parnet, *Dialogues*, trans. Hugh Tomlinson and Barbara Habberjam (New York: Columbia University Press, 1987), p. 139; Gilles Deleuze and Félix Guattari, *Nomadology: The War Machine*, trans. Brian Massumi (New York: Semiotext(e), 1986), pp. 47–49; E. H. Gombrich, "Lessing,"

in *Proceedings of the British Academy*, 1957 (London: Oxford University Press, 1958), p. 134; Pierre Clastres, *Society Against the State*, trans. Robert Hurley (New York: Zone Books, 1989; orig. French ed. 1974), p. 26.

40. Gilles Deleuze and Félix Guattari, *On the Line*, trans. John Johnston (New York: Semiotext(e), 1983), pp. 45–46.

41. Deleuze and Parnet, *Dialogues*, p. 62.

42. Sven Birkerts, *The Gutenberg Elegies* (New York: Fawcett Columbine, 1995), pp. 32, 122–24, 130–31, 137–39, 153–59, 202–3, 208, and 228.

43. Williams, *Ethics*, pp. 198–99; Birkerts, *Gutenberg Elegies*, p. 124.

44. Joel Whitebook, *Perversion and Utopia* (Cambridge: MIT Press, 1995), pp. 5, 68, 89, 172–75, 254, 257, 261, and 264; Bernstein, *Beyond Objectivism*, p. 123; Marianna Torgovnick, *Primitive Passions* (New York: Alfred A. Knopf, 1997), p. 217; George E. Mylonas, *Eleusis and the Eleusinian Mysteries* (Princeton: Princeton University Press, 1961), pp. 284–85; and *The Odes of Pindar*, trans. Dawson W. Turner (London: George Bell, 1881), p. 63. This is similar to the discussion I have in *Coming to Our Senses*, chapter 10, regarding what I call "Creativity II" versus "Creativity III," and the issue of working one's way through the former to get to the latter. Cf. the vignette on this topic in A. S. Byatt's beautiful novel, *Still Life* (London: Vintage, 1995; orig. publ. 1985), pp. 380–83.

Torgovnick's book is a valuable study of the ambivalent legacy of CT no. 1. Thus, while endorsing the need (in civilization, I would add) for the unitive experience, she remarks (p. 217): "Even at the very point where the term 'oceanic' enters the Western vocabulary to describe ecstatic experience—in Ramakrishna's utterances as transcribed in Romain Rolland's *The Life of Ramakrishna*—there are passages that evoke mass death. On the way to ecstasy, Ramakrishna is shown . . . 'heaps of human heads, mountain high.' Such passages have been notoriously literalized by events in our time."

45. I don't know where Lawrence wrote this; it was quoted in an article on him in *Le Monde*, 26 June 1992, p. 31.

46. Octavio Paz, *The Other Voice*, trans. Helen Lane (New York: Harcourt Brace Jovanovich, 1991), pp. 159–60.

SELECTED BIBLIOGRAPHY

Anderson, Walter Truett. *Reality Isn't What It Used To Be*. San Francisco: Harper & Row, 1990.

Bahn, Paul G., and Jean Vertut. *Images of the Ice Age*. New York: Facts on File, 1988.

Balagangadhara, S. N. "The Origins of Religion: Why is the Issue Dead?" *Cultural Dynamics*, 3 (1990), 281–316.

Barfield, Thomas J. *The Nomadic Alternative*. Englewood Cliffs, NJ: Prentice Hall, 1993.

Barnard, Alan. *The Kalahari Debate: A Bibliographic Essay*. Edinburgh: Centre of African Studies, Edinburgh University, Occasional Papers No. 35, 1992.

Barry, Herbert, III, Irvin L. Child, and Margaret K. Bacon. "Relation of Child Training to Subsistence Economy." *American Anthropologist*, 61 (1959), 51–63.

Barth, Fredrik. *Nomads of South Persia*. Oslo: Oslo University Press, 1961.

Bar-Yosef, Ofer, and Anatoly Khazanov (eds.). *Pastoralism in the Levant*. Madison, WI: Prehistory Press, 1992.

Begler, Elsie B. "Sex, Status, and Authority in Egalitarian Society." *American Anthropologist*, 80 (1978), 571–88.

Berman, Morris. *Coming to Our Senses*. New York: Simon & Schuster, 1989.

———. *The Reenchantment of the World*. Ithaca, NY: Cornell University Press, 1981.

———. "The Shadow Side of Systems Theory." *Journal of Humanistic Psychology*, vol. 36, no. 1 (Winter 1996), pp. 28–54.

Bernstein, Richard. *Dictatorship of Virtue*. New York: Vintage Books, 1995.

Berry, J. W. "Independence and Conformity in Subsistence-Level Societies." *Journal of Personality and Social Psychology*, vol. 7, no. 4 (1967), pp. 415–18.

———. "Psychological Differentiation in Cross-Cultural Perspective." *Journal of Cross-Cultural Psychology*, vol. 6, no. 1 (March 1975), pp. 4–87.

Bettelheim, Bruno. *The Children of the Dream*. London: Macmillan, 1969.

Binford, Sally R., and Lewis R. Binford (eds.). *New Perspectives in Archeology*. Chicago: Aldine, 1968.

Bonanno, Anthony (ed.). *Archaeology and Fertility Cult in the Ancient Mediterranean*. Amsterdam: B. R. Gruner, 1986.

Bourguignon, Erika. *Religion, Altered States of Consciousness, and Social Change*. Columbus: Ohio State University Press, 1973.

Bowlby, John. "The Nature of the Child's Tie to His Mother." *International Journal of Psycho-Analysis, 39* (1958), 350–73.

Boyce, Mary. *A History of Zoroastrianism*, vol. 1: *The Early Period*. Leiden: E. J. Brill, 1975.

———. *Zoroastrianism*. Costa Mesa, CA: Mazda Publishers, 1992.

———. *Zoroastrians*. London: Routledge and Kegan Paul, 1984.

Carneiro, Robert L. "A Theory of the Origin of the State." *Science, 169* (21 August 1970), 733–38.

———. "On the Relationship between Size of Population and Complexity of Social Organization." *Southwestern Journal of Anthropology, 23* (1967), 234–41.

Castillo, Jorge Silva (ed.). *Nomads and Sedentary Peoples*. Mexico City: El Colegio de México, 1981.

Chance, M. R. A. (ed.). *Social Fabrics of the Mind*. Hillsdale, NJ: Lawrence Erlbaum, 1988.

Chatwin, Bruce. *The Songlines*. New York: Penguin Books, 1988.

Clastres, Pierre. *Society Against the State*. Trans. Robert Hurley. New York: Zone Books, 1989; orig. French ed. 1974.

Cohen, Mark N. "Archaeological Evidence for Population Pressure in Pre-Agricultural Societies." *American Antiquity*, vol. 40, no. 4 (1975), pp. 471–75.

———. *The Food Crisis in Prehistory*. New Haven: Yale University Press, 1977.

Cohen, Mark N. et al. (eds.). *Biosocial Mechanisms of Population Regulation*. New Haven: Yale University Press, 1980.

Cohen, M. N., and G. J. Armegalos (eds.). *Paleopathology at the Origins of Agriculture*. New York: Academic Press, 1984.

Deleuze, Gilles, and Félix Guattari. *Nomadology: The War Machine*. Trans. Brian Massumi. New York: Semiotext(e), 1986.

Dinnerstein, Dorothy. *The Mermaid and the Minotaur*. New York: Harper & Row, 1976.

Edgerton, Robert B. *The Individual in Cultural Adaptation*. Berkeley: University of California Press, 1971.

Ehrenberg, Margaret. *Women in Prehistory*. London: British Museum Publications, 1989.

Eisenstadt, S. N. "Heterdoxies and Dynamics of Civilizations." *Proceedings of the American Philosophical Society*, vol. 128, no. 2 (1984), pp. 104–13.

Eisenstadt, S. N. (ed.). *The Origins and Diversity of Axial Age Civilizations*. Albany: State University of New York Press, 1986.

Erdosy, George (ed.). *The Indo-Aryans of Ancient South Asia*. Berlin: Walter de Gruyter, 1995.

Fortes, Meyer, and E. E. Evans-Pritchard (eds.). *African Political Systems*. London: Oxford University Press, 1940.

Fried, Morton H. *The Evolution of Political Society*. New York: Random House, 1967.

Frymer-Kensky, Tikva. *In the Wake of the Goddess*. New York: Free Press, 1992.

Gardner, Peter M. "Foragers' Pursuit of Individual Autonomy." *Current Anthropology*, vol. 23, no. 5 (December 1991), pp. 543–72.

Gero, Joan M., and Margaret W. Conkey (eds.). *Engendering Archaeology*. Oxford: Basil Blackwell, 1991.

Gimbutas, Marija. *The Goddesses and Gods of Old Europe*. New ed.; London: Thames and Hudson, 1982.

Goldschmidt, Walter. *Pastoral Production and Society*. Cambridge: Cambridge University Press, 1979.

Harrold, Francis B. "A Comparative Analysis of Eurasian Paleolithic Burials." *World Archaeology*, 12 (1980), 195–211.

Hausfater, Glenn, and Sarah Blaffer Hrdy (eds.). *Infanticide*. New York: Aldine, 1984.

Hayden, Brian, and Robert Gargett. "Big Man, Big Heart? A Mesoamerican View of the Emergence of Complex Society." *Ancient Mesoamerica*, 1 (1990), 3–20.

Jaynes, Julian. *The Origin of Consciousness in the Breakdown of the Bicameral Mind*. Boston: Houghton Mifflin, 1976.

Johnson, Allen W., and Timothy Earle. *The Evolution of Human Societies*. Stanford: Stanford University Press, 1987.

Johnson, Ana Gutierrez, and William F. Whyte. "The Mondragón System of Worker Production Cooperatives." *Industrial and Labor Relations Review*, vol. 31, no. 1 (October 1977), pp. 18–30.

Jones, Grant D., and Robert R. Kautz. (eds.). *The Transition to Statehood in the New World.* Cambridge: Cambridge University Press, 1981.

Kent, Susan. "The Current Forager Controversy: Real Versus Ideal Views of Hunter-Gatherers." *Man* (n.s.), 27 (1992), 45–70.

Kent, Susan (ed.). *Farmers as Hunters: The Implications of Sedentism.* Cambridge: Cambridge University Press, 1989.

Khazanov, Anatoly M. *Nomads and the Outside World.* Trans. Julia Crookenden. 2d ed.; Madison: University of Wisconsin Press, 1994; orig. publ. 1984.

Klein, Richard G. "What Do We Know About Neanderthals and Cro-Magnon Man?" *American Scholar,* 52 (1983), 386–92.

Kurtz, Stanley N. *All the Mothers Are One.* New York: Columbia University Press, 1992.

Leacock, Eleanor, and Richard Lee (eds.). *Politics and History in Band Societies.* Cambridge: Cambridge University Press, 1982.

Lee, Richard. "Art, Science, or Politics? The Crisis in Hunter-Gatherer Studies." *American Anthropologist,* vol. 94, no. 1 (March 1992), pp. 31–54.

———. "Eating Christmas in the Kalahari." *Natural History,* vol. 78, no. 10 (December 1969), pp. 14–22 and 60–63.

Lee, Richard, and Irven DeVore (eds.). *Man the Hunter.* Chicago: Aldine, 1968.

Lewis, Michael (ed.). *Beyond the Dyad.* New York: Plenum Press, 1984.

Mallory, J. P. *In Search of the Indo-Europeans.* London: Thames and Hudson, 1989.

Marinatos, Nanno. *Minoan Religion.* Columbia: University of South Carolina Press, 1993.

Mellars, Paul. "Major Issues in the Emergence of Modern Humans." *Current Anthropology,* vol. 30, no. 3 (June 1989), pp. 349–85.

Monk, Ray. *Ludwig Wittgenstein.* New York: Free Press, 1990.

Murdock, George P. *Ethnographic Atlas.* Pittsburgh: University of Pittsburgh Press, 1967.

Mylonas, George E. *Eleusis and the Eleusinian Mysteries.* Princeton: Princeton University Press, 1961.

———. *Mycenae and the Mycenaean Age.* Princeton: Princeton University Press, 1966.

Nitecki, Mathew and Doris (eds.). *The Evolution of Human Hunting.* New York: Plenum Press, 1987.

Noll, Richard. *The Jung Cult.* Princeton: Princeton University Press, 1994.

Parpola, Asko. "The Coming of the Aryans to Iran and India and the Cultural and Ethnic Identity of the Dāsas." *Studia Orientalia,* 64 (1988), 195–302.

Possehl, Gregory L. (ed.). *Harappan Civilization.* New Delhi: Oxford and IBH Publishing Co., 1982.

Power, Margaret. *The Egalitarians—Human and Chimpanzee.* Cambridge: Cambridge University Press, 1991.

Price, T. D., and J. A. Brown (eds.). *Prehistoric Hunter-Gatherers.* Orlando: Academic Press, 1985.

Pritchard, James B. (ed.). *Ancient Near Eastern Texts Relating to the Old Testament.* 2d ed., corrected and enl.; Princeton: Princeton University Press, 1995.

Reite, Martin, and Tiffany Field (eds.). *The Psychobiology of Attachment and Separation.* Orlando: Academic Press, 1985.

Renfrew, Colin. *Archaeology and Language.* New York: Cambridge University Press, 1988.

Reynolds, Peter. *On the Evolution of Human Behavior.* Berkeley: University of California Press, 1981.

Roberts, Bernadette. *The Experience of No-Self.* Rev. ed.; Albany: State University of New York Press, 1993.

Sahlins, Marshall. *Stone Age Economics.* Chicago: Aldine, 1972.

Salzman, Philip C. (ed.). *When Nomads Settle.* New York: Praeger, 1980.

Sandars, N. K. *Prehistoric Art in Europe.* 2d ed.; New York: Viking Penguin, 1985.

Sasson, Jack M. (ed.). *Civilizations of the Ancient Near East.* 4 vols.; New York: Scribner's, 1995.

Schrire, Carmel (ed.). *Past and Present in Hunter-Gatherer Studies.* New York: Academic Press, 1984.

Simons, Elwyn. "Human Origins." *Science,* 245 (22 September 1989), 1343–50.

Slater, Philip E. *The Glory of Hera.* Boston: Beacon Press, 1968.

Spain, David H. (ed.). *Psychoanalytic Anthropology after Freud.* New York: Psyche Press, 1992.

Spooner, Brian. *The Cultural Ecology of Pastoral Nomads.* New York: Addison-Wesley, 1973.

Spooner, Brian (ed.). *Population Growth: Anthropological Implications.* Cambridge: MIT Press, 1972.

Stork, Hélène. *Enfances indiennes.* Paris: Centurion, 1986.

Tainter, Joseph A. *The Collapse of Complex Societies.* Cambridge: Cambridge University Press, 1988.

Testart, Alain. "Significance of Food Storage among Hunter-Gatherers: Residence Patterns, Population Densities, and Social Inequalities." *Current Anthropology,* vol. 23, no. 5 (October 1982), pp. 523–37.

————. "Some Major Problems in the Social Anthropology of Hunter-Gatherers." *Current Anthropology*, vol. 29, no. 1 (February 1988), pp. 1–31.

Thomas, Nicholas, and Caroline Humphrey (eds.). *Shamanism, History, and the State*. Ann Arbor: University of Michigan Press, 1994.

Trinkaus, Erik (ed.). *The Emergence of Modern Humans*. Cambridge: Cambridge University Press, 1989.

Trinkaus, Erik, and William Howells. "The Neadertals." *Scientific American*, *241* (December 1979), 118–33.

Turnbull, Colin M. *The Forest People*. New York: Simon & Schuster, 1961.

Ucko, Peter J., and Andrée Rosenfeld. *Paleolithic Cave Art*. New York: McGraw-Hill, 1967.

Weigert-Vorwinkel, Edith. "The Cult and Mythology of the Magna Mater from the Standpoint of Psychoanalysis." Trans. F. M. von Wimmersperg. *Psychiatry*, 1 (1938), 347–78.

White, Randall. *Dark Caves, Bright Visions*. New York: American Museum of Natural History, 1986.

————. "Rethinking the Middle/Upper Paleolithic Transition." *Current Anthropology*, vol. 23, no. 2 (April 1982), pp. 169–92.

Whitebook, Joel. *Perversion and Utopia*. Cambridge: MIT Press, 1995.

Whiting, Beatrice B. (ed.). *Six Cultures*. New York: Wiley, 1963.

Whiting, Beatrice B., and John W. M. Whiting, *Children of Six Cultures*. Cambridge: Harvard University Press, 1975.

Wilmsen, Edwin N. *Land Filled with Flies*. Chicago: University of Chicago Press, 1989.

Wittgenstein, Ludwig. *Culture and Value*. Trans. Peter Winch and ed. G. H. von Wright. 2d ed.; Oxford: Basil Blackwell, 1980.

————. *Philosophical Investigations*. Trans. Rush Rhees and G. H. von Wright and ed. G. E. M. Anscombe. 3d ed.; New York: Macmillan, 1958.

————. *Tractatus Logico-Philosophicus*. Trans. D. F. Pears and B. F. McGuinness. London: Routledge and Kegan Paul, 1969.

Woodburn, James. "Egalitarian Societies." *Man* (n.s.), *17* (1982), 431–51.

Zaehner, R. C. *The Dawn and Twilight of Zoroastrianism*. London: Weidenfeld and Nicolson, 1961.

ABOUT THE AUTHOR

Morris Berman is well known as an innovative cultural historian and social critic. He has taught at a number of universities in Europe and North America, and has held visiting endowed chairs at Incarnate Word College (San Antonio), the University of New Mexico, and Weber State University. Between 1982 and 1988 he was the Lansdowne Professor in the History of Science at the University of Victoria, British Columbia. Berman won the Governor's Writers Award for Washington State in 1990, and was the first recipient of the annual Rollo May Center Grant for Humanistic Studies in 1992. His published works include *Social Change and Scientific Organization* (1978), *The Twilight of American Culture* (2000), and his trilogy on the evolution of human consciousness: *The Reenchantment of the World* (1981), *Coming to Our Senses* (1989), and *Wandering God* (2000) (more information on these is available at the web site, http://www.flash.net/~mberman). He lives in Washington, DC, where he works as a writer and editor and teaches part-time in the Master of Liberal Arts Program at the Johns Hopkins University.

INDEX